ACCOUNTING EDUCATION IN
ECONOMIC DEVELOPMENT MANAGEMENT

ACCOUNTING EDUCATION

IN

ECONOMIC DEVELOPMENT

MANAGEMENT

by

Dr. Adolf J.H. Enthoven

Professor of Accounting and Director,
Center for International Accounting Development
The University of Texas at Dallas
Richardson, Texas, USA

with a foreword by

Professor Dr. Jan Tinbergen

Nobel Laureate in Economics

NORTH-HOLLAND PUBLISHING COMPANY
AMSTERDAM · NEW YORK · OXFORD

ISBN: 0 444 86195 5

Publishers:

NORTH-HOLLAND PUBLISHING COMPANY
AMSTERDAM NEW YORK OXFORD

Sole distributors for the U.S.A. and Canada:

ELSEVIER NORTH-HOLLAND INC.
52 VANDERBILT AVENUE, NEW YORK, N.Y. 10017

1440746

PRINTED IN THE NETHERLANDS

Dedicated to friends and colleagues in Third World countries who, in the face of exacting professional responsibilities and at great personal sacrifice, are advancing the education, practice and frontiers of accounting knowledge in the context of their own countries' socioeconomic development.

FOREWORD

In principle, the activity called accounting constitutes the measurement of a number of key variables of revenue and expenditure character and related concepts. Accounting started in single firms, especially corporations, for auditing purposes. As discussed in Professor Enthoven's original doctoral dissertation, accounting spread to much wider areas. Some milestones of this rapid expansion are its application to the activities of public authorities, and from there to national accounting, considering a national economy as one unit.

But there are other aspects which widen the scope of accounting as well. The purposes served are among these aspects. Whereas, in the beginning, checking the consistency of the transactions observed was its task, new tasks evolved such as the evaluation of some measure of efficiency. A further development was an evaluation of some measure of optimality of the welfare created by the set of transactions portrayed. Again, the scope of whose welfare to evaluate broadened the field of application. The scope grew from a study of profits as a primitive yardstick used by firms to the study of the social welfare, however conceived, of a whole nation.

Another aspect concerns the type of transactions observed. These range from material transactions to non-material transactions, such as psychological dimensions—unavoidable as soon as welfare concepts are introduced.

Still another expansion was the spread "downward" from large to small unincorporated business units. Thus, farmers and retail traders were taught to have a more sophisticated look at their own labour inputs and capital used.

As in the best organized sciences, economic science has learned to apply the cooperation or dialogue between measurement and theory. New measurements may falsify existing theories, inducing the theorist to revise his theory, which is again to be checked by observations, i.e., measurements. Increasingly, accounting has contributed to economic science in a way comparable to the astronomer's observation of the physical universe.

Finally, the focus of Adolf Enthoven's work is the expansion from applications of accounting in developed countries to those in developing economies. This is not a luxury; where financial resources are scarce their proper use is even more important than in situations of abundance. Professor Enthoven has succeeded in convincing a number of international institutions, including the World Bank Group, of the necessity of accompanying their transactions with the Third World with accounting operations. As a matter of course, underdevelopment also showed up in the state of the art of accounting. Improvement of that has become a major aim of both the institutions involved and the author of this book. The instrument to be used is education; and that brings with it the enormous complex of activities and problems linked with education, learning and training.

This new study by Adolf Enthoven reflects an impressive series of reconnaissance missions and the ensuing projects for accounting education. These projects have confronted the profession with the existence of a number of different "schools" in the subject, connected with national and even ideological divergencies.

It is again a pleasure for me to introduce this "expanding universe" of the subject dealt with to the reader, and to wish him *bon voyage*.

J. TINBERGEN

TABLE OF CONTENTS

ACCOUNTING EDUCATION IN
ECONOMIC DEVELOPMENT MANAGEMENT

FOREWORD   Professor Dr. Jan Tinbergen

Chapter I   Introduction and Outline 1

PART ONE   AN OVERVIEW OF ACCOUNTING
                AND ECONOMIC DEVELOPMENT

Chapter II   The Significance of Accounting in
                Economic Development Management.................. 11

Chapter III   Elements Influencing the Development of Accounting... 23

Chapter IV   Accounting Education and
                International Economic Activities 29

Chapter V   Accounting Education in the Development Process...... 35

PART TWO   ACCOUNTING EDUCATION IN
                THIRD WORLD COUNTRIES

Chapter VI   An Evaluation of Accounting Educational
                Deficiencies and Requirements........................ 41

Chapter VII   The Role of Accounting Education,
                Training and Research in Development 51

Chapter VIII   Accounting Educational Programs for
                Economic Development 65

PART THREE   A FRAMEWORK FOR
                ACCOUNTING EDUCATIONAL ACTION

Chapter IX   Ways and Means of Enhancing
                Accountancy Education and Training 89

Chapter X   Education for Public Sector Financial Management 99

Chapter XI   Development Banking and Accounting Development... 107

Chapter XII   An International Association for
                Accounting Development 115

Chapter XIII   International and Regional Vehicles for Action 127

Chapter XIV   Potential Financial Resources for
                Implementing Framework 135

Chapter XV   Summary and Conclusion 137

PART FOUR   COUNTRY AND REGIONAL STUDIES

Chapter XVI   Regional Aspects and Developments in the
Asian and Pacific Area 155

Chapter XVII   Accounting Education in the Developing
Island Nations of the South Pacific 171

Chapter XVIII   Accounting Education in the
ASEAN Federation of Accountants (A.F.A.) 187

Chapter XIX   Accounting Education in Indonesia:
Its Structure and Requirements 197

Chapter XX   Accountancy and Accounting Education in Korea 210

Chapter XXI   Accounting Education in Malaysia 233

Chapter XXII   Accounting Education in Pakistan.................... 243

Chapter XXIII   Accounting Education in the Philippines 263

Chapter XXIV   Accounting Education in Thailand 297

Chapter XXV   Regional Aspects and Developments in
Africa and the Middle East 305

Chapter XXVI   Accounting Education in Egypt 309

Chapter XXVII   Accounting Education in Kenya 325

Chapter XXVIII   Accounting Education in Libya...................... 343

Chapter XXIX   Accounting Developments and
Education in Somalia............................... 347

Chapter XXX   Accounting Education in Tanzania 353

Chapter XXXI   Regional Aspects and
Developments in Latin America 367

Chapter XXXII   Accounting Education in Brazil 373

Chapter XXXIII   Accounting Education in Mexico 381

Chapter XXXIV   Accounting Education in Venezuela 391

APPENDIX: Accountancy Education in India..................... 401

REFERENCES.. 433

ABBREVIATIONS 434

INDEX 437

CHAPTER I

INTRODUCTION AND OUTLINE

This study aims to appraise the significance and function of accounting education, training and research in the context of socioeconomic development management, with particular reference to Third World economies. The actual role of accounting in economic development has already been evaluated in various previous publications, for example, Enthoven 1973/1978 and 1977/1979. The first text deals with the influence and role of accounting for socioeconomic analysis and policy, and the latter explores the orientation and practice of accounting in a series of developing countries around the world. Although some attention was given in these texts to the urgent need to improve accounting (e.g., auditing) education at all levels and branches of accounting (i.e., in the enterprise, government and macro spheres), the actual accounting educational and training aspects were not covered to the extent warranted. In a sense then, this new and underlying study is a logical sequence and culmination of the previous ones. Furthermore, while our current thesis looks at both the *existing conditions and desirable improvements* in regard to accounting education serving socioeconomic development objectives and policies, it also takes into account the future *direction* accounting education may have to follow to fulfill an effective prospective role.

From both these points of view, a broad array of related functional topics is dealt with, such as: accounting education and public sector management; development banking and its relation to accounting education; and changing international socioeconomic patterns and their impact on education.

Many of the major deficiencies in accounting standards and practices stem from an inadequate recognition of both the need for good accounting in all socioeconomic sectors of the economy *and* the unsatisfactory educational exposure to the functions and operations of accounting. Our international surveys indicate that accounting education and research tend to be void of relevance, have a monistic orientation (towards financial reporting and taxation), are based on outdated concepts and norms, and are rather poorly transmitted to students and practitioners. Most of these weaknesses tend to be beyond the immediate control of accounting educators and practitioners, due to a series of historical, economic, general educational, cultural and other complementary factors. We therefore hope to clarify in this study why and how special attention can be given to improve accounting education in Third World economies by both internal and external parties. In this context we propose extensive international accounting educational efforts to remedy the situation. Unfortunately, the nature and potential of accounting and accounting education have not been adequately clarified in many countries.

The reader should not gain the impression that improved accounting education—and accounting practices—will automatically lead to economic development. This is not so; the significance of and need for better accounting education and information measurements and reporting for all sorts of socioeconomic activities are, in our opinion, generally not well portrayed. It also needs to be mentioned that accounting education at public and private levels is *not* competing with other economic development policies, such as better income distribution, the "basic needs" concept, and agricultural development; it supplements these policies. Improved accounting education is not a substitute for other socioeconomic development policies, but an integral part thereof, irrespective of the structure, economy and types of economic policies to be pursued. We also should convey at the outset that effective accounting education, hopefully resulting in better accounting/auditing standards and practices, cannot be separated from other levels of education at the primary, secondary and postsecondary levels. Good general educational foundations are prerequisites to better accounting education and practices.

General education has received a fair share of attention and support from local, regional and international agencies, but this not so for *accounting education* in most Third World countries. Governments and international and regional organizations may well pay more attention to the overall significance of good accounting education and accounting methodology in the private and public sectors of the economies. In this regard, accounting education should not merely *follow* socioeconomic development (as has been so often the case) but also to help *shape* it. Such an orientation is badly needed in many countries, and undoubtedly would improve the status of accounting as both a practice and a learning discipline. It requires, however, an extensive appraisal of the aims and contents of the accounting system and its methodology, including the ways and means of transmitting knowledge.

Although each country or region has to evaluate the degree of sophistication required in accounting education, we opine that clear international patterns exist and could be adhered to effectively. Accordingly, we hope this study will assist policymakers and educators in rectifying certain inadequacies, and may lead to a more sound accounting education and research in the context of economic development policy, planning and decision making.

Once the immediate and long-term needs for improving accounting information measurement systems in the public and private sectors of Third World economies are recognized, the role of accounting education will become an integral part thereof. The accounting educational modules may have to be restructured and/or improved. Potential improvements should take into account the countries' socioeconomic objectives and policies, and the past and existing conditions. Different models may have to be developed based upon the type of economy encountered in a country, its eco-political philosophy and the prevailing educational setup and coverage provided for accountants. However, as mentioned previously, certain common required trends and developments tend to exist in all countries, and to a large extent this study sketches divergent but often common educational needs and patterns in different geographical and eco-political regions. The type of accounting system and methodology required should be of a fairly integrated eco-accounting nature, serving a variety of development objectives.

Throughout history, accounting, by and large, has had a micro orientation, and accountants have not looked upon their discipline as serving society as a whole. As stated in a previous study (Enthoven, 1978, p. 21):

> Accounting has passed through many stages: . . . These phases have been largely responses to economic and social environments. Accounting has adapted itself in the past fairly well to the changing demands of society. Therefore, the history of commerce, industry and government is reflected to a large extent in the history of accounting . . . What is of paramount importance is to realize that accounting, if it is to play a useful and effective role in society, must not pursue independent goals. . . . It must continue to serve the *objectives of its economic environment.* The historical record in this connection is very encouraging. Although accounting, generally, has responded to the needs of its surroundings, at times it has appeared to be out of touch with them.

In this context, developing economies have to assess whether their accounting education is "in touch" with its socioeconomic environment, while trying to determine what the needs for accounting education will be five to fifteen years hence. This requires an adequate *educational inventory and planning framework* tied to the country's long-term economic development plans.

The studies of specific countries and the regional observations presented in Part Four will be valuable to Third World countries and regions with similar problems. These country analyses and recommendations serve as the basis for the outlining of certain *general* educational patterns. These in turn are geared to serve action programs of an international, regional and domestic nature. Furthermore, this study hopefully will assist governments, professional and educational entities, international and regional agencies, and international accounting associations or federations, in taking appropriate steps to enhance public and private sector accounting education and developments. A major aim of this study is to assist external agencies to clarify the necessity and scope of accounting education and development in their respective countries and regions, and to help them channel technical and financial aid in this direction. Accordingly, this study can be designated as "A Framework for Action," fully recognizing that the action models may have to be outlined internally before effective internal *and* external programs can be executed. Various vehicles to execute such programs are reflected.

Our study's coverage serves both national and international purposes: national in that it proposes the development of an "accounting inventory and plan" within a country; and international in that it examines methods used to grant technical, manpower and financial assistance, and to execute cooperative accounting development programs on regional and international bases.

Academic and professional bodies in both developed and developing nations have expressed considerable willingness to assist counterparts in countries requiring assistance, and we expect that effective "action programs" can be exe-

3

cuted. Whether the first steps would be country or regional appraisal missions, or the establishment of an international commission along the lines of the United Nations' (UN) Brandt Commission appointed by Robert McNamara, President of the World Bank, will be touched upon in Chapter XV. Undoubtedly, other ideas will emerge which will warrant consideration. Input and suggestions from international and regional development organizations in this connection will be extremely welcome!

Strong impetus for our study was given by the American Accounting Association (AAA) in 1976-1978 with the appointment of a Committee on International Accounting Operations and Education, chaired by the author. This committee prepared a report, published with the financial support of the Price Waterhouse Foundation, which has been very well received in developing, and developed, economies. Feedback on that monograph, and on previous assessments made regarding accounting and economic development, uncovered a great need to appraise, in greater depth and on a broader scale, the education, training and other developmental aspects (e.g., research) of accounting in a variety of Third World countries and regions. Such appraisals needed to be carried out by knowledgeable persons in their respective countries. Subsequently, a framework could be developed to help improve accounting educational modules in these countries and regions. What emerged was the realization of a need for a more cohesive international framework for spurring accounting education in developing economies, with the potential assistance from certain international organizations and institutions in both developed and developing countries. Such efforts would need to be performed cooperatively by educators, professional bodies and practitioners in Third World countries; international and regional development agencies, such as the World Bank, UN, regional development banks; and educational and professional organizations in the so-called developed countries.

This study then focuses specifically on the *scope and methods* of improving accounting education and related aspects in Third World development management. Extensive international accounting assistance programs are envisaged, for which ways and means are also reflected in our current study.

In regard to a proposed accounting development and assistance program, it appears that some immediate vehicles for action warrant implementation:

1. *Set up an International Association for Accounting Development* to serve as a clearinghouse for information, technical assistance, etc., for the benefit of Third World accounting education.

2. As part of the above, send out *accounting educational appraisal teams* to Third World countries which request them. These teams would evaluate needs and outline a program for accounting educational assistance. They would be comprised of experts from a variety of countries with skills in various fields of accounting education and training and would spend from three to six weeks on each study. Our report on Indonesia (Ch. XIX) gives an idea of what can be done for a specific country.

Complementing the above vehicles for action, or substituting for them, would be the appointment by the World Bank and/or UN (or other international agency) of a special "Accounting Development Committee" to explore accounting practices and educational systems and requirements in Third World countries, and make recommendations for action.

A portion of the material presented in this study was originally compiled as part of the Committee Report of the Committee on International Accounting Education and Operations for the American Accounting Association (AAA), and the author is grateful to the Executive Committee of the AAA for permission to use this material. Several chapters are similar to the ones presented in the previously mentioned AAA study, and some of the individual country appraisals previously analyzed by our committee members have been updated by them in this study. However, our AAA Committee Report tended to be somewhat narrow in country/regional coverage, and it was necessary to extend the country and regional layouts, and to pursue the educational elements and requirements in greater depth and more extensively. Accordingly, this study also may help the Executive Committee of the AAA in delineating its role in international accounting education.

A number of persons from Third World countries has spent a great amount of time and effort in appraising their countries' situations for the studies presented in Part Four. In alphabetical order by country, they are:

Brazil	Professor Sergio de Iudicibus
Egypt	Professors Metwalli B. Amer, and M.M. Khairy
India	The Institute of Cost and Works Accountants of India and The Institute of Chartered Accountants of India
Indonesia	Professor Adolf J. H. Enthoven
Kenya	Professor James D. Newton
Korea	Korean Institute of Certified Public Accountants and Professor Sang Oh Nam
Libya	Professor Khalifa Ali Dau
Malaysia	Professor C. L. Mitchell
Mexico	Dr. Ricardo M. Mora
Pakistan	Mr. A. M. Ansari
Philippines	Professor Jesus A. Casino
Somalia	Dr. C. P. Cacho
South Pacific	Professor Roger Juchau
Tanzania	Professor Robert Dinman
Thailand	Professor Sangvian Indaravijaya et al.
Venezuela	Professors Omar Nucete and Mireya Villalobos de Nucete

This study would not have been possible without the active cooperation of these experts. We are very grateful for all their input, and hopefully it will lead to more sound international accounting education. These country and area reports serve the following specific purposes:

- They present an insight into the educational modules and requirements in a series of Third World countries, of potential benefit to other Third World economies and development countries' institutions.

5

- They outline bases for international and regional bilateral technical assistance.
- They set forth vital elements for seeking common accounting educational frameworks in developing regions.

In summation, the objectives of this text are: (1) to appraise, by means of specific Third World country studies in different regions, the need for accounting education in socioeconomic development; (2) to set forth a conceptual and pragmatic framework for enhancing accounting knowledge and education (and related practices) in Third World economies; (3) to assess the role of educational and other institutions throughout the world in disseminating accounting know-how and expertise to developing economies; and (4) to suggest how assistance may be given to Third World countries by way of effective eductional, training, and research programs and projects in conjunction with local, regional, and international educational and development bodies.

Part One of this study gives an *overview of the function of accounting in economic development*. Chapter II looks at the content of the accounting information system and its subsystems to aid in socioeconomic analysis, policy and planning. Chapter III appraises the socioeconomic, professional and institutional, and legal and statutory elements that influence accounting structures and processes. Chapter IV presents a sketch of the significance of accounting education, with regard to overall international economic activities, while Chapter V specifically looks at these educational aspects in regard to the economic development process.

Part Two analyzes the *accounting educational conditions, weaknesses and requirements* in Third World countries. Chapter VI describes the main deficiencies and needs in the area of accounting education, based upon the country studies and additional feedback received from around the world. Chapter VII gives a general presentation outlining the functions of accounting education, training and research for economic development management. This is followed, in Chapter VIII, by an analysis of educational programs for countries in the process of economic growth and development.

Part Three deals with a *Framework for Educational Action* in accounting. This Framework for Action is founded upon the analyses presented in previous parts and the country and regional evaluations (reflected in Part Four). Chapter IV gives an overall assessment of the ways and means for carrying out such an action program. Because training for public sector activities has generally been fairly neglected, a special chapter (X) deals with this subject. The potential task of development banks to spur accounting in countries and regions has also been previously overlooked. Accordingly, a separate chapter (XI) deals with the function of development finance institutions in the growth of accounting educational developments. Considerable interest has been expressed by educators, government officers and accounting practitioners in setting up an "International Association for Accounting Development" to function as a clearinghouse, accounting educational research entity, etc. This association would serve the needs of Third World countries in regard to accounting education, research and related developments. The potential activities and structures of such an international association are presented in Chapter XII.

Various international and regional vehicles exist to help implement such an international association, accounting development centers and other international, regional and country educational programs. These vehicles are set forth in Chapter XIII, while the subsequent chapter (XIV) covers the potential sources of finance to carry out the described programs. The last chapter in this section (XV) presents a summary and concluding observations.

Part Four constitutes much of the *background information* for our previous parts; it covers country and regional studies compiled by experts in the respective areas. This background information has been incorporated in the overall study. Hopefully, the specific information may help officials in the countries concerned to discern similar conditions and requirements. These countries' officials may also benefit from our overall study, as it gives directions to improve educational patterns in individual countries, in regions and internationally. We sincerely hope this study may lead to much needed improvements in the education of accountants, and to coordinate on an international scale an area in which the Third World countries are particularly dire.

This study would not have been possible without the active and dedicated involvement of colleagues of mine in the countries represented in this study. Their ideas are reflected in the respective chapters. However, in addition, a great number of other colleagues, government officials and accounting practitioners at domestic institutions in Third World economies and international organizations have given ideas and observations over the years, which have shaped many of my thoughts as reflected in this text.

Finally, I am highly appreciative that my mentor, Professor Jan Tinbergen, has written again a foreword to this study. His tremendous experience, knowledge and insight into the vast fields of economic development, information measurement and education give particular credence to the need to pursue a more active course in regard to "accounting education and economic development." His wisdom, writings, behavior, and deeds have greatly influenced my pursuits.

PART ONE

AN OVERVIEW OF ACCOUNTING

AND

ECONOMIC DEVELOPMENT

CHAPTER II

THE SIGNIFICANCE OF ACCOUNTING IN
ECONOMIC DEVELOPMENT MANAGEMENT*

1. The State of Accounting Development

1.1 Stages of Growth in Accounting Systems

A brief review of some historical accounting developments may be in order. For centuries after the system of double entry bookkeeping appeared, accounting was devoid of methodology or any form of theory. It was during the nineteenth century that we saw a move from bookkeeping to accounting—a move away from the relatively simple recording and analysis of transactions toward a comprehensive accounting *information system*. The increased reliance on capital as a factor of production necessitated extensive record keeping but, finally in the nineteenth century, a theoretical framework began to develop. This framework or methodology provided a technical means to measure, evaluate, and communicate information of an economic-financial nature.

Financial accounting "theory," building on bookkeeping, has been created from experience. It is essentially descriptive and has a utilitarian bias, and it has been oriented to the recording and verification of microeconomic enterprise information.

In twentieth century accounting, profit calculation is no longer a simple comparison of financial values at the beginning and end of a transaction or series of transactions. It is now related to a complex set of allocations and valuations pertaining to the operational activities of the company. The concept of accountancy or accounting might now be so far extended as to qualify for the description of the recording, processing, classifying, evaluating, interpreting, and supplying of economic-financial information for statement presentation and decision-making purposes. Accounting has been successful technically and methodlogically. However, the development of a comprehensive theory, with a secure intellectual relationship to its operating economic environment, has hardly begun in most countries.

Refinements in cost and management accounting came later in the twentieth century along with mass production techniques and high capital investment. These developments created a need to allocate costs correctly over the units of production, and also to provide a measure of productivity and efficiency. Thereafter, cost accounting evolved naturally to meet recognized managerial requirements of pricing and costing for competitive purposes, and to the determination and setting forth of operational information for decision-making purposes.

Traditionally, government accounting was linked to taxation and revenue control, and to the recording of and accountability for receipts and expenditures. The twentieth century development of budgeting and budgets gave a much

---

*For an elaborate appraisal of the function of the accounting system, and its subsystems, economic development policy c.f. Enthoven, 1973.

larger scope to the area of government accounting. The budget became a managerial and policy-making instrument and developed into a mechanism for the forward planning of receipts and expenditures. Budgeting nowadays has developed in such a manner that it forms one of the bases of, and is closely associated with, economic planning and programming.

The use of enterprise accounting for the purpose of macro (economic or national) accounting is largely a development of the last three decades. For purposes of economic policy and economic planning, these national data—to a large extent derived from commerical data—have become of great importance. They have given rise to a new concept of macro accounting which has presented the professional with a new sphere of operations and perspective. Macro accounting has particular importance in helping to build the bridge between economics and accounting, and thus offers accounting significant scope to make a contribution toward macroeconomic policy.

Accounting, then, has already gone through many phases: simple double entry bookkeeping, enterprise, government, and cost and management accounting; and it has most recently moved towards social accounting. These phases have all been largely a product of changing economic and social environments.

For the newer nations, this historical process and progress is of great significance. Although an understanding and competence in bookkeeping and basic accounting is, of course, necessary in developing countries, a great need exists for cost accounting and the presentation of analyses and various statements for planning purposes and decision-making. The economic development process is in need also of effective cost-benefit measurements for project and program evaluations, and of information for operating measurement, internal organization, pricing, and other management and economic policies. In addition, cost, management, or project accounting; government accounting; and accounting for public enterprises are characteristically even more important for developing countries. It is important to realize that accounting, if it wishes to be of maximum value to society, must not follow its own independent course of action, but should continue to gear itself to the objectives of the socioeconomic environment. This linkage of accounting information systems with socioeconomic analysis, policy and planning has been one of the most neglected areas of accounting.

1.2   Classification of Accounting Systems

The following historical sketch may give insight into the development of accounting. By looking specifically at various developing countries and regions, the impact of different historical "zones of accounting influence" is noticeable. In this respect, some paragraphs from a report of the AAA Committee on International Accounting Operations and Education (Supplement to Volume 52, 1977, of *The Accounting Review*), show that "zones of influence" concept does help explain educational patterns:

   Accounting systems have developed on the basis of an obligation for accountability. This obligation is usually based on law, economic or political or even religious power. There is some evidence that sophisticated accounting and reporting methods evolved only after a high level of industrialization has been attained. This, of course, does not mean that the availability of accounting skills in the early phases of development would not make a significant contribution. The economic development of today's emerging nations will certainly not follow the patterns experienced by the older industrialized countries. One reason is that there is a much greater degree of urgency; it is generally agreed that the rate of development should be more rapid than that experienced by today's industrialized nations. Another reason is that the tools of planning and policy making available today at both the micro and macro levels are far superior to those previously available. Accounting in the broadest sense of the word represents one of these tools.

The accounting patterns in the world accordingly may be classified according to the referred to "zones of influence" based on historical-cultural-socioeconomic circumstances which have influenced the development of the accounting principles underlying financial measurement and reporting in different countries and regions. The concepts and principles applied in these geographic areas are observable in the financial statements of companies. Essentially five distinct historical sources of accounting influence can be distinguished, i.e., British, Franco-Spanish-Portuguese, Germanic/Dutch, U.S., and Communistic.

A preliminary effort (Supplement to Vol. 52, 1977, of *The Accounting Review*) was made to classify the particular features of each of these zones. While generally the sources of accounting influence are known, the identification of characteristics of "sources of influence" in developing countries is less clear, due to stages of development and influences the countries may have gone through. These historical zones of accounting influence may help us to understand the educational structures in the countries analyzed. The study reported:

> The study of comparative accounting systems is lagging behind the developments in law, and is far behind the work being done in economics and political science . . . there is impetus for more rigorous work in the area of comparative accounting systems. This impetus stems from the growing scientific interest (and ability) among accounting academies, the thrust toward international standards of accounting (which requires an articulation and resolution of similarities and differences), and a growing concern by the "Third World" that what is best for the advanced industrial nations—in the way of an accounting system—is not necessarily best (and indeed may frustrate) the goals of developing countries.

A classification of accounting systems should be of value in many ways. First, it sharpens description and analysis. Second, it has predictive power. For example, a country or international body which seeks to impose its accounting system on some other country should be able to ascertain *a priori* whether such an imposition is likely to be feasible and/or desirable. From an ontological perspective, the classification would have predictive value in that it sets forth the most probable path of development of a particular country's accounting system.

Change in Egypt.

Further, in linking accounting with politics and economics, it would help to predict how a change in the latter would most probably affect the former. Accordingly, any program for assistance in the development of accounting in a particular Third World country should take into account its particular historical path of development and a "classification of accounting systems" would be useful. A detailed outline is given in the previously referred to committee report.

There are several structural approaches to the classification of accounting systems. Identifying the appropriate classification systems for a country would have the following benefits:

• It would permit a developing country to specify a classification for the nation's accounts, for economic segments and firms.

• It would help a country to plan the process of replacing the present system, gaining from the experience of other countries.

A developing country may wish deliberately to follow a sequence of changes from one accounting system to another because it has observed that another country has negotiated successfully that route toward what is perceived to be a desirable accounting system.

2. The Nature and Function of Accounting in Development

At this stage it may be appropriate to inquire about the nature of accounting in the economic process.

Accounting, as a measurement and reporting information system, can be seen to cover both micro and macro economic activities; it is composed of various subsystems which relate economic events and decisions. Thus, accounting concerns itself not only with individual enterprises, but also with government administration and national (economic) accounts; and these three systems or branches of accounting are closely related. Accounting then can be conceived and practiced as the identification, selection and analysis, measurement, prediction, processing, evaluation, and communication of information about costs and benefits, both of a direct and indirect nature, to facilitate economically justified decisions regarding activities and resources.

In our society of a highly interdisciplinary and interacting nature, the role of accountancy also has to be more and more conceived and practiced as relevantly and effectively servicing socioeconomic needs of a public and private nature. Especially to spur the development process, accountancy has to become much broader in orientation, measurement, and reporting, i.e., serving individual and social needs. So far, we have not adequately lived up to this challenge; our responses have been meager.

One can grasp the scope of accounting effectively only if one has a clear understanding of the composition of its elements and how the measurement of economic activities are interrelated in three logical branches, namely, business or enterprise accounting, government accounting, and national accounting. The accounting branches serve specific functions, although all three branches work with the same raw economic material (i.e., the phenomena occurring in the socioeconomic environment). The first two, including accounting for nonprofit organizations are often referred to as micro accounting, while national accounting is often referred to as macro, social or economic accounting.

2.1 Enterprise Accounting

A distinction is to be made between financial accounting and cost or management accounting. Financial accounting is concerned primarily with the provision of financial information to outsiders (e.g., shareholders, creditors, bankers, government, economic analysts); management or operational accounting deals with accounting information for managerial and other microeconomic decision-making purposes. This is the application of accounting knowledge to the production and interpretation of accounting and statistical information for assisting management tasks, including planning, control, and budgeting.

Currently, income determination is a primary objective of enterprise accounting. Because of the articulation of the income statement, balance sheet and flow of fund statement, however, rules for measurement of income also affect the classification and valuation of items in the other statements.

Another primary objective of enterprise accounting is to facilitate microeconomic planning and control. In accomplishing this objective, the output of the accounting system is no longer seen merely as a set of historical financial statements, but in addition, as providing information for sophisticated normative management decision models.

More comprehensive and unifying criteria for income measurement, applicable to both micro and macro economics spheres are needed. A collective viewpoint must be adopted to achieve an interdisciplinary concept of enterprise income. For example, data from business income statements are used and should be useful for national accounting purposes; economic programming; and national economic, fiscal and monetary policies.

In most countries financial accounting has an established series of specific guidelines, principles, or rules. These principles form a general frame of reference to judge the acceptability of procedures and practices. Insufficient attention has been given to building a comprehensive and consistent pattern of thought, applying of other disciplines and using normative and deductive criteria. Managerial and cost accounting generally assumes a more economically realistic approach, emphasizing measurement of future values and focusing on the users of the data.

Unfortunately, the principles and rules governing accounting in different countries are so varied and are based on such numerous and contradictory theories that it is difficult to interpret them on an international or even a national basis. It becomes extremely difficult, for example, to compare and assess financial statements reliably; to measure enterprise and industry and efficiency performance adequately; to construct effective budgets; to pinpoint capital needs; to conduct adequate enterprise project and program appraisals in the domestic and international fields; to facilitate investment decisions; to perform satisfactory econometric analyses and projections; to design effective industry, sector and national economic plans; and to establish national accounts soundly.

This is not to say that conventional financial accounting norms, based on historical and legalistic concepts, should be discarded. For accountability and stewardship purposes, these are highly effective, and give a clear idea of what has occurred. But for the most vital task of enterprise accounting, to serve as a framework and tool for socioeconomic decision-making, these concepts are neither effective nor relevant.

2.2 Government Accounting

Government accounting deals with the collection, measurement (classification and valuation), processing, communication, control, and stewardship of receipts, expenditures, and related activities in the public sector. The accounting needs of the government sector are no less urgent than those for the business enterprise sector, nor is sound government likely to exist without sound governmental accounting. Many enterprise accounting techniques and procedures are applied extensively to government sector activities. This is especially true regarding public enterprises (parastatals) and other government undertakings. However, there are distinct aspects of accounting information, classification, and procedures applicable only to transactions in the government sector that make it desirable to treat this as a separate branch of accounting even though it is inter-related with the other branches. For example, statements prepared in the government sector are used for macro accounting purposes.

2.3 Macro (Economic) Accounting

Macro accounting also is known as economic, national (regional) or even social accounting. This study abstains from using the original Hicksian (1942) term "social accounting" as that term nowadays refers to the measurement and reporting of the social effects of their operations. The aim of macro accounting is to describe systematically and quantitatively the structure and activities of an economy or region/sector during a certain time span, and of its stocks (assets and liabilities) at a particular time. While micro accounting deals with the single micro entry (such as the business enterprise), macro accounting covers similarly the economic position, activities, and measurement of efficiency of an aggregation of entities in a community. These units being accounted for, showing costs and benefits at aggregate levels, may be a whole industry, a sector or the economy as a whole.

Macro accounting is concerned with business enterprise, private households, the governments; related accounts such as rest-of-the-world and capital formation; and the derivation of their component. It is concerned with the application of accounting methodology to macro economic analysis. Economic transactions between groups of individuals (households), business enterprises, government agencies, the outside world, and all their respective sub-institutions are covered. The mass of quantitative data is recorded, measured, processed and consolidated into various systems designed to exhibit in accounts and tables the principal national aggregates (e.g., national product and income) and their interrelations. The entities (units)—an industry, a sector, or the economy as a whole—are much larger here than in enterprise or government accounting. Although macro accounting uses the same basic techniques as micro accounting for classifying (revenue, income), summarizing, combining and reflecting data, the underlying procedures vary. *as will be seen in chapter 6.*

Within the macro accounting system, economic data have to be identified, collected, analyzed, measured (e.g., valued and classified) and reported. These are all functions which are part of accounting; macro accounting techniques and procedures, including double-entry recording (the duality principle) and the pattern of account classification (e.g., revenue, expense, income, purchases, assets), show similarity to those in enterprise (micro) accounting. The distinction between flows (activities) and stocks (resources) also is maintained in macro accounting.

The various macro accounts are obtained largely from business enterprises' accounting profit and loss statements and balance sheets, although the macro accountant has to rearrange the data and incorporate additional information of a quantitative and evaluative nature to reflect current activities and changes in stocks for the entities as a whole. Macro accounting is an essential part of the overall accounting system—the parent framework—with its interrelated branches of accounting.

The framework of macro accounting consists of five interrelated versions or segments: (1) the national income and product account, (2) the interindustry (or input-output) account, (3) the flow of funds account, (4) the balance of payments account, and (5) the national balance (sheet) account. Of these five, the first two reflect real flows (transactions in goods and services), the third and fourth cover both real and monetary flows, and the fifth account concerns itself with stock variables (assets and liabilities). The national income and product account and the national balance sheet are comparable to enterprise account's income statement and balance sheet. The flow of funds account compares to the statement of changes in financial position. Input-output tables (matrices) also are encountered in business accounting, but the balance of payments account has no comparable account in the business sphere.

2.4 Auditing

Auditing, an integral part of accounting, is concerned with obtaining and verifying financial and economic facts in order to give an audit opinion about an entity's progress and financial condition. It applies to the public and private sectors. An auditor investigates and comments on the accounting system and methods applied. Some even consider the evaluation of management as part of the auditing task. Audits also are necessary for stewardship determination. As a process, an audit tends to have a beneficial influence on the generation, allocation, and flow of capital from internal and external sources, and enhances efficient administration. The types of audits to be distinguished are: financial, operational, economic, and social.

As for government auditing, a recent monograph by the United Nations (ST/ESA/SER.E8, 1977) touches upon some aspects of relevance to our study, i.e., in a number of developed and developing countries, audit institutions have been set up by the national legislatures, independent of the executive branch of the government, to aid the legislatures in performing these tasks. The traditional concepts of control and accountability were, however, somewhat narrowly defined in terms of verifying whether the government transactions were in accordance with the sanctions of the legislatures. Consequently, audit functions were limited and concentrated on checking the financial correctness and legal propriety of government transactions.

This purely fiscal or financial audit sufficed when governments played a minimum role in the economic life of their societies and confined their transactions largely, if not exclusively, to the maintenance of law and order. In recent decades, however, governments have assumed major responsibility for and a dynamic role in the acceleration of the economic and social development of their societies, and many of them have adopted planning as an integral approach to decision-making. As a result, the public sector continues to grow in size, and public activities continue to increase in their diversity and complexity. Within this process of planned development, managerial dimensions other than the propriety and regularity of government transactions have surfaced prominently, and governments today are concerned, *inter alia,* with ensuring that the limited resources at their disposal are being used as economically as possible for the attainment of program goals and objectives.

Within this context the question of performance audit has been discussed in recent years. It is widely recognized that government audit has an expanded role to play in planned development. Performance audit entails examination in terms of appropriate cost efficiency, and effectiveness of government transactions. The principal idea is to analyze the effectiveness of public outlays in terms of their expected contribution to stated goals and objectives and in terms of the costs incurred in doing so. Thus, unlike fiscal audit, the emphasis is shifted from purely financial considerations to cost, output, and goal fulfillment.

The development of performance audit, however, raises a number of issues which merit further investigation and analysis. The first and foremost question relates to the formulation of performance criteria and methodology. Different projects have different objectives, designs, and impacts. Policies and projects often have multiple objectives and sometimes give rise to results which may be unintended. It is, therefore, essential to distinguish between principal and subsidiary objectives, direct and indirect benefits, and externalities (external effects). It would be fruitless to prescribe a standard methodology for this purpose, but it would be constructive and helpful to develop suitable methodologies for sets of projects and sectors, and sets of policies having a common focus.

An equally important issue relates to the choice of audit techniques. The use of appropriate techniques has relevance both to the patterns of project organizations and management and to the timeliness of audit. Development projects are becoming increasingly complex, and organizations such as public enterprises are assuming greater significance. Because a comprehensive audit is almost impossible, owing to considerations of time and resources, suitable techniques are essential to evaluate at least the projects and policies which constitute the core of the development effort. The task is, therefore, to establish such cores in terms of groups of countries and to devise techniques for investigation and reporting which are expeditious, effective, and least demanding in terms of their draft on scarce critical inputs.

Both the auditing and accounting functions also have a major bearing on capital markets, finance, and capital formation. While universal accounting and auditing methods are of great importance, legislation should be standardized also, for example, regarding commercial reporting and disclosure requirements and company laws (although the existence of a commercial code does not guarantee that it will be applied). Furthermore, legislation is needed for the protection of the auditing and accounting profession, whether operating as an independent or government-supervised body for private and public sector activities.

3. Accounting as a Parent Framework

Accounting has been viewed as a dealing with entities of enterprise, government, and macro nature. It covers the entire administration or management of information for all socioeconomic activities and conditions in the micro and macro economic sector, covering internal and external information needs of various groups. It may be classified in broad terms as including (1) the recording of economic facts based on real world phenomena involving measurements and their further appraisal and interpretation, in the form of cost and benefit measurements, to enable effective evaluations and decisions about activities and the allocation of resources, and (2) the communication of the results of evaluations and decisions made for present and prospective purposes. Such an orientation involves focus on both (a) micro and macro managerial decision-making and economic planning and control content and (b) an accountability or stewardship content.

There is a great need to integrate all forms of accountancy into a coherent framework. The scope for such a framework makes the separation between micro and macro accounting somewhat artificial. Micro data are used for macro accounting, while the latter is used for evaluations and decisions at the enterprise and governmental accounting level.

The demands made on accounting for information to serve socioeconomic needs and aims requires a better framework and better subsystems for organizing the information, and an economically sound and comprehensive set of fundamentals to cater to and guide the dynamic force of accounting. Accounting objectives have, thus, to be served by a useful and relevant primary framework. We believe that a completely new direction or dimension regarding the whole *scope* and *contents* of accounting is warranted to serve more effectively the socioeconomic needs of countries.

What is necessary is a more integrated evolution in line with the changing and expanding public requirements of society; for example: measurement of social benefits and costs of economic activities, realistic current value appraisals, and projections regarding future individual and social costs and benefits. Furthermore, a better set of accounting systems involves a carefully appraised general accounting theory of information. Development of the theory might precede practice, but the theory should be practical and feasible, involving evaluation of the cost and effort with regard to the results.

4. Accounting and Economic Policy

Accounting systems and procedures, furthermore, are used within a whole range of macro and micro economic analyses, policies and plans. These activities will be appraised briefly.

4.1 Economic Planning

To better allocate the scarce human, financial, and material resources, all countries require some form of economic planning or programming. Economic planning, which is a preparatory evaluation and decision-making process, requires alternative measurements and evaluations for the determination of priorities in resources allocation.

4.2 Project Appraisals

Every economic plan consists of a series of projects which require the compilation of information relating to the production of specific goods and services. The feasibility and justifiability of such projects must be appraised because they are the building blocks for the development plan. Thus, there is a continuous dialogue between the micro and macro phases.

The most rational basis for project decision-making is sought. Project appraisal requires extensive present and future data, and direct and indirect quantifications and measurements. Extensive cost-benefit calculations and evaluations are incorporated in the decision model, which requires information that is economically realistic, comprehensive, and standardized.

4.3 Other Socioeconomic Studies

These studies include accounting for socioeconomic facets dealing, for example, with ecology, poverty, social security, and a whole range of other aspects in a society for which accounting measurements and reporting are warranted. This area is nowadays also referred to as "social accounting." To date, accounting has been reluctant to get involved in socioeconomic areas, but logically this is an essential extension and function. A great deal of coordination with other disciplines will be necessary, and measurements may not be easy. Standardization requirements, for example, concerning measurement of indirect effects (e.g., social cost-benefit studies), also will need to be appraised.

4.4 Capital Formation

The availability, formation and use of capital are important factors in the economic growth and development process. Reinvested and distributed profits in the business sector, and savings in the household and government sectors, constitute the principal sources of capital formation.

Corporate growth, and the corporate form of organization, which enables small amounts of savings to be coordinated through the capital market, make heavy demands on legal, fiscal, and accounting procedures. Accounting and auditing have to meet these demands; company statements have to be reliable, helping to instill confidence in corporate operations. The necessary funds may not be forthcoming if inadequate accounting and auditing standards and practices prevail. The need for sound accounting, however, is not limited to the larger corporate entities. Small-scale operations might have even greater need. The requirements of small industry are too often neglected, and this can have serious repercussions on the country's potential for economic growth.

Accounting plays an important role in improving the organization of both tax administration and the responsibilities of taxpayers, enabling more equitable and effective tax policies and procedures to be implemented. Furthermore, accounting is able to assist in appraising the best forms of taxation to achieve necessary objectives.

Accounting techniques, such as information accumulation, measurement, processing, recording and verification (auditing), are all essential to a well-designed tax structure and smoothly operating tax administration. Also, a sound tax auditing structure is imperative. Closer integration between taxation and accounting undoubtedly will be beneficial to the economic community as a whole.

CHAPTER III

ELEMENTS INFLUENCING THE DEVELOPMENT
OF ACCOUNTING

Accounting structures and processes are influenced by socioeconomic, professional, institutional, statutory, legal, and other considerations. Some of the critical elements may have a bearing on the improvements considered necessary.

1. Socioeconomic Influences

Because accounting operates in a socioeconomic framework as a "service" function, the socioeconomic activities and policies have a major bearing on accounting. In Chapter II, accounting was seen as adapting itself to the changing requirements of society. These requirements are differentiated in so-called capitalistic, socialistic or communistic societies with their different emphases on how economic transactions are to be pursued and priced (e.g., economic planning of a mandatory or indicative nature).

Most countries want to pursue an active policy of economic development, which constitutes economic growth plus structural social and economic changes. Structural change is composed of a whole series of social, political, legal, administrative, organizational, and other environmental factors.

Economic development cannot be expressed in purely quantitative economic terms; it is a transformation and adaptation process. Within this adaptation process is found the need for deliberate and coordinated actions by governments to spur economic development owing to scarcities of factors of production, income disparities, population pressures or other structural disequilibria identified by governments. Accordingly, governments may pursue direct actions involving extensive economic planning and programming.

Different planning forms are encountered as part of economic policy in a nation, and economic development planning can be referred to as a decision-making process of a forward-looking nature in which alternatives have to be measured, weighed, and outlined. An economic plan is a coherent whole of facts and figures indicating the most desirable coures of events. Economic policy, of a short-, medium- or long-term nature, is characterized in turn as desired acts of economic behavior, directed towards changes in quantitative and qualitative aims, and intended to attain an optimum socioeconomic pattern for the nation. The briefly sketched socioeconomic framework and activities will have a major bearing on the accounting structures and processes to be pursued.

2. Professional and Institutional Structures

In many developing countries, either no accounting profession exists or the profession is in infancy and suffers from many shortcomings. A word of caution is in order. There are significant exceptions to many of the general statements made in this report. India and Pakistan, for example, are usually classified as developing countries, yet they have developed accounting professions and also have well-developed systems for accounting education. Nevertheless, the generalizations apply to most developing countries. When there is no accounting profession, the country usually looks to its former colonial motherland for a model. Thus, a number of countries of the British Commonwealth try to establish professions and professional qualifications modeled after British examples. Former French colonies and protectorates follow the French model. Establishing a soundly based accounting profession in developing countries is extremely important. The accounting needs (of developing countries) generally involve three main elements: (1) relevant accounting and auditing standards, (2) effective training of accountants, and (3) recognition of the accounting function as a tool for national economic development. Dynamic and potent professional organizations may help serve these needs.

Professional institutes or societies in developing countries tend to be fairly weak, but most countries recognize the need to improve the institutional functions. There is an increasing awareness in most (developing) countries of the need for soundly functioning accountancy institutes that set standards in accounting and auditing, design codes of practice, run training and educational programs, give qualification tests, and do research and exchange information with other accounting bodies. Many of the existing institutional frameworks tend to be somewhat outdated and not enough attention is given to the future direction of accountancy tasks, plus ways to introduce new approaches to the institute's members.

Often the existing professional and practitioner bodies in financial accounting, managerial accounting and government accounting form independent organizations, while the statisticians and national accountants also may have their own groups. In most countries, the field of cost or management accounting has not been professionalized. Far greater attention should be paid to management accounting, accountancy systems and cost-benefit measurements. For example, an inverse relationship exists between better systems and procedures and auditing, to the extent that the audit work will be facilitated and less detailed when good systems of internal control and internal check exist.

Extensive efforts should be made to build or strengthen an indigenous (local) profession in all countries. For this purpose, domestic registration, regulations, laws and citizenship rules are being passed, and usually a national board of accountants, a registration board or similar body is set up to localize the profession under the supervision of a government ministry.

Regulations covering accountancy measurements and reporting may be designed and enforced by a government or by a semiprivate or private accounting association or institute. The existing institutional accountancy structures frequently suffer from insufficient professional interest, inadequate government encouragement, and lack of support and compliance by private and public institutions. In addition, a variety of professional accounting bodies may be organized without much substance and influence.

Professional accounting service generally has not been geared adequately to economic development needs of the countries, while the professional training programs and research are neither linked effectively to these needs nor do they portray future requirements of accounting. The programs tend to give limited attention to such areas as long-range projections, shadow price measurements, value-added concepts and the measurement/reporting of indirect costs and benefits. Auditing, too, has not given necessary attention to efficiency of operational audits, economic audits, and social audits. Only recently have several accounting institutes incorporated economic decision-making and analysis programs as parts of their institutional courses. Most professional institutes have not had the time, nor felt the need to establish an "inventory" of skills and related medium- and long-range requirements. But in several countries an accountants registration act has been passed to set up a board of accountants to regulate qualifications, administer examinations, register accountants and function as a professional nucleus under the supervision of a ministry.

In most countries a strong accountancy act is lacking. An act should incorporate not only accounting and auditing standards but also codes of conduct and the operational aspects of accounting firms. Such an act could help the profession both internally and externally. A separate accountancy act could be set up to cover these elements, and such an accountancy act may be necessary in addition to a company's act. The latter generally is not geared towards incorporating detailed accounting standards and a code of ethics.

An accountancy board may function as the planning body and spur an atmosphere of learning and research, hold conferences, arrange publications and promote the sound functioning of accounting tasks. The board's rulings often are unenforceable, however, and may not be backed by government. This, the absence of professionalism and a weak or non-existent accounting institute, may impede the development of accounting and auditing standards and may prevent accountancy from becoming an effective force within the nation.

In general, the institutional accountancy structure warrants strengthening, whereby, *inter alia*, due care should be given to publications, journals, promotional aspects, research and developmental matters, student coaching, lectures and seminars. Many institutes are fairly passive, for reasons often beyond their control, and they may be forced to keep low profiles due to lack of financing, status and real interest from members. The existing or newly established institutes or societies will have to become involved heavily in these areas instead of merely providing a low profile secretarial office. These developmental activities entail extensive financial requirements, and perhaps the assistance of foreign experts to create a viable and dynamic profession.

Accordingly, strong associations or institutes of accountants need to be encouraged and they should have their own articles of incorporation, rules of conduct, standards of performance, and membership requirements. Various degrees of memberships are feasible and desirable. It may be useful to set up a "parent body" for various accounting interests and involvements. An accountancy act may have to set the necessary qualifications, accounting and auditing standards, standards for admittance to membership, and codes of conduct. The one or more accountancy titles established should be protected by such an act.

The institutes preferably also should form closer bonds. Technical assistance from other institutes would be desirable, whereby "clearinghouse" activities might take place, involving exchange of study materials, accounting programs, tests and personnel. A building(s) and library(ies), including rooms available for seminars and self-study should be considered. The institutes should have adequate facilities, in the major cities and elsewhere, for encouraging and helping students to study.

The institutes, furthermore, may well want to get more involved with socio-economic requirements of the countries and build close linkages with government agencies, economic and social planning offices, and ministries of education to link accounting development and training with the country's socioeconomic demands. The institutes, in turn, should receive official recognition from the government. In this regard, the accounting titles and the profession should have legal recognition, and the institutes may be partially or wholly responsible for the standards applied. These standards will have to be outlined by the profession and government, and cover accounting, auditing and the code of ethics.

A trend in professional training is for a person to obtain an academic or other basic formal training degree before being admitted to sit for a professional accounting examination. Such a program appears desirable as long as the programs of the formal (academic and other) institutes are relevant to local needs. As the institutional training programs are given a wider base, the upper level accounting training gradually makes a university or comparable degree compulsory. The old style "on-the-job" training and articleship have shown certain deficiencies for the development of effective accountants.

3. Legal and Statutory Requirements

Accounting theory, methodology, and practice are influenced strongly by requirements in companies' acts or in legal and tax decrees. The absence of regulatory aspects in many countries does limit the comparability and usefulness of accounting information. The functions of capital markets and capital formation may be hampered and the users of financial statements may be deprived of adequate protection. On the other hand, rigid adherence to company or taxation acts, with their heavy accountability aspects, may cause inadequate development of a sound and economically relevant discipline based on useful norms.

It is very unlikely in most developing countries that an accounting profession will evolve, as it did in Great Britain and the U.S., without government involvement. Even if it did, the process would take too long and urgently needed professional services would not be available on time. The development of accounting should, therefore, be promoted by appropriate laws and regulations on accounting. This would include laws that regulate the accounting profession, auditing laws that regulate financial reporting and accounting (uniform charts), and tax laws that affect accounting. In most developing countries, it is hard to visualize an orderly development of the accounting function without such legal underpinnings. In developing countries where professional organizations exist, they are much too weak to develop and enforce their own standards of reporting and auditing. There are many countries where there is no professional organization of any kind.

Taxation in developing nations should be considered from two basic points of view. Firstly, an adequate amount of taxation is needed to provide the government with revenue to finance not only its regular public services but also badly needed investments, especially in the infrastructure. Taxation is one of the important sources of capital formation. Efficient tax systems are often also a prerequisite for the availability of foreign credits to the public sector and public enterprises. Secondly, the tax structure of developing countries must give particular attention to the probable affects of different taxes on private incentives to work, save and invest.

The accounting statutes in countries which set forth accounting standards (principles) and auditing standards often reflect the legal, statutory, and tax requirements. Also, accounting standards and rules frequently follow foreign guidelines with little domestic relevance. Other countries lack effective legislation covering accounting and auditing standards and procedures, and accounting practices may vary at the behest of those who prepare the statements.

Companies' acts in some countries set forth the economic significance, scope and content of financial statements, and the classification, valuation and other measurement procedures to be applied with sample reporting layouts for industrial and commercial sectors. Accounting measurement, classification and reporting may be standardized usefully either by industry or on some broader scale. The involved norms are to be outlined in the accountancy and/or company's act.

In other countries, a central accounts office, by act or decree, may be set up as part of the accountant-general's office to design and implement accounting procedures for government and semi-government operations. This may embrace procedures concerning the treasury, central bank, public enterprises, and other agencies and the linkage, by means of uniform layouts and measurement criteria, of all public and semi-public entities. By law, the government audit agency (by means of the auditor-general) also may extend its activities to other than financial audits, i.e., operational (efficiency), economic and legal audits.

In any case, the socioeconomic influences, the professional and institutional structures, and the legal and statutory requirements are important factors in any assessment of a country's accounting service.

The factors affect the needs of the accounting education function in a country.

CHAPTER IV

ACCOUNTING EDUCATION AND INTERNATIONAL ECONOMIC ACTIVITIES

1. Accounting in the International Environment

Although our study focuses on accounting education within Third World nations, the economic interphase between and among Third World and other countries also has a bearing on the development of accounting methods and education. Reference was already made to the changing role of accounting involving extended dimensions, e.g., "societal responsibility accounting." This is brought about by both pressures originating within countries and international demands towards further disclosure and reporting, and the associated measurement techniques applied.

International operations require a wide range of information for domestic and foreign parties. In this regard, the U.K. "The Corporate Report" (Accounting Standards Steering Committee, London, 1975) suggested for example that disclosure requirements preferably should include: a value-added statement; an employment report; statement of future prospects; and statement of corporate objectives. Other disclosures would cover: flow of funds statements, efficiency and performance indicators, directors' interests, corporate pension funds, etc. Such reporting is an indication of the move towards "societal responsibility accounting" around the world, built upon stewardship and decision-making accounting. Similar information and disclosure reports have emerged in France, Germany, Sweden and The Netherlands. Such trends also go hand in hand with greater accounting standardization of both measurement and reporting elements. Several international bodies are involved in such efforts, i.e., the accounting profession's International Accounting Standards Committee (IASC and the UN's Centre on Transnational Corporations). The European Economic Community is setting forth its own disclosure and standardization guidelines (directives). These regional efforts also will have transnational impacts as economic integration tends to spread beyond national-regional borders. Accordingly, regional and international developments have educational implications, and in order to improve international economic flows (especially between developing and developed nations) accounting educational structures also require improvement. Not only the previously referenced organizations should be involved but also such institutions as the World Bank, IMF and regional development organizations.

To restate and clarify our position, the changing international economic scene, influenced by the growth of multinational enterprises (MNEs) and international economic interdependence, demands better international accounting standards and practices, accompanied by business laws, codes of conduct, etc. Critical techniques and norms for international accounting operations will have to be developed. This would apply in particular to value-added data and statements, transfer pricing, current values, currency translations, cost accounting standards, planning and budgeting, performance measurements, operational auditing and management information systems, and other valuation and classification criteria. International economic activities also demand a deep insight into whether financial, material and human resources are allocated and used in the most efficient manner. This requires sound management accounting and management controls and audits. In turn, effective project cost evaluations may lead to better pricing structures.

Prospective measurements also will be required, such as those pertaining to feasibility studies, capital budgeting, and economic programs. Such measurements must also be integrated with the regional or global strategic planning framework. Furthermore, cost-benefit measurements need to be audited—an area of particular concern to management accountants.

Consequently, both management and financial accounting will need to become more heavily involved with socioeconomic aspects, based upon economic plan or program activities. Sound economic planning—of a micro and macro nature—in turn must be based on carefully evaluated feasibility studies. Accounting may have to become better aligned with the economic policies and plans of all governments, and to appraise these policies by taking into account taxation, capital formation, cost-effectiveness, and so on. Accounting could effectively assist in enhancing public analyses, policies, plans and programs.

Accounting also will have to be more closely linked with other disciplines, such as economics, statistics, sociology, and quantitative methods. Various disciplines will have to jell together to make international accounting more relevant and useful within the context of our socioeconomic framework. The inputs have to be relevant for the required outputs, whereby everything must prove itself in terms of its usefulness for analysis, policy and decisionmaking. All this has wide educational, training and certification implications.

2. International Accounting Requirements[1]

The need to identify, measure and report economically relevant and comprehensive information regarding international transactions and resources requires a sharpening of tools in several areas. Critical demands are made for accurate readouts in transfer pricing, current values, value-added cost accounting standards, planning and budgeting, performance evaluation, control, management audits, macro-accounting and so forth. Somehow these developments and their associated techniques must be linked with the future impact and role of accounting for international activities.

Several critical techniques have considerable bearing on the development of international accounting. International transfer pricing refers to the establishment of prices of goods and services between corporations and their affiliates located in different countries. Ideally, "arm's length" prices are to be established for such transactions, and the "cost-plus" concept is extensively followed. This

---

[1] This appraisal was partially based on a paper written by the author for *Management Accounting* (Sept. 1980 issue), published by the National Association of Accountants, New York, U.S.A.

entails the cost of production plus a margin for each supplier within the corporate network. But cost-plus may be difficult to apply. For example, uncertainty about the best allocation of research, depreciation and management overhead costs may arise.

In addition, transfer prices may be distorted by either internal or external factors. Examples of internal factors include the reduction or increase in the apparent profits (profit switching) in a particular affiliate for purposes of income leveling, wage bargaining, taxation and so on. External factors can include many things. There may be diversities in the rates of taxation or in the rules of assessment between countries covering payment of capital, dividends, interests, royalties, the ability to transform taxable income into non-taxable costs, and exchange rate differences and risks. Furthermore, accounting policies and standards may vary considerably, affecting transfer pricing methodology.

Related questions are whether direct costing procedures are considered valid as a costing method, and whether incremental marginal costing can be defended as an acceptable procedure by divisionalized companies in countries. Although integral costs are the preferred method for intercompany cost-based transfer pricing, goods and services could justifiably be transferred to other countries at direct costs plus mark-up.

A number of international agencies have been concerned with transfer pricing procedures, among them the UN Centre on Transnational Corporations and its Expert Group on International Standards of Accounting Reporting, the United Nations Group of Experts on Tax Treaties, the International Fiscal Association, the Organization for Economic Cooperation and Development (OECD) and the Commission of the European Economic Communities (EEC).

In regard to the accounting attitude to current values (costs), this is still mainly one of an adjustment to year-end financial statements rather than a total integration of current values in the accounting information system for all sorts of costing, pricing and other analytical or decision models.

The need for managerial or performance audits has also become strong in international operations. While it may be difficult to compare international results data submitted, operational audits could appraise more closely the efficiency and effectiveness of international operations. Management certainly wants a clear insight into all the cost-benefit aspects for evaluation and decision-making, as part of the planning and control framework. The tools necessary to make such appraisals or reports tend to go beyond the financial auditor's scope and expertise, and extended (managerial accounting) expertise may have to cope herewith.

Many private companies find themselves dealing with foreign governments and government operated public enterprises or parastatals. The accounting systems and standards at these public entities may be different from our procedures. Where joint international operations are contemplated, a clear understanding has to exist regarding norms for costing, pricing and other measures. Most frequently disagreements occur regarding depreciation, inventory valuations, changes of management costs, and research and development charges.

Enterprises also need to be aware of the statutory cost standards that may exist in a foreign country.

3. Accounting and the Multinational Enterprise

An accounting oriented criticism often cited is that an MNE's cost and pricing structure may create limited value-added in a foreign country. Transfer pricing policy, for example, is an extremely sensitive issue for a country, whose people may not know the real costs of the inputs and reasonable prices for the outputs.

International accounting is faced with several measurement demands. Firstly, a greater degree of uniformity in cost and financial accounting would be desirable. These more standardized accounting systems would preferably be carried out on an international basis under the auspices of an international agency, in conjunction with international accounting organizations, professional accounting bodies and industrial associations.

Secondly, value-added statements may also have to be prepared. These statements would give a clearer picture of the contribution an MNE makes in its activities in a foreign country. Both the company and government could then more effectively assess the benefits and costs of MNE operations. A breakdown may be given as to sources of ownership, financing methods, or export sales (see Exhibit 1).

EXHIBIT 1

Operations	(Current a/c)

Payments to other countries - by country of source
    (foreign inputs)
        1. to affiliates
        2. to other
+Local Purchases
+Local Value Added
+Total Sales Value

Sales to other countries - by country of destination
        1. to affiliates
        2. to other
+Local Sales Value

Ownership	(Capital a/c)
Ownership	-by country of sources
Other Financing	-by country of source
Assets	-by country of location

Other aspects of international accounting concern, relating to MNE's activities, are:

1) Social indicators and corporate socioeconomic audits may be necessary to convey an MNE's contribution to social and economic development. It would be desirable to reflect a series of social indicators such as health expenditures, welfare, schooling and other services. Furthermore, a corporate social and economic audit could be carried out by professional management accountants and public accountants, as well as by other qualified persons. A government audit service could also undertake this task. The outside auditors could attest to the amounts spent on social and economic services and show these in evaluation reports. Performance audits would be used for both internal and external purposes.

2) Measurement of externalities will have to be made. The indirect and secondary costs and benefits of MNEs have been largely neglected, although they constitute one of the most significant factors in appraising impact. The direct and secondary effects (both positive and negative) also need to be considered in order to appraise the significance of the MNE.

For example, inputs and outputs from or to other industries create in turn other costs and benefits through a sort of multiplying effect by means of "backward" and "forward" linkages that include infrastructure developments such as utilities and roads. The output prices of industries may be lower than original inputs, increasing national benefits which are not necessarily reflected in enterprise statements. The need for skilled workers may also create training requirements that result in a company's subsidizing outside education and related facilities. Finally, MNE employees and their families may be covered by medical services and other social security benefits that have a major impact on sickness prevention and health control in host countries. All these things and more must be taken into account when evaluating the impact on an MNE.

4. International Involvement in Setting Accounting Standards

Such international organizations as the UN's Centre on Transnational Corporations and the OECD have outlined specific standards applicable to transnational operations (enterprises). These norms are of a financial accounting, managerial accounting and social accounting nature. They involve, for example, the above referred to value-added statements, transfer pricing policies, and valuation and classification criteria. Such a broadening move in accounting has wide educational implications, as the accountant, domestically and internationally, has to extend his horizons and body of knowledge. He has to grasp international social, economic, financial and specific monetary facets pertaining to doing business across borders. For example, foreign currency translation and inflation accounting has affected the international accounting community.

The rapidly growing involvement of international (multinational) enterprises in Third World countries also poses heavy demands upon the educational and training facilities and resources in Third World economies; it therefore is desirable to pay attention to the accounting implications from an educational point of view. Furthermore, it appears warranted to focus on certain structural changes which have emerged in transnational enterprise accounting, whereby the need for better (international) management accounting has been particularly pronounced. For example, there are increased demands for realistic and comprehensive measurement of costs and benefits, which demands have arisen from the above referred to changing international socioeconomic and political environments. Attention was paid hereto in the previous section.

5. Accounting Education and International Operations

The changing international and regional scenes pose a challenge to our existing accounting educational patterns, involving an understanding of international socioeconomic conditions, zones of accounting influence around the world, and the historical development of foreign accounting systems and procedures. Courses in "international accounting" should give attention to these aspects, along with the necessary technical accounting elements or techniques mentioned.

Although such courses have to be carried out partly within colleges and universities, more elaborate international accounting sessions and programs should be offered. In addition, a study could be prepared to cover specific international accounting aspects, e.g., managerial accounting. Such a study would be of use to domestic and international parties, e.g., foreign accountants, governments, international agencies and so on.

Accounting education itself then is subject to extensive modification. In addition to the technical and structural-organizational factors cited previously, it must be more involved with its socioeconomic environment. This requires a redirection or expansion of our course programs and contents. Furthermore, courses in accounting should reflect comparative international accounting systems. Research in management accounting needs to be encouraged on an international basis, taking into account the criteria outlined above. This research should be used for developing accounting techniques, standards and educational programs at home and abroad.

The changing demands upon accounting may have major educational implications; they require internal country restructuring, while from an international point of view, it makes clear the scope for assistance and clearinghouse matters.

CHAPTER V

ACCOUNTING EDUCATION IN
THE DEVELOPMENT PROCESS

1. The Economic-Accounting Environment

Accounting systems operate within the socioeconomic framework, and have to be in tune with it. This environment is made up, *inter alia*, of interrelated micro and macro economic activities. Because accounting covers the entire administration or management of information for all socioeconomic activities in both the micro and macro economic sectors, covering internal and external information needs of interested groups, a clear analysis and assessment of this accounting environment is of prime importance. This involves examination of the structure of the economy, the economic aims and means (including welfare or well-being concepts), and the economic policies to be pursued. As will be seen from the country appraisals in Part Two, the political forms, such as capitalistic, socialistic, or communistic, have a bearing on adherence to the various micro and macro accounting systems.

Just as accounting practices have been shaped by these cultural and political zones, so equally have been the educational patterns for accounting. This applies to all levels of education, and what is referred to in Anglo-Saxon countries as "articleship" training. The stewardship concept in traditional *laissez-faire* "capitalistic" societies has had a major influence on the latter form of training. Economic demands in more centrally controlled nations have given accounting a different direction.

The accounting educational pattern to be followed or set up must take into account economic aims and means. Merely to copy educational systems from abroad, without assessing them in the light of the countries' requirements, is not very useful. Furthermore, much that is adhered to abroad in education does not have general applicability in a technological age. It needs to be adapted in order to be adopted.

The lack of this correlation between educational requirements and the socioeconomic environment is one of the great weaknesses in many Third World economies. This also applies to the materials used and tests (examinations) given, which are not necessarily geared towards a country's objectives.

2. An Educational Appraisal

In the area of education a distinction is drawn between (a) general education requirements and (b) those pertaining more particularly to the accounting framework and its activities. Part Two shows that the forms of general education vary considerably by country, dependent on such factors as type of economy, stage of development, future needs, finance, physical facilities and available skills.

A country's accountancy training programs may have to focus more on management and decision-information systems, capital budgeting, cost-benefit analysis, project appraisals, national income accounting, government accounting and budgeting, and other planning and control aspects to enable future accountants to be more useful in both the micro and macro economic sectors. At both academic and institutional training levels, accountants may have to be exposed more heavily to economics, management accounting and sciences, and statistics, etc. University education ought to be more case-method oriented and more relevant textbooks should be used. The "climate" surrounding academic accounting may require improvements, and efforts should be made to reduce the loss of academic accountants to industry and abroad. Domestic teaching salary scales may have to be increased in this connection. Translations and adaptations of texts and professional journals must be stepped up, although the choice of texts should be appraised carefully by a review committee as part of an effective national program.

2.1 Academic Education Needs

Accounting education requires, in the first instance, a good general educational setup at the primary and secondary levels. Unfortunately, the general educational system and its teaching methods, available skills and curricula, might not be relevant, or not geared *inter alia* to the present and future economic development patterns and the involved accounting needs of the country and/or region. The training of higher grade accountants also requires a good general upper-level education, as accounting makes more and more use of other behavioral and exact disciplines such as economics, mathematics, statistics, and sociology.

In regard to accounting education, educators have to answer such basic questions as: What are the country's accounting informational needs?; What is available *qua* skills and data?; What sort and how many accountants do we have to educate for the short-, medium-, and long-term?; Can they be trained partly in conjunction with other related disciplines (economists, business administrators, lawyers, financial analysts, statisticians, government administrators, etc.)?; Where and how shall we educate them?; What to teach and what materials to use?; How to procure the finances?; Where to get the staff, etc.?; and how to go about all these systematically. It is impossible and unnecessary to educate and train all accountants equally well in the various accounting branches and areas.

In most developing economies, a certain restructuring of the various branches of accounting (enterprise, government and national) is badly needed, and a series of functional improvements is warranted. Such improvements, which are often hampered by a variety of social, economic, legal or organizational "roadblocks," tend to be of an educational, professional, and legal and statutory nature within a national, regional and international context.

Significant divergences in accounting training at academic, institutional, and other training center levels exist in most developing countries. The general notion prevails however that, to train highly qualified accountants, a bachelor's degree program is desirable. From such basic university or academic foundation, further academic training may be pursued leading either to the master's degree, or graduates can participate in further training through an accounting institution's program. This latter form of organizational setup does not exist in all countries, however. It needs to be determined whether university training should become a requisite for taking the professional examinations, and whether professional and technical training institutes should grant their own certificates. The latter may well lead to an undesirable proliferation of technical and professional titles.

2.2 Economic Development Accounting

To cater effectively to the needs of socioeconomic development, a distinct body of knowledge called "economic development accounting" may be required. Economic development accounting can be described as the application of existing and potential accounting systems, techniques, procedures and data to enhance economic development within a nation and among nations. While this area of accounting is geared particularly to serve the objectives of Third World economies, it is relevant also for all countries involved in the planning, evaluation and implementation of an economic growth and development pattern, conducive to improving human and material welfare.

Economic development accounting does not constitute a separate branch, but applies to all existing branches of accounting for economic development purposes. It covers the application of accounting structures, processes and data visualized from an integrated accounting framework point of view. To serve micro and macro socioeconomic decisions more effectively, the interrelations and integration between the various branches of accounting, other functional forms and related planning and control activities have to be more pronounced in economic development. Economic development especially requires the selective use of resources for which quantitative micro and macro economic appraisals are necessary.

Economic development accounting pertaining to accountancy for economic analysis, planning and policies also warrants separate educational focus. Its body of knowledge is particularly applicable to people working in the central planning organizations, statistical offices, development banks, and other national institutions who use accounting information in the context of national or sectoral economic analyses and plans. A dynamic economic planning framework requires extensive assessment of forecasted national and international financial-accounting data, which are reflected in cost-benefit statements, etc.

Many countries recognize only one type of "official" accountant, i.e., the financial certified accountant-auditor, while other professionally trained accountants are not (yet) considered "accountants." This is unrealistic for the future. Various official accounting designations should be given for various levels of skills according to (1) the specialization referred to and (2) the level of sophistication. For example, at the upper level are the certified or registered (financial) accountant, certified management accountant, and certified government accountant, while at the middle (diploma) level are the licensed (diploma) or approved financial, and cost accountant, and the public sector accountant. Lower bookkeeping levels are also to have a diploma or certificate. Not all "accountants" have to be trained academically. Diploma level training carried out at academies, polytechnics or other institutions may have to be increased greatly, based upon an "accounting development inventory and plan."

2.3 Accounting Educational Methods

The accounting educational modules required for economic development activities demand (1) a conceptual socioeconomic foundation of accounting education and training, (2) a further specialization in the various areas (branches) of accounting, (3) a closer linkage between the institutional, professional, and educational programs, and the need for continuous education, and (4) a greater focus on forecasting techniques, of both an internal and external nature. This also involves the ability to audit such areas effectively, including the measurement and verification of performance, social and economic aspects, and external effects (externalities). The actual educational demands, however, are of a different magnitude.

The various specializations in economics (micro economics, macro economics, development economics and quantitative economics) are gradually to be linked, once a base has been established, with the accounting specializations at the graduate level. The accounting specializations involve the following: (1) internal or operational accounting, which focuses on planning and control systems, management accounting, cost-benefit analyses, systems and procedures, and systems analyses requiring the development of mechanized accounting systems including computers; (2) external accounting, which deals with the direct financial aspects, and also with the measurement and reporting of externalities, including secondary and indirect aspects; (3) auditing, which can be considered a separate area, although it is an integral part of financial accounting. (This does not imply that those who want careers in public accounting should not have to pass a special auditing examination.) Auditing may have to cover, in future years, operational auditing, financial auditing, and economic and social auditing. In addition to the above three categories of specialization, there is a need for a fourth area: governmental accounting and public enterprise accounting. Governmental accounting, auditing, and budgeting, as a separate branch of accounting, plays such an important function in most Third World countries (and others as well) that it now requires special educational concentration at the graduate or even undergraduate levels.

PART TWO

ACCOUNTING EDUCATION IN

THIRD WORLD COUNTRIES

CHAPTER VI

AN EVALUATION OF ACCOUNTING EDUCATIONAL DEFICIENCIES AND REQUIREMENTS

Extensive feedback was received in connection with our 1976-1978 A.A.A. Committee Report "Accounting Education and the Third World." We have summarized in this chapter the comments gathered from international parties concerning this study. In addition we have given our own interpretations to many of these reactions received. Two principal proposals warrant mention at the outset:

- Considerable international enthusiasm was expressed for establishing an "International Association for Accounting Development," whose major aim would be to cater to the needs, especially of Third World countries, in the area of accounting education, training, research, related developments, and other "clearinghouse" activities. The scope and functions of such an international association are the subjects of further comment in Chapter XII.
- The setting up of "Accounting Development Centers" in regions and/or countries to upgrade accounting instructors, and carry out research and writing, was uniformly felt as being of prime significance for improving the levels of accounting training and knowledge (see further Part Three, Chapter XIII).

1. A General Appraisal of Conditions and Needs

An extensive degree of quantification by country is to be attempted, for example, concerning the implementation of warranted changes, amount of funds involved, timetable, institutional reforms, education (long- and short-term), legislation, plus other items lending themselves to quantitative (cost-benefit) analysis. It was also pointed out by representatives from the World Bank (I.B.R.D.) that of the 185 countries in the world (of which 130 are World Bank members) only 20 percent (35 countries) can be considered to have a satisfactory accounting educational setup. The issue was raised by them as to how much manpower from the 35 countries could be effectively diverted to needy Third World countries.

Quantitative appraisals of "educational assistance projects" are required for international, regional, and bilateral agencies. Domestic country assessments are needed, in first instance, because the initiative has to come from the developing countries. All data are to be outlined in well prepared feasibility studies; these may be carried out with support from the U.N., UNESCO, World Bank, I.M.F., regional development banks (Asian, African, Latin American), and other international agencies or foundations.

A macro view of training capabilities and requirements is warranted, with an evaluation as to how and where to start. In conjunction, an assessment is to made of the priorities for the types of accounting skills needed, and its cost-benefit (effectiveness) involved to serve the needs. Quantitative appraisals are to include a layout of existing and required instructors, teaching methods, institutional demand and other supply (demand) projections. From an international agency point of view such a model is furthermore needed to compare with alternatives; for example, demands for engineering, legal, medical or public administration training.

In the context of the previous paragraphs, each developing country—with assistance from outsiders—requires a comprehensive "inventory" of available skills and needs. Such an inventory is to be broken down by types and levels of accountants, and accounting training institutions. The inventory is to form the basis for "educational planning," whereby the latter is to be based on the current and future needs. Many indicated that prevailing training patterns were too "traditionally oriented" and not relevant for the countries' current and near future needs. Concern was expressed that their (developing) country was not focusing adequately its accounting training on the envisaged near-future needs (several expressed a need to look five to ten years hence). Careful accounting educational planning therefore was considered necessary, involving an appraisal of the existing educational system and available or required vehicles to achieve planning aims and objectives.

The respective appraisals also should delve into the respective countries' objectives of accounting and auditing, which could diverge considerably by type of eco-political system. Accounting education is to be seen as part of the national philosophy (see, for example, Tanzania). Furthermore, it was indicated that accounting education lags behind other forms of education in many Third World economies. A lack of awareness exists in many developing countries regarding the significance and role of accounting in the micro and macro economic sector. (Many thought that a "selling" job needs to be done regarding the importance of good accounting in the socioeconomic environment.)

Regionalization is to be spurred, and centralized by region, and regional assistance programs are to be pursued. In this context, some mentioned that assistance from many advanced developing countries in a region could be more useful than assistance from the Western world. Regional training, development and research centers are considered to be both very efficient and effective, and often more relevant than sending persons to the U.S., Canada, Europe, and Australia for training, except for special upper-level skills and advanced (Ph.D.) training. Regional development centers presumably also could incorporate international and bilateral assistance efforts. Within the region efforts are to be combined, not only by educational institutions, but also with the aid of professional institutes and accounting firms, and their training activities. Regionalization may take the form of a geographical region (for example, in Asia), a linguistic one, i.e., English and French speaking Africa, or combination. Regional aspects also are to be quantified, according to cost-benefit criteria.

Ways and means to pursue accounting training could be achieved by means of the following vehicles: (1) colleges, polytechnics and commercial schools; (2) training houses, i.e., accounting firms, companies, and/or governments. The point was made that training should be more "practice" oriented, while foreign assistance should not merely be in supplying advanced theoretical texts and ir-relevant cases. levels of accounting training and education are to be specifically outlined. This applies to enterprise (financial and managerial) and govern-mental training, and even accounting for national purposes. Government accounting (e.g., public enterprise accounting) is highly neglected in most devel-oping countries. Well trained government accountants tend to be scarce, and the U.N., World Bank, *et al* could play a greater role here. Cost accounting (at the governmental and enterprise level) is often poorly taught and practiced in their countries. Training should be split by degree and non-degree programs and levels; for example, non-degree (bookkeeper, systems analyst, cost clerk), and degree (accountant, auditor, management accountant, government accoun-tant). Accountants could move through various stages for a degree or certificate, by level of competency. Also greater practical exposure (e.g., case-method approach) is needed in the training patterns. These also are to be linked regional-ly, if possible, while there should be certain "centers" for updating and special-ized training.

Some countries place too much emphasis on the production of certified, chartered, or qualified accountants only, and if a person does not reach the "level" of a qualified accountant, he/she is labeled a failure instead of a person competent to do less difficult work. Another issue mentioned was the widespread fragmentism in accounting.

Research and developmental aspects constitute a major problem in most countries. There is a great lack of local reference materials, relevant books, adequate and competent teachers (most are part-time). The status of accountants (in the private and public sector) and accounting teachers generally is low; teachers may have to find alternative means to generate income. Little time is generally spent on preparing lectures, guiding students and doing research (articles or books). Teachers are largely deprived from upgrading and updating themselves.

In a number of countries a wide disparity in quality of training at institutions does exist (for example, Brazil and India) and the qualitative outputs may differ considerably nationwide or regionally. Furthermore, in Latin America, for example, a tremendous gap exists between academic accounting training (very theoretical) and practice needs. Practical exposure and training are not pursued effectively in most countries.

Better linkage is to be established between enterprise, government and nation-al accounting, and the respective accounting professionals. Better ties should be developed between the accounting profession (where one exists), educators and governmental agencies; joint committees could be usefully set up to develop standards and practice requirements. No continuous education modules exist in most developing economies. As for the profession itself, institutional develop-ment may have to be spurred, including appraisals regarding the type of organi-zation warranted, qualifications and tests, control over the profession, statutory accounting auditing requirements. Professional institutes may have to concern themselves better with the dissemination of information, and development of accountants and auditors in both the private and public sectors. Institutes also should develop effective international and regional links. Institutional development tends to be highly neglected.

Development banks (regional and domestic) are considered as being potential sources for enhancing education/training, practice and other accounting developments. They are in a position to require and stimulate better procedures and training for firms they finance, are in contact with, or for capital market registrations. They also are able to influence national accounting and auditing standards, levels of competence and certification/education requisites. Several development banks already are offering "in house" courses in accounting. Some public enterprises, co-financed by many development banks, may have fairly good accounting methods. (Development banks are found on a regional and local basis. Their economic significance is vast in most developing countries; they may be publicly or privately owned, or a mixture of the two.) For further details on the role of development banks in accounting, see Chapter XI.

The need for "pilot" projects in developing countries—with inputs from developed countries' educational bodies, universities and governmental colleges—requires high priority. Such pilot projects might be established at a university or center in a region, catering to both domestic and regional needs. Courses and seminars should be offered in various areas of financial, managerial, governmental and even macro accounting, with preferably text materials supplied—but adapted—from abroad. Specific needs to be served would be in management science (cost-benefit analysis), controllership, computer know-how, auditing, public sector financial management (e.g., performance budgeting, feasibility studies, etc.). The "pilot training program" should cater to the development of various levels of competence, and have both a theoretical and practical focus. It should, however, be post-secondary and near-future oriented. A major function would be the upgrading of existing teachers and administrators. Included therein should be programmatic aspects, i.e., how to administer accounting programs. A full-scale pilot project should cover about two years, and have commitments from international, regional, and academic organizations. Summer or regular semester pilot projects, in the form of three-month seminars, could be another alternative initially. Such a test project, in one or more regions, might well be best performed on a trial run basis.

2. An Evaluation of Educational Elements

This section specifically focuses on the educational components covered in the commentaries:

• Better upgrading of teachers, development of adequate staff and better pay for teachers (part-time or full-time) is badly needed. Many competent persons in accounting firms, industries or in the government show a reluctance to teach due to a lack of incentives, poor facilities, and outdated materials.

• Teaching aids (texts, cases, laboratories, projectors, etc.) tend to be deficient, while not enough funds are set aside to cater to these needs. Students may have to share books, while library facilities may be inadequate. Current international or regional literature is frequently not available for a variety of reasons.

• Training may be too much geared towards small practitioners' problems; the more relevant economic analytical and decision-making aspects of accounting and auditing are not well covered. The training focus tends to be retrospective. Accounting "laboratories" barely exist, and are not well staffed.

• Generally no clearinghouse for information and publications exists, and students have to feel their way around. The professional institutes and firms also tend to be of limited use to students, educators, and administrators. Contacts with accounting and industrial firms are mostly poorly developed; professional publications may not be made available to educators and students.

• Accounting as an intellectual discipline is not in good focus; it is still too often taught as a technical skill only. Newer areas of accounting such as controllership, feasibility studies, management accounting, computer know-how, etc., are mostly poorly covered, if taught at all, although knowledge of these fields was considered badly necessary for the respective countries. Accounting systems and procedures are also poorly catered to in courses.

• Special fields of accounting, for which a great need may exist may not be taught at all, for example: farm accounting, bank accounting, industrial development accounting, performance budgeting, controllership, cost-benefit analysis, and other planning and control methods.

• The field of auditing, e.g., operational and managerial auditing, also tends to lag behind. Auditing training is essentially financial accountability oriented only. Exposure to practical cases is also limited.

• Most governments take a limited interest in accounting training and upgrading. At governmental levels (inhouse) training is also very weak, or nonexistent. The significance of good accounting education for public sector activities, e.g., public enterprises, is not well recognized.

• Workshops for accounting educators, practitioners and students often do not exist; they could bring together educators, practitioners and government officials to discuss issues and developmental requisites. More inputs from industry, government and service sectors are felt desirable.

• Conferences and seminars, to expose students, staff and practitioners to developments in accounting are not usefully pursued. Interest in such activities may be limited and many feel that accounting training lags in content and motivation. Part of the lack of motivation and interest is due to inadequate teachers, and unavailability of periodicals and other materials. Many implied that better education would gradually spur the recognition of accounting for enterprise and governmental operations (at national, district, and local levels). According to many, the governments could play a more effective role in enhancing the training and status of all accountants, and spur developments in accounting.

• Educational institutions, in conjunction with the government agencies, may have to set forth *manpower plans* for training and practice needs, including methodological needs and plans. Special "accounting development centers" could concern themselves with such tasks. Each country is to develop its own "educational plan" covering educational aspects in the private and governmental sectors. Such a plan and related planning elements could be linked or integrated regionally pertaining to courses and activities. The plan should quantify needs and developmental aspects on a cost-benefit basis.

International educational needs were conceived as follows:

• The need was expressed to set up an international "clearinghouse" for publications, materials, course outlines and accounting program and theoretical developments. Many educators are inadequately aware of what is going on outside their own borders, or even inside their own regional sphere. Exchange of staff was considered extremely desirable and it was suggested such visits should be for periods of between three to nine months. Such exchange would help develop new insights.

• Many in Third World countries are deprived of the publications and information, for example, pertaining to the A.A.A. activities, the National Association of Accountants (N.A.A.), (International) Institute of Internal Auditors, Association of Government Accountants, etc. These organizations possibly could have their publications made available to academic institutions in the Third World at "low cost." Better dissemination of such materials, although not always relevant, was felt to be of great importance.

• Universities in Western nations could usefully "adopt" schools in Third World countries. Such a bilaterial *exchange* was considered very effective Details as to how and what need to be presented.

• Assistance from one developing country to another needs to be encouraged. Such exchanges are currently largely neglected, as there is a certain bias against other developing countries' skills. There should be a proper balance between regional assistance from other developing countries and assistance, at higher levels, from western nations.

• Retired persons, especially from the U.S., could play a very useful role in these countries. Assignments for one to two years would greatly help Third World private and government institutions. They would be senior advisors, perform some teaching, but essentially help develop and administer programs. Retired persons could be part of a staff exchange program, also. Educational advice is considered badly needed in most Third World countries; proper channeling of such persons is considered very important. Such type of assistance was also found applicable for governmental staff colleges or other governmental training programs.

• Inputs from such countries as the U.K., Germany, France, and The Netherlands also should be better tapped. The developing countries often have these former colonial systems at their base.

• The U.N. (and its agencies), the World Bank and regional development banks could be very effective in enhancing accounting developments at national, regional, and international levels. They could help evaluate regional requirements and give financial and material assistance. They also could be useful in setting up and administering uniform tests for certain accounting skills. Such tests could become international qualification tests. The U.N. also could sponsor accounting seminars and conferences in their region (as happened sporadically in the past). This could be done in conjunction with regional development banks (Asian, African, Inter-American), World Bank, I.M.F., etc. International agencies are currently not actively involved in assisting accounting developments in Third World countries.

• Advisors may be sent to assist accounting developments. The need exists to get international agencies (U.N., World Bank, etc.) and governmental bodies involved in "accounting assistance programs."

• An international accounting publication would be extremely desirable and circulated for the benefit of the Third World. It should focus on educational and practical accounting aspects, including administrative and programmatic aspects.

• Other observations/suggestions made were:

-a separate newsletter should be prepared outlining items of interest to educators in Third World countries

-conferences/workshops should be scheduled for educators on a regional and international basis, for example, for one to three weeks during summers or other convenient periods. International workshops, seminars, conferences could be used to help distribute accounting materials and accounting ideas.

3. Scope for an "International Association" for Accounting Development

Many commentators extensively referred to the desirability to: (1) disseminate more effectively information and literature between developing and developed nations, and (2) exchange and develop faculty, students, and administrators. Developing nations often feel "deprived" of knowledge and developments taking place in both developed and other developing countries. Developments in other Third World countries could be of great relevancy to their own model. Regional training and regional centers could usefully be established, while regional exchange programs for both educators and students are to be promoted. Of particular necessity were "clearinghouse" activities for: materials, knowledge, research, exchange of faculty, and technical assistance (financial, human and material). Such clearinghouse activities may be undertaken in the form of a society or an association, essentially geared towards assisting Third World nations. For a variety of reasons such an *International Association (or Society or Institute) for Accounting Development* is to have inputs from developed nations private and public sector accounting institutes, international development organizations, governmental agencies, international and regional accounting bodies, and regional development banks. The association should be geared towards the benefit of Third World economies.

The establishment of an "International Association for Accounting Development" warrants further exploration with a variety of agencies (e.g., U.N. and its agencies, World Bank, I.M.F. foundations, development banks, A.I.D., etc.).

Such an association or agency is not envisaged to be a separate dues-paying body, but a vehicle for bringing developed countries and developing countries together to assist the latter in developing their educational patterns, and help spur accounting training developments in the private and public sector. The specific ways and means of the international association/society should be to serve, on a more unified basis, Third World educational, training, and institutional developments. Inputs in such an association would not only come from existing academic associations, but also from professional accounting bodies (e.g., I.F.A.C., International Consortium on Governmental Financial Management, International Organization of Supreme Audit Institutions, N.A.A., C.A.P.A., I.A.A.C., U.E.C., E.A.A., etc.). Its activities are to be pursued in conjunction with international/regional development organizations, development banks, etc. Accordingly, such an association could serve as a central clearinghouse for knowledge, information, exchange, other activities, etc. It may issue combining know-how developments from a variety of countries, and serve the gaps that currently exist in Third World nations.

An international association also could serve as a medium for technical assistance efforts and coordination, possibly in cooperation with the World Bank, U.N., regional bodies, etc. International competency tests, etc., may gradually be part of its function, also. Regional chapters of such an association are to be explored and set up, pending the interests and needs; such regional chapters may well form the cornerstones of the international association. Regional conferences and seminars are an active element of such a regional chapter, in addition to all previously listed clearinghouse activities. It is quite feasible and even appealing to set up such regional educational associations in close cooperation with regional accounting organizations (for example, C.A.P.A. in Asia).

4. Summary of Regional Observations

Set forth below are summaries of inputs received pertaining to three different geographic regions, i.e., (1) Asia and Pacific, (2) Africa and Middle East, and (3) Latin America. A greater delineation should have been made within regions, for example in Asia by ASEAN, India Continent; Africa by English and French speaking territories; Latin America by Central America and South America, etc. The original comments did not give an adequate distinctive separation, but in Part Four we have presented additional regional observations and suggestions.

4.1 Asia and Pacific Region

Language barriers and gross inadequacies in both text materials and facilities were considered major deficiencies. In regard to materials and facilities, accounting students are frequently taught with materials that are printed with only local interests in mind. In general there was not enough exposure to Western ideas. Without improved communications with developed countries, accounting education in the Third World will continue to suffer.

Another major deficiency was a gross lack of accounting research and development in the region. Accounting issues, such as farm accounting, construction accounting, and functional accounting (for banks, insurance companies, hospitals, and schools) should be given expanded scope; currently they are not emphasized enough. Furthermore, not enough focus is given to the linkage of accounting research done in the academic world and that done in the business world. Unless academic research can be applied to the business community in general, it will not be useful to students.

Other deficiencies referred to are: (1) countries are missing the projected demand and supply for trained personnel at different educational levels; (2) tendency exists for some accountants to collect too much data and thus making accounting information confusing; (3) in many instances, accounting records do not reflect reality; and, (4) high cost of qualified personnel keeps businesses and educational institutions from employing very many of them.

In the Asia and Pacific region, the following recommendations were conveyed as able to help solve the bulk of the deficiencies listed previously: (1) exchange of students and teachers; (2) financial assistance from both governments and from professional organizations, such as the A.A.A.; (3) exchange of books, journals, magazines and materials; (4) conferences and seminars; (5) international training programs; and (6) establishment of regional accounting organizations, such as CAPA and an educational association.

A need exists for short-, medium- and long-term plans in accounting education. The establishment of separate departments of accounting at different universities, providing common forums for academics, could supplement accounting education to a high degree.

4.2   Africa and Middle East Region

A major deficiency referred to in accounting education is the view of the profession in the eyes of both the government and the private sectors, e.g., a lack of awareness by government authorities of the role and necessity of accounting. There is a problem of over-emphasis on financial enterprise accounting and little emphasis on managerial, governmental, and even macro (national) accounting. The private sector does not seem to place as much effort on accounting as on other disciplines. This leads to a gross shortage of qualified professional accountants and other problems such as a shortage of materials, texts, and teachers.

Other major deficiencies noted were the general lack of accounting principles and auditing standards. The standards and principles of one country may be completely different from another country and thus we would tend to have data that do not lend themselves for qualified comparison. It appears evident from the replies that if accounting education is to be improved in this region, standard accounting principles and auditing standards are to be established. Another shortcoming apparently was that in using American textbooks, for teaching students of Anglo-Saxon origin at the intermediate level, the differences in terminology, institutional arrangements and the development of generally accepted accounting principles has introduced confusion into an already demanding course. These problems may occur without language differences and/or cultural differences.

Africa is a very heterogeneous region consisting of many different nations having their own identities, cultures, and religious backgrounds. In this situation, it could be difficult to achieve a rate of accounting education which would be the same for all countries concerned.

A grave weakness exists in how the students themselves look upon accounting. Many students assume that accountants are expected to function much in the manner of head bookkeepers. Also, there is a gross misunderstanding of the controller's function in an organization. This is evident because of the gross lack of professional management training programs.

In order to correct governmental accounting deficiencies, suggestions were made for implementation of suitable educational and training courses. Governmental accounting could be taught in these courses, and thus help to eliminate the oversight of the profession by the national governments. Accounting principles and auditing standards could be established by an international or regional body and followed by any country that wishes to follow them.

In regard to the text materials now in use, American publications are to be adapted to local conditions. This could be supplemented by a more extensive use of visual aids. Also, there remains a possibility for the adoption of standard teaching materials.

General recommendations for the region are as follows: (1) assist countries/ regions to achieve their own development; (2) develop research teams, seminars, conferences, and other like organizations; (3) encourage retiring businessmen and teachers to accept positions to teach in underdeveloped nations; (4) set up scholarships for students; (5) have international and regional agencies divert funds to accounting developments in Third World countries; (6) establish an educational coordinating body; (7) exchange professors; and (8) set up effective management and educational training courses.

4.3 Latin America

One of the major problems noted was a gross lack of textbooks, materials, and qualified instructors. Other deficiencies are: (1) gross limitations of funds; (2) lack of an effective organization like the AICPA; (3) many students who know theory but never had the opportunity to apply it; (4) no unified system of auditing; (5) lack of electronic data processing systems to supplement accounting education; and (6) lack of human resources for all levels of instruction.

Possible solutions to the problems would be: (1) have the Latin American Institute of Auditing Services (ILACIF) continue its emphasis on effective and professional government auditing; (2) conduct exchanges of professors and students; (3) exchange texts, materials, journals, and magazines; (4) establish courses and seminars to better educate professionals; (5) create an international accounting education association; and (6) establish laboratories to develop English as a second language.

CHAPTER VII

THE ROLE OF ACCOUNTING EDUCATION, TRAINING AND RESEARCH IN DEVELOPMENT

1. The Types of Accounting Education and Training

In this section the educational deficiencies and needs are looked at more specifically by levels or patterns of training.

The following types of training patterns in Third World countries will be assessed: (1) academic, mostly within university departments of economics or commerce (business administration); (2) institutional, at the institutional offices, polytechnic institutes or other administrative centers—also covers foreign postal (correspondence) courses; (3) technical, mostly for middle and lower levels, whereby programs are given orally and/or by correspondence; (4) in-house training and articleship; and (5) vocational and other centers, e.g., management institutes.

1.1 Academic Training

Training for accountants at the bachelor's or master's degree level is generally carried out within university departments of economics or commerce or, in a few cases, a separate department of accountancy. The link with economics may be close, especially with business eocnomics, or very loose as in British or U.S. oriented accounting schemes. Accounting within the economics department may be "buried" and very theoretical; as part of a college of commerce it may be overly oriented towards finance.

In many countries accounting at the academic level is biased toward financial enterprise accounting and auditing, operational, and economic circumstances. In regard to the latter, accounting as an instrument for effective economic (development) analysis, policy and planning tends to be neglected.

The exposure of students to government accounting and budgeting, cost-benefit analysis, national income accounting and management sciences tends very much to be deficient. The reasons are often beyond the control of the institutions (e.g., inadequacies in teachers and texts), but these accounting fields are also not properly appreciated. A traditional stewardship/accountability approach prevails, with historical cost verification content, even though this should not be the sole function of accounting. Not enough attention is given to such important topics as: (1) project appraisal studies, including project planning, programming, and control; (2) development finance, including capital market development; (3) financial management and finance; (4) government financial management and control; (5) international finance and international enterprise activities; (6) quantitative techniques; (7) accounting and economic analysis, policy and planning; (8) foreign investment; (9) forecasting, and (10) cost-benefit analysis.

Graduate schools, covering accounting training, should be more seriously considered when we recognize that in many Third World countries engineers, lawyers, economists, etc., may want to focus on one of those specialized areas of accounting. For example, an engineer may also want to become a management accountant, an economist, a governmental accountant or an economic development accountant; lawyers may want to become auditors or tax specialists. Instead of returning these people to undergraduate accounting training programs, they should be able intellectually to follow a fairly intensive graduate accounting and/or business course for up to three years. A serious problem is the availability and competence of faculty to teach adequately in these specialized and intensive programs.

1.2 Institutional Training

Institutional training refers to training under the auspices of the accounting institutes or government. These programs, following either high school or a university bachelor's degree, can be very useful in helping fill the major accounting gaps in many countries. The teaching may be oral or via correspondence. From a financial accounting and industrial (cost) accounting viewpoint, such programs enable more people to become accountants at the various levels, and to hold different types of certificates. Many of these institutional programs have a tendency to be legalistically rather than practically oriented, especially for training financial accountants, but in several countries, broader training programs are being implemented.

Institutional centers are distinguished as (1) professional training centers, (2) governmental or private polytechnic institutes and (3) government administrative centers. They generally focus on professional certification, either for upper or middle levels.

A deficiency in many institutional programs is the lack of adequate, broad exposure, and background necessary for accountants to be useful in various functions in society. Often proper coordination between the academic and the institutions/centers is also deficient, resulting in duplication and lack of coordinated accountancy programs.

Several institutions have "sandwich" and evening programs which seem very beneficial from an accounting training point of view, because relatively few students are able to attend courses full time. Moreover, the unavailability of teachers and inadequate teaching space tends to prevent good full-time teaching. Professional institutes often do not have their own training programs, and students studying for professional examinations must go to various centers or take correspondence courses to qualify. Consequently, qualification for professional accounting comes slowly and the failure rate usually is high. Sub-professional levels also are faced with numerous dropouts.

Some "in-house" training is performed by various accounting firms and organizations, but this tool for training accountants is still used inadequately. It is, however, extremely hard to carry out in-house programs when a scarcity of trainers exists.

Training for government accountants is carried out largely by government operated financial-administrative institutes; these show a tendency to stress existing practices and methods and to neglect focus on newer and more relevant government administrative developments, requirements and techniques (e.g., budgetary techniques, adequate systems and procedures, flow of funds accounting). However, several government training institutes attempt this focus in separate advanced administrative courses covering a period of several weeks to several months.

1.3 Technical Training

Technical training refers to the lower and middle level programs given by bookkeeping and commercial training centers. There is a great need for basic clerical and bookkeeping courses, in conjunction with correspondence programs, especially away from urban areas.

Good basic bookkeeping courses consequently are needed, but these must be visualized as part of an overall "accounting plan." In several instances a number of commercial schools have been set up in an uncoordinated manner and sometimes in competition with each other. Due to the scarcity of teachers these efforts have resulted in a certain waste of internal and human resources. Educational planning in the whole field of accounting and bookkeeping seems an urgent matter for most countries.

1.4 Vocational and Other Training

Vocational training is applicable to the basic bookkeepers, cost clerks, and the lower level financial administration. Shortages of these levels of accountants often constitute a block in implementing more effective accounting procedures, and greater attention to such training is necessary. Presently, however, these levels constitute a fairly neglected group in several countries, and often they are deprived of upgrading facilities and texts. Training at basic accounting institutions and correspondence schools is often directly under the ministries of education, and improvements in curricula tend to come slowly. At the same time, teachers fail to update themselves or to give adequate attention to the students.

The low status of accounting in several countries has left much to be desired in the quality of trainees at these levels. The quality of teaching often is below desired standards due to low pay and to the pressure for good accountants elsewhere. Qualified persons in industry, government or accounting firms may be reluctant to spend valuable time preparing and giving courses. Furthermore, the educational and administrative structure of many teaching centers may hamper the efficiency and development of sound curricula. New programs often are adopted with reluctance, and effective exchange of materials between institutions and teachers may be rare. Obsolete texts may be used because useful foreign texts are unobtainable and good local texts are lacking. Teachers and students also may be deprived of (expensive) foreign accounting periodicals, while local accounting publications (if any) may not be an effective forum for research, exchange of ideas and information about international developments.

Vocational accounting training is carried out either over long periods or in programs of several weeks through seminars given at management institutes and local and regional development centers (offering especially project studies; industrial cost and efficiency measurements, teacher training and performing advisory services). Most training is at the industrial/commercial project and program level, i.e., essentially efficiency oriented. This type of training at industrial, managerial, and development centers does fulfill a great need in countries that are coping with problems related to project and program evaluations, accounting planning, and control matters. Although international and regional agencies do conduct valuable programs, accounting aspects generally are covered unsystematically.

2. Research and Development

In most countries research and developmental activities are extremely weak. Both the funds and well-qualified personnel are scarce, and the regular accounting practitioners at both government and private levels are too occupied with daily tasks. In many instances, accounting research and related functional developments are limited to copying foreign accounting research and pronouncements without effectively determining domestic relevancy.

Accounting research could assist in developing appropriate financial accounting models and their underlying legal requirements. Research could also be undertaken to determine what accounting curricula would be necessary to discern accurately a country's particular accounting needs. Such research might lead ideally to the development of an "accounting development plan." Within such a plan the requirements for educational and training programs for different accounting levels would have to be analyzed. Decisions concerning educational methods (apprenticeship or university training) would have to be researched. The desirability of developing uniform charts of accounts and their possible integration with the national accounts would have to be investigated. These are only some of the specific research needs of developing countries. Some of the research undertaken in advanced countries also could be profitably replicated in developing countries.

3. Continuing Educational Needs

Various levels of education and training should be identified, while research must be considered part of education too. At all levels accountancy education and training programs frequently tend to use outdated texts and may not be geared adequately to managerial and economic circumstances and needs. Training at the governmental level may be biased towards stressing existing practices and methods, while training at the national (economic) accounting level generally is neglected. The training format for government accountants also is to be appraised clearly in view of the needs of the economy in five or fifteen years, while the teaching content and methodology should be subject to research study and revision. Vast efforts on a national and regional scale, therefore, will be necessary to improve accounting education at all levels. Correspondence training may have to be spurred. All this may require extensive human and material resources from foreign institutes and international organizations.

Academic, professional-institutional, and technical training may have to be accelerated, and more effective coordination instituted between universities, between other disciplines, and regional and international bodies in order to develop effective programs in the various fields of accounting. Institutional training for financial, cost (management), and government accounting can be better coordinated among various countries. In several countries, training centers have been exploring and experimenting with new programs and texts, and the exchange of experiences, materials, and even instructors would be one area in which educational coordination could be very useful. Coordination and harmonization of tests and examinations, and the gradual recognition of certificates and diplomas of other countries would be another.

A substantial degree of specialization is generally both feasible and desirable in order to fulfill particular accounting needs within the economy. Moreover, specific area concentrations will facilitate training, and help alleviate staff and financial burdens in developing countries. To this extent the use of more standardize and uniform accounting procedures and systems for micro and macro economic purposes appears also to be of real benefit; accounting education also should be more uniform by region. Due to local and regional differences, however, a totally detailed uniform accounting education pattern is not feasible.

Education and training should not be concerned solely with upper level training by means of academic institutions, because middle and lower level skills and training also need extensive expansion and improvement. It is often at the middle and lower levels that accounting training—and practices—break down due to the lack of proper training institutions or programs for middle level internal and external accountants, and at the lower level for good bookkeeping training by means of commerical schools, polytechnics and/or correspondence programs. Middle level training also can be carried out at polytechnics or other professional or academic institutions, and possibly universities, and may lead to a recognized diploma or certificate, or even a bachelor's degree. Some form of concentration or specialization could take place also, leading to assistant or adjunct financial accountants, auditors or cost accountants. These constitute the much needed paraprofessionals. The "accounting development plan" should delineate all these required levels.

Specialized elementary training and vocational centers, for example, may be set up to cater to the more basic bookkeeping and accounting tasks, while higher levels may be trained at middle or higher institutions, either domestic or foreign. Foreign training, however, does not have to be merely academic, but may be more vocational (for example, in the use of electronic data processing equipment) in industry, government, statistical and planning agencies, etc.

Accountants can also be trained effectively by means of correspondence courses, evening or weekend classes, all of which have the advantage that participants can carry out their regular jobs in the daytime. A futher benefit of evening classes is that they relieve financial burdens on the institution and its students; staff members can be more easily attracted from government, indus-

55

try, etc., while international firms operating in the country can effectively assist in the training process. On the other hand, part-time study is a fairly lengthy process, and the country's needs may demand full-time day training for the larger group. Qualified full-time teachers, however, are difficult to find, as they can generally obtain far better salaries in government, industry, or elsewhere. Training centers for part-time courses preferably should then be in the vicinity of industrial areas.

Correspondence course training has already been extensively applied in various accounting fields in developing countries, largely in enterprise financial and cost (management) accounting.

CHAPTER VII - ANNEX

THE NEED FOR SYSTEMS EDUCATION IN DEVELOPING COUNTRIES

by John S. Chandler and H. Peter Holzer

People familiar with accounting practice in the developing countries will readily agree that there is a dire need for developing efficiently operating accounting systems at all levels. This includes particularly small-, medium- and large-sized indigenous companies, all governmental units as well as many partly foreign-owned companies operating in developing countries. These basic deficiencies have been explored and discussed on both a general level (Enthoven 1977) and in numerous reports on the status of accountancy in numerous developing countries (Holzer and Tremblay, 1973; Chu, 1973; Perrera, 1975; Mepham, 1977; Juchau, 1978; Whittle, 1980). This paper discusses a problem that most studies fail to address directly, namely the need for systems training that is specifically directed to the needs of developing countries.

1. Statement of the Problem

The differences between accounting systems in developed countries and those in developing countries are not differences in the basic conception of the systems but differences in their operation. Both environments use the basic double-entry system, thus the concepts of income and financial position do not differ greatly from those used in developed countries. Even the basic notions of product costing and management accounting are quite comparable. In both environments, accounting measurements are based on identical events. Purchases, sales, production, distribution and financing transactions in developing countries are quite comparable to similar transactions in fully industrialized environments. It is in the implementation of these basic accounting concepts that differences of accounting in the two environments become strikingly apparent. The accounting cycle of data collection, processing, and reporting will be used to point out the fundamental problems in developing countries.

When a transaction takes place there should be documentary evidence. This documentary evidence must be generated, i.e., there must be an invoice, a receiving report, a receipt, a voucher, etc. Without these source documents, the first stage of an accounting cycle is necessarily incomplete. Even if source documents are produced, problems will occur when their information content is incomplete, ambiguous or incorrect. When these deficiencies are not corrected, all further processing will suffer from the afflictions of the source document errors. In developing countries we frequently find that deficiencies in accounting information can be traced to deficiencies in source documents. Why are these source documents inefficient? In many cases shortages of adequately trained personnel can be blamed, but very often contributing factors are poor form designs and the absence of simple but effective instructions.

For these accounting documents that correctly enter the accounting cycle, another tenuous journey now begins within data processing. Data processing in this context does not necessarily mean, and for developing countries probably will not mean, computer-based data processing. Here it means the storing, classifying, retrieving, summarizing of basic data along a path that eventually leads to reports for use by internal and external decision makers. The elements of this processing of accounting data are a chart of accounts, journals, ledgers, and worksheets. The mechanics of this system, which should include internal control features, are based on the flow of data between the different subsystems such as purchases, accountants payable, cash disbursements, sales, accounts receivable, cash receipts and payroll. A sound system will provide for detailed, precisely timed procedures for the preparation and verification of source documents, their recording in appropriate journals, and their posting to ledger accounts.

In developed countries, it is sometimes forgotten that the timely and accurate implementation of these procedures requires a carefully designed system. The components of such a system may be described as follows:

1. Forms: the design of the documents necessary to store and transmit data through the accounting system.

2. Records: the media and structure for data storage, including journals and ledgers.

3. Procedures: the actions that must be performed to record, store, retrieve, and summarize the data. These may be performed manually, mechanically or by EDP equipment.

4. Personnel: the skills and manpower required to operate the system. Obviously, the less mechanized or automated a system the larger the involvement of people in the flow of data. Personnel must be adequately trained to perform these functions. Written and verbal instruction will play an important role in the effective implementation of the above procedures.

In developing countries even a superficial observer can readily diagnose deficiencies in each of the components. We shall briefly touch upon the most important ones.

Good form designs can make an important contribution to the proper operation of the accounting system. Besides transmitting data, forms are needed: (1) to document responsibility for initiating, implementing, and recording of business transactions, and (2) to reduce the possibility of errors. Deficiencies and errors on forms not only make other records unreliable, but usually are evidence of internal control weaknesses. Poorly designed forms, including the use of plain paper for frequently used documents, can be regularly observed in developing countries.

Records, such as journals and ledgers, serve their intended purpose only when the data recorded and summarized in them is complete, accurate and up to date. That these requirements are not met is again something readily observed in most developing countries. Shortage of qualified personnel is a fact that cannot be changed in the short run for most developing countries. The preparation of simple instructions (written or verbal) on the implementation of accounting procedures is probably not beyond the available resources in many countries.

Given the state of the first two stages of the accounting cycle, it is no surprise that the final stage, reporting, is also in disarray. Internal performance reports and interim financial statements are rare indeed as has been found in Fiji (Juchau, 1978) and Thailand (Holzer and Tremblay, 1973). Annual reports are produced very late and are of questionable reliability. In Pakistan, there is an average of a six-month delay until publishing of the financial reports (Qureshi, 1974). The reporting and processing stages are in such sad shape that in Tanzania, for example, according to a report by Director General of the Tanzanian Audit Corporation, over one-third of the Tanzanian corporations "could not produce their accounts for audit within one year or more after the closing of their financial year." (Sekoro, 1979)

2. Consequences

The consequences of such a state of affairs are obvious. Sekoro summarized the situation of Tanzanian corporations in 1978 as follows:

> Only thirty percent follow sound financial controls and maintain proper books of accounts; ten percent have very poor financial controls and their books of accounts cannot be relied upon, and the remaining sixty percent are in between. (Sekoro, 1979, p. 8)

Besides being inauditable, such systems invite irregularities. Because essential internal control features are not present, fraud and misappropriation of funds become frequent occurrences.

A lack of effectively functioning accounting systems affects much more than interim reports and annual financial statements. In practically all cases it indicates serious deficiencies in organizational discipline. It affects, therefore, the basic functioning of management and will impact the effectiveness and success of management. In the Tanzanian example nearly forty percent of the firms that were audited suffered losses in 1978. Such results occur in part because all levels of management are affected by the absence of an effective accounting system.

As a minimum, management needs accounting data to develop financial budgets, to evaluate performance and to plan operations. It should be emphasized that the discipline of a good accounting system impacts the entire organization. Enforcing the deadlines of an accounting system, e.g., required monthly trial balances, budget sumission dates, production reports, etc., will automatically improve management practices. Most observers of managerial practices agree that without a minimum of accounting, effective management becomes very difficult, if not impossible. Without speculating as to an effect, one finds that in poorly managed companies, accounting systems are usually also very deficient. These shortcomings are not confined to commercial and manufacturing establishments but are equally prevalent in governmental and public service organizations.

3. Reasons for Accounting Deficiencies

The reasons for these deficiences described are numerous. The operation of a good accounting system depends on the availability of people trained to design, install, use and maintain them. The shortage of people with such training at all levels is, of course, the major problem in developing countries. First there is a critical shortage of accountants. This includes both those trained internally and those who received their training elsewhere (Juchau, 1978); Holzer and Tremblay, 1973; Enthoven, 1977). Second, there is a shortage of clerical support personnel. A well-designed accounting system needs clerical personnel to generate and complete documents, maintain accounts, ledgers and journals, and produce routine reports. With a low literacy rate, as we find for example in many African countries, the national work force has a woefully inadequate supply of qualified personnel even for the simpler clerical tasks of an accounting system.

Sometimes the introduction of computer systems is seen as a panacea for improving accounting systems in developing countries. The problems encountered in most companies in developed countries when computerized systems were first introduced should be recalled. In many companies these transitional problems took years to overcome. Yet in all these cases computerized systems replaced well functioning manual or mechanized systems staffed by qualified personnel. It should be obvious that the introduction of computerized systems in the average developing country would require an incomparably larger training effort and the required adjustment time would be a multiple of that required in developed countries. In addition to these problems, developing countries would need to make large investments in extremely scarce foreign exchange to acquire the necessary hardware and software. It is, therefore, not surprising that only few computerized systems have so far been introduced in developing countries.

Obviously the accounting problems in developing countries can be overcome only through educational efforts at both the clerical and the professional levels. Educational and training programs should be adapted to meet the specific needs of each developing country. Yet an examination of present programs for the training of accountants in many developing countries shows that they are frequently copies of Western, usually U.S., programs which obviously do not address the problems of the developing world. This is particularly true with regard to the training in the design and operations of accounting systems.

Teachers of accounting in developing countries have usually been trained in developed countries and have been exposed almost exclusively to current Western textbooks and other teaching materials. This exclusive orientation leads to the following: the typical systems courses taught in developed countries and the related teaching materials are of a highly abstract nature and their limited practice orientation focuses on computer systems. Except for some exposure in the introductory courses and in courses on auditing, Western institutions of higher education long ago ceased to teach the simpler aspects of manual accounting systems such as form designs, document flow, flow charting, systems and procedures analysis and so on.

The implicit rationale for no longer teaching these down-to-earth subjects is that they are best learned on the job. Upon graduating, the student in an industrialized society will go to work in an environment in which good systems and procedures prevail, and he has no difficulty learning these practices on the job. The student in a developing country, however, has no such opportunity for on-the-job training because efficient systems do not exist in the indigenous working environment he will enter when leaving school. Given their lack of experience and lack of practical, useful relevant knowledge, the accounting graduates are ill-equipped to bring about improvements in existing systems and procedures. Thus, the deficiencies of existing accounting systems are not likely to be remedied in the near future.

4. Recommendation for Systems Training Education

Our brief discussion shows that the young accounting graduate from a developing country has no opportunity to learn some of the basic aspects of systems design and operation. If he graduated from a Western university, he was exposed to management information systems courses which included some discussion of the computer's function in organizations, but probably no discussion at all of the elemental systems problems he will encounter in his own country. If he graduated from a university or college in his own country, he is no better off because the courses on systems will most likely have the same orientation as those offered in the developing world. How can such basic systems knowledge then be transferred to the place where its application is so badly needed, the typical business entity in a developing country?

We would recommend the problem be attacked in each country at three levels: (1) the university or college; (2) professional associations or productivity institutes; and (3) the individual enterprise.

At the university level, courses and textbooks need to be developed to teach students the basic concepts of accounting systems (see appendix for a typical outline). This training should be practice-oriented and should include case studies and practice sets. Furthermore, this training should be attuned to the particular industries, laws and needs of the country.

Professional associations or productivity institutes should develop standardized systems for typical manufacturing and commercial enterprises. This would include standard procedure manuals, standard forms, and flow charts. Intensive short courses should be offered at both the clerical and the professional levels. At the professional level such courses would enable practicing accountants to become acquainted with well designed standardized systems. Much of what is learned should, with some modification, be applicable to their individual enterprises. Clerical personnel would be given intensive instruction on the implementations of accounting systems procedures and their role in the accounting system. Familiarity with basic systems concept should be required for all professional accounting levels (CPA, CA or equivalent) and, where available, for lower level qualifications. This would force all candidates for professional examinations to study or review the material and practices identified as basic to the operation of accounting systems.

At the enterprise level, organized efforts should be undertaken to adopt and apply the systems knowledge taught at the universities and by the professional associations and productivity institutions. Steps would include (1) analyzing and flow charting the existing system; (2) writing simple procedural instructions for each accounting systems related task; and (3) designing new forms or improving the design of existing ones. Chief accountants and supervisory personnel should develop a systematic approach to on-the-job training programs for the clerical personnel involved in accounting related chores. Furthermore, enterprises should begin a reciprocal liaison with the universities and profession by providing work-study programs, case material, financial support and qualification standards.

It is suggested that a systematic effort along the lines indicated would represent a cost-effective attempt at solving a problem that may otherwise not be solved in the foreseeable future. Our recommendations could be implemented in most countries with already available resources. For some countries, however, outside consultants may need to be employed in developing courses and case material in order to expedite the implementation of the program.

APPENDIX: TYPICAL COURSE OUTLINE

I. Overview of Accounting Systems
    A. Identification of Components: Forms, Records, Procedures and Personnel
    B. Definition of the Accounting Cycle and Double-Entry Bookkeeping
    C. Role of User in Accounting System Design
II. Design and Analysis Tools
    A. Analytic Review of the Organization
    B. Flowcharting, General Techniques
    C. Flowcharting Applications
        1. Document flow
        2. Accounting data flow
        3. Material flow
        4. Decision flow

III. Fundamentals of an Accounting System
    A. Accounting Data Sources and Events
    B. Input: Accounting Data Collection
        1. Source documents - forms design
        2. Data collection procedures
        3. Charts of accounts
        4. Personnel requirements, qualifications and training
    C. Data Processing
        1. Books of first entry - journals
            a. Forms and types of journals
            b. Procedures for entering data
        2. Books of final entry - ledgers
            a. Forms and types of ledgers; general and subsidiary
            b. Procedures (posting)
        3. Personnel requirements, qualifications, and training
    D. Output: Reporting
        1. Procedures
            a. Work sheets
            b. Trial balances
            c. Pro forma statements
        2. Output forms
            a. Financial users
                (1) Income statement
                (2) Balance sheet
                (3) Funds statements
            b. Management control users
                (1) Budgets
                (2) Cost analyses
                (3) Production reports
        3. Personnel requirements, qualifications, and training
    E. Internal Control Considerations
        1. Input control
            a. Document control through form designs
            b. Procedural controls over data collection
        2. Data processing
            a. Reconciliation of specific accounts
            b. Separation of duties
        3. Reporting
            a. Distribution of reports
            b. User verification of data accuracy
        4. Personnel requirements, qualifications and training
IV. Functional Applications
    A. Sales
    B. Production
    C. Payroll

    D. Purchasing
V. Representative Case Studies of Business Applications
    A. Manufacturing
    B. Merchandising
    C. Mining
    D. Shipping
    E. Banking
    F. Governmental

REFERENCES

Jose Manuel Chu, "Accounting Principles and Practices in Panama," *The International Journal of Accounting Education and Research*, (September 1973): 43-52.

Adolf J. H. Enthoven, *Accountancy Systems in Third World Economies*, (Amsterdam, North-Holland, 1977).

H. Peter Holzer and Doria Tremblay, "Accounting and Economic Development: The Cases of Thailand and Tunisia," *The International Journal of Accounting Education and Research*, (September 1973): 62-80.

Roger Juchau, "Accounting Practice Problems in Papua New Guinea and Fiji," *The Australian Accountant*, (March 1978): 111.

M. J. Mepham, "The Accountancy Profession in Jamaica," *The Accountant's Magazine*, (November 1977): 468-470.

M. H. B. Perera, "Accounting and its Environment in Sri Lanka," *Abacus*, (June 1975): 86-96.

Mahmood A. Qureshi, "Private Enterprise Accounting and Economic Development in Pakistan," *International Journal of Accounting Education and Research*, (Spring 1974): 125-141.

H. K. Sekoro, unpublished text of a lecture, Dar Es Salaam, Tanzania, June 1979.

J. D. Whittle, "The Accountancy Profession in Thailand," *The Accountant's Magazine*, (March 1980): 112-115.

CHAPTER VIII

ACCOUNTING EDUCATIONAL PROGRAMS
ECONOMIC DEVELOPMENT

1. Accounting Education and the Development Process

This chapter appraises various aspects of international accounting education and their potential significance for Third World countries.

First we shall look at the broad role of accounting education in economic development. In this regard, Prof. Norton Bedford ("The Role of Accounting in Economic Development," S.I.D. 1976, p. 75-77) stated:

> Given the existence of a basic international core of accounting concepts as a reference point and using the accounting education roles making auditing and cost control measures meaningful; emphasizing measures of efficiency as well as of accomplishment; and developing an updated qualified body of record keepers and accountants, it seems reasonable to propose the following as an overall role for accounting education in economic development: the task of developing and constantly improving, through research and study, a basic information system that will provide verifiable data useful for planning and controlling economic activities at the micro level. Part of this role is the transmission of newly developed knowledge, as well as of the accounting knowledge accumulated by past generations, to students and accounting practitioners on a continuous basis.

> It is in the research role that accounting education can make a significant contribution to economic development. Of particular importance is behavioral and motivational accounting research, which if coupled with research on the cost and value of accounting information, should result in a flow of new accounting knowledge that would enable a society to maintain accounting information appropriate to a continuous program of economic development. To be effective, an organized system for transmitting this knowledge would have to be maintained at the university level.

> While the universal nature of basic accounting thought indicates that it is an international discipline, at the national level considerable variation exists, because accounting procedures are adapted to the needs of the particular economic society in which they are developed. Since the appropriate procedures are, according to the theory of social relativity, relevant to a particular social and economic environment, and since each economic society is constantly changing its relative place in the world order of nations, it seems imperative that some type of international exchange of accounting procedures be established immediately. This is a role that accounting education should assume. Operation of an international accounting information center is another role of accounting education, whether or not the center is associated with an educational institution. The international exchange would include both descriptions of accounting procedures used in different coun-

tries and evaluations of the appropriateness of various accounting procedures to various types of economic societies and endeavors.

The notion that an economic society operates no better than the information it has available to guide and control the actions of the economic entities which direct that society is not without merit. But, as we have seen, it is the role of accounting education to select, adopt, and apply the elements of the basic accounting information systems to the needs of particular countries. Nevertheless, next to the natural resources of an economic society, relevant economic information is probably the most important requirement for economic development, and the accounting role in that process has and is expanding rapidly.

Broadly speaking, it seems that for societies at the lower level of economic development, accounting control information is more relevant than planning or accountability information. For societies at a more advanced level of economic development, accounting information for planning future activities and for accountability reporting on multiple social goals seems to be more important. It is the role of accounting education to see that accountants have the qualifications necessary to assure that the accounting information system supplies the information relevant to the needs of the specific economic society.

Increasingly, it appears that economic development at all levels can be significantly improved if the accountability or planning role of accounting is given greater emphasis. It is the role of accounting education to prepare society and accountants for this aspect of economic development.

It is these changing roles of accounting in the development process which warrant the attention of both educators and accounting professors, for without such an awareness, accounting will remain stagnant, as it unfortunately has been in many countries. The various levels of education have to be geared accordingly.

Formal accounting education should focus on concepts instead of purely techniques, although the latter are necessary for carrying out the accounting functions. The educational program of professional institutions and training centers tends to concentrate on the more technical aspects. A major objective of education is to develop students who can think in accounting concepts, norms and procedures; it involves a conceptual appraisal of systems and models, and an awareness of the socioeconomic environment in which accounting operates.

Accounting for economic development has been conceived by us in a broad context as (cf. Part One): an information measurement and reporting system for both micro and macro economic activities of a retrospective and prospective nature, and covering both internal and external aspects. In assigning to accounting the task of reflecting various socioeconomic aspects, involving the portrayal of externalities, accounting educators will have to reappraise the scientific foundations of our discipline instead of focusing on purely technical-procedural aspects. The demands of society also pose a need for specialization and concentration.

Our challenge is to make accounting more relevant and useful for all sorts of economic analyses, policies, planning and decision-making. This in turn raises the question whether our accounting discipline and the accounting educational setup are able to cope with the anticipated needs. A major educational question is whether the present accounting programs are suitable to educate the people for future societal, managerial and professional demands. We may have to break the present vicious circle between existing (e.g., professional) practices and educational training. In this regard we should question: (1) the training of the external accountant, (2) the professional aspects, and (3) the didactics of accounting. Although the training of accountants (in most countries) already offers the possibility to become a financial accountant or auditor, the internal accounting training has been neglected, and does not adequately focus on the various specializations required in the years ahead. Again we have the micro and macro accounting systems in mind.

Furthermore, our *philosophy of accounting education* may have to be rethought and recast based upon a solid interdisciplinary basis, and reflecting the socioeconomic structure and process in which accounting functions. Currently, we really do not have an adequate accounting philosophy nor an accounting theory to serve the profession and academic interests (we have a series of "theories"), and this absence of a philosophy and theory that links the micro and macro aspects presently makes us, to a large extent, technicians. A better philosophy will have to bring in newer and extended dimensions of accounting, such as human resource, behavioral, environmental, socioeconomic, national and accounting for economic policy and planning, etc. Also, the information explosion and the information needs require private and social cost-benefit measurements to make relevant analyses and decisions. But it is unfortunate that many accountants are completely adverse toward these required extended dimensions and problems, while few recognize that the micro and macro aspects are not only interwoven but form an interactive process. A great failure in both accounting philosophy and theory is that we have not brought these within a broad socioeconomic structure. Our educational programs are to be oriented toward the more prospective character of our society's needs. Accordingly, we will have to think not only of the strictly financial demands but also of the socioeconomic, macro and multidimensional requirements.

The rapidly developing and dynamic changes in the real world reflect a further need for continuous education of practitioners, and to obtain better cooperation and coordination between the accounting practitioners and the academic environment. Otherwise, our students could well emerge from our educational system without the qualifications suitable for a dynamic society. The determination of this suitability is not something the universities alone can solve but has to be a truly coordinated process. These elements pose a particular problem to Third World economies.

2. The Structure and Process of Accounting Education

Education for accountants essentially comes at various levels for different tasks: the technical, the conceptual and the research, and in this respect we shall quote a respectable group, the Arthur Young Professors' Roundtable, "Accounting Education" 1977, p. 91.

Skousen's views that education for accountants comes at three levels (technical, policy, and research) were generally accepted. The technical education aimed at training students to apply accounting fundamentals, rules, and procedures, is typically taught in the undergraduate program or the first year of a two-year graduate program. The professional policy, environment, and interaction education, aimed at relating accounting information to others, involves the study of professional ethics and organization operation, and enables the student to relate to diverse interests and groups. The third level of accounting education is accounting research methodology, aimed at creating new accounting knowledge. It is typically Ph.D. work, and is the means by which the professors of accounting are developed.

In regard to the *structure of accounting*, Prof. Louis Perridon of the University of Augsburg (Germany) conveyed in a paper called, "Development and State of Conventional Accounting Education Systems" (delivered at the Fourth International Conference on Accounting Education held in Berlin, Germany, in October 1977) the following:

The importance of accountancy as a tool of management in the control of the economy and of the public administration has increased a great deal since it abandoned its "historiographic" function, in favour of its prognostic function. So long as it served only to enable the businessman to have an account of his business activities for himself and others, it had to be based on the past. Irrespective of other factors, mainly legal (and later, also political and economic), the latter objective also shows why the principles of historic costs (input costs) for measurement in the accounts were until recently seen as an unshakeable axiom for accountancy and in the preparation of accounts. First and foremost, the present world-wide inflation has caused the accountancy profession to abandon this principle in practice, although (and this is significant) historic values continue to be stated.

The development of the accountancy profession must also be seen in the light of this evolution. In the "historiographic" age of accounting, internal accounting was mainly directed towards collecting and preparing information for submission of external accounts and a necessary consequence of this was the auditing of these accounts, which was orignally done by the shareholders as partners. Because of the technical knowledge needed to fulfill this task, it soon led to the creation of a new profession, namely public accountants or auditors.

With regard to so-called "internal accounting," the emphasis on the prognostic function has led to a diversification of tasks. Budgeting should be mentioned first. Thanks to the fact that modern quantitative methods have improved prognosis, budgeting has become an indispensable instrument of forward-thinking management. This has had the result that through the use of budgetary control, accounting has not only received new tasks, but has thereby become an integral part of the management decision-making process. The necessary analysis of the variances between planned and actual performance leads to the fact that the historiographic function of accounting is no longer exclusively directed towards the submitting of external accounts, but from now on can be utilized for internal purposes.

Progress can also be observed in the area of cost accounting, which is at least partly attributable to the development of economic theories. Without exact knowledge of costs and cost structure, a rational business policy is unthinkable. In this way, cost accounting has led to an ever closer bond between accounting and the management process.

The importance of accounting is not limited to the private sector. In public enterprises, insofar as these are not obliged by legal or other requirements to use a determined accounting system, similar developments can be observed. The task of accounting in the public sector cannot any longer be limited merely to submitting accounts, as decisions on public investment are to be made with the aid of such techniques as cost/benefit analysis.

The importance of accountancy as a scientific discipline, and as an instrument of management, and of economic and social policy, will increase more than ever as the economic sciences expand into the field of behavioral sciences, and will entail a fundamental change in the approaches in research and the solution of economic issues. Such a development would be conducive to interdisciplinary research and solution of practical issues. Having stated what has been obvious, it should be apparent that accountancy education will be influenced by this evolution. It is above all the tasks of education to introduce students to the relevant areas of knowledge, so that they are able to solve the problems they are faced with in the best possible way in their professional careers. A central question is: Are the curricula used today adequate, i.e., do they give enough preparation for professional life? In posing these questions, one raises also the question of the task of the universities. (For the present, it is enough to point out that accountancy education is not left to the universities alone since professional organizations are active in this field and even set forth teaching standards.)

Perridon sent out a questionnaire to professional organizations, and to teachers, to gather information on the education of auditors and accountants in various countries. This questionnaire was divided into three sections: (1) Education of internal and external accountants; (2) Questions about professional issues and ethics; and (3) Didactics of accounting.

Because of the wide range of specialization within the accounting field and the absence of a uniform terminology of the different accountancy functions, a distinction has only been made (in his analysis) between "internal accountants," (i.e., specialists who work in responsible positions in management, financial, cost accounting, or internal audit) and "external accountants" (those who give an independent opinion on the annual accounts required to be published).

In most countries there are several ways of becoming an accountant or an auditor. In principle, there are two modes of procedure: a university education, perhaps expanded with practical training or a non-university training given either directly by the relevant professional organizations or by independent courses. It is this diversity of educational opportunities that makes international comparison difficult, and does not allow for a meaningful "qualitative comparison."

Because of the lack of recognized professional bodies around the world, there is in this area of training no "professionalization" in the proper sense, although attempts to achieve this are being made. For this reason there are not any generally recognized guidelines given by professional bodies for the content and scope of entry qualifications which could serve as a basis of an academic curriculum. This means that the universities have a completely free hand in many countries. This situation is unfortunate because the universities do not always know what the real needs of the profession are in this respect. More than in the past, the universities have three vital tasks to fulfill: scientific-based teaching, practice-oriented teaching and research. The majority of students expect to receive a training tailored to their later careers, and are less interested in theoretical and analytical training. Industry and profession (which have to fit the graduates into jobs) wish, understandably, to get graduates ready-trained for practice from the universities. If there were professional bodies for the different accountancy fields, the universities would be spared a great deal of trouble and criticism. It would facilitate a more unified approach towards accounting education and training.

From the answers to the international questionnaire, it appears that, although there are possibilities for specialization into, say, financial or management accounting, one gains the impression that the curricula are not altogether geared to the profession. Curricula appear to provide rather more scientifically-based and limited areas of knowledge which then (together with other subjects) lead to a certain academic grade, which does not always indicate the specialization or denotation of the profession chosen.

A major university's task is certainly to prepare students for a profession. As the students generally, according to their talent and professional opportunity, reach a position of responsibility eight to ten years after completion of their studies, the education must have a prospective character, i.e., there must be included in the teaching program those problems with which the student will be confronted in ten years. Not only subjects such as inflation accounting, but also social and macro accounting need to be addressed. This area affords us valuable scope for a prospective teaching program. In France, for example, the publication of a social balance sheet is now compulsory for certain companies. It can be expected that this obligation will not be confined to this one country. However, how should accountants present such balance sheets when there are no generally accepted principles for the drawing up of social balance sheets? It will certainly be the task of interdisciplinary research to develop this area further. Today's students should be presented with these problems now, so that later in their careers they will be able to solve the practical issues associated with them.

With regard to further education (post-experience programs), the answers to the questions contained some interesting information. In general, it can be said that mainly the professional bodies are concerned with the problem, whereas the universities, especially in developing countries, with a few exceptions, are behind here. One must differentiate here between post-experience educational programs within business entities and outside it. Post-experience education within business fulfills two functions: on the one hand the course presents solutions to technological, legal and tax problems occurring in the company, business or accounting firms, while on the other hand it draws attention to possible future issues. They are basically oriented to the internal problems of the company and are often associated with internal development. Post-experience educational programs outside the companies deal with more "general" problems, but are also oriented towards practice. Often the programs, usually two to five-day courses, have the purpose of giving information on new developments in the particular subjects or their application in practice.

It has become generally recognized almost everywhere that in order to carry on professional practice efficiently, whether it be as an internal or external accountant, continuous education is required.

Perridon in his writeup also addressed himself to the problem of the pedagogical and didactical education of teachers. As far as is known, no university didactics exists. Attempts have been made in this direction which have obviously not led to the desired success. In spite of this, the question is whether an academic teacher, just as the teacher in elementary and secondary schools, needs such training. This question also has an economic aspect. Could the absence of a suitable general university didactics and didactics for the various disciplines not be the reason for the failure of many students? When the efficiency of the university is measured against the drop-out ratio, we find a problem which we cannot bypass.

From the answers to the questionnaire, it was also found that almost everywhere the main emphasis in programs was placed on the so-called "technical" subjects, such as bookkeeping, financial and cost accounting, etc. These disciplines are supplemented by subjects such as tax law. Quantitative methods, including financial mathematics, are on most programs. EDP was cited everywhere. A subject which in general was considered a useful basis for accounting training was economics. However, it is striking that with few exceptions both the universities and the professional organizations ignore the teaching of new subjects such as human resource accounting, behavioral accounting, social accounting and profit centre accounting, among others.

The questionnaire contained a question about attempts for reform, in the first place in the training of external accountants. Although in general such reforms are contemplated, they appeared mainly to be concerned with minor issues. Hardly any indication was given about their content and aims.

In any case, it is certain that no comprehensive reforms are foreseen even by the professional organizations. Does this mean then that all is well in this sphere of education? Could it not mean that universities and professional organizations think of training too much retrospectively or traditionally and not enough prospectively? What is at stake here is not the adequacy of the education of today's accountants, but those of tomorrow. On the basis of his activities outside the university, Perridon and others have come to the conclusion that accountancy in all its forms should arrive at a point of paramount and dramatic change. This will mean that many subjects which are presently being taught will soon find themselves overtaken by events; and then large and costly efforts will be required to bring those in the profession up to the new standards required. A reconsideration of our teaching programs may well be long overdue.

In our opinion academic study geared to a profession will fail in its duty if it merely endows the student with the current state of knowledge and this on the foundation of a traditional perspective. Study should be prospective, i.e., it should reflect not only present developments in the disciplines concerned, but above all the changes in society and its organizations which may possibly lead to new tasks for those in the profession. The future accountant must be so familiar with modern mathematical and statistical techniques that he will be able, with their help, to solve on his own the economic problems pertaining to businesses.

Academic research and education both require a prospective content, as it should envisage the economic-accounting requirements five to ten years hence to prepare students for the world they will be facing. Also students should be made aware of the role and impact of accounting in society and the aligned techniques necessary to make accounting an effective discipline. This also includes socioeconomic analysis and plans; a great dose of non-accounting courses is to be reflected in the curriculum as these constitute the foundation upon which the accounting program should be built in the years ahead.

It is remarkable that the largest gap, at an international level, in the education standards of accountants can be traced back substantially to the differing importance of various subjects, especially hard-core economics in accounting education. Many accountants have little knowledge of the problems of micro and macro economics. They are not always in a position to see the consequences of economic decisions taken by a company on the economy and vice-versa.

Accounting therefore will need a better theoretical foundation, and accounting education should help supply such a basis. There can be no good practice without a sound theoretical foundation and education. We have been rather deficient in these respects. In this context, the function of an academic institution and "education" is not merely to teach, but also to do research and related development matters. Research helps in constructing specialized courses.

In addition, a better bridge needs to be built between academicians and practitioners. In many countries the gap between these two is very wide, hampering the proper development of accounting in all sectors. Collaboration between these levels would be of equal benefit. For tnis, academicians could beneficially serve for periods of time in practice, while practitioners could usefully teach and do research at institutions of learning. Often we see that practitioners only read what practitioners write, while the same applies to academicians. The dialogue between these groups is a major prerequisite for dynamic accounting enhancement; without it accounting stagnation may occur.

3. International Accounting Education and Economic Development

Some further specific observations on international education are warranted as part of our appraisals, and we may touch, first of all, on European elements.

The Union Europeenne des Experts Comptables Economiques et Financiers (UEC), an institution grouping European professional accounting bodies, has set itself the task of developing a common European education program for accountants. The program is based on the philosophy that harmonization of the profession at the European level is necessary and that this aim is best achieved by a common education of the next generation of (public or external) accountants.

The UEC Committee for Education and Professional Training has suggested a framework for theoretical and practical professional training, which will be expanded with concrete proposals in the near future for individual subjects. The proposed system is represented by a diagram as shown in Exhibit 1.[1] We feel this framework of education and training has relevance for many Third World economies.

The whole program is divided into four circles. Circles 1 and 2 are basic education and 3 and 4 represent professional education proper. The UEC committee's explanation of the diagram is, " ... The knowledge and skills covered by the third circle of the framework are to be obtained through a combination of theoretical studies and practical experience, which together would normally extend over a period of five to eight years. Having acquired this common body of knowledge, which should be evidenced by the possession of a certificate granted by a recognized body, the qualified accountant should be encouraged to gain additional experience and training in the areas in which he intends to specialize." The framework shows in Circle 3 a common body of knowledge, while Circle 4 shows some of the specialization which might be undertaken. The position in Circle 3 does not indicate any priority, nor does the size of the sectors indicate their relative importance.

From this presentation, it is clear that the subjects suggested are without exception to be included in the training program. It is also noteworthy that the committee has striven to include international aspects of the relevant subjects. More important is that this project apparently confirms the desire on the part of this professional organization to bring about not only a harmonization of accounting education at European level but at the same time to bring about an improvement and more thorough treatment of individual subject matter.

The "Framework of Education and Training" as given in Exhibit 1 involves a broadening of activities (with all its specializations in the outer circles), but we may well ask whether the extended and prospective dimensions of accounting are properly cast in this framework. The circle may not be complete as for international (multinational) comparative aspects; social, socioeconomic and extended dimensions of accounting; macro and public sector accounting; economic development accounting. But this diagram and related observations make us aware of this need for a broader insight into all the dimensions of accounting, and greater specialization and concentration.

Perridon, for example, raises the issue whether in order to make allowance for the increasing and changing requirements of practice in the theoretical teach-

[1]Journal UEC, Vol. II, No. 1, 1976, p. 42-52.

EXHIBIT 1

Framework of Education and Training

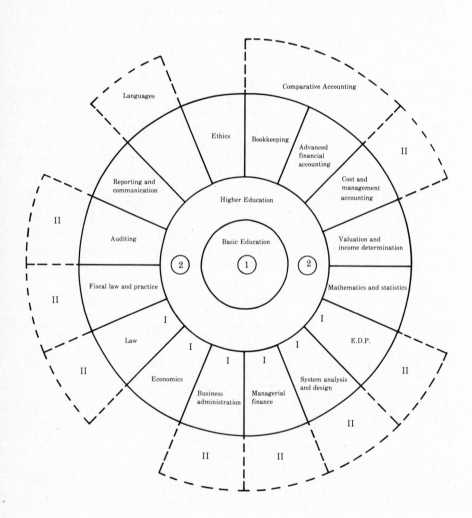

ing, the UEC framework should be supplemented by the following:

(1) Accounting in the public and private sectors should be differentiated.
(2) The audit function should be expanded in reference to social accounting and ecological reports.
(3) For internal accountants in particular, more emphasis should be placed on budgetary control, cost accounting and internal audit.
(4) Because of the intensification of international commercial relations, certain legal subjects of international private law should be expanded.
(5) Because in the future every accountant will be expected to gauge the consequences of business decisions on the economy, economics should take on a greater importance.

The accounting educational pattern required for economic development activities does largely conform to this presented model, i.e., (1) a conceptual socio-economic foundation of accounting education and training, (2) a further specialization into the various areas (branches) of accounting, (3) a closer linkage between the institutional, professional and educational programs, and the need for continuous education, and (4) a greater focus on prospective accounting, of both an internal and external nature. This also involves the ability to audit such areas effectively, inclduing the measurement and verification of performance, social and economic aspects, and externalities. The actual educational demands, however, are of a different magnitude, which we elaborate on in the following text.

Previously we described the necessity for close linkage of accounting with economic decision-making aspects of both a micro and macro nature. Accordingly, the educational setup in Third World countries requires a similar orientation.

The interaction between economics and accounting may well have to be enlarged, especially at the undergraduate level. In addition, the various specializations in economics—micro, macro, development, and quantitative—are gradually to be linked with the accounting specializations, at the graduate level, once a sound base has been established. The accountancy specialization might be in line with the referred to categorization whereby: (1) internal or operational accounting should focus on planning and control systems, management accounting, cost-benefit analyses, systems and procedures, and systems analyses, including the development of mechanized accounting systems including computers; (2) external accounting would deal with the direct financial aspects, but also the measurement and reporting of externalities, including secondary and indirect aspects; (3) auditing can be a separate area, although we may conceive it as an integral part of financial accounting. (This does not exclude that those who want to be in public accounting may have to pass a special auditing test.) Auditing may have to cover in future years: operational auditing, financial auditing, economic and social auditing. In addition to these three categories of specialization, there is a need for a fourth area; (4) governmental accounting and public enterprise accounting. We feel that governmental accounting, auditing and budgeting, as a separate branch of accounting, plays such an important public sector

75

function in most Third World countries (and others as well) that it now requires special educational concentration at the graduate or even undergraduate level. The fifth area of accounting concentration, (5) "economic development accounting," pertains to accountancy for economic analysis, planning and policies, and as such also warrants separate educational focus. Its body of knowledge would be particularly applicable to people working in the central planning organizations, statistical offices, development banks, and other national institutions using accounting information in the context of national or sectorial economic analyses and plans. A dynamic economic planning framework requires extensive assessments of forecasted national and international financial accouting data, to be reflected in cost-benefit statements, etc.

Many of these more sophisticated courses, however, should be taught at the upper level and in specialized (electives) forms. Some of these subjects also need to be taught as part of "continuing education" efforts for practitioners. Specialization should follow a good fundamental generalistic approach covering a wide range of subjects and topics. Too early a specialization may lead to training too narrow an accountant.

In many countries, a good international understanding of business and accounting is required; to this extent some comparative international business or accounting courses should be built into the programs. It is fair to say that a course on "comparative international accounting systems," including zones of accounting influence, forms the capstone course. Such a course would enable students to think better in international terms and gives a more relevant dimension to their own (domestic) accounting strengths and weaknesses. Research efforts also need to be internationalized and regionalized.

The above educational ideas may sound contradictory: (1) a greater economic base and (2) a subsequent greater specialization, with three to five areas of concentration over the years. But both a broader interdisciplinary base and greater scope for concentration are necessary, in our opinion, as the accountant gradually should be more than a general practitioner to cope with future demands. To portray these demands, we require an "accountancy development plan," based upon a comprehensive "accountancy inventory" to help outline the type of specialization to be offered at educational and training institutions.

Education and training should not be solely concerned with upper-level training by means of academic institutions, as middle and lower level skills and training also need extensive improvement. It is often at the middle and lower levels that accounting training and practices break down, caused by the lack of proper training institutions or programs for middle level internal and external accountants, and at the lower level for good bookkeeping training by means of commercial schools, polytechnics and/or correspondence programs. Middle level training can also be carried out at universities, polytechnics or other professional or academic institutions, and may lead to a recognized diploma or certificate, or even a bachelor's degree. Some form of concentration or specialization also could take place, leading to assistant or adjunct financial accountants, auditors or cost accountants; these constitute the much needed paraprofessionals.

Many countries recognize only one type of "official" accountant, i.e., the financial certified accountant-auditor, while other professionally trained accountants are not (yet) considered "accountants." We consider this not realistic for the future, and we advocate various official accounting designations for various levels of skills according to the (1) specializations referred to and (2) the level of sophistication. For example: the upper level certified or registered (financial) accountant, and a certified management accountant and a certified government accountant, while at the middle (diploma) level we can have the licensed (diploma) or approved financial and cost accountant, and the public sector accountant. Lower bookkeeping levels are also to have a diploma or certificate. It is to be recognized that not all "accountants" should be academically trained, but diploma level training carried out at academies, polytechnics or other institutions may have to be greatly enhanced based upon an "accounting development inventory and plan."

From an educational-structural point of view, graduate schools, covering accounting training, should be more seriously considered. In many Third World countries engineers, lawyers and economists, etc., may want to focus in one of these specialized areas of accounting. For example, an engineer may also want to become a management accountant, an economist, a governmental accountant or an economic development accountant, and lawyer, auditor or tax specialist. Instead of returning these people to undergraduate accounting training programs, they should intellectually be able to follow a fairly intensive graduate accounting and/or business course for approximately three years or less. A serious problem is the availability and competency of faculty to teach adequately in these specialized and intensive programs. Furthermore, one of the weaknesses in many Third World countries is the adequacy of teaching staff, materials (e.g., books, cases, etc.), teaching aids (labs) and facilities. This requires vast technical and financial assistance programs, for the establishment of accountancy development centers. As we saw, one of the functions of such accountancy development centers by countries or regions would be to upgrade existing teachers and to expose them to more effective and relevant teaching methods, materials, etc.

A related function of the accountancy development centers should be research, writing local text material and cases, translating articles and books, issuing bulletins and magazines and everything associated with the development of accounting education, training and practice including educational reorientation and restructuring. It also could include the evaluation of public and private accounting and auditing standards and procedures and the evaluation of pronouncements pertaining to international accounting, while the composition of an accounting development plan constitutes another activity.

4. The Accounting Curriculum

The design of an accounting curriculum has to be seen in the context of the objective(s) of accounting, whereby its function is a broad socioeconomic one. It has to be treated as (part of) a science, instead of merely a technique. We addressed this problem previously.

Another principal question to be posed is, what should be the basic accounting curricula in colleges and universities? This may be called the body of common accounting knowledge, together with various areas of specialization and concentration to serve the respective environments. Within this framework adequate emphasis needs to be given to both conceptual knowledge and technical competence.

The accounting core should cover the areas of:
(1) Financial accounting: practice and theory
(2) Managerial and cost accounting
(3) Auditing: financial and operational
(4) Public sector and not-for-profit entities accounting
(5) Taxation
(6) Information systems and procedures
(7) Macro accounting and economic development accounting
(8) Business and commercial law
(9) Comparative accounting

In addition to the accounting core, each country and institution has to select the accompanying subjects with which students should be familiar, especially such areas as: economics, quantitative methods, communications and skills, statistics, sociology, and finance.

Within each of the above core areas further levels can be distinguished, for example, in financial accounting: principles, intermediate, and advanced, while within each of those, special topics are to be covered. Financial accounting topics may include:

- Accounting and reporting standards
- Income measurement: revenue and expense recognition
- Balance sheet valuation
- Flow of funds statement
- Transaction analysis
- Information needs of statement users

In the area of managerial accounting the following topics may have to be included:

- Standard costs
- Responsibility accounting
- Variance analysis
- Budgeting, flexible budgets and capital budgeting
- Planning and control reporting
- Direct costing; variable costing

- Performance evaluation
- Corporate planning models
- Overhead control
- Management information systems and needs
- Computer know-how
- Controllership issues
- Behavioral measurements
- Segment reporting and divisional appraisals
- Operational appraisals and audits
- Cost-volume-profit analysis
- Short-, medium- and long-range plans
- Process costing

Taxation should include both a good understanding of the taxation rules, and also deal with tax planning, tax research and methodology, international tax agreements, foreign tax credit and taxation of international operations. Auditing will have to cover auditing standards to be applied, internal control principles and evaluation, audit evidence, computer auditing, internal vs. external audits, operational and management audits, audit planning, statistical sampling techniques, audit reports, audit administration, the audit process, legal responsibilities of auditors, standard forms of reporting, comparative international auditing standards, management letter.

It should be apparent that the listing of these topics is not all-inclusive nor that each developing country should focus on all of these elements. As we mentioned previously, accounting course planning should be based upon: (1) the needs of the country, (2) resource availabilities, and (3) the direction the country wants to go, i.e., geared towards socioeconomic planning, and (4) inventory of current courses and programs. Adequate material is available internationally to outline and evaluate the topics to be covered in each area of accounting. However, in our opinion, a systems appraisal first needs to be made of the objectives and scope of accounting education in the country and region.

5. The Internationalization of the Accounting Curriculum

Due to the greater international economic interdependency, partially influenced by the spread of multinational enterprises, the need exists to develop accounting programs in both developed and developing countries which have international relevance.

Such internationalization is to occur both at the undergraduate and graduate levels, and two ways are open to deal with international accounting in the training programs:

(1) Build gradually into the various courses, such as: basic, intermediate and advanced financial accounting; accounting theory; management (cost) accounting; planning and control; and auditing and taxation, etc. (Exhibit 2 sketches how such courses could be built in.)

79

EXHIBIT 2

Course	Hours	
	Minimum	Maximum
1) Financial, intermediate accounting	3	9
2) Advanced financial accounting	3	6
3) Accounting theory	3	6
4) Managerial accounting and planning and control	3	9
5) Auditing	3	6
6) Taxation	3	6
or		
7) Governmental accounting	(3)	(6)
or		3
8) Macro accounting	(3)	(6)
	18	45

(2) Set up a separate course (elective or required) to deal with the various dimensions of international accounting, including comparative international accounting systems and procedures.

The selection may have to be based on faculty resources. For example, in the first case it requires an insight in international accounting at each teaching level. In the second case, a question is whether the scope exists for including such a course and whether a person is available to cope with the respective elements. It becomes important to "sensitize" the accounting instructors to international accounting operations in their countries. A third alternative would be to set up a separate international business course, combined with economics, finance, marketing and business policy, whereby approximately 25 to 30 percent of the course time would be spent on international accounting standards. Another approach would be to have a combined international course with only finance or economics.

To offer such courses, teaching materials need to be developed; to some extent this can be done on an international scale. It also is to include case materials and specific problematical issues, for example, currency translation, consolidations, transfer pricing. It would be desirable that each country, and their institutions, would evaluate the need and content of such a program, in view of greater international economic interdependence.

A separate monograph, for international use, would serve a useful purpose, while the regular accounting textbooks gradually are to incorporate international accounting aspects, pending upon the needs of the country concerned.

At the professsional training and examination level, such an international accounting course may be required or optional; the same could apply to the continuous education setup. In both cases it can be catered to by separate papers or monographs. Many professional texts in Third World countries leave little scope for incorporation of additional educational materials, although the professional bodies may well (gradually) require better coverage of comparative and international accounting.

6. Accounting Education in The Netherlands

Because Dutch accounting and accountants are very highly regarded internationally, it would be useful to comment briefly on the accounting educational setup in The Netherlands. The basis of accounting is the science of economics, and especially business economics. In many other countries as well, the recognition exists that accounting needs a broader economic learning base.

Accounting education in The Netherlands takes place in two separate institutions, either via the university or via the professional accountants organization— The Netherlands Institute of Registered Accountants (NIVRA). They are separate institutions with their own responsibilities, but agreement exists between them concerning the overall contents of the study.

In Dutch universities, accounting is being taught in the Department of Economics, and is a post-master's degree specialization. By means of choosing the proper courses within the department of economics the students are able to acquire the necessary qualifications in order to be admitted to the specialized post-master's courses in accounting. The university study of economics is full-time study. The whole university study in order to become a qualified Registered Accounting (R.A.), i.e., equivalent to chartered or certified accounting, takes about eight to ten years.

As for accounting education via the professional accounting organization, the non-university accounting education is a part-time study with classes mainly scheduled on Fridays and Saturday mornings. Thus the study may be combined with a job with an accounting firm or business enterprise.

The Act on the Registered Accountants (1967) prescribes that every year an examination on academic level must be organized for non-university educated accounting students. The Netherlands Institute of Registered Accountants (NIVRA) is appointed by this act to attend to the non-university accounting education. A new education structure was introduced in 1972, leading to a nominal period of study of eight years. However, the actual number of years tends to be between ten and twelve.

7. Some Observations on Professional Education

Professional education in many developing countries is also undergoing rapid change. Recently, for example, the Institute of Chartered Accountants of India prepared a study (June 1979) called "Report of the Review Committee for Accounting Education." Some principal features of this report of potential interest to other Third World countries are:

> The more important changes anticipated in the economic environment of the country include an increasing emphasis on the small scale sector and the public sector, greater realization of the need for management accounting techniques in all sectors, changing role of the private sector.

The objective of modern education is to integrate the individual into the society of which he is a part. This has resulted in an increasing awareness of the social content and purpose of education. It has also resulted in reducing the gap between purely academic education and vocational training.

The objective of accounting education and training is to produce a well-rounded professional, rather than a mere technician. This requires a proper blending of liberal education with technical competence and professional integrity.

In view of the increasing specialization in various disciplines, our (Indian) members should be able to develop a coordinated approach with the members of other professions and disciplines. They should also be able to comprehend and evaluate professional developments on the international scene.

Initially our profession was concerned mainly with accountability for honesty and integrity but it is now concerned also with accountability for efficiency and productivity. While recognizing the need for legal compliance we should also not be oblivious to the economic basis and justification for financial reporting. Similarly, our system of education and training should achieve a harmonious blend between legal and the economic streams of thought.

There has been an increasing degree of specialization in the different facets of the accountancy profession. Such specialization must be achieved within an integrated and unified profession.

Specialization is much more a function of continuing education than of education and training at the qualifying level.

The research activities of the institute have contributed not only to professional development but also, more specifically, to the continuing education of our members. Our research efforts can now shift emphasis towards creative and basic research. The continuing success of research and professional development demands that the institute should develop its own research department manned by qualified experts in different fields.

Some extensive "thinking" in the area of accounting professional education has also been taking place in the U.S., and its features may have some significance for our readers. Initially, a study called "Horizons for a Profession" (AICPA, 1967, New York) was prepared and the developments are stated in a AICPA publication.[2] The recent study mentions:

Following the publication of "Horizons for a Profession," the president of the American Institute of Certified Public Accountants appointed a committee on education for CPAs (the Beamer committee). The Beamer committee was charged with reviewing the conclusions of "Horizons." In March 1968, the Beamer committee prepared a paper entitled "Academic Preparation for

[2] "Education Requirements for Entry into the Accounting Profession," AICPA, May 1978, New York.

Professional Accounting Careers." In early 1976, the education executive committee of the AICPA appointed a task force to review the recommendations of the Beamer committee to determine whether its curriculum proposals were appropriate in light of current practice and education conditions.

The Beamer committee noted the expanding role of the accountant in society and expressed the belief that the suggestions in "Horizons for a Profession" be adopted if accountants are to fill this role. The Beamer committee noted the trend toward placing greater reliance on formal education than on on-the-job training for professional preparation. It agreed this was a desirable development and believed that the body of knowledge necessary fo entrance into the profession should be acquired as part of the collegiate education. The Beamer committee concluded that mastery of this body of knowledge would require not less than five years (referred to as 150 semester hours) of collegiate study.

Education for professional accounting is to be composed of three segments: general education, general business education, and accounting education.

A sample program is set forth below in the referenced AICPA publication:

A Sample Program

General education	Semester hours
Communication	6-9
Behavioral sciences	6
Economics	6
Elementary accounting	3-6
Introduction to the computer	3
Mathematics and statistics	12
Other general education	24-18
	60

General business education	
Economics (theory and the monetary system)	6
The legal and social environment of business	3
Business law	6
Marketing	3
Finance	6
Organization, group, and individual behavior	3-6
Quantitative applications in business	6
Written communication	3
	36-39

Accounting education[1]

Financial accounting theory ⎫	
Applied financial accounting problems ⎬	15
Contemporary financial accounting issues ⎭	
Cost determination and analysis ⎫	
Cost control ⎬	6
Cost-based decision making ⎭	
Tax theory and considerations ⎫	6
Tax problems ⎭	
Audit theory and philosophy ⎫	6
Audit problems ⎭	
Computers and information systems	6
	39 [2]
Electives	15-12 [2]
Total semester hours	150

The above sample program refers to a five-year program; most colleges have a four-year program leading to the bachelor's degree. The former is also tied into the professional schools of accountancy, which have five-year programs.

8. The Role of the Profession

In conjunction with professional development, we may well ask what can be the potential role of the accounting profession itself in enhancing economic development in Third World regions. We are enumerating a few here, as outlined by the author in a presentation (May 1979) delivered at the annual "Accountants-dag" of the Netherlands Institute of Registered Accountants (NIVRA):

(1) Developed countries' institutes can be helpful in developing professional institutes, and its organizational, administrative, training, publications, registration, clearinghouse and other aspects. Developed countries' institutes may effectively establish technical assistance working parties in different areas (formal and practical education, accounting standards, auditing, administration) by branches of accounting.

(2) The focus of accounting should be the various systems of accounting and auditing in the private and public sectors. Governmental accounting may need strong emphasis. One overall parent organization, with sub-groups, may well be the most effective setup, at least initially.

(3) Close liaison may have to be established between the profession and governmental agencies, as exists already in many countries. Legislative requirements, accounting norms and rules, auditing standards may have to be jointly developed.

---

[1] Includes accounting for both profit-oriented and not-for-profit entities.
[2] Three semester hours of the thirty-nine hours of accounting education and six hours of the twelve to fifteen hours of electives, or both, might be allotted to an area of specialization.

(4) Assistance can be given in developing an "accounting inventory" and the various "accounting planning" aspects.

(5) Educational and training center assistance (e.g., universities, polytechnics, colleges, commercial correspondence) will be needed. "In-house training" and practical local country education also needs to be developed more efficiently. Care should be taken not to blindly transplant developed countries educational patterns, examinations and standards.

(6) Greater attention may be given to value-added measurements, measurement and reporting of costs and benefits for micro and macro purposes, management planning and control. Auditing may cover multiple facets based upon the demands of society. It may also be necessary to focus on information generation and verification for national analyses and planning purposes.

(7) Exchange of personnel and information needs to be drastically enhanced. All forms of technical assistance and exchange could be most effectively activated by means of an "International Institute for Development Accounting," which would be closely associated with IFAC, the various country and regional bodies, and educational associations.

9. Summary

The accounting educational content requires both solid theoretical and technical elements, the former to be geared towards the socioeconomic objectives. In this regard, the search for a good accounting theory (conceptual framework) is still going on. The techniques of a financial, managerial, governmental and macro accounting nature require better coordination and standardization. In both, "education" can play a significant role; however, it should broaden its scope and not only include teaching but also research and accounting developmental appraisals. The structure of accounting education also warrants reappraisal, as too often we have been sticking to a traditional, but non-relevant, pattern. Several programmatic thoughts and frames of reference were sketched, to show that a close linkage exists between academic and professional training.

Accounting training can be carried out both in daytime and evening colleges, and by means of correspondence (postal) courses, the latter often is associated with articleship or on-the-job learning. As experiences in, for example, India and Pakistan have shown, correspondence programs can be highly effective at various levels. However, even these programs have a tendency to become more formalized whereby students take classes at night or during certain periods of the year. Furthermore, in many countries, e.g., The Netherlands and U.K., accounting training is pursued by two streams, i.e., via the university or the professional accountants' organization.

PART THREE

A FRAMEWORK FOR

ACCOUNTING EDUCATIONAL ACTION

CHAPTER IX

WAYS AND MEANS OF ENHANCING ACCOUNTANCY EDUCATION AND TRAINING

1. Mechanisms of Transferring Know-How

1.1 An Overview

In order to get a clear idea of the accounting requirements of each developing country or region, an accounting "inventory" must be made of: (1) the environmental conditions of accounting, (2) the status of the branches and activities of accounting in the micro and macro economic spheres, and (3) the necessity and feasibility for improving all forms of accounting. It is necessary to focus on the educational, administrative, technical, social, and economic requirements, of both a domestic and international nature, which will affect the future development of accounting within the context of the national and regional socio-economic objectives. An initial appraisal of these requirements provides a proper insight into, and clear delineation of, the needs and scope for domestic and international improvements and assistance. The principal domestic requirements, enumerated previously, are socioeconomic, professional and institutional, legal and statutory, and educational, training and research development.

Whether personnel should be educated/trained abroad should be the subject of careful study. A particular problem in this connection is that such accounting education may not cater sufficiently to the developing country's needs. It may, for example, be too much concerned with sophisticated mechanized processing techniques. Furthermore, these trained persons may not return to their home country, or may demand too much upon their return by way of salary and position, and consider themselves part of an elite, disdainful of local institutions and unwilling to perform practical accounting work. The selection of any personnel to be sent abroad should take such matters into account, in addition to the candidates' personal qualifications and functional needs.

To a limited extent, some foreign academic institutions, especially North American, have set up branch schools in developing countries. These may be resented, however, by local institutions which may feel consequently downgraded to second class. It would seem better to assist through existing local institutions, although special departments might be set up therein for servicing special groups of students. Notwithstanding such problems, international assistance (bilateral and multilateral) will be very much needed for carrying out extensive and systematic accounting education programs at various levels and sectors in the economies of the developing countries.

The need arises for the following procedural educational accounting steps: (1) to survey and outline technical assistance requirements on a country and regional level; (2) to determine how to cope with these needs in view of available resources (involving a cost-effectiveness appraisal); and (3) to seek ways of coordinating educational technical assistance at country and regional levels.

Related to education is theoretical and applied research. Accounting requires extensive research in order to appraise the ways and means by which it can best serve economic development planning and policy. International requirements are equally significant for a proper implementation of economic development accounting. Both domestic and international requirements can be divided into two categories: (1) technical assistance and (2) international coordination and unification of an educational, and institutional/professional, nature.

The various mechanisms for transferring educational, training, technical know-how are now discussed.

1.2 Universities and Other Post-Secondary Institutions

Bilateral educational assistance from one educational institution to another, and exchange of visits of one or more instructors have been effective to some degree. This assistance frequently is not well structured, however, and tends to be a patchwork operation without a proper "philosophy" and framework. Unless such assistance efforts are better thought through and coordinated in view of longer-range needs, effectiveness may be minimal. An effective framework and sound planning will have to be based on this study's suggested inventory of educational requirements. The mere exchange of academicians and other teachers without a proper "plan" may be ineffective. It should be determined, for example, where and for how long teachers and students (and other officials) from developing countries should study and/or obtain experience in order to acquire the additional and appropriate knowledge. Furthermore, extensive institutional interchange might take place, not only with respect to personnel, but also with course programs, texts, etc. Accounting research is needed in the economic development sphere, which might best be coordinated at academic institutions. Preferably, national and international research efforts should be carried out jointly and results exchanged, and recommendations submitted to international accounting and development bodies.

In all fields of accounting the use of adaptable texts and teaching materials generally poses serious problems in both language and content. Good accounting books in the local language may be few; pure translation does not suffice, because the texts need to be adapted to local conditions (for example, government regulations and taxation, illustrations and problems, economic conditions). New text materials may have to be created, but this should not be done by accountants alone. Examinations, too, should be locally relevant and not merely copies of foreign tests based on foreign problems.

1.3 Professional Institutes

Foreign institutes, active in enterprise, governmental or social accounting, can be highly beneficial in helping to promote not only institutional aspects (e.g., laws, standards, code of ethics) in developing countries, but also the related aspects of education and training, and examinations and certificates. Institutional aspects may be transferred directly on an institutional basis or by individual "experts." All assistance might be channeled effectively, for evaluation and control, through a central accounting organization. Professional assistance might involve developing institutional training; certification and practice requirements and programs; insuring quality of examinations; designing accounting systems; establishing standards and rules (fundamentals); translating professional literature and case materials; organizing professional workshops, seminars, and conferences; exchanging personnel and other clearinghouse activities; and advising on managerial (advisory) services.

Comprehensive courses for various branches, areas, and levels of accounting relevant to the needs of the countries should be established based on cooperation with professional accounting organizations, management and economic institutes, and the government. Examinations preferably should be designed and supervised by national authorities to ensure that they meet standards and cater to various levels of need. A particular problem is that where performance standards have not been very high in developing countries, accounting is not usually held in high regard. This makes it difficult to improve standards, while low standards hamper the image and status of accountants and decrease the attraction for competent persons to enter the field (a sort of vicious circle).

Various classes of certificates may well be introduced to demarcate the various levels of skill. The granting of certificates and/or licenses may justifiably comprise several functional types and levels, ranging from so-called accounting processors (bookkeepers) to information system specialists (top grade accountants and systems builders) in the various fields of accounting, all dependent on the needs and skills available in the country.

1.4 International Development Organizations

Organizations such as the World Bank group, IMF, UN (and its agencies) and OECD might be effective vehicles for channeling technical and financial educational accounting assistance.

1.5 Development Banks

Regional development banks (such as the Asian, Inter-American, Islamic, African Development Bank) and local development banks (partly financed by international agencies) constitute significant vehicles with which to build better accounting at all levels. Where professional accounting associations are inadequate or lacking, such local development finance corporations may perform a vital initial and promotional task in this connection.

Regional development banks could perform effective accounting training either directly or indirectly (see above). They could do this separately or preferably in conjunction with the "accountancy development centers" to be created regionally. Regional development banks in Asia, Africa, Latin America and the Middle East could above all give financial support for spurring accountancy training. In-house programs, as carried out by the World Bank and IMF, could also be geared towards accountancy.

1.6   Training at Multinational Enterprises

In the industrial, commercial and service sectors, multinational enterprises often have substantial operating activities in developing countries, with many qualified accountants and other information specialists who could be of service in training local people. Banks, insurance, and transport firms also have talent available for training and even part-time educational assistance in developing countries.

In the different accounting fields, i.e., enterprise (financial and management), government and social accounting, and at various levels, expatriate accountants already operating full time or on temporary assignment in a host country can assist effectively by giving instruction at local institutions, and by contributing to the accounting and economic literature. A different teaching approach may be necessary, less oriented, for example, toward highly industrialized situations. These experts have to keep in mind that local conditions, customs, and needs may deviate considerably from their own home circumstances. The assistance of such expatriate experts, who should be replaced by nationals in due time, is distinguished from professional foreign institutional assistance. Extensive financial accounting and auditing know-how may be found in the foreign chartered or certified public accounting firms which operate in developing countries.

In-house training in multinational enterprises will gradually help the whole level of accounting in the Third World countries. Part of such training is pursued abroad, while part or most of it is generally done at the office in the host country. These enterprises generally have good training programs and this knowledge could be further disseminated in Third World countries. These entities also could help by staffing and supplying materials for local accounting training centers. The possibility of obtaining accounting educational assistance from multinational enterprises should be investigated.

1.7   Other Entities

Apart from academic institutions, professional institutes, government organizations, business firms, etc., valuable accounting assistance can be secured from labor unions, cooperatives, other professional societies, private foundations and other service groups; international accounting firms operating in Third World countries also can play an instrumental role in enhancing accounting education and practices. Further statistical and economic research entities are useful in supplying assistance and guiding various aspects of accounting training and development. The administrative and accounting experience, skills, and programs of all these entities in developed countries should be made available through proper channels to their Third World colleagues.

In addition to the above forms of direct or indirect foreign training, a "peace or executive corps" of accounting instructors should be considered. A well-organized peace corps of accounting instructors could be highly effective in transferring all forms of accounting skills and techniques. Many of these accountants may function as "accountants for accountants," i.e., a counseling role in working with other accountants. Accounting peace corps and executive corps efforts preferably should be internationally coordinated, i.e., through an "international accounting education association."

In connection with the channels described above, separate country and/or regionally integrated educational/training programs should be created and evaluated, and a central record of programs and experience kept. Importantly, thought should also be given to building a group of educational experts in the various fields of accounting to be made available to developing countries upon request. This could be channeled through and supervised by accounting educational "clearinghouses" on a central or international level.

Although educational accounting assistance has been often of an *ad hoc* nature, concerted efforts should be applied to make it more systematic, comprehensive, and long-range, involving all aspects of accounting necessary for economic development. Such assistance, to be linked with financial and eco-technical aid, may have to be accompanied by educational, administrative, institutional, and even social reforms.

In the subsequent sections, the focus is on more specific ways and means for enhancing accounting educational development.

2.   Training at and by Means of Developed Countries' Institutions

2.1   Exchange of Faculty, Students and Materials

There is a need for training educators, specialists and certain students at institutions in the so-called more developed countries. Both the persons and the type and duration of training to be pursued in the latter countries needs to be carefully evaluated. A few examples are:

- Educators at various levels could effectively pursue three- to six-month "brush-up" or specialized courses in the various areas and also study new developments of accounting, for example, computer science, socioeconomic accounting, and teaching methodology.
- Specialists in certain areas, for example, auditing, management science, computer know-how, could enroll at academic institutions or other training or practice centers to achieve greater understanding and depth in certain fields.
- Students could usefully spend several years abroad, particularly at the Ph.D. and master's levels, to develop knowledge of specific use to their countries. However, the students and programs should be carefully selected, as there is often a tendency for students either to fail to return to their country or to study materials of minimal relevance.

Sending persons abroad should be determined on a cost-effectiveness basis, and careful assessment should be made as to whether such persons could not equally well be trained either locally or through regional "accountancy development centers." Training at developed countries' institutions should not be limited to educational institutions but could also be usefully performed by or in conjunction with, and assistance from (1) professional institutions, (2) accounting firms, (3) governmental and private agencies, (4) international development

93

organizations, (5) development banks, and (6) multinational enterprises.

Faculty and student exchange is to be encouraged. Such exchanges may be for short periods of time such as three to twelve weeks, or longer periods of up to a year. It appears important to us that such exchanges be carefully planned, whereby both faculty and students are presented with specific programs of what is expected and/or what they intend to do. Mere exchange for the sake of exchange has little merit. It must contain substance. Exchanges should be based on a "plan" whereby it is determined where and for how long such persons should study. The exchanges can be on (1) a bilateral institutional basis, (2) by means of an international accounting education association, or (3) by means of the International Association for the Exchange of Students of Business and Economics *(Association Internationale des Etudiants en Sciences Economiques et Commerciaes* (AIESEC). Exchanges, of course, also need to be carried out at other training levels (private and governmental) and at practical operating levels. Visits by foreign practitioners and educators to institutions are another means of disseminating ideas and information.

Exchanges of faculty and students between developing countries and possible regions could, under certain circumstances, prove of significant value to strengthen staffs particularly where specializations are concerned.

In-house training programs at accounting firms, generally at the larger and international ones, also enable the practitioners to keep up to date. In industry and commerce, internal ("in-house") programs in accounting also need greater improvement. It should not be forgotten, however, that adequate practical training in industry, government, or the profession needs to go with continuing formal education.

Materials (books, course outlines, articles, etc.) also need to be better disseminated and translated. It appears an urgent task to us to make available such materials to Third World countries, as few educators and practitioners are able to subscribe to current literature. Their own upgrading in terms of continuous education is severely hampered. A relatively inexpensive way to help improve accountancy education in Third World countries would be to make available teaching and reading materials, books and publications, course programs and teaching outlines and didactics. It could be one of the functions of an "international educational association" to help make such materials available.

Translations of texts pose a more serious problem because the means are generally lacking. Also mere translations seldom suffice; there is significant need for adaptation to the particular economic environment.

An integral part of the exchange is curriculum development assistance, i.e., the adaptation of courses to the aims of education and the socioeconomic requirements of the particular developing country. This matter has already been discussed under educational planning. Such curriculum development may be part also of short- or medium-term seminars in both developed and developing nations (regions).

In general, the problems must first be studied on an individual country and regional basis before specific courses of action can be prescribed and resources mobilized. The tocsin should be sounded against prescribing other countries' accounting educational systems and procedures, notwithstanding that much of what is taught and practiced in developed countries may be relevant.

2.2 Professional Institutions

Professional institutes, operating in various branches of accounting, could bring in foreign counterparts to provide them with insights into operations, and the development of standards, course materials, research, bulletins, etc. Professional organizations with their own appraisals of standards are an urgent necessity for Third World countries.

Furthermore, professional groups, such as the American, French, British, German and Dutch accounting institutes, could provide valuable human and material aid, but such aid should be geared to the specific country or region receiving it. Aid should be broadly based, well coordinated, and void of self-interest.

2.3 Accounting Firms

International accounting firms, with an extensive network of international operations, could be highly effective in providing training assistance and other services at all levels in the private and public sectors by bringing persons to their home countries' offices. Furthermore, international accounting firms operating in Third World countries could spur the training of local staff and encourage their advancement. They can also provide valuable working experience (practical training) for accounting teachers in the academic institutions during vacation or longer term leave periods. These firms could help promote a domestic profession and institutes, and actively participate in the affairs of such professional bodies.

2.4 Governmental and Private Agencies

Accounting related assistance also can be given by sending persons overseas to train in various governmental departments, semi-governmental agencies, and private bodies; industrial and trade associations; employers and employee organizations, etc.

2.5 International Development Organizations

Organizations such as the IMF and World Bank could provide indirect and direct training assistance. The training institutions at these organizations, i.e., Economic Development Institute of the World Bank and the IMF Training Institute, could incorporate more accounting oriented programs for government and private personnel.

Furthermore, such agencies as UNIDO, ILO, UNESCO and UN-headquartered departments (e.g., the Fiscal and Financial Department, the Committee for Development Planning, Statistical and National Accounts Department, Public Administration Department, and the Institute for Educational Planning) could supply valuable accounting training and assistance, separately or in coordination. The UNDP could be instrumental in authorizing and financing such programs.

3. Accountancy Development Centers (Regional and Local)

3.1 A Mechanism for Educational Exchange

Undoubtedly, the greatest weakness in accountancy training in Third World countries is the basic inadequacy of teaching staff, and of materials (i.e., books, cases, etc.), teaching aids (labs) and facilities. Satisfying these needs requires substantial technical and financial assistance programs. Such organizations as the World Bank, International Monetary Fund, United Nations and regional development banks (African, Asian, Inter-American Development Banks) could be instrumental in the establishment of accounting development centers. An accounting development planning center would be part of educational/accounting planning, to be tied in turn into national economic, social and manpower planning. The accounting educational system is of course to be socioeconomically realistic and relevant.

A main function of such "accounting development centers," whether of countries or regions, would be to upgrade existing teachers and to expose them to more effective and relevant teaching methods, subject content, techniques and materials. The upgrading, reorientation and development of a competent core of instructors is a *sine qua non*. Accounting teachers generally teach what they themselves have learned (sometimes out of date and inadequate), resulting in an in-breeding process which is detrimental to the development of modern accountancy education and practice.

The composition of an "accounting development plan" would constitute another high priority activity. A related function of the "accounting development centers" should be research, writing local text materials and cases, translating articles and books, issuing bulletins and magazines and everything associated with the development of accounting education, training and practice, including educational reorientation and restructuring. It could include also the evaluation of public and private accounting activity and of auditing standards and procedures, and of pronouncements pertaining to international accounting.

Accounting development centers, working in close liaison with the professional practice world to determine the needs of the society, industry, and government, could also offer continuing education programs by means of seminars and correspondence courses. However, this may also be the function, either separately or jointly, of professional accounting institutions where existent. In many countries, however, the institutional setup is rather weak, and the professions are not able to develop good material on their own, and conduct upgrading seminars, correspondence type programs, and technical courses, of a formal or informal nature.

Accounting centers, which should have full-time and visiting staff members from developing and developed countries, might be set up by region, for example, Latin America, West and East Africa, Southeast Asia, and the Middle East, and/or by country. They should cover one or more forms of accounting and their integration for economic development purposes, largely on a practical (case-method) basis. The practical approach in the teaching of accounting, and its correlation with economic aspects, should be encouraged because this gives clearer insight into the problems and promises more effective results.

Accounting development centers might be financed by (1) accounting organizations in both the developed and developing countries; (2) international organizations; (3) foundations, and (4) public and private organizations in the developing countries.

3.2 Accounting Research and Development

Within the countries and the regions, more extensive and broader based accountancy research should be undertaken, e.g., accountancy aspects pertaining to harmonization of accounting standards and practices, capital formation, national accounting, government and municipal administration, quantitative methods, economic programming and planning. The accounting bodies should consider a joint regional research and evaluation center for matters of mutual interest where topics are evaluated and outlined for the benefit of the countries concerned.

A research and accounting training/development center and group could possibly be financed initially by the respective national institutes together with international and/or regional organizations and foundations. The center could be small but manned with high caliber personnel who receive relatively high salaries, so that top personnel can be attracted on a full-time basis. Assignments may be for a period of five years or less. In addition to a small staff of permanent personnel, experts in various fields of specialization, e.g., national accounting, government budgeting and management sciences, may be hired for specific periods or on special assignment.

As can be inferred from previous analyses, continuing education and research are a vital factor in professional development. But, because most accounting practitioners are individuals or in small firms, their degree of formal training may be limited. A professional institute may have to take the lead regarding establishment of new formal courses for members, by means of seminars, lectures or meetings. Adequate training material should be available, possibly obtained partly from other national institutes. Case materials could be extremely beneficial. Having adequate material ready is important, but means should be available through regular publications (journals or bulletins) to communicate effectively with practitioners, educators and students. In addition, adequate library facilities should be available for reference and study. Such facilities are an urgent necessity in most developing economies. The developed nations and their publishers may be able to assist in this area by selling text materials at reduced (overseas) rates.

CHAPTER X

EDUCATION FOR PUBLIC SECTOR
FINANCIAL MANAGEMENT

1. A General Appraisal

Extensive reference has been made to the growing significance of the public sector in Third World Economies, the tremendous deficiencies that exist in public sector financial management, and the necessity to spur better practices and training in this vital sector of the economy. The public sector will cover the national, provincial and local government agencies and departments, and the public enterprises, while for our purposes it also covers the not-for-profit public entities such as hospitals, schools, etc.

The significance of improving public sector and especially governmental accounting was most recently set forth in a United Nations publication "Governmental Accounting in Economic Development Management" (ST/ESA/SER.E.10, 1977).

Furthermore, most recently (1974), the Comptroller General of the United States (Mr. Elmer B. Staats) hosted a symposium in Washington to appraise ways and means by which U.S. agencies could assist in improving public sector financial management training in Third World economies. The results of this symposium (where the author participated as a panelist), together with additional surveys, were reflected in a report to the Congress of the U.S. by the Comptroller General. This report of the General Accounting Office (G.A.O.) is ID-79-46(1979) - Staats (pi-vii), in summary form:

> The absence of effective financial management in developing countries is a major obstacle to the optimum use of resources, both internal and external, that are available to improve the standard of living in Third World countries. Effective financial management is essential because anything less dissipates available resources and thwarts development. To improve financial management, developing countries must:
> --develop effective accounting and auditing practices,
> --insure the presence of skilled personnel to effectively run their financial management systems,
> --develop a comprehensive and up-to-date training program at both the national and regional level of the developing countries, and
> --increase their commitment to the realization of an effective training development program and work more closely with the international donor community in this effort.

A severe shortage of trained financial managers exists in the public sector of Third World countries. The G.A.O. study showed that the relatively small number of trained and experienced people in developing countries are often reluctant to work for the government. Reasons for this include low pay and ineffective civil service systems which neither protect career employees from political actions nor provide for merit promotions.

Governments of developing countries need skilled personnel who can plan and budget public programs, develop and operate management information systems (e.g., data processing), account for expended funds, and evaluate program results and relate this factual information to future budgets and plans.

Government interest in providing training in accounting, auditing, and program evaluation outside the Comptroller General's office is currently quite low in most countries.

Training offered by developing-country institutions in financial management and control is often inadequate and of poor quality.

Most developing countries prefer establishing or improving national and regional training to sending people to developed countries for training. One reason training given in industrialized countries is not very popular is the loss of these personnel to the country that trained them ("brain drain").

Major donors and recipient governments should work together to upgrade public sector financial management primarily through improved training. A national training plan is a necessary and vital part of this effort. Long-range plans should provide for (1) the training of people to overcome existing deficiencies and (2) other types of assistance, including the provision of facilities and staff to improve the in-country capability for meeting future training needs.

There is a need to improve and expand training offered at institutions serving only one country as well as regional institutions serving the nationals of several countries. Additional assistance will be needed for this effort, both by providing more resources and by demonstrating to high government officials how improved financial management and control can help save scarce public funds.

There is general agreement that the international community must assist Third World countries in improving financial management in government; however, agreement on the precise measures to insure these improvements is needed.

The GAO has recommended that the U.S. Congress amend the foreign assistance act, as follows:

> It is the sense of the Congress that improvement of governmental financial management should be given a higher priority within the development process. More of the development assistance resources being made available to Third World countries should be directed toward improving financial management capabilities through more effective training and technical assistance in this field.

Accordingly, it recommends that the U.S. Government should act to improve the financial management in developing countries by:

--cooperating more fully with other major donors, such as U.N. organizations and the multilateral development banks, in an effort to strengthen regional and national institutions that provide financial management training to Third World countries;

--determining, at the time of authorizing assistance projects and programs, to what extent the developing country implementing agency requires training and technical assistance in general management, and particularly in financial management, in order to carry out the U.S. assisted effort;

--strengthening the U.S. capability to plan, program, and assist in implementing financial management programs and projects;

--instructing U.S. representatives and delegates to international organizations and other forums to emphasize the benefits to be gained by improving financial management in developing countries and to propose and encourage that the necessary resources be directed toward this objective.

We feel that these observations and recommendations by Mr. Staats and his G.A.O. staff are very laudable and warrant close scrutiny by the international community. Although there is agreement that the community is willing and able to assist Third World countries in improving financial management of the public sector, more precise measures to insure such improvements are required.

The G.A.O. report lucidly states:

Before any effective assistance programs can be considered, however, governments and many existing training institutions must first realize the importance of resource management and its potential role in the development process.

Once an increased commitment has been made, governments, with the help of all interested parties, should identify present training in these areas and additional training needs and types of assistance required to satisfy these needs. It should be possible then to provide assistance in a more coordinated manner. Specific steps could then be developed by the host government with as much input as possible from international and regional assistance organizations.

The U.S. Agency for International Development (AID) has recently begun to consider the role that administrative and management development should play as an integral part of the development process. The U.S. Congress should emphasize the need to improve financial management and public administration because administrative and management capabilities are necessary for poorer countries to achieve maximum benefit from their development projects.

2. Governmental Accounting Training

As the U.S. G.A.O. (p. 25-26 1979) also appropriately conveys:

Before a government upgrades its training programs, it should take stock of existing human resources, identify present training programs, and determine future needs. This process should first include preparing a national inventory that would list all current training relevant to both public and private accounting, auditing and other areas related to financial management. Once an inventory of existing training is developed, the government should prepare an inventory of future training needs, based on available human resources, anticipated future resource requirements, and current ongoing training programs. This inventory could be used to prepare a national plan for upgrading training so that anticipated future requirements can be fulfilled. The plan should include the role of international donors and foreign institutions.

This entire process of developing a national training plan should be done by a centralized government agency having access to all government offices such as the national planning office. The office of the Comptroller General might also be a logical choice because of its government-wide contact and its interest in this type of training.

Training is to be carried out primarily on in-country or regional basis, and by concentrating training at the country level, more attention could be given to the specific needs and problems of each country. It is difficult to consider the developing countries as a totality; country-specific approaches are needed for almost everything that is done. Disparities between the countries in terms of their level of development are great, including development in terms of financial management. It is difficult to generalize in a way that will fit the extremes of the developing countries.

Training at the regional level should also be strengthened and encouraged. Regional training centers could be established under the jurisdiction of the United Nations or other organizations or by a separate regional organization comprised of the involved governments. Such training programs should be more effective and relevant to local conditions because they could cater to specific regional requirements. Regional institutions tailored to fulfill certain specific needs could provide better instruction in more narrow technical subjects than country-level training institutions which may have to teach more general subjects. They would also save time and money compared to sending students overseas to developed countries.

Such regional centers could also assist in the development of procedural manuals, accounting concepts, and auditing standards. These centers might also be an ideal vehicle for carrying out research programs on a mutually beneficial basis, and for sponsoring regional gatherings which provide a good opportunity for the exchange of country experiences, practices, and ideas. Students, teachers, and instructional materials could also be exchanged through these centers.

3. A Training Program for Public Sector Accounting

As the U.N. manual (1977 p. 52) outlined:

Training for government accountants and auditors is different from training for chartered or certified public accountants, i.e., those in private enterprise accounting. Furthermore, the managerial accounting focus encountered in programs is not always suitable for public sector accounting, due to its need to measure social costs/benefits, for example. Although many of the basics are the same and, accordingly, could be taught simultaneously, divergences arise at a later stage.

A training program for governmental accountants would have to cover the following topics of an administrative accounting nature:

- Government accounting within an overall parent accountancy systems framework
- Government accounting systems, methods and procedures
- Government financial accounting, including fund accounting
- Managerial accounting for public sector accounting, e.g., cost-benefit analyses, standard costing
- Budgetary techniques, including program and performance budgets
- Public enterprise accounting: financial and managerial
- Auditing for government activities and parastatal units
- Mechanization of accounting systems, e.g., electronic data processing, computer auditing
- Economics and public finance
- Tax policy and administration
- Government accounting and its relation to national accounting and planning, including economic development accounting
- Financial and operational management requirements of ministries, departments, government boards and public corporations
- Statistical analyses and quantitative methods

Not all of these topics would, or should, be taught in a government accounting training course; depending upon the specialization of the individuals, deeper concentration in several of them may take place. Several courses may be run simultaneously. Suitable institutional arrangements should be made for conducting the courses and lectures arranging examinations for certificates and diplomas. Various qualification levels may be instituted, and certificates or diplomas granted accordingly.

Training could take place at separate government training centers (staff colleges), at universities and colleges, or by means of various short- or medium-term courses at separate local and regional institutions. Using separate institute of public administration, as is done in several countries, appears to be highly effective. Other channels for the training of government accountants need to be explored, for example, including it as part of academic training or giving it in conjunction with other professional instruction, e.g., for chartered accountants or management accountants. In essence, an "inventory and plan" needs to be prepared to assess the best kind of training, based upon existing needs and resources (training manpower, facilities, funds).

Whether the courses should be offered for several years in a row or whether a step-by-step ("sandwich") approach should be adhered to (whereby participants go back to government service for several months or years) must be the subject of careful scrutiny in every country, based on a "cost-effectiveness" model. In the step-by-step approach, the official lecture program could be supplemented in the intervening months/years by correspondence courses. Tests would be given accordingly. Various other alternatives for government training exist and need to be appraised, before a definite program is set up. A mixture of various types of programs, depending upon the level of training, should be part of such an appraisal.

There will remain a need to train certain persons outside their own country, i.e., elsewhere in the region or in developed countries. Regionalism in the training of government accountants needs to be encouraged, for it can effectively serve the requirements of the countries concerned. Regional training centers could be established under the auspices of the United Nations, IMF and other international agencies, or the government bodies themselves. Qualified persons from both developed and developing countries could teach for periods of time at such centers. Regional centers for training would not only be effective and relevant but also timesaving and money-saving, because they would tend to cater to specific regional requirements. Regional coordination of procedural manuals, accounting concepts and rules, auditing standards, research, etc., would be beneficial. Attached to the training center might be a research and implementation center, which could provide technical assistance to needy countries in the region.

International centers would be needed to appraise new developments in government accounting and budgeting, mechanization of accounts, etc., although such efforts might be limited to top or specialized personnel.

It seems desirable, as was reflected in the U.N. manual (1977 p. 51), to establish or encourage a government accounting association or institute in developing countries, because government accounting methods, procedures and training tend to deviate from those of other systems, and coordination could be beneficial. The institutionalization of a profession is necessary for achieving progress in it. Such an association or institute would perform, *inter alia*, the following tasks:

(1) Promote research on government accounting and auditing procedures;
(2) Issue regular bulletins and publications pertaining to up-to-date methods, international aspects, etc.;
(3) Circulate, discuss and publish material in areas of government accounting interest;
(4) Give training courses and examinations concerning government accounting and auditing; and grant, by means of tests, etc., protected titles in government accounting;
(5) Give correspondence courses and short courses in conjunction with institutes of public administration, accounting institutes, planning organizations, etc.

The existing International Organization of Supreme Audit Institutions (INTOSAI) and its regional branches throughout the world may well be the most suitable vehicle, at this juncture, to execute training programs on an international and regional scale. In addition, the U.S. G.A.O. program to bring individuals from developing countries for one-year training at G.A.O. may well be actively followed by other countries, and possibly be coordinated.

In our opinion, greater attention is to be given to help develop, at the request of the countries concerned: (1) national governmental accounting programs and/or (2) regional programs.

The contents of such a three- to ten-month program could be, for example, as follows:

(1) **General Development Areas**
   Economic concepts
   Financial management and control
   Areas of accounting (enterprise, government and national)
   Linkage between accounting and economics
   Decision theory and quantitative techniques
   Accounting concepts, principles and practices
   Normalization and valuation
(2) **Enterprise Accounting**
   Public enterprise aspects
   Feasibility studies and project appraisals
   Budgeting and planning
   Control and audits
   Legal, institutional and professional aspects
(3) **Financial Analysis and Management**
   Analysis of reports/statements
   Source and application of funds
   Financial intermediaries
   Capital market development
   International financial aspects
   Multinational enterprise facets
(4) **Government Administration**
   Government accounting
   Budgeting and performance budgeting
   Tax administration and tax policy
   Government finance
(5) **Macro Accounting**
   Systems of national accounting
   Macro accounting and economic planning
   Macro accounting for project studies
   Regional accounting
(6) **Education and Training**
   Forms of training and training levels
   Training methodology
   Certification
   Research

CHAPTER XI

DEVELOPMENT BANKING
AND ACCOUNTING DEVELOPMENT*

1. Some General Considerations

This chapter covers material beyond the confined educational aspects *per se*. It looks at the institutional setup of development banks which are able to help shape both better accounting practices and financial management (accounting) education and research.

Development banks play a very significant role in Third World economies (cf., William Diamond, 1957, 1968, and Enthoven, 1973, Chapter X). A development bank (D.B.) is primarily a financial institution sponsored, although not necessarily owned, by the government. These can be private, public or jointly owned. They have proven to be a proper vehicle for enhancing capital market activities, and having an institutional arrangement well suited to spur accounting developments. The accounting importance of these banks was already well recognized by the World Bank (W. Diamond, 1968), where it is stated (pp. 34-5):

> A development finance company can have a direct hand in correcting business practices ... by setting high standards of performance in its own operations, for instance, by observing high standards of accounting, by observing thorough control procedures, and by making meaningful reports available to its shareholders and the public, it can serve as a model ... Sometimes the development finance company will be able to make a start toward upgrading business practices by imposing auditing and reporting requirements on its clients ... it can assist in upgrading accounting practices, first by example, and then by supporting accounting firms that do have high standards. In one case, a development finance company associated with the World Bank Group assisted in the formation of a new accounting firm, with the understanding that if the firm would follow international accounting standards, the finance company would, in turn, underwrite the accounting firm's business until its operations were profitably established. The firm was an almost immediate success and is helping to establish a new norm for accounting practices in the country concerned.

The D.B.'s can be influential in seeing to it that accounting methods and practices are soundly conceived, and well adhered to. From a direct point of view, they are especially able to have firms adhere to good accounting standards and practices. This would apply to financial accounting, managerial (cost) accounting, management services, computer accounting/auditing, accounting systems and procedures, and accounting for national purposes. D.B.'s can carry consider-

*Much of the material covered in this chapter was originally worked up by the author in a paper on "Accounting and Development Banking" presented at a World Bank/UNIDO Global Symposium on "Development Banking in the 1980's," held in Zurich (Switzerland), June, 1979.

able clout in such matters, and they may want to exercise their influence. In these instances, where D.B.'s are involved in managing enterprises, their impact could be even more vast. It should be clear, however, they only could do this if they themselves have an adequate grasp of accounting needs and developments; and, therefore, they themselves should direct such expertise to attract such efforts. They may well create a separate "accounting development unit" serving relations with firms they intend to finance, and with national professional and governmental agencies, to promote better accounting.

D.B.'s can influence that adherence to an adequate control system by firms they finance, including review of financial systems and practices by an internal audit committee and/or an audit committee/person of the board of directors. Such a committee/person should work closely with the outside auditors. In many countries, the value of an audit review is not well perceived. This may be due to several factors, i.e., the inadequate recognition of the value of an audit review and lack of competence of the auditors.

Previously (Chapter VII), we indicated that underlying potential improvements in accounting is the need for an "accounting inventory," i.e., an analysis of the accountants operating in various functions and levels, the current legislative and institutional setup, educational and training elements and the antici· pated accounting requirements in the next five to fifteen years. Based upon an accounting inventory, "accounting planning" can be executed involving institutional, legal, educational, and practice oriented aspects. The preparation of such an "inventory" and "plan" constitute the first phase for improving accounting in developing economies; D.B.'s could play a major direct or indirect role in the development of the accounting inventory and plan.

2. The Role of Development Banks (D.B.'s)

After these general considerations, whereby the indirect function of D.B.'s was outlined, our attention will now be directed toward areas where D.B.'s can more directly influence accounting methodology and education.

We may distinguish two such areas of direct concentration, i.e., 1) internal accounting at D.B.'s, and 2) accounting at enterprises financed by D.B.'s. In addition, we have certain general tasks of accounting in development banking, i.e.:

(1) Satisfactory financial reporting and meaningful full and fair disclosure, for internal and external purposes, supported by sound accounting legislation, methods and practices.

(2) Ensuring that funds are distributed according to priority criteria, involving effective cost-benefit measurements.

(3) Granting accounting (educational assistance) to firms and institutions, which will help these entities in their financial and economic appraisals.

Accordingly, the general role of accounting in regard to investment and capital formation can be seen as twofold: (1) to generate sufficient investor and lender confidence to stimulate the flow of capital, and (2) to ensure the continued efficient use of capital.

2.1 Accounting at Development Banks

The aspects which require attention within the operations of the Development Bank itself are of the following nature:

• Clearly laid out accounting policies and procedures, preferably in the form of accounting, budgeting and operational manuals. Such guidelines are to be better harmonized (standardized) to facilitate measurement, reporting, comparison and evaluation, by both internal and external parties. There is far greater scope for accounting normalization in this area; it should pertain to all areas of the accounting system, e.g., the planning, decision-making, and control elements. Greater standardization would also facilitate the installation and application of computerized accounting systems. For all these purposes adequate "development banking accounting manuals," are to be prepared—possibly on a regional or international basis—while accounting development issues also can be explored better jointly. Accordingly, it may be desirable to develop and disseminate accounting methods, procedures, and practices for development banks.

• Training of own personnel in accounting systems and methods would be another important aspect. It appears desirable to conduct, on a local or regional basis, a three- to six-week condensed course in "Accounting for Development Banking," where financial officers can be further exposed to, or updated in, various areas of accounting. The contents of such programs may include, for example, standardized financial measurement and reporting, feasibility studies and cost-benefit analyses, computer accounting and auditing, controllership, regulatory aspects, financial and operational auditing, budgeting including performance budgets, analysis of financial statements, source and application of funds, international accounting developments, macro and governmental accounting requirements, professional enhancements, legislation, etc.

Such updating or even further (specialized) accounting training presumably could best be carried out under the auspices of regional development banks for upper level training, while secondary accounting training may be pursued at the local (country) level by means of outside instructors. Such courses could be run as part of a "sandwich" training program.

The importance of sound systems and training is not only applicable to the bank itself, but also has a bearing on the practices of the customers of the DB's. It has a catalytical effect.

2.2 Accounting of Enterprises Financed by Development Banks

A financially well-run D.B. will set an example for enterprises it finances, while the D.B.'s officers can assist accounting personnel at enterprises in improving their accounting structure. However, the significance of good accounting and auditing needs to be recognized by these enterprises; deficient accounting is often considered a major reason for not obtaining necessary funding. D.B.'s may prepare "standard accounting forms" for enterprises, applicable to financial and managerial accounting, and even assist them (directly, or indirectly by means of professional firms) in improving their measurement and reporting system. Such efforts may be done as part of the "prefinancing study" or as a separate "technical assistance" project. The latter may be done only for enterprises considered to be likely financing candidates, and the charge for such technical accounting assistance may later on become part of the project financing. There definitely is a need to assist many firms in improving their accounting system before a clear assessment can be made whether financing is required. A sound accounting system is able to identify the specific projects to a far better degree than a loose set of accounting (bookkeeping) practices. Accordingly, an effective accounting system will facilitate, from an enterprise, D.B. and national point of view, the effective and efficient allocation of resources. Various vehicles exist regarding the ways and means for executing accounting assistance to enterprises either during the (1) pre-feasibility study phase, or (2) as part of this phase and/or (3) as part of the project financing. Furthermore, an effective accounting system facilitates the auditing task, and helps reduce the cost of having an audit carried out; there exists an inverse relationship between accounting and auditing. The value of audit reports and its use by management therefore also needs to be better appraised.

The D.B.'s may well insist upon an adequate system of accounting control and check, related accounting planning methods, and on a series of financial reports of the following nature:

> Balance sheets, income statements, and statement of sources and application of funds, giving a past five-year record and a pro-forma appraisal. The statements preferably should be audited by a recognized accounting/auditing firm. Adequate explanations and footnotes are to accompany these statements. The audit report itself preferably should be a "long form" report, and weaknesses are to be set forth therein for management and board of directors purposes. The measurement (e.g., valuation) procedures adhered to by the firm are to be reflected. The statements should reflect more than the report submitted to tax authorities. As stated before, some degree of "standardization" as to both measurement criteria and reporting format would be extremely desirable. Such normalization efforts for enterprises financed by D.B.'s (and D.B.'s itself) is a matter which warrants due attention in the years ahead.

2.3 Feasibility Studies

A standard layout covering the project study is equally warranted. They are to convey systematically and quantitatively the costs and benefits (of a direct and indirect nature) regarding the projects. It may be necessary to reflect shadow (equilibrium) prices for the factors of production, while macro or sectoral economic analyses may be an integral part of the study. To the extent possible, these analyses are to be tied to an input-output statement covering the industry and the nation. The measurement of input-output tables of a macro and micro nature, the quantification of shadow prices and the reflection of relevant (current cost) feasibility studies has, more and more, become a function for accountants. In this context, upgrading of persons at enterprise levels also becomes a significant task. "Accounting training development centers" may handle such updating or up-grading of accounting programs and personnel.

It may be apparent that development banks can be very helpful in enhancing accounting norms, practices and training as they generally can impose stringent requirements in their lending patterns for statement presentations and feasibility studies.

2.4   The Technical Assistance Function of Development Banks

Development banks, as we saw, can help improve accounting systems, methods, practices and education. It may also be useful to appraise three perspectives, i.e., the internal, external, and national.

Internally, the need exists to set up good accounts and hire competent accountants and auditors. Outside consulting firms may be attracted to help achieve these objectives. Management of D.B's should recognize the value of an effective internal accounting system for a variety of accounting and auditing tasks. Regional and international development finance agencies may be helpful in securing the services.

Externally, D.B's may not only insist upon good accounting of firms they finance, but see to it that adequate financial and managerial accounting systems are installed at these entities. Audit reports should be comprehensive, and should clarify deficiencies. D.B's can be helpful in identifying the weaknesses, setting forth requirements, and aiding in securing technical assistance. The latter may be done directly by the D.B., or the development bank may be an intermediary for obtaining such services. D.B.'s should keep a record of firms that can grant various types of accounting services, pending upon the nature of the industry, needs, and coverage. D.B.'s may make arrangements with reputable accounting/auditing firms to perform such services. However, development banks may also want to appraise to what extent they should set up an "accounting service unit" for limited or extensive accounting identification and technical purposes. Such units also could be set up nationally or regionally.

As stated before, auditing is dependent upon good accounting systems, and the better such systems are at D.B.'s, and the firms they finance, the more productive the auditing task will be.

Nationally, the main thrust will be to spur: an accounting/auditing profession, an accounting institute(s), legislation, training, education and other developments. The function of the D.B. can be direct or indirect, i.e., to become directly involved in the development and financing of such activities or serve as a vehicle or catalyst to help implement these activities. This may be done by means of the government, professional associations or groups, and training institutions. The D.B.'s may well have to play a more active role in developing and improving the accounting infrastructure, by means of the government, professional associations or groups, and training institutions. The D.B.'s may well have to play a more active role in developing and improving the accounting infrastructure. They can do this in cooperation with regional and international organizations, e.g., World Bank, United Nations, regional development banks (Asian, African, Islamic, and Inter-American).

Institutional and educational aspects are of great significance. D.B.'s may want to set up "appraisal teams" to determine the most effective ways and means to develop as rapidly as possible a useful accounting infrastructure (including professional, institutional, educational components). D.B.'s, in conjunction with others, also may appraise accounting and auditing standards, related accounting acts, and reporting systems. D.B.'s are in an excellent position to play a strong role in accounting growth, and their involvement is badly needed in many Third World countries.

Regional and larger local development banks may add accounting experts to their staff who would serve industrial clients in setting up accounting systems, give accounting advice to these entities and development banks, and appraise with them the ways and means to improve accounting methods, procedures and training of personnel. They also could give advice on the audit scope to be pursued, and help develop internal auditors. Furthermore, they may be useful in selecting qualified outside auditors and review financial management matters with them.

In many countries the ability of the D.B.'s to play such roles may be limited; however, in such cases regional or international efforts may be pursued to cater to the needs. The ways and means to activate these activities in turn should be appraised regionally, and a "planning framework" designed accordingly.

Accounting improvements in a country, and technical assistance required, should be a joint effort between the D.B.'s, the borrower, the accounting profession, certain public regulatory agencies, and above all, the country's educational institutions. D.B.'s can be catalysts for change and agents for improvements in accounting, as they constitute significant vehicles with which to build up better accounting at all levels.

Auditing activities also need reassessment. Auditing firms often perform services at high cost, and development of better domestic auditors and audit firms is an urgent task in many Third World countries.

Accordingly, the general accounting improvements tend to be of a methodological, professional, and educational nature, and may require extensive technical assistance. These requirements will have an internal and external country component.

3. A Summary of Development Banking's Impact on Accounting

The function of development banks in improving accounting/auditing can be seen from a triple point of view:

(1) Install good financial and cost accounting, e.g., systems and procedures, at their own units, which enables them to make effective external and internal appraisals and reports. These operational and financial statements are to be audited by qualified external, and preferably internal, auditors. Good accounting and auditing go hand in hand; an inverse relationship exists between improvements in accounting and the need for (costly) auditing work.

(2) Require effective accounting and auditing methods and practices at firms they finance. Furthermore, D.B.'s may finance or help install accounting/auditing procedures at these entities either as part of a technical assistance effort or as part of a pre-financing program.

(3) Serve as an agency to spur accounting systems and auditing standards, practices and institutional and educational developments throughout the economy. They may achieve this as a catalyst, and help promote technical assistance in these areas.

In our opinion a vast concerted effort is necessary by development banks, commercial banks, the government, the accounting profession or practitioners, and other bodies to enhance accounting and auditing methodology in Third World countries. International agencies, and regional development banks (Asian, African, Islamic, Latin American) are able to play an important function in spurring accounting improvements at all levels. Development banks may attract accounting experts to their staff to assist accounting improvements of local development banks and firms they help finance.

It is hard to conceive how development banks (and for that matter, a country) could function effectively in the 1980's without a sound and updated accounting infrastructure of systems, procedures and practices, which aspects in turn are based upon a series of elements of a professional, legal statutory and educational nature.

The technical assistance and educational elements will play an important role at various levels: (1) larger development banks may attract accounting experts to help guide industrial and financial establishments in setting up accounting systems, (2) regionally training and development activities may be carried out to assist smaller development banks, and (3) international agencies may help promote domestic educational efforts. A major requisite is that D.B.'s put their own accounting house in order. As such they are able to carry out better appraisals and assist enterprises they help finance. The auditing element is also of considerable significance for such improvements.

As a first step, each development bank may prepare an "inventory" of it's own accounting system and procedures, list its needs, set forth the requirements of the firms they finance and give a brief appraisal of the national accounting requirements. They may constitute the basis for an accounting development "program" for the D.B., which could be extended to the country/region concerned.

The educational and training aspects are of a dual nature: (1) those that are to be influenced directly and indirectly by development banks in the form of training its own personnel, clients' personnel and supporting accounting training centers for such tasks, and (2) those that assist existing or new educational institutions, whereby attention is to be given to the development of accounting programs. Aligned with these aspects is the improvement of accounting and auditing standards, which require a sound research and educational base.

CHAPTER XII

AN INTERNATIONAL ASSOCIATION FOR ACCOUNTING DEVELOPMENT

Currently no proper vehicle exists to bring together all the accounting educational entities, having as its major objective the improvement of accounting education, training and development on an international scale. Furthermore, no relevant international educational publication exists for the exchange of materials and ideas. These matters are explored in this chapter.

1. The Structure and Activities of the Association

Previously (Chapters I and VIII), we referred to the desirability to set up an international accounting educational association, whose task it would be to assist Third World economies (e.g., educational institutions) in improving their accounting educational elements.

An outline of a proposal for the establishment of an International Association for Accounting Development (IAAD) is presented below. This association is envisaged to be structured as an autonomous international accounting educational body, but, preferably, it will pursue its activities in close cooperative relationship with the educational associations in the developing and developed world (such as AAA, EAA), and the educational activities (Education Committee) of the International Federation of Accountants (IFAC).

1.1 Orientation

It has become apparent that a great need exists (1) to build closer ties between accounting educational bodies and institutions around the world, and (2) to aid accounting educators and institutions in developing and developed countries in their efforts to improve their accounting education, knowledge, research, development, and practices. To accomplish these dual objectives, the establishment of a coordinating body in the form of an "International Assocation for Accounting Development" (IAAD) may be considered the most effective vehicle.

1.2 The Aims

The principal aims of the proposed international association can be described as:

(1) Fostering of closer ties between accounting educators throughout the world, the exchange of information, research efforts and knowledge, and the stimulation, by mutual effort, of post-secondary accounting education and training in both developed and developing nations of the world, in order to make accounting more relevant and useful in the socioeconomic process of nations.

(2) Assistance, by various means, to Third World countries' accounting-oriented educational institutions and associations to spur the qualitative and quantitative output of accounting students, and to aid in the furthering of know-how, teaching skills, research, publications and other developmental and clear-

inghouse activities in these countries or regions.

These aims are not intended to infringe upon the status of existing accounting associations but to assist and complement their activities, and to link the educational bodies and teachers closer together, and build such bodies in Third World countries.

Accounting as a discipline and body of knowledge, for purposes of the international association, is considered to encompass (1) enterprise accounting of both a public and private sector nature, geared towards both financial and managerial (cost) accounting, (2) government accounting (e.g., taxation and budgeting) including all sorts of governmental agencies, parastatal units and not-for-profit entities, (3) macro accounting and accounting for economic growth/development and planning, and (4) auditing for all sectors.

The more specific objectives of such a contemplated international association would be (in due consultation with and/or request from national educational or professional entities) to:

(1) Serve as a medium for exchange of information, knowledge and ideas, in relation to educational, research, and accounting training aspects.

(2) Coordinate research, training, and accounting development activities in the various branches and functions of accounting (e.g., enterprise, government and national accounting and auditing).

(3) Assist in, and encourage, the translation and adaptation of current accounting/auditing texts.

(4) Help develop local courses, course materials, programs and teaching methodologies in the various areas (branches) of accounting.

(5) Help develop text materials (e.g., cases) of relevance to specific regional and local environments.

(6) Assist in exchanging faculty personnel and students between countries and regions. Direct exchanges between post-secondary educational institutions will be sought.

(7) Sponsor conferences and seminars (workshops) in various regions/countries of the world pertaining to educational and research aspects, including methodologies for accounting training plus course and program developments.

(8) Support and/or sponsor extensive programs, mostly in Third World regions, to update and upgrade accounting educators. Such programs can be short (one to three weeks), medium (one to three months) and long (three to six months), and cover specific accounting educational fields.

(9) Assist in locating competent expatriate teaching or research staff needed by accounting training institutions in developing countries.

(10) Help find staff for regional and country "Accounting Development Centers," which centers will focus on development of teachers and research activities.

(11) Establish other ways to spur technical assistance programs by means of joint committees, and encourage exchange of teaching, research and administrative personnel.

(12) Spur cooperation and linkages with other international, regional, and local accounting practitioners' bodies to coordinate training of an ongoing or

extensive nature, and carry out joint research and other activities.

(13) Coordinate the evaluation of international accounting and auditing standards.

(14) Sponsor the development of courses, programs and examinations to provide greater international comparability and more uniform qualifications.

(15) Help evaluate and unify examinations by region and/or internationally. The determination of the comparability of international qualifications may become one of IAAD activities.

(16) Issue regular newsletter and other publications pertaining to accounting information of an international educational, research, developmental, and training nature.

The implementation of these objectives is to be carried out in conjunction with existing national educational accounting associations, or other institutions, and be developed in cooperative relationship or association with the educational activities of IFAC, IAAC, CAPA, UEC, etc. These activities should not infringe on the individual national association's sovereignty, rights and functions, but should serve essentially to better coordinate these, and jointly devise ways and means to (1) enhance international accounting education and research and (2) help develop Third World countries' educational structures and processes.

1.3 Membership

Two types of membership can be envisaged for the international educational association, i.e., full and and individual membership.

1.3.1 Full Membership

Full membership (on a voluntary basis) would be composed of:

(1) National or regional associations of teachers in post-secondary institutions.

(2) Professional organizations (most professional accounting institutes are concerned nowadays with improvements of education at the post-secondary levels). These can be of a governmental or private nature.

1.3.2 Individual Membership

Individual members would be composed of:

(1) Academic and other post-secondary accounting educational institutions.

(2) Groupings of individual educators and practitioners at private and governmental agencies, institutions or firms interested in education (where no national entities exist).

(3) International, regional and local development agencies, foundations and other interested bodies. It is assumed that where groupings of accounting educators form an association, the latter will become a full member.

1.4 Funding

Funds for carrying out the activities of assistance activities for Third World countries presumably will be funded by various types of membership fees and other sources. Roughly stated, the annual financial requirements of the International Association may be expected to be generated from:

(1) Membership fees; separate fees for full, and individual members (fees will be minimal).

(2) Profit on sale of publications (it is hoped the support for publications can be obtained from international bodies).

(3) Support (extra) support from professional accounting bodies, domestically and internationally.

(4) Foundations and other institutions.

(5) International and regional development agencies, such as the World Bank, Asian Development Bank, Inter-American Development Bank and the United Nations (UNESCO/UNDP).

The initial two to three years may have to be used to explore and develop the various coordinating activities with accounting associations, encourage memberships, set up study and education programs and form certain committees.

During the initial exploratory period, a regular newsletter and/or other publicationss may be issued stating the progress being made in establishing the international educational association. A newsletter or journal may be issued (free of charge) during this period.

An approach can be made to foundations, development organizations and/or other institutions for assistance towards initial exploration and start-up costs.

1.5   Accounting Education for Economic Development

The major and integral part of the activity of the IAAD should be to help accounting education, knowledge, research, translations, and publications in Third World countries and regions. It is anticipated that the IAAD can function effectively as a "clearinghouse" for such activities, and work in close cooperation with international/regional development agencies (World Bank, UN, etc.) in channeling such assistance, finding the right personnel, evaluating countries' accounting needs and plans, and pursuing related matters. Accordingly, the technical assistance aspects of the IAAD as a coordinating body, can give accounting educators and institutions an international entity through which to channel technical assistance requests, and aid to the various countries. The IAAD gradually may put together or assist in locating technical assistance teams to appraise countries' needs (at their request), and work together with international organizations in delineating requirements and supplying qualified manpower, materials, texts, and other needs. It is envisaged that such joint efforts will become the major function of the International Association for Accounting Development.

The setting up of international accounting tests and examinations, and granting internationally comparable certificates at various levels, is another function that could be enhanced. Support can be given to develop and help grade examinations in Third World countries at various institutional levels.

As accounting is considered to encompass (1) enterprise, (2) government, and (3) national accounting, which require different focus, it is to be recognized that governmental and public enterprise accounting, macro accounting and accounting for economic development is of relatively greater significance to Third World countries than to Western (free enterprise) nations. Therefore, the emphasis in education may have to be different. All these needs will have to be taken into account in pursuing the various activities of an international association.

2. A Potential International Role for the AAA

The American Accounting Association (AAA), one of the foremost accounting educational associations in the world, and comprising the largest body numerically of academic accountants, could play a vital role in spurring accounting education, research, development, and technical assistance to Third World nations. In addition, it could help foster better coordination between the existing educational associations, and assist in the process of setting up local and regional accounting educational bodies in both developing and developed nations. Although the focus is primarily on potential accounting educational improvements in Third World nations, better international accounting coordination is an inherent part thereof. AAA's role may be as a vital promoter for the proposed IAAD.

The potential roles of the AAA in regard to Third World economies are seen as (1) setting forth short-, medium-, and long-term programs, (2) finding ways and means to implement such programs, and (3) executing potential pilot projects. A discussion of each of these follows.

2.1 Types of Programs

In setting forth the programs, an assumption is that the AAA has "something to offer" the Third World nations in the area of accounting education (as was conveyed in the country studies in Part IV), although it does not necessarily imply transferring U.S. know-how and techniques. The determination of what to convey and how to do it must be subject to careful assessment by the countries and regions, as part of their educational "inventory" and "planning" framework.

We visualize the following programs, program contents and the means for pursuing them. These programs may well become an integral function of a separate coordinating body, i.e., the International Association for Accounting Development.

2.1.1 Short- and Medium-Term Programs

The components of the short- and medium-term programs are:

(1) To assist in carrying out accounting "inventories" (manpower surveys) and accounting "plans" as a vital element for improving accountancy education, knowledge, and practices.

(2) Identify projects of an accounting educational nature for implementation and submission to international agencies (such as the World Bank, IMF, UN agencies, regional development banks).

(3) Assist in locating competent and experienced teaching and research manpower.

(4) Assist in setting up accounting courses, course outlines and teaching methods.

119

(5) Make available U.S. course materials, cases, etc.

(6) Serve as clearinghouse for requests and publications (including translations), teacher exchange, etc.

(7) Make available AAA newsletters and *The Accounting Review* to educational institutions (e.g., libraries) abroad.

(8) Facilitate and encourage international membership in the AAA to educators in Third World countries at a nominal fee (to be paid in local currency but converted by means of UNESCO coupons).

(9) Prepare special international newsletters on a quarterly basis, setting forth items of relevance to Third World nations, such as course developments, teaching experiences, exchange programs, new texts, etc.

(10) Encourage articles from Third World nations to be compiled in an annual *International Accounting Review*.

(11) Compile and exchange accounting educational materials, research publications, teaching experiences, etc., and make these available at a nominal fee.

2.1.2 Long-Term Program

The envisaged long-term program basically covers the same aspects as the short/medium terms, although on a more extensive and structural basis. In addition, we visualize the following long-range or general programs in which the AAA could play a part:

(1) Faculty (and programs) exchange between U.S. academic and other institutions with counterparts in Third World nations.

(2) Joint programs for writing texts, translations and case materials of relevance to Third World countries and regions.

(3) Research programs and course content development linked with the countries' socioeconomic development programs.

(4) Setting up a permanent clearinghouse on an international or regional basis, and spurring the activities of an International Association for Accounting Development.

(5) Harmonization of international educational activities and development, including examinations, degrees, and certificates.

The AAA itself does not have funds available to carry out accounting assistance to Third World nations, and the activities that could be pursued by the AAA would have to be those that involve a minimum expenditure of funds. The AAA could assist in the various programs pertaining to Third World countries, making its talents available and offering its publications at a nominal fee. The funds that could be generated by Third World country institutions and educators also would be minimal. Accordingly, the funding for such activities have to be seen in the context of funding for the international association.

To get such an effective accounting educational assistance program started to evaluate the accounting needs in respective Third World countries (together with country bodies and academicians), and to set forth the "accounting development plans" (based on the "inventory") is a major task. To execute such programs in a series of countries, presumably in conjunction with international and regional agencies, may cover a period of between one to four years. To set up these programs and carry out the initial evaluation phases, issue publications and materials, and implement a limited international exchange and technical assistance program may require outside funding of $200,000 (estimated), covering the one-to four-year period.

As for the long-term, no estimate can be made (as yet), as it will depend on the extent, coverage and duration of the various countries' requirements. In addition to international sources listed, it can be expected that the Third World countries themselves and the institutions would gradually supply a larger portion of the finances required, foreign and domestic. Additional local and regional facilities may have to be constructed, for example, accounting development centers, and these funds should be principally financed locally.

The execution of accounting assistance to Third World countries and other coordination efforts potentially could be carried out by means of an international association with extensive inputs from the AAA and other educational associations around the world.

2.2 Proposed Pilot Project(s) in Third World

In addition to or in conjunction with the above programs, and in cooperation with a contemplated International Association for Accounting Development, country pilot project(s) may be set up initially, as referred to in our country studies. Such "pilot" projects in a Third World country, at the request of that country, would involve the accountancy educational system at post-secondary levels. The project would involve the following components:

(1) The developing country itself would request such a technical assistance program, covering a two- to three-year period, and have, if possible, its own counterpart team work up the needs and requirements.

(2) Establishment of an "Accounting Development Center," whereby the main focus will be on:

-developing and upgrading accounting instructors;
-developing course materials, textbooks and translations;
-outlining teaching approaches of relevance to the country;
-carrying out seminars and other courses for the other post-secondary teachers in accountancy and practitioners;
-pursuing research and other developmental work;
-issuing newsletters and other publications; and
-preparing an accounting inventory and accounting development plan.

(3) The pilot program, initially covering a two- to three-year period, is to be pursued in close coordination with the country's ministry of education and other governmental and academic agencies and international/regional development agencies, such as the World Bank-IMF, UNESCO, UN, etc. The latter agencies can effectively help shape the direction of the programs.

(4) Funding for the pilot study(s) is to be secured from international agencies and foundations; while it can be expected that part of the domestic financial requirements will come from the local governmental agencies. To carry out such

a pilot country program over a two- to three-year period, with the services of two or three expatriate professors, the total cost would be around U.S. $200,000. In this context, it is important that such accountancy projects become part of the economic development plans and projects of the country concerned, as envisaged by international development agencies. Countries, for example, like Egypt, Indonesia, Mexico, Pakistan, Tanzania, Syria, Zaire and Burma, may be most suitable candidates for such pilot programs as in contrast with other countries; limited programs have been carried out already in these countries to enhance post-secondary accountancy education and training (see country studies).

3. Feedback on the Potential Role of Developed Countries

Based upon the feedback received in connection with the AAA study, "Accounting Education and the Third World," the following is a combination of reactions received and our own inferences.

• Many respondents from developing countries mentioned that the publications of the AAA (*Accounting Review* etc.) and other developed countries were not adequately available in their country, although this material was considered of great significance for some of their accounting courses, and for updating educators. (Not all of it was considered relevant.) Some better means should be found to distribute journals and newsletters at a minimal cost, whereby possibly dues could be paid in local/regional currencies (e.g., Unesco coupons).

• American, European and Australian accounting literature and teaching methodology were considered by many respondents as being most useful to them, although they do need to be adapted. Accordingly, many urged that both literature and instructors be made better available to their educational system (locally or regionally). No clear pattern emerged as to the means to do this.

• Exchange of faculty for short periods of time (3-9 months) was considered extremely desirable; many felt that bilateral exchange between universities should be explored. The suggestions were made that developed countries' universities "adopt" universities in Third World countries. Professors from developed countries were considered particularly desirable for master's and Ph.D. programs. The AAA and others may, in due time, arrange for scholarships for accounting teachers from Third World countries to study at other universities. It may well be that some form of clearinghouse for exchange of teachers more palatable. This may be part of the proposed international association.

• Many suggested that developed and developing countries' universities, or a consortium of universities, send out appraisal teams for periods between four to six weeks to Third World institutions to help them evaluate the courses, and jointly outline literature and better teaching methods and approaches. Visiting faculties would be useful in trying to adapt literature to current situations, and in helping develop "case method" teaching. Accounting educational advisors are in short supply in the Third World.

• Visits by faculty to Third World countries, for short periods of time (one to six weeks), would be desirable for conducting seminars and workshops. Such visits, however, should be well announced in advance, and well planned. (Currently many professors on overseas trips merely drop in or do not visit with faculty and students.)

• The most frequently mentioned topics for required advice and assistance were: management (cost) accounting, controllership, computer (EDP) know-how, operational auditing, management information systems and procedures, management science, financial reporting for specialized agencies, accounting theory, case method teaching, and management advisory services.

• Educational assistance (advice) should also be extended to public sector accounting (government administrative management, budgeting, tax administration, public enterprises), as many felt they could learn from the developed countries. (The public sector is often the largest sector in developing nations.)

• Although respondents made it clear that U.S. and other international assistance in the area of accounting education (e.g., literature) would be highly appreciated, they also stressed they did not have funds to finance some of the suggestions made. They expressed the hope that adequate means could be found to disseminate literature, send out technical assistance terms, develop exchange of faculty and conduct joint seminars.

4. "International Accounting Educational Survey"

One of the great needs for adequate international accounting education development is the evaluation and exchange of activities pertaining to course materials, textbooks, programmatic developments, curriculum structures, articles published, research in progress, faculty availabilities, and related aspects concerning educational, training and research activities. No such medium currently exists for the dissemination of international information. Especially, many Third World countries have been less than adequately exposed to activities which could have been, and could be, of benefit for their proper educational pursuits. There are not only certain activities taking place in developed countries that may be of benefit to all parties concerned, but many developing (and developed) countries are not aware of, and informed about, educational/research matters of interest taking place in developing nations, and other non-Western nations. In turn, many accounting practices, which have an educational impact, are not properly disseminated and evaluated from an international educational point of view. In essence, a vehicle has to exist to improve and coordinate accounting and auditing education and to communicate such activities to educators and institutions around the world.

Recognizing the need for such a proper international forum, the Center for International Accounting Development of The University of Texas at Dallas (U.S.A.), has initiated a semi-annual publication, "The International Accounting Educational Survey," to cover such materials. This publication will be free of charge initially and interested parties can obtain this survey by writing to the Director, Center for International Accounting Development, The University of Texas at Dallas, P.O. Box 688, Richardson, Texas 75080 U.S.A.

The material to be covered in this survey will be of the following categories/modules:

(1) **Accounting Educational Programs and Courses:** Study programs and courses at post-secondary institutions will be outlined and reveiwed, and their potential applicability assessed for other (Third World) nations and regions.

(2) **Course Materials: Textbooks, Articles and Other Learning Aids:** The use of materials in countries/regions will be appraised in view of the objectives of countries (and internationa/regional) accounting programs.

(3) **Research Aspects Pertaining to Various Branches of Accounting** (enterprise, governmental and national/macro), and the relationship between accounting and other disciplines, accounting for economic analysis, policy and planning, etc.

(4) **Training of Accounting Faculty** i.e., ways and means to upgrade and update new and existing faculty. This includes faculty training programs (e.g., Ph.D.) in various regions.

(5) **Review of International Articles and Books** especially those which appear to be of interest to accounting educators.

(6) **Information Regarding Faculty Exchanges,** availabilities, salaries by regions, and other items covering faculty clearinghouse matters.

(7) **Updating Programs** of a long-term, medium-term or short-term nature being offered in various regions. This may include specialized programs pertaining to oil and gas accounting, computer accounting and auditing, executive management programs and other more general programs.

(8) **Funding availability** from international and regional organizations for accounting development.

(9) **Accounting Educational Pursuits and Programs** carried out, or to be explored, by international and regional bodies such as UN, World Bank, regional banks, IFAC, CAPA, IAAC, African Accounting Council, and UEC.

(10) **Clearinghouse Matters** of a miscellaneous nature, essentially of an educational, training and research content.

This publication will be issued semi-annually, starting with the first issue during the spring/summer of 1981. It is expected that the proper exchange and distribution of developments and pursuits gradually will help in improving the still sizeable educational and practice deficiencies that currently exist in Third World economies. Reaction from international and regional agencies for such a publication has been very favorable, and it is expected that gradually the survey will fill a real international educational need.

5. Conclusion

The necessity for an international educational association has become apparent, and it is expected that such an association will come off the ground in the near future. Essentially it should be to serve the Third World countries, where the needs for such an international clearinghouse are the greatest. It also should benefit the developed countries, who are now recognizing that accounting assistance is of vital importance for many Third World nations. The association should be a forum for all countries and institutions, irrespective of their economic, political or social form of government. Hopefully, international agencies, such as the World Bank, IMF and UN will gradually actively support such a body.

While such an association in due time will issue various publications, the Center for International Accounting Development of The University of Texas at Dallas has taken the initiative in publishing an "international educational survey," which would fill an immediate need regarding educational and re-search clearinghouse matters. It is expected, however, that such a journal gradu-ally will be part of the proposed international association, and may constitute one of its major functions.

CHAPTER XIII

INTERNATIONAL AND REGIONAL VEHICLES FOR ACTION

Our previous appraisals already covered the various vehicles that exist to execute an effective "framework for action." The various approaches we have in mind are briefly summarized here. In addition, we now have an active International Federation of Accountants (IFAC) with a sub-committee on education. The latter, in our opinion, also could be a major force in enhancing educational pursuits. Furthermore, regional accounting organizations, such as CAPA, ASEAN, IAAC, UEC are paying due attention to educational and training aspects (e.g., continuing education), as will be noticed from the writeups under Part Four.

In this chapter, two principal items will be reviewed: (1) general approaches of a domestic and international nature to implement accounting educational programs, and (2) the function of international professional accounting organizations.

1. Domestic and International Approaches for Action

The domestic means can be categorized and described as follows:

(1) Layout of an accounting inventory and plan covering the quantity and quality of accountants by sections and functions, manpower availabilities, and functional and educational aspects. The inventory and plan hopefully will result in educational, institutional, professional, and legislative programming of accounting.

(2) Professional and institutional enhancement, preferably to be done by existing practitioners and educators, initially with governmental backing. Professional activities are to involve training, certification, practice requirements, accounting standards, translating and developing materials, seminars, exchange of personnel, and other clearinghouse activities.

(3) Governmental support and/or supervision is necessary in developing accounting and auditing norms, regulations, practices and training.

(4) Accounting/auditing firms, often one-man operations, may be merged to give better all-around services and improve training. Contacts with foreign firms may be useful in this connection.

(5) Domestic enterprises and firms may have their accounting personnel teach at colleges and in seminars.

As for the international and regional (i.e., external) means, the following would be the most suitable:

(1) Regioanl and international development organizations.

(2) International and regional accounting development centers where persons from Third World countries could be updated and trained for short periods of time.

(3) International accounting firms, in supplying expertise and assistance for

professional enhancements.

(4) Multinational enterprises to help conduct training programs at various centers.

(5) International and regional accounting service corps of retired accountants to function as counselors. Exchange of personnel may be part of such service also.

(6) Governmental assistance, for example, in the area of government accounting and other public sector accounting aspects, e.g., regulatory agencies.

Internal and external programs can pursue the following joint vehicles:

(1) Domestic and regional accounting development centers involving theoretical and organizational assistance. Such centers may constitute the core of accounting training, development and planning in the private and public sectors. A major task will be the upgrading of teachers, generation of text materials, development of standards and examinations, research and other clearinghouse matters.

The need is particularly great for the establishment of such accounting development centers for the upgrading and further development of accounting educators in Third World countries and/or regions. These accounting development centers could be usefully linked with clearinghouse activities for educators (as part of the international association referred to in Chapter XII). These programs may require extensive financial support. It is quite feasible that agencies like the World Bank, U.N., Regional Development Banks (Asian, African, Latin American, and Islamic) may look upon such centers as projects and programs effectively serving economic development purposes.

(2) International and regional harmonization and coordination pertaining to institutional developments, accounting and auditing standards, and other programming aspects.

(3) An international association for accounting development to function as association or clearinghouse of accounting for economic development purposes. It would deal, *inter alia*, with the coordination of accounting activities for the benefit of Third World countries. The mentioned internal and external programs could partially be channeled through such an international association. The latter could be tied to international and other regional accounting bodies, and have inputs from such educational entities (c.f. Chapter XII). Strong regional chapters would be warranted, for example, in East and West Africa, Middle East, Latin America, Asia, and Southeast Asia. Such an international association should have the backing, at least initially, of various international and regional bodies such as the World Bank, U.N., UNESCO, and Regional Development Banks. [In Part Four, we return to the developments taking place in various world regions.]

2. The International Federation of Accountants (IFAC)

The IFAC was set up in October 1977 during the meeting of the 11th International Congress of Accountants.

Joseph P. Cummings and Michael N. Chetkovich in an article called "World

Accounting Enters a New Era" in the Journal of Accountancy, AICPA, April 1978, made the following observations, which we feel are of interest in order to get a clear picture of these international coordination activities.

> The IFAC started out with a membership of 63 professional accountancy bodies from 49 countries. Of the 99 accountancy bodies from 71 countries eligible to become founder members of the IFAC, 63 accounting bodies have already joined the IFAC, accepted its objectives and agreed to work toward implementing its guidelines and standards. Other accountancy organizations will also be eligible for membership if (1) the organization is nominated by a member body and (2) the organization is recognized, either by law or general consensus within its country, as being a substantial national organization of good standing within the accountancy profession (but not a governmental body, although it may be established under the laws of its country).

Personally, I am skeptical whether this rule is in the best interest of many Third World countries whose professional institute is now excluded from IFAC.

The IFAC has developed a 12-point program to guide its efforts. This program is designed to:

(1) Develop statements that would serve as guidelines for international auditing practices.

(2) Establish a suggested minimum code of ethics to which it is hoped that member bodies would subscribe and which could be further refined as appropriate.

(3) Determine the requirements and develop programs for the professional education and training of accountants.

(4) Evaluate, develop and report on financial management and other management accounting techniques and procedures.

(5) Collect, analyze, research and disseminate information on the management of public accounting practices to assist practitioners in conducting their practices more effectively.

(6) Undertake other studies of value to accountants such as, possibly, a study of the legal liability of auditors.

(7) Foster close relations with users of financial statements, including preparers, trade unions, financial institutions, industry, governments and others.

(8) Maintain close relations with regional bodies and explore the potential for establishing other regional bodies as well as for assisting in their organization and development, as appropriate. Assign appropriate projects to existing regional bodies.

(9) Establish regular communication among the members of IFAC and with other interested organizations through the medium of a newsletter.

(10) Organize and promote the exchange of technical information, educational materials, and professional publications and other literature emanating from

member bodies.

(11) Organize and conduct an International Congress of Accountants approximately every five years.

(12) Seek to expand the membership of the IFAC.

"The constitution of the IFAC provides for governing bodies consisting of an assembly of representatives from each member body and a council of 15 members elected by the assembly. To assist these bodies, a three-member permanent secretariat has been established."

"An important objective of the IFAC is to encourage the formation and development of regional organizations. Regional organizations provide opportunities for accounting organizations to cooperate in the development of the profession in their regions, in the solution of common problems and in the exchange of information. Also, such groups have important resources and skills available to them.

"IFAC's council formed seven standing committees to forward its objectives. These committees are: Auditing Practice, Education, Ethics, Management Accounting, Regional Organizations, International Congresses, and Planning.

The education committee has been asked to survey each member organization's entry requirements, examinations and alternative educational and practical experience requirements. It also is intended that the committee will review and publicize developments relating to basic training and continuing professional education as a basis for developing recommendations in these two key areas.

The educational activities of IFAC have, as yet, been rather narrowly oriented, eseentially towards professional (public) accounting training. The question of the types and levels of education to promote general accounting development for the member countries and regions has not been coped with. For that reason, we currently have a somewhat reserved attitude toward IFAC's educational pursuits, although hopefully this will become a major area of its activities.

3. The International Accounting Standards Committee (IASC)

Although the IASC is concerned with the harmonization of accounting and reporting standards, the ability to appraise and implement such standards is, of course, highly dependent upon the sophistication (education) existing in the countries. Furthermore, the philosophy and nature of accounting standards to serve economic decision making has to have a broad educational base; standards should be more than mere technical standards. The educational setup in a country is, therefore, important, and in this context we should evaluate whether the development of accounting standards can also be a means, or vehicle, to spur the body of knowledge of accounting and related accounting practices. First, the structure of IASC will be looked at.

The IASC in its October 1977 publication, "The Work and Purpose of the International Accounting Standards Committee" states, p. 2:

Three developments can be identified which demonstrate the need for international standards: the growth in international investment, the increasing prominence of multinational enterprises, and the growth in the number of accounting standard setting bodies.

The primary source of information for investors' decisions on their shareholdings in an enterprise is the published financial statements. There is rapid growth in international investment, and investors in international capital markets currently have no assurance that the financial statements on which they base their decisions are compiled using accounting policies which are recognized in their own country. The harmonization of international accounting standards will assist the investors in making their decisions more efficient. Consequently the flow of new funds into productive enterprises may improve and the investor's return on his investment may be maximized.

The multinational enterprise must produce information for the countries in which their shareholders reside, as well as information to satisfy the requirements of the local country in which they operate. Accounting principles may vary from country to country, resulting in the publication of different information to describe the same activities. The harmonization of accounting standards will assist in avoiding the misunderstanding and confusion and in reducing the cost of preparing multiple sets of financial statements.

A further matter which is of concern to the accountancy profession and affects its relationship with business and the general public is the proliferation in recent years of accounting standard setting bodies. An effort to coordinate and harmonize these separate rule-making efforts is essential to avoid increasing confusion and differences in financial reporting between countries.

In regard to the objectives of standards, Cummings and Chetkovich (Journal of Accountancy, April 1978, p. 52-61) continue:

> The founding members of IASC distinguished between standards that were likely to find universal acceptance readily and those that would require more time and greater effort to win acceptance. They recognized that standards being developed in their own countries probably were more highly advanced than those of other countries and would not necessarily be considered appropriate by all countries. Accordingly, their eventual acceptance and implementation on a worldwide basis would be, at best, difficult.

> With this concept in mind, the group defined its immediate objective as the development of standards capable of rapid and broad acceptance, thus contributing to a tangible improvement in the quality and comparability of corporate disclosure on a multinational basis at the earliest possible time.

> Although there can be no question that achieving agreement on the harmonization of accounting principles is a task, there would appear to be general agreement that the IASC has made substantial progress in addressing itself to a number of basic topics that entail major conceptual, reporting and disclosure differences.

> Moreover, even when it may not be possible to achieve universal ac-

ceptance of a single method of accounting and reporting, the fact is that the promulgation of an international standard reduces the alternatives available under varying circumstances and that the required disclosures facilitate understanding and comparison.

In our opinion, we may well have come at a certain impasse in developing international accounting standards. Although the development of coherent international accounting and auditing standards is highly desirable for economic and financial activities, such standards also have to serve the economic aims and conditions of the respective countries and regions. It is quite apparent that socio-economic circumstances greatly vary, as yet, around the world. Accounting and auditing standards, therefore, have to be in tune with the specific economic conditions and objectives. Such a trend is already noticeable in the European Economic Community (EEC) where the directives are geared to the prevailing circumstances, while in the U.S. the Financial Accounting Standards Board (FASB) is trying to develop standards suited to the U.S. conditions.

Such trends, however, should not run contrary to the aims of the International Accounting Standards Committee (IASC), but could effectively be linked herewith. It does require, in my opinion, a stage or "phase approach" for the IASC. For example, the international standards to be developed should, first of all, be in the nature of "common concepts" based upon a more homogeneous international accounting framework. The accounting measurement and reporting elements may find a commonality within such a framework, but setting international standards without such a framework would be somewhat like operating in a vacuum.

Within the above context also should be mentioned the various structural economic developments that have taken place in the last decades which require standard setting, but which are based upon different purposes. Such developments are:

(1) Rise and growth of multinational enterprises.

(2) Economic integration taking place in certain regions.

(3) Industrialization of many Third World countries.

(4) Extension of accounting to make it useful for a variety of socioeconomic purposes.

So far, it appears that the IASC has had above all the first item in mind. While the need for such commonality of standards for international enterprise operations is apparent, the other facets are not to be neglected. Therefore, it may well be warranted to focus on the following:

(1) Development of certain primary standards for international operations, taking into account the different economic-financial objectives and circumstances.

(2) Development of a set of secondary standards pending upon the regional or country circumstances, for example, the needs of the EEC in its integration, and the purposes of many Third World countries in developing a better accounting framework. For example, standards pertaining to value-added measurements and reporting and the portrayal of indirect costs and benefits play a vital role

in many economies. In essence then the secondary standards could be developed in greater coordination with economic regions and Third World economies, whereby the latter would be forced, jointly or separately, to think through and set forth their accounting structure and requirements. Such standard setting would not only be more effective but also would involve more beneficially Third World and other economic regions. For example, in Asia, the ASEAN group or CAPA; in Latin America, the Inter-American Accounting Association, and in Africa, the African Accounting Council, plus others, could give their inputs. It could involve restructuring or amending the IASC, taking into account these interests, without however making IASC an impotent entity. For the long range, it would serve better the International Accounting Standard purposes; it could be patterned along lines of the IFAC.

It also should be clear that standards should not be limited to financial accounting measurement and reporting elements, but also take into account the managerial or cost accounting needs, for example, regarding transfer pricing, price level or current values, imputation of cost of capital, value added, etc. In many countries the needs for such cost standards may be even greater, to serve the aspects of control, decision-making, pricing, and performance evaluation. Such standards may have to be incorporated in the primary and secondary standards to be developed. They should be part of the accounting conceptual framework. While auditing standards also are to be seen in conjunction with the accounting standards, they may be treated for our purposes as a somewhat distinct area of standard setting.

A major element in standard setting is the question of accounting education and training, since the education of accountants is to be seen in the context of the economic needs to be served. Merely translating foreign standards would not be very useful. (Unfortunately, this is what has happened in many countries.)

Accordingly, the IASC could serve a useful purpose by laying out a sort of "accounting conceptual framework" which is to be evaluated within countries and regions, and then to link the standards it outlines (primary and secondary) to this framework. Rule setting by itself would not serve the accounting discipline in the most beneficial way; the fundamentals or concepts underlying these rules are to be portrayed in first instance. The discipline would be better served internationally if the rule or standard setting would be based upon or linked with an "international accounting conceptual framework," requiring evaluation by professional accounting bodies, educators, and other institutions.

Maybe we have been too monistic and at the wrong end of the scale in setting international standards. While the overall aims are laudable and should be actively pursued, our current means may not be the most effective. This needs to be carefully appraised in first instance, and an attempt must be made to develop a somewhat more systematic approach towards international standards. Also, when we think about standard setting, we should not necessarily identify it with "harmonization," because the standards may be geared, according to primary and secondary norms, to different socioeconomic requirements.

As we conveyed above, standard setting, international accounting organization, economic environment, and education constitute a closely interwoven pattern. As such, the latter (education) is linked to the first two items.

CHAPTER XIV

POTENTIAL FINANCIAL RESOURCES
FOR IMPLEMENTING FRAMEWORK

1. General Proposals

Our "framework for action," dealing with the improvement of accounting education, and training and practices in Third World economies, poses heavy demands of a technical, personnel, material, and financial nature. Financial resources are extremely significant for accomplishment of the objectives.

Although we have referred in other chapters to the need for funding of the respective activities, we are briefly outlining here the potential sources for executing the general framework. The potential financial resources can be distinguished as being 1) internal and 2) external.

1.1 The Internal Resources

Internal resources constitute 1) government budgets—capital and development; 2) academic and other educational institutional funds generated from various sources (e.g., development banks); and 3) private funds, companies, and other endowments.

Governmental resources constitute the largest input, but in general not enough funds are being set aside by governments for accounting education, including adequate salaries in particular, scholarships, training materials, texts, and physical facilities. Governments in Third World countries should have a more thorough look at their requirements, based upon the previously described "accounting inventory and plan." The "planning framework" and its cost-effectiveness (benefits) models reflected therein can provide the authorities with a better insight into the need for additional resources.

Governmental resources to be provided are for both capital and operating expenditures. The capital budget may be partially covered by medium/long term borrowings guaranteed by the government. The capital and operating budgets preferably are to be drawn up covering a five to ten year period, a period necessary to accomplish the desired qualitative and quantitative output of students. As indicated, the accounting (capital and operating) budget is to be seen in the context of the total planning framework.

Other public and private resources will have to be tapped, but again proper feasibility studies (project evaluations) need to be set forth outlining the aims and needs over the medium- and long-term periods. One of the great weaknesses in many Third World countries is just this absence of adequate accountancy feasibility studies to be presented to governmental and private organizations for consideration. The feasibility studies must include detailed source and application of funds statements, setting forth what resources will be generated from student fees (gradually to be increased), and what other fund sources are to be used.

1.2 External Resources

External resources can be separated into 1) regional and 2) international.

(1) *Regional bodies.* Such development institutions as Asian Development Bank, African Development Bank, Islamic and Inter-American Development Bank can play an effective role in supporting accountancy development plans and training programs. Regional divisions of the UN organizations also are to be approached, while regional firms (multinationals) may supply additional support.

(2) *International bodies.* The principal international agencies are the World Bank (IBRD), International Monetary Fund (IMF), United Nations (UN), together with various foundations (Ford, Rockefeller). Again, any approaches to them should be based on carefully prepared feasibility studies, and with adequate layouts presented.

The subsidiaries of multinational enterprises could play an effective role also in supporting accounting training. In addition to financial support they can provide technical support, i.e., training personnel and materials (especially case studies). International professional accounting firms are another logical candidate for additional support of financial and material nature.

2. Specific Suggestions

It would be beyond the scope of our study to enter here into the specifics of how each country and region could secure the necessary financial resources to execute an accounting educational framework. Our study essentially covers the general means, while in Part Four we have given certain suggestions for procuring finances for the respective countries and regional programs. In our opinion, financing may not be the primary problem, the issue is whether we can convince local, regional and international agencies, institutions and governments of the need (and its impact) for accounting educational improvements in the context of the socioeconomic development process. We opine if this can be made clear, more then half the battle is won. In this regard, this study hopefully will contribute while our specific country and regional appraisals give specific coverage for execution. It is up to the local and regional accounting educational entities, in conjunction with international, regional and governmental bodies, to evaluate the specific ways and means, and design their own action program. The norms and guidelines presented in this study could help both parties in its implementation. It should be clear that such a framework for action has to be specifically geared to the local/regional needs; based upon such a specific "plan," the financing would be facilitated.

CHAPTER XV

SUMMARY AND CONCLUSION

This chapter reviews the previous appraisals of accounting education in economic development, and makes additional suggestions concerning the direction of accounting education in Third World economies. A fair amount of space has been allotted in our study to the relationship between economic development accounting methodology and accounting education. This interaction also will be summarized here.

1. Accounting and Economic Development

1.1 The Nature of Accounting

Accounting is being viewed as an "information measurement system" dealing with the generation, verification and reporting of relevant data for micro- and macro-economic activities and resources with increasing frequency. In this context, accounting standardization is considered desirable in order to improve the reliability and consistency of information for internal and external enterprise operations, for sectoral and national accounting, and for other socioeconomic purposes. Extensive efforts are being made at the international level, by means of the International Accounting Standards Committee (IASC) and the UN's Centre on Transnational Corporations (CTC) to develop more uniform international standards of measurement and reporting. In addition, regional coordination such as the European Economic Community (EEC) also exists. Greater uniformity of valuation norms (historical versus current costs) is another accounting issue which requires attention at both national and international levels to facilitate better analysis, evaluation and decision making. For example, current values tend to reflect more relevant costs and to enhance capital formation.

1.2 Accounting and Development Activities

Accounting methods are important for a series of economic analyses, planning and policy aspects, such as development planning, project appraisals and capital formation. Economic development planning utilizes measurement tools in the process of resource allocation. Among the most important of these are capital-output ratios, dynamic input-output analyses, and shadow pricing. Capital out-put ratios, which reflect the relationship between capital investment and the likely resulting growth of real national product, serve as a crucial guide for economic policy. Dynamic input-output models reflect altered economic and technical conditions. To be effective, cost inputs and outputs should be put on a standardized basis, preferably using current cost (value) criteria. Shadow pricing attempts to price the various factors of production as if market equilibrium existed in an economy in order to try to show society's preference for, and relative scarcity of, factors of production.

Every plan consists of a series of activities or projects involving the production of specific good and services. Appraising the feasibility and justification of such projects and their components requires extensive use of past, present, and future data, and their measurement in the form of direct and indirect costs and benefits. The necessary cost-benefit calculations demand information which has an economically realistic, comprehensive and standardized content if accurate projections of items such as sources and applications of funds (cash flow) are to be made.

Accounting can help shape the climate of investment; well-devised systems and controls inspire investor confidence, which in turn leads to healthy growth. Thus, the role of accounting in investment and capital formation is twofold: first, it generates sufficient investor confidence to stimulate the flow of capital; and second, it helps insure the continued efficient use of capital once it has been accumulated. If the fundamentals of accounting and auditing simultaneously become more uniform, the economic business community would have a much more refined instrument with which to measure performance, to pinpoint capital needs, and to further capital formation.

The availability, formation and use of capital are important factors in the economic development process. To improve the capital market mechanism and to mobilize domestic and foreign funds into productive activities may require changes of an institutional, legal, sociocultural or eco-technical nature. Intermediary financial institutions can contribute to better capital flows. They act not only as sources and catalysts for investment, but also provide all kinds of technical assistance, including sorely needed help in various fields of accounting.

Capital formation and development finance would clearly benefit from the professionalization of accounting and auditing. The patronage of government and development institutions may be necessary to persuade the accounting profession to address itself to the problems and challenges of the process of capital formation and economic development.

Taxation can be seen as both (1) a form of capital formation and (2) an instrument to facilitate transfers of money and capital flows, enabling the financing of the public and private sectors' short- and long-range programs. Accounting can enable more equitable and effective tax policies and procedures to be executed. Accounting techniques, such as information accumulation, measurement, processing, recording and verification (auditing), are all essential to a well-designed tax structure and smoothly operating tax administration.

Accounting also plays an increasingly important role in socioeconomic studies of problems of ecology, poverty, social security, and human resource development. Any examination of such areas demands effective cost-benefit analysis.

1.3 Accounting Influences and Practices in Third World Countries

In most countries, accounting began as a requirement established by a legal, economic, political, or religious power. Certain accounting patterns can be distinguished by the "zone of influence" under which they were developed. The British, Franco-Spanish-Portugese, Germanic-Dutch, U.S., and Communistic zones all have characteristic differences. Classifying countries using these zones is helpful for analytical and descriptive purposes. Such classification also aids in the charting of possible deficiencies existing in current accounting and auditing standards and practices.

As for Third World countries, enterprise accounting and auditing methodology and practice have been strongly influenced by the acts, laws, and tax decrees of foreign companies. These tend to be geared toward custodianship. Accounting in the Third World thus may lack consistency and relevancy in both practice and theory, making it difficult to compare financial statements, pinpoint capital and finance needs, measure efficiency, prepare feasibility studies (project appraisals) and construct budgets. Limited focus is generally given to accounting systems and procedures in these countries. Professional accountants may be hired for tax computation or bookkeeping purposes only. Auditing may be subject to extensive and detailed checking, largely due to the absence of good internal control and check systems.

Government accounting (e.g., public enterprise) in the Third World is often seen solely as an accountability device for public receipts and expenditures. Methods used are frequently antiquated, with little attention paid to sound estimation procedures and budgetary controls. Effective auditing standards and practices are not sufficiently stressed for government accounts, programming and performance activities, and public enterprises.

Macro-accounting often lacks a good data base (e.g., quantification and valuation). Accountants may not be aware of the macro-accounting requirements, such as value-added measurements, imputations, and current valuations.

In Third World countries professional institutes generally tend to be weak. No recognition may exist of the need for a professional institute to set standards for accounting and auditing, to establish codes of conduct, to compile training and qualification tests, or to disseminate information. The institutional setup may also suffer from insufficient professional interest, inadequate government encouragement, and lack of support by private and public institutions.

1.4 Accounting Infrastructure Improvements

The aspects that warrant improvement in Third World economies are:

(1) *Professional and Institutional.* A well-functioning institute with related professional activities is needed to evaluate the status of accountants, to develop accounting and auditing standards, to establish codes of conduct, to supervise professional training and updating, to guide research, to disseminate reading materials, and to act as a clearinghouse for activities.

(2) *Legal and Statutory.* Laws and statutes must be clearly spelled out. A company's law or an accounting act should set forth the economic significance, scope and content of financial statements, and the classification, valuation, and other measurement procedures to be applied. An accounting act should also outline the qualifications and tests necessary, the requirements for registration, the accounting and auditing norms required, and the reports to be filed with the government, etc.

(3) *Accounting Inventory and Planning.* Underlying any potential improve-

ment in accounting, is the need for an "accounting inventory." This inventory would include a layout and an analysis of: 1) the activities of an accountant at various functions and levels, 2) the current legislative and institutional setup, and 3) the educational and training elements. It would also anticipate accounting requirements for a period of five to ten years. Based upon such an accounting inventory, a plan can be executed, involving institutional, legal, educational, and practice-oriented aspects. The preparation of such an "inventory" and "plan" would contitute the first phase of a schedule to improve accounting in developing economies. The "planning framework" should cover the following areas: education and training; institutions and professions; and legislation. It may also cover regional planning in regard to regional harmonization and standardization or the development of regional "accounting development centers."

1.5   Accounting and the Long-Term Development Process

Too often accounting, and accounting improvements, are visualized within a short-term model, with income determination as its goal. For economic development, accounting methodology requires a long-term perspective. In this regard, a sharpening of tools and techniques is necessary, especially for management (cost) accounting in both the micro and macro sector. Merely looking at micro-sector activities may not give the best long-range development picture. The micro- and macro-accounting sectors must be seen in conjunction with each other; they influence each other and interact, and the accounting information has to be seen accordingly. Furthermore, "accounting for economic development" needs to be viewed from a systems point of view, whereby the respective sub-systems (e.g., enterprise, government, societal and national accounting and auditing) are to be properly linked by means of basic standards and classification models.

1.6   A Move Towards Meta-Accounting

Accounting is generally adapting itself (admittedly, rather slowly) to economic circumstances and behavior. However, far too little research (if anything) has been done on the topic of how accounting could influence and direct socio-economic development. Our basic methods of accounting have not changed radically, and we may well question whether a partially reoriented accounting methodology, measuring broader and deeper phenomena, (e.g., externalities and social cost-benefit items) of significance for socioeconomic behavior would be desirable. For example, the long-range socioeconomic goals and objectives of a society are studied by existing measurement methods, while extended and multi-dimensional measurement criteria are required. Accordingly we are suggesting that research in accounting information systems and methods should delve into the area of meta-accounting. This will be especially applicable to countries in various early stages of economic development.

As we have seen in this study, accounting education generally follows existing foreign modules and is void of proper interaction with long-term development needs. But accounting should anticipate the changing requirements of society and take action accordingly, especially in the area of education. It is important for Third World countries in particular, to evaluate and establish their own accounting goals and not to follow uncritically the frameworks set up by developed countries, although much can be learned from the latter.

2.   Aspects of Accounting Education in Third World Economies

Certain educational "soft spots" will be discussed before some suggestions for improvement are presented.

2.1 Educational Weaknesses

(1) *Academic training* for accounting generally has a strong accountability orientation, while management accounting, systems and procedures, control, government accounting, cost-benefit analysis and economic development accounting tend to be neglected and underrated in the educational process of many Third World economies. Teachers teach what they have learned; updating is infrequent. Specialized training will be needed in the various branches and areas of accounting.

(2) *Institutional training,* for chartered (certified), cost and governmental accounting is often void of adequate teachers, learning materials and teaching aids. Many accounting professional institutes have no training programs at all, and continuing education is mostly nonexistent. "In-house" training at firms is generally inadequate, while correspondence programs and accounting training centers are poorly developed.

(3) *Vocational and other training* constitutes a fairly neglected group in many countries. Insufficient development of these levels forms a stumbling block in executing accounting improvements. Bookkeeping and commercial colleges for lower and middle levels are only found in certain urban areas. In general, accounting has a low status and is poorly paid in many countries. This discourages qualified people from entering the teaching field as full-time or even part-time instructors.

2.2   Educational Improvements

Effective training is needed at various functional levels (upper, middle and lower) and must focus on various qualification levels (such as cost accounting, financial accounting, government-oriented accounting, auditor) as well. The needs of the country or region may have to be carefully considered in the design of the training program.

Academic, institutional, technical and vocational training and research all have separate features:

(1) *Academic training* must be made relevant from functional micro and macro points of view. The macro economic-accounting orientation should be geared to the needs of the economy. Furthermore, it will involve concentration in: external or financial accounting; internal or operational (management) accounting; and auditing (financial and operational). Courses in government accounting and budgeting, cost-benefit analysis, national income (development) accounting, and controllership are also to be incorporated in the curriculum to

the extent possible. Financial accounting expertise is often considered th sole accounting qualification for certification. It is desirable to establish various levels of competence (degrees and certificates) by separate concentrations (financial, managerial, and government). In many countries, there is a great need to rethink and recast the structure of accounting training at academic and other levels.

(2) *Institutional training* demands an institutional setup, which may need to be developed. Institutional training refers to training under the auspices of the (professional) accounting institutes in both chartered or certified accounting and management, cost and industrial accounting. These programs, following either high school or a university bachelor's degree, often warrant improvement. This pertains to the regular lecture programs and the correspondence programs. Many professional accounting institutes do not have their own training programs, and students studying for professional exams must go to various centers or take correspondence courses to qualify. These programs frequently are in short supply. Institutional programs have a tendency to be legalistically oriented, especially for training financial accountants and auditors. Some "in-house" training is performed by accounting firms and organizations, but this tool is still used inadequately to train accountants. However, it remains extremely hard to carry out in-house programs when a scarcity of trainers exists.

Training for government accountants is largely guided by government-operated financial-administrative developments and requirements (e.g., budgetary and performance techniques, systems and procedures, flow of funds accounting).

"Accounting development centers" may have to be promoted, whose main task will be to impart theoretical and practical knowledge regarding problems and issues found in both private and public sector financial management and auditing. This may be done by country or region. These centers also should cover developmental aspects of administation, research, publication and information dissemination. Included should be evaluations regarding training methodology and legislative requirements, resulting in administrative reforms where necessary. Computer techniques and procedures applicable to accounting and auditing will be important, and manuals need to be developed. A part of the training pattern should deal with operational auditing, and the development of learning materials in this area.

(3) *Technical training* refers to lower and middle-level programs given by bookkeeping and commercial centers. The need for basic clerical/bookkeeping courses, in conjunction with correspondence programs, is very strong, particularly in rural areas. Few countries have good technical training programs.

(4) *Vocational and other training.* Vocational training applies to the basic bookkeeper, cost clerk and financial administration levels. These levels constitute a fairly often neglected group in many countries, and participants often are deprived of upgrading methods and texts. Inadequate development of these levels may constitute a stumbling block for implementing more effective accounting procedures in the private and public sectors.

The low status of accounting in several countries is often a hampering factor, while the quality of teaching often is below desired standards due to low pay. Qualified persons in industry, government or accounting firms may be reluctant to spend valuable time preparing and giving courses.

2.3 Accounting Education and the Profession

To enhance the image of professional accounting, an awareness must exist regarding the significance and impact of good accounting systems, practices and education at all functional levels. The following constitute some of the underlying features needed:

(1) The focus of accounting should be on the various systems of accounting and auditing in the private and public sectors. Governmental accounting may need strong emphasis. One overall parent organization, with sub-groups, may well be the most effective setup, at least initially.

(2) Close liaison may have to be established between the profession and governmental agencies; this already exists in many countries. Legislative requirements, accounting norms and rules, and auditing standards may have to be jointly developed.

(3) Greater attention may be given to value-added measurements, measurement and reporting of costs and benefits for micro and macro purposes, management planning and control. Auditing may cover multiple facets based upon the demands of society. It may also be necessary to focus on information generation and verification for national analysis and planning purposes.

(4) Educational and training center assistance (e.g., universities, polytechnics, colleges, and commercial correspondence) will be needed. In-house training and practical local education also needs to be developed more efficiently. Care should be taken not to blindly adopt the educational patterns, examinations and standards of developed countries.

(5) Exchange of personnel and information needs to be drastically increased. All forms of technical assistance and exchange could be most effectively activated by means of an "International Institute for Development Accounting," closely associated with country and regional bodies, and educational associations.

2.4 International Development and Accounting Education

International economic development requires a broader range of information. This applies, for example, to value-added information, performance and efficiency statements, future projections, and private and social cost-benefit appraisals. The allocation of our scarce international material and financial resource demands that comparative assessments be made, setting forth specific accounting data of a financial and managerial nature. The broader international needs and required appraisals have been sketched in such studies as *Reshaping the International Order*,[1] and the Brandt Commission Report dealing with the North-South relations in the years ahead.[2] The greater international economic

---

[1] *Reshaping the International Order*, a Report to the Club of Rome, Jan Tinbergen, Coordinator, E.P. Dutton & Co., New York.

[2] *North-South - A Programme for Survival*, Report of the Independent Commission on International Development Issues, Pan Brooks, London, 1980.

interdependence also demands that accounting (and other business) students become aware of the socioeconomic issues facing the world. Such understanding and knowledge might lead to the desired improvements in accounting methodology; generally, accounting has been too narrowly oriented. Gradually we may move toward better international accounting methods and education, but this must be based on a clearer understanding of the issues and objectives desired. It is, however, necessary to measure the social rate of return on accounting education. Merely to lay out the needs without such quantification—to the extent it is possible—does not make a strong case. A separate monograph will lay out the cost-effectiveness framework for accounting education, and will cover *inter alia* the social rate of return regarding accounting education development.

2.5 Educational Programs for Development

Educational programs have to suitable for the country and region, and where possible take into account future international requirements. Merely copying educational programs from abroad will not serve most Third World countries. These programs must be carefully developed internally, based upon the accounting aims to be achieved. In this respect, greater focus needs to be given to such areas as management accounting, systems and procedures, budgeting, government accounting, and performance auditing. Generally, the discipline of financial accounting is fairly well covered, but the more decision-making and evaluative accounting courses tend to be neglected.

Educational content needs both theoretical (conceptual) and practical (applied) emphasis; the case method approach should be spurred. Research in the various fields of accounting also demands improvement; good teaching without accounting research of a basic and applied nature is rather empty. It tends to be retrospective. Furthermore, training and research coordination between institutions of learning and professional institutes would serve the whole future accounting framework. In many countries, a more effective accounting educational approach is required and greater attention needs to be given to reappraising the structure and content of accounting education. This may require, for example, that a student have a degree program with a broader base in economics but subsequent specialization in major areas of accounting.

Education, however, should not be solely concerned with upper level training at academic institutions; the middle and lower levels also need vast improvement. At the lower levels especially, correspondence courses and other types of institutional programs may have to be reshaped or developed.

Future accounting programs, in both developing and developed countries, must undergo changes in curriculum and structure due to changing international developments and environments. More emphasis should be given to issue-oriented approaches, an interdisciplinary body of knowledge, and a strong pragmatic orientation. As accounting training will find itself increasingly a part of the total socioeconomic scene, it also needs to respond to dynamic changes and to be future oriented. Research in accounting will have to be viewed as the key to future developments and improvements. Continuing education also will become a major force in accounting education, consequently the institutions of learning will be supplying both a general and specific base. Continuing advanced knowledge also may be given in short-term specialized courses by professional institutions and other agencies. Cooperation between the institutions of learning, the profession, and industry and government also will become closer. There will be a trend to broaden, deepen, enlarge and enhance the academic curriculum. Greater importance will be given to the results and effectiveness of the courses offered.

Most accounting education will continue to be pursued at daytime/nighttime institutions, with direct teacher-student contact, but great scope also exists for training by internal institutional-company means and articleship. This should be better explored and outlined in Third World economies.

3. Country and Regional Evaluations

Part Four of this study focused on the educational accounting systems, developments, and requirements in eight countries in Asia, five in Africa and the Middle East, and three in Latin America. The regional developments of each of these were also sketched. The deficiencies and requirements in those countries/regions tend to have the following fundamental commonalities:

(1) Accounting education has a strong traditional orientation, largely concentrating on stewardship accounting, while such topics as managerial accounting, planning and budgeting, controllership, systems and procedures, public sector accounting, accounting for economic analysis and policy, and operational auditing are relatively poorly pursued. This is largely due to the lack of suitable texts and instructors in these topical areas.

(2) Not enough awareness exists at the government and private levels of the need and potential of good accounting, and the corresponding requirement to improve accounting educational levels. Better linkage needs to be established between government, the accounting profession, industry and educational institutions to enhance accounting training, research, and developmental activities.

(3) Education and training at all levels (upper, middle and lower) and sectors of the economy (private and public) require a reappraisal and restructuring. Extensive assistance from both other Third World countries and developed countries would be needed. Assistance is needed in the form of texts, teaching aids, cases and manpower.

(4) To enhance education by region and country, *accounting development centers* are to be established. Such centers would serve to upgrade and train the scarce body of accounting teachers (at all levels), develop text materials and cases, evaluate teaching methodology, and carry out relevant research and development activities. Regional centers should be linked to national development centers. Regional centers are to focus on specialized topics, such as computer accounting, computer auditing, accounting for economic development, and social responsibility accounting. A certain number of teachers are to be sent to Western nations for specialization and certain Ph.D. degrees.

(5) Exchange of accounting educational developments needs to be improved. In this respect, regional accounting organizations are to establish active *Educa-*

145

tional Clearinghouse Centers. Internationally, it has been suggested that an *International Accounting Development Association* be established to cater to the educational, training and other accounting development needs in Third World countries. This association would also serve as a clearinghouse for educational pursuits, such as the exchange of faculty, reading materials and texts, and the development of courses.

(6) International and regional development agencies, such as the World Bank, UN, IMF, and regional development banks are to be approached, by means of carefully laid out feasibility-project studies, to help finance accounting development activities in Third World regions.

The approaches for spurring accounting education differ to some extent in each region. The developments taking place in CAPA and ASEAN region may be the most encouraging, while the African Accounting Council still must get its feet wet. However, assistance from Asia could be of great benefit to coordinating accounting education in African territories. The restructuring of the Inter-American Accounting Association (IAAI) gives great hope for the future. Regional developments and pursuits tend to be promising; however, the restructuring of education in most countries has not adequately been linked regionally.

The countries covered in this study do not include all countries in the region, and many major ones were left out. However, the ones outlined tend to give a fairly representative view of the region, while sketching international requirements. Accordingly, we opine the country studies presented are intended to ments. Accordingly, we opine the country studies presented are intended to serve educators and others, (1) within these countries, in order to compare their accounting education structures in the light of other countries and the general appraisals, (2) in countries not incorporated in the study to evaluate these reflected country systems in view of their own patterns, and (3) within regions, to link accounting educational pursuits. This study has fairly broad international, regional and country significance. The specific country and regional appraisals are of particular interest to the respective regions and countries concerned, because they were written by persons (mostly nationals) fully familiar with the local educational scene. Exchange of ideas by local, regional and international educators may well result in more specific country appraisals.

Based upon these analytical frameworks, it can be expected that better educational models and policies will emerge. Such comparative appraisals have been highly neglected, and this study must be considered a primer in the attempt to evaluate accounting education models on a comparative country, regional and international scale.

4. A Framework for Action

4.1 Ways and Means to Improve Education

Various vehicles exist to improve education, and the transferring of know-how (technical assistance) will have to play a major role in the years ahead. Such transfers should be based first of all upon internal evaluations composed of an accounting inventory and plan. Furthermore, the country/regional training patterns may have to be altered, with the assistance of *centers for accounting development*. Multilateral and bilateral assistance will have to go hand in hand; technical assistance and international coordination of accounting programs will also have to be linked. Mechanisms for transferring know-how will include universities and other post-secondary institutions, professional institutes, international development organizations, development banks, multinational enterprises and other organizations such as foundations.

The actual training elements would cover: the exchange of faculty, students and materials; an interchange between professional accounting institutions; assistance by accounting firms operating in Third World countries; governmental accounting exchange programs; and program assistance by means of such organizations as the World Bank, UN and regional development banks. Another major element in the transferring of know-how will be the establishment of *accounting development centers*, as mechanisms for educational training, exchange and related accounting development matters (such as texts, research, curriculum development). These centers would also deal with the pursuit of relevant—and country related—accounting research and development. Such research/development needs to be domestically oriented and pursued, but have adequate international and regional inputs in view of closer international integration and coordination.

4.2 Education in the Public Sector

The growth of public sector activities in Third World countries puts heavy stress on the financial management training of the public sector (e.g., parastatals). The focus of such training should be on improving the government accounting and auditing systems, budgets, fiscal administration and other administrative *practices*, and on training *personnel* in better public financial management. Training programs need to be developed at the national, regional and international levels, the latter essentially by means of programs through the UN and foreign government bodies like the U.S. General Accounting Office. Public sector service has to be made more attractive for university graduates, while more extensive government accounting exposure should be built into the curriculum. Furthermore, separate international government accounting and auditing associations are useful vehicles to exchange experiences and know-how. In the international government auditing field the International Organization of Supreme Audit Institutions (INTOSAI) is doing very commendable work on many broad public sector aspects. It has effective regional organizations. Recently an international financial management grouping was proposed, i.e., *Consortium on International Governmental Financial Management*. The proposed policies of this consortium are geared to improve governmental financial management. Such improvement must be based upon the practical application of sound principles and practices within governmental financial management. The consortium seeks, wherever possible and practicable, to achieve uniformity, consistency and harmony with the best practices of financial management in the private sector.

The consortium has been established primarily as an international grouping of already established, operating, and active organizations functioning within the public sector at the international, regional, national, provincial, state, or local level.

The following areas constitute the disciplines of governmental financial management and provide the general frame of reference for the programs, activities and operations of the consortium, as well as the delimitations of areas of interest of its individual and organization members. The areas of interest are accounting, auditing, budgeting, data processing, debt administration, retirement administration, and treasury management. One means is to encourage the exchange of information and ideas on government financial management on an international basis. The eventual long-range goal is to assist in the establishment of international standards in accounting, auditing, and other financial management areas in government. Hopefully, this consortium will work closely with INTOSAI, and other international, regional, and local governmental bodies, and will accordingly also serve as a vehicle to help enhance educational and training programs and clearinghouse activities.

A major technical assistance role may fall on the UN, and a workshop will take place in 1981 focusing on the transfer of governmental know-how and its educational elements. This program, called "Government Accounting and Auditing for Development" and sponsored by the UN's Department of Technical Cooperation for Development at the authorization of the ECOSOC, will focus on the following aspects:

(1) Substantive issues such as the nature and scope of government accounting and auditing.

(2) Institutional and organizational dimensions.

(3) Government accounting, education, training, research, and personnel development, e.g., certification and standards.

The efforts of the UN and other organizations to improve governmental accounting and auditing training should interest professional accounting bodies and universities; it is through the educational curriculum that government improvements materialize. *Accounting development centers* can also function as effective vehicles to upgrade teaching at public sector levels and serve as mediums to improve training in the public sector. It also covers research and exchanges of material and personnel, and related public sector accounting development aspects, including the activities of parastatal units.

The U.S. Association of Government Accountants (AGA), a member body of the international consortium, has an International Affairs Committee which can explore international technical assistance efforts. The AGA serves the interests of governmental financial management through involvement with other national organizations.

4.3 Accounting and Development Banking

National and regional development banks play a major role in economic development. They have considerable clout in spurring accounting developments (such as norms, practices, and training), as they are able to impose stringent requirements on their financing patterns. They can influence the financial planning and control systems of the firms they finance, or are in contact with, and can secure adequate audits. These banks may create separate "accounting development units" to serve present and prospective clients, and other outside parties.

The technical assistance function of development banks (DB's) has internal and external components. Externally, they may require that adequate systems be installed, audit reports submitted, etc. DB's may keep a record of accounting firms that can grant such services, while they also may set up their own "accounting service units" to cover local and regional assistance requirements.

Nationally, the main thrust of DB's in this area will be to spur an accounting/ auditing profession, accounting institute, legislation, training and education, clearinghouse, and research and development activities. DB's can become directly involved in the development and financing of such activities or act indirectly, as a vehicle or catalyst, to spur such implementation. International and regional development institutions have extensive clout in these matters. DB's may want to set up "appraisal teams" to determine the best ways to develop a useful accounting infrastructure in countries. They may help assess the accounting and auditing standards, accounting acts, and the reporting system. DB's may work closely with the educational institutions of regulatory agencies; accordingly, they can function as catalysts for change.

In training of DB personnel (who will, in turn, transfer their knowledge to industries), it is desirable to conduct, on a regional or local basis, condensed courses on "Accounting (Financial Management) for Development Banking." Such courses should include: feasibility studies and cost-benefit analysis; financial measurement and reporting; computer accounting and auditing; controllership; budgeting; regulations; international and regional accounting developments; and professional enhancement, etc. Regional development banks and international organizations may carry out or support such programs. Upgrading and updating of accounting personnel may also be undertaken at the *accounting development centers.*

4.4 International Association for Accounting Development

The establishment of an International Association for Accounting Development will have great international value, as indicated previously. Separate attention is given to it here. Such an international association can have a dual purpose:

(1) The *fostering of closer ties* among accounting educators throughout the world. This would facilitate the exchange of information, research efforts, and knowledge, and would stimulate by mutual effort accounting education and training in both developed and developing nations of the world.

(2) The *assistance,* by various means, to the accounting-oriented educational institutions of Third World countries to improve the productivity of accounting students, and to aid in the furthering of know-how, teaching skills, research,

publications, and other developmental activities in these countries or regions. Principal focus will be on assisting Third World economies.

The international association, initially in the form of a clearinghouse, would build close relationships with IFAC, regional bodies, international development groups and governmental agencies. Membership would be quite open. The international association would essentially function as a central organ for coordination, dissemination, and technical assistance for Third World nations.

The *International Association for Accounting Development* could serve as an international association for a variety of accounting education clearinghouse and developmental activities. Strong regional chapters would be warranted for areas such as East and West Africa, the Middle East, Latin America, Asia, and Southeast Asia. Such an international association should have the backing, at least initially, of various international and regional bodies such as the World Bank, the UN, UNESCO, and regional development banks.

Inputs in such an association would not only come from existing academic associations, but also from professional accounting bodies such as IFAC, the International Organization of Supreme Audit Institutions, NAA, CAPA, IAAC, UEC, and EAA. Its activities are to be pursued in conjunction with international/regional development organizations, and development banks. Accordingly, such an association could serve as a central clearinghouse for know-how, information, exchange, and other activities.

Just as the Brandt Commission, *North-South: A Programme for Survival*, stressed that "international coordinated action" is warranted in economic affairs, the same appears to apply to accounting and its educational elements.

The development of accounting development centers for the upgrading and further development of accounting educators in Third World countries and/or regions, could be usefully linked with clearinghouse activities for educators of such an international association. Such programs, however, require extensive financial support. It is quite feasible that such agencies as the World Bank, the UN, and regional development banks (Asian, African, Latin American, and Islamic) may look upon such centers as projects and programs serving effectively economic development purposes and worth their support.

4.5 External Vehicles for Action

The principal vehicles to execute educational improvements have to be sought within each country. These vehicles would include the institutions of learning, the accounting professional bodies, government and regulatory agencies, and development banks. However, external vehicles will be necessary, and these include the principal international agencies (the World Bank, the UN, IMF, etc.), regional development organizations, and international and regional accounting bodies (IFAC, IASC, UEC, CAPA, etc.). It should be apparent that such "accounting programs" have to be clearly laid out, setting forth future benefits, effects, and costs. As much as possible, quantitative information should be supplied outlining the inputs and outputs of such programs in the years ahead, and their linkage of the economic development programs. Training patterns need to be spelled out in detail by level and area. The aforementioned "International Association for Accounting Development" can well play an effective assistance role in such efforts.

4.6 Sources for Implementing Framework

Financial requirements will be heavy. However, we feel the potential flow of funds will be facilitated if it is shown that improvements in accounitng education are a necessity for the countries and regions concerned, and enhance international economic development. Financial sources will have to be, in first instance, internally generated from government budgets, academic and institutional funds, development banks, and private and foundation funds. External sources would be regional bodies, international agencies, and bilateral funding arrangements (technical assistance programs such as AID).

While financial sources are a means to improve the accounting educational structures, the nonfinancial aspects ("software") is of equal concern. There needs to be a strong awareness and commitment internally and externally to improve the accounting set-up and training. Once such commitments for change have been made (see, for example, Indonesia), we believe that internal and external funding will be forthcoming with relative ease. In this respect, the study hopefully has given useful leads to all parties concerned.

5. Some Concluding Observations

Although the main thrust of this study has been to outline accounting *educational* patterns, requirements, and suggestions, these cannot be separated from the accounting *systems and methods* in Third World countries, in regions, and even internationally. Furthermore, the accounting systems are to be tied to economic and social policies. It is necessary therefore to evaluate more profoundly the accounting educational structures in the context of the economies and projected needs of a period five to fifteen years hence. Accounting should not merely *follow* economic events, it should also help shape them. This area of accounting methodology and education, based upon theoretical and applied research, is one of the most neglected areas in accounting development.

In a number of countries, regions, and on an international scale, extensive economic projections and plans have been set forth. Accounting inventory and planning should be geared to them. Such planning should involve the types of accountants required (for example, industrial, financial/auditing, governmental) and also the skills they should possess. This is an extremely important aspect facing accounting education in Third World countries, and facing the countries/organizations supplying technical assistance. Accounting education in many countries tends to be rather haphazard, as our study indicates; more sophisticated frames of reference (planning models) are needed. Such studies constitute the basis of technical assistance projects and programs for international and regional agencies, the accounting profession, and the governments.

Not only are improvements needed within countries, but global interdependence and the spread of multinational enterprises also demand better international accounting and auditing practices. Educational setups could supply the necessary inputs. Underlying these educational improvements is the ability to pursue sound theoretical and applied research in accounting. This research should deal with the *objectives* of accounting and the *methodology* to be applied. Such research and developmental pursuits need to be well coordinated and findings exchanged; this coordination is currently absent. Research is also to be linked with professional activities. In this regard, IFAC is an encouraging development, although its base and educational operation need to be enlarged.

While there is much that worldwide accounting education and the profession can do to improve Third World accounting education, a major thrust will have to come from such vital organizations as the UN, the World Bank, IMF, and regional development banks. So far, these have not shown great interest in helping improve the accounting educational infrastructures of Third World nations. Accounting education should be considered a vital form of capital investment necessary to enhance socioeconomic growth and development. But accountants themselves must present the need for improvement in education and training to these organizations. Unfortunately, too many educators and practitioners are so absorbed in their day-to-day affairs that they have neither the time nor the exposure to get involved in such appraisals.

This study would not have been possible, or as useful, had it not been for the active involvement of many dedicated educators and practitioners around the world. We are sincerely grateful for their dedicated involvement; hopefully their suggestions will bear fruit. All these analyses and suggestions, it is hoped, will add up to a worthwhile "framework for action" in accounting education and development. This framework by itself will not solve the national and international development issues, but it can greatly contribute to their solutions. In a way, it is regretable that "programs for survival" (e.g., the Brandt Report) do not pay more attention to this vital need for technical assistance and the need to see accountancy education as a necessary area for domestic and foreign investment on a greater scale.

Hopefully the studies of individual countries will help other Third World countries to improve their own educational models, to ask for advice and assistance from others, and to aim for better coordination in their educational organizations. These analyses may also serve regional and international organizations in delineating their support. Furthermore, they can effectively help bilateral assistance between developed and developing countries.

PART FOUR

COUNTRY AND REGIONAL STUDIES

ASIA AND PACIFIC

CHAPTER XVI

REGIONAL ASPECTS AND DEVELOPMENTS IN THE ASIAN AND PACIFIC AREA

1. Regional Background

Regionalization has taken great strides in the Asian and Pacific region, and these regional developments will be extensively outlined because they may prove to be of benefit to other regions around the world, showing how to link the educational elements in such regional efforts. Two regional entities warrant our attention: (1) Confederation of Asian and Pacific Accountants (CAPA), and (2) The ASEAN Federation of Accounts (AFA) as an affiliate of the Association of Southeast Asian Nations (ASEAN).

2. Confederation of Asian and Pacific Accountants (CAPA)

The first Far East Conference of Accountants held in Manila on November 28 to December 1, 1957, actualized the concept of a regional conference of accountants in Asia and the Pacific. This conference was the first step toward the formation of a federation of accountants in the Far East. The Philippine Institute of Certified Public Accountants hosted this first conference.

Three significant issues emerged during the conference: (1) a proposal for the establishment of a federation of accountants in the Far East; (2) holding conferences at regulat intervals, and (3) dissemination and interchange of ideas and information among the member countries.

The formation of a federation of accountants in the region was thought to be premature at that time, due to the absence of accounting organizations in several countries in the Far East. Consideration of the proposal, therefore, was deferred.

In 1960, the second conference was held in Melbourne and Canberra. To reflect the extended membership, the description of the conference was aptly changed from the Far East Conference of Accountants to the Conference of Asian and Pacific Accountants (CAPA). Thereafter, the conferences that followed used the name CAPA. Succeeding conferences were held in Japan in 1962; India in 1965; New Zealand in 1968; Singapore and Malaysia in 1970; Thailand in 1973, and Hong Kong in 1976.

During the intervening years, further changes in representation were made because of the formation of new accounting bodies and the merger of some existing organizations in some countries.

The objectives of CAPA were likewise defined. Basically, it sought to bring together official representatives of various professional bodies in the area for the purpose of discussing means of developing their own services to their own members and their own communities, in education for accountancy (including continuing education for professional men in accounting research) and in ethical professional conduct and associated activities. Moreover, CAPA committed itself to the identification and promotion of means of developing professional standards, practices, and techniques at national and international levels.

For sometime, CAPA was a loose formation of accounting institutes and societies that came together periodically at conferences on accountancy matters. However, in 1973 at the 7th CAPA in Bangkok, the idea of a regional federation of accountants in the area was revived. The chief delegates at the conference met and proposed the expansion of CAPA into a full scale confederation complete with a constitution, a president, and a secretariat. Toward this end, an Executive Committee was formed to study the proposal and make appropriate recommendations.

In 1976, at the CAPA in Hong Kong, the Executive Committee presented its proposed constitution for the Confederation. The proposed constitution was approved and officially adopted on September 23, 1976.

The governing body of CAPA is the Assembly of Delegates consisting of one representative from each member organization. An Executive Committee is appointed to take all practicable steps to achieve the objectives of CAPA.

To facilitate its work, the CAPA Executive Committee has created four subcommittees: Education and Training, Technical, Ethics and Finance.

CAPA is one of the three major regional accounting bodies of the world. The other two are the European Accounting Union (UEC) and the Inter-American Accounting Conference (IAAC). Together with the UEC and IAAC, CAPA has pledged to fully support the newly formed International Federation of Accountants (IFAC).

CAPA has a seat on the Council of IFAC. In addition, it has been invited to join the Education and the Regional Bodies Committees of IFAC. CAPA also represents all three regional bodies in the Planning Committee of IFAC. All these indicate the high standing of CAPA in the accounting world.

CAPA has a present membership of 28 accounting organizations from 21 countries in Asia and the Pacific.

Member Organizations of CAPA are:

Australian Society of Accountants
The Institute of Chartered Accountants in Australia
The Institute of Cost and Management Accountants of Bangladesh
The Institute of Chartered Accountants of Bangladesh
Institute of Incorporated Commercial Accountants (Burma)
The Society of Management Accountants of Canada
Fiji Institute of Accountants
Hong Kong Society of Accountants
The Institute of Chartered Accountants of India
The Institute of Cost and Works Accountants of India
Indonesian Institute of Accountants
The Japanese Institute of Certified Public Accountants
Korean Institute of Certified Public Accountants
The Middle East Society of Associated Accountants
The Malaysian Association of Certified Public Accountants

Malaysian Institute of Accountants

New Zealand Society of Accountants

The Institute of Chartered Accountants of Pakistan

Institute of Cost and Management Accountants of Pakistan

Philippine Institute of Certified Public Accountants

Singapore Society of Accountants

The Institute of Chartered Accountants of Sri Lanka

National Federation of Certified Public Accountants Association of the
    Republic of China

Institute of Certified Accountants and Auditors of Thailand

American Institute of Certified Public Accountants

American Accounting Association

National Association of Accountants

Western Samoa Society of Accountants

Essentially CAPA consists of four broad groupings: (1) the developing countries of Southeast Asia (ASEAN), (2) the Indian subcontinent countries, (3) the developed countries (U.S., Australia, Canada, New Zealand), and (4) Hong Kong, Japan, Korea, and the People's Republic of China (not yet a member) and Taiwan.

The conferences of CAPA have been excellently organized, the topics evaluated were highly relevant and it has brought closer together the accounting bodies, practitioners and educators in the region. However, certain weaknesses of CAPA are felt in the heterogeneity of its participating bodies, the different stage of economic development (i.e., developed and developing nations), the wide dispersion of economic and social interests and its geographic spread. These factors undoubtedly hamper its closer integration at this point of time, although the various working activities, conferences, clearinghouse activities and technical assistance should be actively pursued.

CAPA's role should be further strengthened, especially in regard to:

(1) Design of accounting concepts (i.e., a framework of accounting) to serve the economic development structures of the countries and region. CAPA may set up a study committee to work on such a project. However, the purpose should be essentially to serve the developing nations within CAPA.

(2) Evaluation and layout of accounting and auditing standards, whereby attention needs to be given to better management accounting norms. CAPA should bring these inputs to the IASC and IFAC.

(3) Setting forth a technical service group to assist small- and medium-scale industries in the area, to prepare operating manuals for such entities and render various types of accounting service for financial institutions, cooperatives, etc.

(4) Establishing regional training center(s) for updating and upgrading accounting practitioners and educators. This is a task of great priority. It should involve textbook writing, case studies and other developmental and research activities.

Regional cooperation, however, could be further strengthened within the sub-areas of CAPA. A good example is already the AFA within ASEAN. However, similar moves could be made by the Indian Sub-Continent countries (e.g., India,

Pakistan, Sri Lanka, Bangladesh).

3. ASEAN and the ASEAN Federation of Accountants (AFA)

The Association of Southeast Asian Nations (ASEAN) was formed in 1968; its purpose was to accelerate the economic development of the member countries and to promote stability and cohesiveness of the region as a whole. ASEAN has five member countries: Indonesia, Malaysia, the Philippines, the Republic of Singapore, and Thailand. The countries are different in, among other things, educational and legal systems and culture and business requirements due to geographical situations and historical background. Regional diversity is not as wide, however, as within the CAPA countries.

It was only logical that the expanded trade and investments taking place within ASEAN would have to be followed by better accounting harmonization and integration. Cognizant of the need for a formal structure to consolidate harmonization efforts in the ASEAN region, a series of organizational meetings were held among the representatives of the various ASEAN accounting organizations beginning in 1976. The result was the formation of the ASEAN Federation of Accountants (AFA) on March 12, 1977, in Bangkok, Thailand.

AFA has a permanent secretariat in Manila and has already undertaken several programs of professional activity. At the present time, AFA has four standing committees: Accounting Principles and Standards, Auditing Principles and Standards, Education, and Professional Development. Most notable to date has been the work of the Accounting Principles and Standards Committee whose charge is to promulgate accounting standards applicable to conditions in the ASEAN region. However, many obstacles still have to be overcome. Accounting principles among the ASEAN countries are still far from uniform; the accounting and reporting standards are divergent within and among the countries in the region. Currently different sets of accounting standards may have to be prepared to accommodate the internal and external country reporting needs.

The force of the ASEAN Federation of Accountants (AFA) has been written up by Frederick D. S. Choi in an excellent article in the Fall, 1979 (Vol. 15-1) issue of *The International Journal of Accounting* (University of Illinois, Urbana) and also printed in the September 1979 *A.F.A. Newsletter*. We are citing the accounting differences as it reflects the educational and training challenges we are facing in this region.

> *Historical Ties.* ASEAN countries were formally under foreign rule, Thailand being a notable exception. As a result, accounting practices in these countries have been significantly influenced by those of the respective "mother countries." Accounting practices in the Philippines are largely patterned after those generally accepted in the United States. Accounting standards in Malaysia and Singapore reflect the British influence, while Indonesian accounting practices largely mirror the influence of the Dutch. Foreign-based multinational companies (mostly American) are also a growing feature of the ASEAN scene. The reporting practices of these companies add yet another dimension to accounting norms in Southeast Asia. Finally,

accounting education systems in ASEAN have also been influenced by historical ties. This factor will, no doubt, continue to perpetuate differences in accounting practices in the region.

Government Laws and Regulations. Existing laws and regulations of ASEAN governments also impact the development of financial reporting standards. National legislation affects the types of accounting records to be maintained, the form and content of financial statements to be filed, reporting periods to be observed, and the manner of recognizing revenue and expense for tax purposes. Tax laws in certain ASEAN countries, for example, do not permit deductions for depreciation on buildings. Consequently, depreciation of buildings for financial reporting purposes is likewise uncommon in these countries, a practice that may be difficult to change.

Environmental Differences. Differences in environmental circumstances also promise to complicate ASEAN harmonization efforts. Thus, public ownership of corporate securities in a country like the Philippines suggests financial reporting and disclosure principles different from those applicable to predominantly family-owned corporate interests as in Thailand. Similarly, agrarian economies such as Indonesia and Thailand may require accounting systems that differ from those utilized by an economy based largely on trade and financial institutions, such as Singapore.

Choi (1979) further examines the differences in accounting and financial reporting differences among the respective countries and enumerates a series of elements:

Disclosure Legislation. Malaysia, Singapore, the Philippines, and Thailand possess national regulations requiring the publication of annual financial statements by groups or individual companies. While this is not the case for Indonesia, companies listing their shares on the Indonesian stock exchange are required to do so. In both Indonesia and the Philippines, this publishing obligation relates to reports of individual companies only. Consolidated statements are not required. The publication of annual financial statements of the parent company as well as consolidated financial statements of domestic companies are required in Malaysia; whereas, in Thailand only annual financial statements on the parent company must be disclosed. Singapore stands alone in mandating the publication of parent company as well as consolidated financial statements of the worldwide group. This no doubt is due to Singapore's role as leading financial center in the Pacific.

Financial Statement Principles. Uniform principles underlying the publication of financial statements is present in four of the five ASEAN member countries. Thailand, being the exception, follows generally recognized non-codified principles, i.e., certain accounting concepts are considered so fundamental to the reporting process that they are considered mandatory by the profession even in the absence of statutory or professional pronouncements.

Professional Involvement in Standard Setting. Professional accounting associations play an active role in the development of accounting principles in all ASEAN countries. However, decision-making authority with respect to the promulgation of accounting standards is not enjoyed by the Thai accounting profession to the same extent as the professions in the other four countries. The profession in all five countries are reportedly exerting efforts to harmonize local accounting principles on an international basis with Thailand implicitly adopting principles prescribed by the International Accounting Standards Committee (IASC).

Application of Accounting Principles and Practices. Contrasting the application of specific principles and practices in a five-nation setting is a major undertaking. Therefore, the principles/practices chosen for analysis are highly selective. It should also be noted that the data analyzed represent the responses of national accounting organizations surveyed in each of the respective ASEAN countries. These responses reflect the attitudes and views of these organizations and simply provide a general overview of what is and what is not applicable from country to country.

Consider, first, the area of consolidation principles. In Malaysia, the Philippines (for companies wishing to consolidate), and Singapore, ownership of more than 50 percent of the equity capital of an investee company is a condition for preparing consolidated financial statements. This criterion is employed by only a handful of companies in Indonesia and Thailand where consolidated statements are not mandated. Consolidation is also required in Malaysia and Singapore when an investor has effective control of an investee even though ownership is less than 50 percent. Investment in unconsolidated subsidiaries is carried on an equity basis by a majority of companies in Malaysia with about half the companies in Singapore also adopting this practice. The other 50 percent of Singapore companies carry these investments at cost with separate disclosure of the parent company's equity in related net assets. Companies in Indonesia and the Philippines also subscribe to this practice.

In accounting for enterprise assets, inventories are carried exclusively at cost in Indonesia and Malaysia while the lower of cost or market rule is generally accepted in the other three ASEAN countries. Indonesia stands alone in valuing long-term receivables at their discounted present values and recognizing imputed interest income thereon. Unlike Malaysia and Singapore, fixed asset depreciation methods for financial reporting purposes in Indonesia, the Philippines, and Thailand conform strictly to the requirements of tax law. Moreover, companies in the Philippines and Thailand do not customarily consider estimated salvage value in calculating periodic depreciation charges.

Interestingly, accounting responses to inflation are not entirely new to ASEAN as revaluation of fixed assets in excess of original cost is permitted in Malaysia, Singapore, and the Philippines. For example, special Bulletin No. 2.71, issued in November 1971 by the Philippine Institute of CPAs, recommends that companies revalue their assets using appraisal values whenever price levels, as measured by a consumer price index, increase by at least 25 percent since the last revaluation. In cases where assets have been revalued, all three countries require that the basis of revaluation be disclosed and an owner's equity account credited for the amount of the write-up. Malaysia and Singapore require that depreciation expense for financial reporting purposes be based on the revalued amounts. Although the Philippine Institute also encourages such treatment, few companies follow this prescription as depreciation on revalued assets is not yet recognized by the Philippine tax authorities.

With regard to liabilities, discounts on bonds payable is usually amortized over the term of the outstanding obligation in the Philippines, Singapore, and Thailand, whereas it is written off in its entirety in the year in which it occurs in Malaysia. Long-term lease payments are recorded as periodic rental charges in the Philippines and Singapore whereas they are capitalized in Indonesia, Malaysia, and Thailand when the substance of the lease arrangement transfers the usual risks and rewards of ownership from the lessor to the lessee. While deferred tax accounting is generally accepted in Malaysia and Singapore, this is not the case in the Philippines and Thailand. In Indonesia, tax referrals (owing to timing differences) are generally disclosed in footnotes to the financial statements.

Accounting for owner's equity in ASEAN also offers some interesting contrasts. The use of owner's equity reserves to transfer income between reporting periods is actually required in Indonesia and Malaysia. Revaluation reserves created following the write-up of fixed assets, mentioned earlier, are not only available for stock dividends in both Malaysia and Singapore but also for cash dividends in Malaysia.

Turning now to items of income, whereas sales and cost of goods sold are generally disclosed in four of the five ASEAN countries, one is hard pressed to find such disclosures in the income statements of Singapore companies. And, while earnings per share figures are disclosed in Malaysia, the Philippines, and Thailand, only a minority of companies do so in Indonesia and Singapore.

Owing to the fact that most countries in ASEAN are still in the early stages of their industrial development, foreign direct investment activities by ASEAN companies are not extensive. This, no doubt, accounts for the accounting emphasis on foreign currency transactions as opposed to the translation of foreign currency financial statements. In this regard, translation losses arising on foreign currency liabilities incurred in relation to the import of inventories are capitalized as part of their cost if the corresponding items are unsold when the translation loss occurs. This "single transaction" perspective is followed in Indonesia, Malaysia, and the Philippines. Similarly, the cost of fixed assets is also increased by any translation loss arising on foreign currency debt incurred for the purchase of the asset, subject to a realization test. About one-half of the companies in Thailand also subscribe to this treatment. Translation gains and losses on all other unsettled transactions are generally taken to income in the period in which they take place.

161

Malaysia is reportedly the only exception here.

As a final contrast, consider the funds statement. A statement of changes in financial position is included in the general purpose financial statements in only three out of the five ASEAN countries—Indonesia, Malaysia, and the Philippines. In the former two countries, attention is directed primarily at changes in cash or its equivalent. The Philippine Institute of CPAs, in contrast, adopts a broader view and recommends that companies disclose all important aspects of its financing and investing activities regardless of whether cash or other elements of working capital are directly affected.

As for the relationship between AFA and the IASC and CAPA, Choi continues:

AFA and IASC. While the prospects for ASEAN accounting cooperation and harmony seem bright indeed, one may rightfully question the appropriateness of this endeavor in light of IASC efforts to establish and secure the adoption of more global accounting norms. Specifically, will AFA's regional efforts prove to be redundant or perhaps even work at cross purposes with those of the IASC? Probably not. Accounting must respond to the changing needs of a society (or societies) and conform to the social, economic, and legal-political mores of its environment. If we accept the proposition that accounting will differ geographically and justifiably so. In a similar vein, accounting standards issued by the IASC may not always apply to the ASEAN context. Gerhardt Mueller has observed that international standards, as they are slowly emerging through the efforts of the International Accounting Standards Committee (IASC) and the influence of capital markets as well as other international financial institutions and organizations, are really directed at the large multinational enterprises rather than at the local small-to medium-size closely held companies. As an example, the IASC now encourages consolidation of the accounts of subsidiaries owned or controlled by a parent company. This practice makes good sense for companies whose shares are widely held. This condition, however, is not the general case in ASEAN. Similarly, IASC's 20 percent ownership test as a condition for use of the equity method of accounting for non-consolidated subsidiaries makes little sense in ASEAN countries where the stock of related companies are often owned by a few families.

AFA's efforts, therefore, will no doubt prove to be complementary to those of the IASC rather than competitive. An important function of AFA will be to buffer individual ASEAN countries against the wholesale adoption of international accounting pronouncements that may not be suitable to local circumstances. More importantly, active participation in the work of the IASC and constructive reaction to proposed IASC dicta would enable AFA to sensitize the committee to the views and concerns of the less industrialized world.

AFA and CAPA. What then are the implications of AFA for other international accounting organizations in the Pacific such as the Confederation of Asian and Pacific Accountants (CAPA)? While one can only speculate in this regard, an examination of CAPA's country membership provides some possible clues. At the present time, CAPA's membership consists of 28 professional accounting organizations from 21 countries in Asia and the Pacific. The sheer size of such an organization probably does little to facilitate a spirit of togetherness and congeniality among representatives of each of the member organizations. Coordinating the professional affairs of such a regional venture, furthermore, would seem ominous if not a "mission impossible." National membership in CAPA also runs the gamut from highly industrialized countries such as the United States and Japan to developing economies such as India and Sri Lanka. In an organization of such size and contrasts, there is the omnipresent danger of some members being "lost in the shuffle." Under such conditions, progress in achieving regional cooperation and a coordinated regional accounting profession would be slow. When viewed in this context, AFA constitutes a natural evolution or "partitioning" of a regional confederation that is perhaps too large and varied in its makeup to be fully responsive to the needs of all of its national contingents.

With a new regional organization of their own, will the ASEAN countries now withdraw from CAPA? One would hope not as the increasing interdependence of nations through trade and expanded investment flows together with the pervasive influence of multinational enterprises will heighten rather than lessen the need for regional cooperation in the Pacific. Accordingly, dual membership in both AFA and CAPA would seem both necessary and desirable. Should the ASEAN five withdraw from CAPA and pursue an independent mode of operation, the International Federation of Accountants, whose objective, among others, is to encourage and promote the development of regional organizations, will have a very significant role to play in coordinating the activities of these two Pacific Basin accounting federations.

Choi concludes:

The ASEAN Federation of Accountants (AFA) promises to be a constructive force in the international accounting standards movement. As a regional accounting organization, formally recognized by each of the ASEAN governments, AFA will play a leadership role in the quest for harmonized accounting and reporting standards in Southeast Asia. While AFA will undoubtedly benefit from the experiences of the industrialized countries in the promulgation of accounting standards, it will also serve as a vehicle for tailoring international standards to the ASEAN framework. Coordination of harmonization efforts in ASEAN and active participation in the formulation of international accounting standards will enable AFA to help buffer the mammoth IASC influence on its member countries. In so doing, AFA will foster a greater sense of confidence within ASEAN and a sense of not being dominated by what is often perceived as an extension of the former "mother countries." If nothing else, AFA should produce higher visibility and social and professional status for independent accountants in Asia. In all of these areas, let us wish them well.

Extensive efforts are now also underway to coordinate accounting education and training, and a separate ASEAN university (e.g., School of Accountancy) will be operating in Indonesia in the next couple of years. Furthermore, various professional development programs and literature have been developed. The *AFA Newsletter*, issued quarterly, is abound with new activities taking place in the ASEAN region.

In our opinion, the AFA, only a few years in existence, has made considerable headway. We are very encouraged by this development, and it proves that regionalization of accounting is feasible as long as: the economic and social needs are there; the region is manageable; and the will is there to pursue regionalization actively. The efforts taking place in ASEAN may need close scrutiny by other sub-regions from a practice, training and development point of view.

ASEAN also should develop accounting standards that have an ASEAN identity to enhance the understandability, meaningfulness and comparability of the financial measurements and reports. Greater emphasis needs to be given towards incorporating macro accounting for economic analysis and policy. Research should focus on adaptation of micro accounting techniques to macro economic analysis. These are to reflect the economic substance of flows and stocks.

The ASEAN School or Institute of Accountancy, as a regional training and development institution, could well serve the objectives we have previously enumerated in regard to regional training centers (see Chapter VIII). The function of such an institute, to enhance formal and continuing education and research, would be highly significant to gradually integrate better accounting at the private and public sector levels.

In regard to this vital area of accounting education, the AFA Committee on Accounting Education has prepared a report (1978) of which certain excerpts are quoted:

> All ASEAN countries require well qualified accountants in both the public and private sectors. Each country has determined the stringency of its required qualifications for accountants based on a cost-benefit assessment peculiar to their individual environments.
>
> At present, to be qualified as a certified public accountant, candidates are required to obtain a formal education ranging from three to five years and a period of work experience with or without a professional examination.

The AFA report's prime objective is to recommend a minimum common body of knowledge required for the preparation of public accountants. It is not intended to interfere with the existing traditional educational system of the various countries, which the AFA committee clearly intended to avoid. The recommendations reflected in the report comprise three parts:

(1) the formal education necessary to provide for the common body of knowledge in accounting,
(2) the qualifying experience, and
(3) the CPA examination.

To be successful in his professional career the prospective certified public accountant should acquire:

(1) A comprehension of the total system of financial information flow and its relations to other systems in generating, analyzing and communicating data useful to management, the public, or governmental agencies.

(2) Habits of analytical thought which permit identification, accumulation, and interpretation of information required for decision making and control in both the private and public sectors.

(3) An ability to present financial information in conformity with generally accepted accounting principles.

(4) Proficiency to audit in accordance with generally accepted auditing standards both for a critical evaluation of the system used in developing the financial data and for fair presentation of the information in financial statements.

In view of the recommendations it is believed that, to be most effective, the education required should be broadly conceived and should provide for a variety alternative of accounting careers and to develop those qualities that will enable accountants to achieve success in their professional careers. Moreover, standards should be established as to the level of quality in various aspects of accounting educational programs that would give the graduate a capacity for growth and development within the accounting profession.

The accounting curriculum must be specifically relevant and responsive to the needs of the profession. Education for professional accountants is composed of three parts, namely, general education, general business and accounting discipline.

The broad general education in humanities and sciences, including a knowledge and understanding of topics relevant to accounting, should provide the students with a disciplined foundation for the successful study and practice of accounting. The foundation is intended to provide:

(1) The capability to continue to learn, develop and grow and the foundation on which to build.

(2) An understanding of the content and process of scientific thought and systematic approach to problem solving.

(3) Facility in the use of mathematics and statistics to measure and express economic events in quantitative terms.

(4) An ability to communicate effectively orally and in writing.

(5) An appreciation of the institutions and forces of the behavioral decision process, legal, economic and political considerations that influence and interface with accountancy.

Supplementing and building upon the knowledge gained in the general education courses, the general business courses provide an understanding of the major functions of business society and the discipline of accounting and an understanding of some of the social forces which influence business and extend the student's understanding of some of the topics having business application.

The number of courses devoted to this part are:

Course	Semester Hours
Economic Analysis (advanced micro-macro economic theory including the monetary system)	6
Marketing	3
Finance	3-6
Production or Operational Systems	3
Business Law	3-6
Organization (the working, group and individual behavior)	6
Quantitative Applications in Business (optimization models, statistics, sampling, Markov chains, statistical decision theory queing, PERT, simulation)	9
Accounting (financial, managerial)	6
Written Communication	3
Business Policy	0-3
Total	42-51

The accounting portion of the total curriculum should cover concepts and skills required in several areas of accounting, including financial, managerial and governmental accounting, auditing, tax advising, management advisory services, data processing, and systems analysis. The overall objective is to provide an understanding of the function of accounting, the underlying body of concepts that comprises accounting theory, and their application to accounting business problems and situations.

The advanced professional program should also cover the impact of regulatory agencies and professional bodies on current and emerging accounting issues.

The committee recommends a range of 30-45 semester hours of accounting study beyond the two introductory accounting courses as follows:

Accounting Course	Semester Hours
Financial Accounting Measurement Problems, Financial Reporting: Theory and Problems, Contemporary Financial Accounting Issues	12-12
Cost Determination, Cost Analysis and Control, Cost-Based Decision Making	3-6
Tax Theory, Computation and Problems	3-6
Audit Theory, Standards and Problems including Ethics and Responsibilities	3-6
Electronic Data Processing	3-6
Accounting electives	6-9
Total	30-45

The suggested program would of course permit only limited specialization within the four-year program (minimum number of 111 credits) and the five-year program (minimum number of 135 credits); additional study would be required to achieve substantial specialization with the case and/or problem method of instruction to be intensively used.

The professional preparations that now exist within the five ASEAN countries vary rather widely, ranging from the three-year to five-year university level of accounting education with the following alternatives:

Within the College of Business Administration
(or other equivalent names)

1) The three-year program
   -with qualifying work experience
   -with and with no CPA examination
2) The four-year program
   -with and with no qualifying work experience
   -with only one-subject examination (in auditing practices) and the full-fledged CPA examination
3) The five-year program
   -with qualifying work experience
   -with no CPA examination

To the administration of the professional program through the College of Business Administration (or other equivalent names) at the undergraduate level it can be added to the program in a separate school of accountancy (usually a five-year program).

The present general acceptance of the MBA type of educational program in business does have some implications for accounting as well as other business disciplines. The focus centers on the existence of the two contrasting avenues of study of the business disciplines—one at the undergraduate level and the other at the graduate level.

The committee believes that the undergraduate accounting education will continue, for many years to come, to be an important avenue of education for professional accounting, although the MBA type of graduate program will expand in absolute and relative measures. It is reasonable to believe that the MBA-type program will prove itself to be the most effective way of professional preparation and will eventually become more attractive to the prospective CPAs. With regard to the administration of the program, the committee is not prepared to recommend any model program of study.

The CPA certificate is evidence of basic competence of professional quality in the discipline of accounting. This minimum level of competence is demonstrated by acquiring the common body of knowledge (by passing a college accounting program) and by passing the CPA examination. The committee recommends that the CPA examination comprises five sections of six papers as follows:

Section	Number of Papers	Hours of Examination
1) Accounting Practice: Part 1	1	4
Accounting Practice: Part 2	1	4
2) Accounting Theory	1	3
3) Auditing	1	3
4) Taxation	1	3
5) Business Law	1	3

Due to the socioeconomic environment and total educational system of the member countries being widely different, the committee was not prepared to recommend change that would substantially affect the now existing traditional system. Thus, in one respect it makes specific recommendations, while in the other, it only brings to notice of the member some observations. The committee's report can be summarized thus:

(1) The role of the professional accountants in society is expanding, making necessary a need for more rigorous education for the common body of knowledge required for all professional accountants.

(2) The body of knowledge necessary for entrance into the profession will and should be required as part of the college education.

(3) The committee has no definite recommendation on the duration of the college professional accounting program, instead it recommends the structure of the accounting programs in terms of work (semester hours).

(4) The structure of the professional accounting program consists of 39 semester hours of work of general education courses as specified, in addition to other general education courses as required by the college and university; 42 to 51 semester hours of work of general business courses, and 30 to 45 semester hours of work of accounting courses. In all, a minimum total of 111 to 135 semester credit hours as specified plus other general education courses would make up for the full four- or five-year programs respectively.

(5) Qualifying experience seems to be regarded as part of the college accounting education in some member countries; the effectiveness of the value of the practical experience should be thoroughly reviewed.

(6) Changes always take place in business and the accounting profession. Educational programs must be flexible and adaptive and this is best achieved by entrusting their specific content to the college and university. However, the committee believes that the scope, purpose and general concern of the formal education for professional accounting are proper concern of the professional body.

(7) The CPA examination is considered to be of great value, and the real test for the mastery of the body of knowledge. The examination papers should cover the main areas of accounting discipline, namely, Accounting Practice and Theory, Auditing, Taxation, and Business Law. Candidates should be allowed to take such examination as close to their graduate dates as possible.

(8) The committee has no recommendation on the administration of the accounting program. However, it regards the setup of a separate school of accountancy as the least appropriate. While the undergraduate accounting program will remain the main source of supply of the professional accountants, the MBA-type program is becoming the most effective means for professional preparation.

The committee expressed that accounting education is on the threshold of change and the high quality of the professional accountants is clear and evident. A review of forces for change suggests that the education of the professional accountants of the future will require, in some member countries, a tremendous effort. The change would undoubtedly be affected by the college and university educational philosophy and the country's total educational system. In view of these forces, colleges ought to carefully review their present curriculum and long-range goals.

The AFA Committee on Education has furthermore been asked to look into the following matters, which items we feel are to be investigated for any type of regional accounting educational-professional education:

(1) That an inventory be undertaken of each country's accounting capabilities to identify the respective needs for accounting professionals.

(2) That accounting education be studied both as regards pre-qualifying and post-qualifying requirements in the light of AFA's objectives; and accounting and auditing standards.

(3) That work experience be made compulsory before a certificate to practice accountancy is issued since formal education is not sufficient preparation in the actual practice of a CPA.

(4) That post-qualifying education be made on a purely voluntary basis considering that CPAs are responsible professionals, and considering further that this is the concern of the professional organization.

(5) That faculty exchanges and establishment of professorial chairs be promoted and their funding studied.

(6) That appropriate awards be given to ASEAN authors of accounting texts and training materials which meet ASEAN conditions, develop ASEAN awareness, and promote ASEAN spirit.

(8) That a junior AFA or an ASEAN Federation of Accounting Students organization be organized in each member country.

Continuing education, in our opinion, also is part of the educational process; it needs to promote post-qualifying education and training. As for research in the ASEAN area, this is to focus on:

(1) Standardization and harmonization of accounting practices.

(2) Improvement in the standard of disclosure in financial reporting.

(3) Search for suitable alternatives to the historical cost basis.

4. Conclusion

The efforts that have taken place in the Asian and Pacific regions are extremely encouraging. We have found here a great trend towards regional self determination in accounting, whereby it became practical to establish sub-regions of greater commonality (ASEAN-AFA). This was a logical and pragmatic approach, as the whole CAPA region itself was too wide-ranging economically, geographically and from a development point of view.

As the AFA will be growing in stature over the years, we equally expect that other accounting regionalization efforts will take place, for example, in the Indian subcontinent and Japan-Korea-China. This also should be encouraged by CAPA, while CAPA itself should remain the proper vehicle in which these countries and sub-regions have their "clearinghouse" activities, and other developmental aspects, pursued. Such regionalization, in our opinion, makes much greater sense than so-called internationalization.

As for the educational-training-research aspects, the great diversity encountered within the region and sub-regions poses a great challenge to educational establishments. Not only have these institutions to serve expanded domestic training needs but also take into account regional aspects. Therefore, we believe it is essential that in the sub-regions accounting training centers are set up to upgrade, update and develop accounting instructors. Furthermore, such centers are to concern themselves with exploring regional accounting harmonization, text materials, exchange of lecturers, course developments and other clearinghouse matters.

There is a need for an ASEAN institute—or school—of accounting education. Such a school of accounting could be a training and examining body; it could also look after continuing education. It could initiate research of an academic and practical nature for the region, e.g., inventory of needs, accounting plans, and the development of standards.

It also should develop literature for the area, i.e., textbooks and case studies.

The lessons of CAPA-AFA, in our opinion, are also to be of benefit for Africa and Latin America; gradually (hopefully), further knowledge gained there may also return to the Asia-Pacific areas.

CHAPTER XVII

ACCOUNTING EDUCATION IN THE DEVELOPING ISLAND NATIONS OF THE SOUTH PACIFIC

by

Roger Juchau*

1. Introduction

In the island economies of the South Pacific, accounting has a crucial role in enabling these economies to look at their attainments critically, as well as determining pathways for more efficient and effective organization, both in the public and private sectors. The pressures for critical assessment and efficient organization are strong. With growing populations in a limited resource and development context, where the goals of economic and social progress are pursued, there has long been a realization that a greater emphasis has to be placed on effective utilization of resources and their equitable allocation. There is for many of the economies little prospect for large secondary basic industry, so that resource utilization must focus on the primary-tertiary dimensions of development with fishing, light secondary industry, minerals and tourism emerging strongly as income supplements to rural production. The brief of accounting thus issues from this setting. Public and private organizations require a financial information base that enables them to assess the effectiveness of past and present resource utilization, as well as controlling and planning future dispositions of resources in some production or service generating activity. In the island economies reviewed here, the level and amount of accounting services to provide such work tends to be inadequate. And for accounting education and training, a sizeable brief exists to increase and upgrade accounting manpower at all levels.

2. Background and General Economic Profile

The islands considered here are located in the Southwest Pacific Ocean and are distributed from the equator to the Tropic of Capricorn. Table 1 shows the islands referred to in this chapter as well as their populations. The islands are inhabited by three major ethnic groupings, Micronesian, Melanesian and Polynesian (distribution shown in Table 1) and have, in addition, residents and citizens of European, Chinese and Indian origins. All non-indigenous groups make a crucial contribution to the commercial life in the islands and naturally perform many accounting services.

*Professor Juchau is Head of the Division of Finance and Information Systems, School of Business at Nepean College of Advanced Education, Kingswood, Australia.

TABLE 1

Population (1977) and Dominant Ethnic Groupings

		(000)
Fiji*	(Melanesian)	600
Kiribati	(Micronesian)	56
New Hebrides	(Melanesian)	100
Papua New Guinea	(Melanesian)	2,910
Solomon Islands	(Melanesian)	210
Tonga	(Polynesian)	90
Western Samoa	(Polynesian)	150

*More than half the population is now of Indian origin.

Sources: 1) The Courier, No. 58, Nov. 1979, pp. 51-53.
2) Pacific Islands Year Book, 13th Edition, 1979.

The economies of the islands listed are partly characterized by subsistence production which meets many personal consumption requirements. The cash economy has traditionally related to international trade. Most capital goods are imported and the growth of urban populations has meant that there is a rapidly growing demand for imported consumer goods. The import bill is mostly met through the sale of agricultural and mineral produce overseas and is being increasingly supplemented by the earnings from tourism. Frequent deficits on current account are largely offset by remittances from islanders residing abroad and by foreign capital, either in the form of private or aid investment. For all islands, trade depends on a limited range of goods and services and is vulnerable to world market conditions. This is accentuated by the fact that the market areas for the supply and sale of products are also limited in number.

Table 2 gives a view of the wealth of each island economy and the major export items.

TABLE 2

Island Wealth and Export

Islands	Year	G.N.P. Per Capita ($U.S.)	G.N.P.	Major Export Items
Fiji	1977	720	1220	Sugar, Fish, Gold, Tourism, Copra
Kiribati	1977	39.4	649	Phosphate, Copra
New Hebrides		N.A.	N.A.	Copra, Fish, Manganese, Meat
Papua New Guinea	1977	1410	480	Copper, Copra, Coffee, Cocoa
Solomon Islands	1977	53	260	Copra, Timber, Fish
Tonga	1976	30	330	Copra, Tropical Fruits
Western Samoa	1977	50	320	Copra, Cocoa, Bananas

Information Source: The Courier, No. 58, Nov. 1979, pp. 51-53.

Fiji and P.N.G. are the strongest economies and naturally are focal points for regional ventures (e.g., airlines, shipping, higher education) and for the development of manufacturing and processing industries. In the islands the larger scale agricultural projects (fisheries, timber, sugar, beef, copra) together with the mining and tourist ventures require the services of skilled manpower, including accountants. Growth in all islands tends to be tentative rather than aggressive. Incentives for foreign investment notwithstanding, there is a constant fear throughout the islands that the real "takeoff" is yet to eventuate. Some people wish to deny growth but an urbanizing and growing non-subsistent population cannot accept such a view.

Whatever the outcome of future investment plans, there is a clear pursuit in all islands of economic and social progress, which means resources must be effectively used and equitably deployed. There is for most of the islands little hope for large manufacturing industry, and future development plans focus on minerals, tourism and new agricultural schemes; effective development in these areas will require well managed enterprises with sound accounting services and backup. There is little leeway in these limited economies for inefficient enterprises, haphazard management and poor planning. Any one failure of a major enterprise in any one island nation could seriously impede the progress and prospect of its people. In this context the role of accounting is quite critical.

3. Specific Accounting Contexts

3.1 Fiji

Fiji is an island group lying latitude 20 degrees south in the South Pacific Ocean. The principal island is Viti Levu where the most populous towns are centered. Suva is the principal center (major port) on the eastern side, and Nadi (international airport) and Lautoka (port) on the western side constitute other major centers. External trade earnings flow from the sugar, tourist, copra and gold mining industries and great hopes are placed on the further growth of earnings from minerals, timber and tourism. The dependence on secondary products from overseas places a substantial burden on foreign exchange earnings, and efforts are continually being made to expand local secondary industry both to reduce the volume of imports and to provide a further source of foreign exchange through exports to neighbouring island communities. By island standards, Suva provides a well-developed commercial infrastructure and all city oriented services are available. Foreign investment is encouraged and subsidies and allowances are provided to attract new industry. Pressure on urban employment remains high, and the rural-urban drift coupled with a large number of school leavers (10,000 per annum) is aggravating the unemployment scene.

The thrust of private and public investment has meant that business and government operations have continued to grow, placing a severe demand on specialist and skilled manpower among which accountants are included. In all sectors the lack of trained accountants at both the sub- and full-professional levels is apparent, and some serious problems have emerged. Accounting services are undermanned and often accounting work lacks sound preparation and analysis.

173

Accountants are paid premium salaries and the scarcity of local accountants has meant that expatriates are brought in to bolster a local and largely unqualified work force. Government has felt this problem as well, and the Public Accounts Committee has expressed grave concern over the shortage of qualified accountants in government and has pointed to the possible dangers of a poor and ineffective accounting service. Most qualified personnel work in the private and quasi-government sectors.

To meet the shortages of sub-professional accountants the Derrick Technical Institute runs a Diploma course in Accounting. Some undergraduate or chartered training[1] in accounting takes place in Australia and New Zealand, yielding no more than or or two qualified accountants a year to Fiji. It is envisaged, however, that the full degree programme in accounting at the University of the South Pacific will rapidly raise the number of fully qualified accountants (see education section).

The concern for the development of accounting training and accounting practice in Fiji is reflected in the fact that the Fiji Institute of Accountants is currently supporting existing and proposed programmes to train and develop unqualified and qualified accounting personnel. The age-old problems of time, resources and opportunity restrict development in this area. Some overseas funds and resources have been made available and both the institute and university are now in a position to provide more resources for training and professional development. Close contact with neighbouring professional bodies in New Zealand and Australia will afford greater opportunity for professional exchange of ideas. But all these problems are seen in terms of the major one, to increase the supply of accountants at both levels. Reliance on expatriates will continue. The limiting factors of few suitable school-leavers and inadequate tertiary resources in education will continue to be present and must affect the level and pace of localization.

Fiji, although one of the wealthiest of the island communities under review here, has yet to experience fully the benefits of having an adequate number of trained accounting personnel to service ips accounting needs. Current professional and educational developments will provide the necessary scope and stimulus to shift training along at a greater pace. Fiji must take the lead in the South Pacific in furthering accounting development. The English speaking peoples of Southern Micronesia, Polynesia and Melanesia have a right to expect that the larger islands of Fiji and New Guinea will play a growing and significant role in expanding the level of technical expertise in accounting. They provide more suitable and appropriate venues for study by enabling island value systems to be accommodated and preventing cultural disaffection which so often arises where students venture to study abroad.

3.2 Papua New Guinea

Papua New Guinea (P.N.G.) is one of the largest countries in the South Pacific (land area 465,000 square kilometres) and comprises the eastern half of the

---

[1]The labels "Chartered" or "Graduate" are simply representative descriptions of fully qualified professional accountants; other qualifications, e.g., A.A.S.A., C.P.A., would be included here.

island of New Guinea (the western half being Irian Jaya) and various islands to the north and the east. Urban population represents 16 percent of the total population. Centered principally in the towns of Port Moresby (capital), Lae, Wewak, Rabaul and Madang, urban population is expected to double within the next decade. Communications raise many difficulties. There are about 1,000 different languages and whilst English is the official language, the language understood by the majority of the nationals is the so-called Pidgin English. Overland communication is poorly developed. The difficult topography has meant that air and ship are the main facilitators of trade and commerce.

P.N.G. is largely an agricultural nation. The monetary sector has rapidly expanded but as yet has not replaced subsistence agriculture as the principal economic activity for the large majority of Papua New Guineans. The money economy, traditionally dependent on export of primary products, has diversified rapidly within the last decade. Sectors which have developed include mining, fisheries, forest products and manufacturing. Agricultural products (coconut products, cocoa, coffee) and copper constitute the major source of export earnings to which Japan has become the largest contributor. Richly endowed with natural resources, the country is fast becoming a highly attractive location for foreign investment.

An active private, corporate and business sector has emerged in P.N.G. and is sustained by more than 30,000 expatriates and their families (total work force 1.25 million). High level accounting work is largely in the hands of expatriates and critical audit, systems, and regulatory work is handled by expatriate personnel. There is a pronounced shortage of fully qualified accounting personnel and despite free tertiary education only a small number of accounting graduates (see education section) have emerged to ameliorate the situation. Larger enterprises continue to recruit accounting personnel from Australia and New Zealand.

Many large enterprises and accounting firms operating in New Guinea see two major problems affecting future accounting services. One is the flow from national high schools of suitable candidates for entry into the profession and university courses. The quality of candidates is generally of not a high standard and tends to affect adversely the level of performance in work and study. Allied to this problem is the fact that registrations in primary and secondary schools are not growing in pace with the population. The shortage of candidates for professional training is likely to be exacerbated in the future. The second problem relates to the standard expected from students who complete tertiary education (degree level) in accounting. There is a view among certain sections of academia that the standard should be pitched to local conditions and not relate to some Western/international standard. Such view, if fully reflected in programme standards, is seen by the business sector as a serious threat to the standard and proficiency of accounting work. A general consensus in this sector is that P.N.G. is part of the international business community and growing investment from Asia and Western economies requires a standard of accounting and accountants commensurate with the conditions and demands of advanced and international commercial relations.

The particular accounting contexts and their associated problems for both Fiji and P.N.G. have been explored by this author through a survey of accounting practice problems (1977, respondents: accountants working in Fiji and P.N.G.). The survey revealed that from the perspective of working accountants, there was large agreement between the islands on the importance of various accounting practice problems. The problems and agreement levels are indicated in Table 3.

TABLE 3

Evaluation of Importance of Eleven Accounting Practice Problems

Fiji and Papua New Guinea

Problems	Agreement on Importance of Problems	
	Fiji	Papua New Guinea
Shortage of qualified accountants in all operational areas of accounting	Extreme	Extreme
Accounting profession and its members have low status amongst the profession	Low	Low
Inadequate legislative support for accounting and auditing standards	Moderate	Moderate
Accounting information for operational decisions is often unobtainable, untimely, and/or incomplete	Extreme	Extreme
Inadequate financial reporting and auditing standards	Extreme	Moderate
Accountants' role primarily devoted to assisting enterprises evade tax and manipulate financial results	Moderate	Moderate
National accounting profession has limited impact on professional activity	Moderate	Moderate
Accounting practice tends to be geared towards bookkeeping routines and pays little attention to systems and control accounting	Moderate	Moderate
Lack of adequate accounting in government and government agencies	Extreme	Extreme
Application of Western techniques and concepts that are unsuited to local conditions	Low	Low
Conflict between international and local accounting firms	Low	Not Important

3.3 Tonga

Accounting activity in Tonga is concentrated in government and quasi-government operations. The private sector offers, at the present time, limited employment for accountants at both the professional and sub-professional level. Most financial operations are centered in Nuku'alofa, the capital, which is the seat of government and the only significant commercial center. Most trade is carried out in Nuku'alofa and is based on primary and tertiary activity. Copra and tropical fruits sustain the primary sector, whilst wholesaling/retailing and tourism dominate the tertiary sector. Funds flowing in from Tongans abroad and from mission station headquarters add a substantial amount to foreign exchange earnings.

For accounting practice there would seem to be little room for expansion and much development of the financial sector will depend on the flow-in benefits of the jet capacity airport and the furthering of hotel investment to tap an increasing tourist market. But whatever perspective is taken of private and public investment it would be safe to assert that a relatively static condition is an appropriate description of the present Tongan economy. Investment levels do not indicate any future dynamism in financial undertakings. Population growth is also a containing force and threatens an already meagre per capita income.

A limited scale of operations in accounting thus prevails. At the present time there are a few active qualified accountants and a scattering of people who have part qualifications from New Zealand university and professional courses. Although the number and shortage of accounting personnel are both small, they do not convey the true significance of the great lack of accounting expertise in crucial positions. Strategically placed accountants throughout the government and commercial sectors could do much to raise the level of efficiency and effectiveness of resource utilization and allocation. Tonga can ill afford mismanagement of its financial undertakings, and failure to control and plan in one undertaking can have dire consequences for the economy as a whole.

Certainly, there is no lack of concern for getting accounting expertise into key positions. Wherever suitable and willing students emerge, then scholarships can be provided for study abroad. The difficulty is that many employees wishing to undertake accounting training lack formal secondary schooling. The only possible means of promoting accounting knowledge in this context is to give very basic courses in commerce and accounting with the hope that some able students can subsequently be identified for further training abroad.

Outside observers may tend to dismiss a case for finance-accounting expertise in an economy where people are largely self-supporting from their rural endeavours, and whose life-styles blend with the rural economy. Population pressure, growing education levels, and urbanizing of values and tastes quickly scotch any notion of the continuing of the idyllic life in the south seas where all is abundant. Unemployment is an emerging problem and investment is needed to stimulate the labour market. Whatever new investment emerges will need to be administered judiciously and effectively, not only to encourage further investment, but to ensure resources are efficiently employed.

3.4 Solomon Islands

The Solomon Islands form a scattered archipelago stretching over 900 miles on the eastern side of P.N.G. The principal commercial and government center is Honiara, which is situated on the island of Guadalcanal. Honiara, being the major port and administrative center, provides the only location where accounting expertise can be suitably employed. External trade earnings stem from three major commodities, copra, timber and fish, the latter two items assuming greater significance as far as future earnings are concerned. Palm oil, rice and beef are other primary activities that are attracting further local and foreign investment. Most accounting activity is generated from the secondary benefits of public and rural investment. It serves the growing needs of the government and commercial sectors whose growth has been further stimulated by an increasing population and a steady rise in local purchasing power and investment. An optimistic feeling abounds about the growth of investment in all sectors and the possibility of mining and tourism ventures is in part contributing to this growth of optimism.

The prospect and growth of accounting practice seem good, and for the next decade the demand for accounting staff will expand. At the moment there are fewer than 20 qualified accountants in work and there is a considerable shortfall in both sectors of full and sub-professional level accountants. To cope with a growth situation, further accounting expertise is clearly warranted throughout all sectors. There are Solomon Islanders presently undergoing further training and attending courses in accounting and auditing abroad. The University of Technology at Lae in P.N.G. has been the main recipient of accounting students and it is expected that, with an increasing urge for localization, more students will be identified from the ranks of employees and school-leavers to undertake training either in Fiji or P.N.G. However, it is unlikely that the gap will be filled by the turn of this century.

There has long been a view that persons becoming accountants in government service need only assimilate the rules and regulations of government accounting procedures and be familiar with the fund-cash accounting system. This view is not peculiar to the Solomons. Governments in other islands have hitherto taken similar views. However, the demands for economy and greater information for management decisions, require that present accounting systems in government switch to a modified accrual basis accounting and that expenditures be classified functionally rather than simply under object headings. Further, government has to regulate, tax and guide private sector enterprises. For these purposes it is clear that government accountants need to have commercial accounting training in order that government effectively manage and regulate the private sector. In the Solomons, the presence of joint equity undertakings between government and private enterprise clearly adds another reason for government accountants to have commercial professional skills and know-how which would enable them to match the contribution and skills of their private sector counterparts. Joint equity implies joint participation and undertaking. It is thus important that, in the training of their accountants, governments (Solomons and others) do not

continue to follow their previously short-sighted and selfish posture on accounting training.

The Solomons present a typical picture of a rural developing country seeking
routes for growth that are compatible with the rural orientation of its people.
Employment and investment must be expansionary and be accompanied by an
emphasis on localization, together with a regulated and participatory foreign
investment in local undertakings. Accounting expertise must be contributive
and incisive if investment ventures are to be sustained, and for the growth of an
effective government service both at the central and district levels, a wider
perspective of accounting training needs to be adopted. Accelerated training in
accounting must take place if such plans are not to be thwarted.

3.5 New Hebrides

The New Hebrides consists of about 80 islands with the island of Efate being
the main focus of trade and communication. Vila (Efate) is the principal administrative center and has achieved a place on the list of international investment
markets offering tax haven facilities. Naturally, a small but growing commercial infrastructure has arisen and the presence of banks, trust companies,
legal and accounting practices are quite evident. Although the take-off benefits
of a tax haven have yet to fully materialize, there exists considerable scope for an
active and growth-conscious commercial community. Traditional exports of
copra and fish (and short-lived manganese) will no doubt be substantially
boosted by beef and tourism for which export earnings are growing. For accounting activity it is clear that the developing commercial services and government
administration are providing, and will continue to provide, most employment
opportunities. Private investment growth will, apart from private and tourist
industry interests, depend on the marketing skill of tax haven operators.
Accounting service firms' growth will thus depend largely on the promotional
skills and success of these operators.

At present there are few New Hebrideans occupying qualified accounting
posts. Output from high school of suitable recruits for professional training is
small and it is unlikely that this century will see anything like a 100 percent
localization of accounting jobs. As an initiating step some elevation of New
Hebrideans presently employed needs to take place. A concentrated adult education programme of basic accounting and business practices needs to be implemented in order to raise the level of commercial skills and knowledge and to
serve as a basis for identifying suitable students for study abroad. This will be
an arduous and painstaking venture but a start has to be made, and the only
candidates immediately available are mature employees.

A problem common to the New Hebrides and elsewhere in the South Pacific
is the one of localization. Whether newly independent or not, a common and
natural concern of local people is to govern their own destinies, and to occupy
the strategic positions held by expatriates. Now, in one or two cases, expatriate
procrastination and dishonesty have held back justified localization of jobs. However, as a general case, it can be argued that forced and premature localization

can produce disastrous consequences as has been evidenced in Africa and the South Pacific. Accounting positions, as a case in point, cannot be justifiably localized unless local expertise in accounting is available. Instances may arise where expatriate accountants are unfit for positions they hold (in terms of age, competence, motivation, etc.), and of course, pressure to localize is difficult to resist in such circumstances. The presence then of an adequate supply of qualified and technical accountants is one guarantee against wastage, bankruptcy, poor pricing policies, uneconomic production activity and mismanagement both at the local and national levels. And in most islands it is clear that the presence of expatriate expertise in accountng will be necessary right into the next century.

The New Hebrides is critically positioned for rapid growth. Local manpower limitations in accounting pose a significant problem. If private investment expands at the levels envisaged, then expatriate staffing must continue to grow. The road to localization in accounting will need to be very long in the case of the New Hebrides.

4. Accounting Population

The development of accounting practice in the islands has been linked to foreign investment, branch development of major accounting and auditing firms (staffed in the main from New Zealand and Australia), and the colonial administrations of Britain, New Zealand and France. Until the last decade most accounting work was carried out exclusively by expatriate labour and only a small number of local staff were given formal training in accounting. The supply-demand situation[2] for accountants in the islands is set out in Table 4.

TABLE 4

Supply/Demand Accountants
(Based on surveys conducted by the author)

Islands	Year	Demand		Supply	
		Degree (i.e., fully qualified)	Sub-Degree	Degree	Sub-Degree
Fiji	1973	280	550	139	150
Kiribati	1973	10	17	4	6
New Hebrides	1980	30	60	20	30
Solomons	1980	20	150	15	80
Tonga	1973	10	24	5	8
W. Samoa	1980	25	90	12	60

Current indications are that the core supply of fully qualified personnel will continue to depend on expatriate sources, especially from Australia and New Zealand. Their continuance in the islands will be a matter of how issues of local-

[2]Figures for 1980 and for P.N.G. are not all obtainable. Currently over 200 expatriate qualified accountants are employed in P.N.G. Since 1973 the gap in supply would have closed only slightly because of growth in demand, especially in the larger island economies.

ization and the problems of non-indigenous management of local economic entities are handled in the political arena. The issue of localization would seem only capable of a satisfactory resolution when the training of local accountants is firmly established and the flow of these trained personnel can be clearly predicted.

The current demand picture reveals considerable problems for educational and training endeavours in accounting. In the degree category a serious deficit is apparent especially when it is realized that most of the present supply are expatriate. The island governments are naturally concerned with such a deficit and it would appear that this deficit will not be breached in the short term, given the moderate flow of graduates from the universities (see education section) and retirement/emigration factors. The sub-degree category reveals an even more significant deficit, given their vital role of supporting accounting practice throughout the many small enterprises and government agencies in the islands. For this category the training contributions of local institutions of accountants (see next section), and the educational establishments of the islands will be crucial. Further, the generosity and investment in accounting training by local and expatriate enterprises will have an equally important role to play and will need further expansion.

5. Accounting Professional Associations

Traditionally the New Zealand Society of Accountants has been for many islands the prominent professional body in the southwest Pacific. It has offered its annual exams for professional qualifications to islanders who have had the requisite secondary education, and many New Zealand accountants working in the Pacific have kept strong links with their professional body. In recent times, Australia has developed greater interest in the Pacific, where both the Institute of Chartered Accountants and the Society of Accountants have made contributions to professional development courses and lectures. Further, the Confederation of Asian and Pacific Accountants (C.A.P.A.) has admitted island institutes into its ranks and regional assistance for accounting development may be forthcoming when C.A.P.A. organizes itself in this direction.

The development of island professional bodies must necessarily be limited. Still, three bodies have been formed to generate and improve accounting services and standards. In Western Samoa the Western Samoan Society of Accountants has been active for over a decade and at a local level conducts foundation and intermediate accounting courses on a part-time basis. Its most significant role has been the training of accounting personnel to a level suited to a range and scale of enterprise in Western Samoa. As a relatively small organization the Western Samoan body has not the resources to take on the full range of roles normally undertaken by its sister professions in New Zealand and Australia.

The second professional body to emerge has been the Fiji Institute of Accountants (formed June, 1972), which through legislation (February, 1972) has been given wide powers to regulate accounting standards and training in Fiji. The institute, which is coming into its eighth year of operation, currently has over

200 members and has issued standards relating to financial statement presentation and content. It conducts an annual congress and has invited and attracted speakers and participants from New Zealand and Australia.

The institute's standard of admission to full membership equates with Australia and New Zealand and confers charter status. Its accounting standards follow closely Australian and British lines and will continue to do so as the resources of the institute cannot provide for research and development into new standards for Fiji. Business conditions follow Australia and Britain and most standards are easily transferable. The institute has good liaison with Australian and New Zealand bodies whose various services have been willingly offered to Fiji on gratis or heavily discounted terms.

The Fiji Institute is set to play an incisive role. Fiji, being a natural focal point of commerce for the smaller islands, needs to support an effective accounting profession whose standards and members are to provide one of the foundation blocks for continued growth of successful enterprise in Fiji and beyond.

Unlike Fiji, P.N.G. is less advanced along the road of having a vigorous and independent accounting professional body. To promote the interests of the accounting profession, a P.N.G. Association of Accountants has been formed and membership comprises suitably qualified national and expatriate accountants. A more active role is sought for the association, especially in the areas of public relations and lobbying. Legislators and the community need to be apprised of the value of a profession in assisting the development and growth of enterprise and diversified investment.

6. Accounting Education

Accounting education* for islanders has been traditionally sought in New Zealand, Australia and British tertiary institutions or through correspondence courses from these countries.

The difficulties of having islanders studying abroad are considerable. Two warrant mention here. Firstly, many students find it difficult to study and relate to a cosmopolitan and urban setting. Pressures are immense and many islanders find that their limited financial means and their previous social and cultural background place them at some considerable disadvantage. Secondly, many islanders who complete courses become unsettled when they return home. They desire the life of the large cities and as a consequence emigration occurs, depriving the islands of many skilled accounting graduates. To offset the problem of overseas study and to promote accounting education sensitive to local and regional needs, two major accounting degree programmes have been established in universities in Fiji and P.N.G.

Degree-level education is conducted by the University of the South Pacific (Fiji) and the P.N.G. University of Technology. Though relatively recent institutions, they have made a promising start in accounting education and

*Reference in this section relates only to degree-level education. Sub-degree education and bookkeeping training obtains throughout the islands on varying scales. There is not sufficient space in this current brief to deal with all these endeavours.

together they have placed over 200 graduates into the local and regional work force. Like other tertiary institutions in developing countries, they find difficulty in maintaining a full complement of high quality faculty to sustain the growth of accounting education.

Each institution attracts students from neighbouring countries and apart from the perennial problems of lack of finance and resources, face a number of problems arising from a mixed student population (ethnic and high school background, literacy and numeracy level, cultural and social motivation), who demand a varied and sensitive education provision. But in respect to the accounting curriculum, the provision closely follows the three-year degree pattern operating in Australian and New Zealand universities and includes an array of subjects drawn from the disciplines of accounting, economics, management, law and mathematics. The degree programme in P.N.G. is however, a four-year degree to provide sufficient time to accommodate the diverse educational backgrounds of new degree registrants. Students completing the three-year B.A. degree in accounting at the University of South Pacific qualify for entry into the Fiji Institute of Accountants. The programmes for both institutions are set out in Table 5.

TABLE 5

Course Composition of Accounting Programs

	U.S.P.	P.N.G. University of Technology
	%	%
Financial Accounting and Auditing	20	21
Law	10	12
Mathematics	10	10
Finance	10	8
Management Accounting*	10	13
Economics and other Social Sciences	40	36
	100	100

*Includes Data Processing and Systems Studies.

Given the current economic status of the island economies and their dependence on modern professional accounting services, both these institutions serve a critical function in supplying accounting manpower and raising the level of accounting expertise in the South Pacific region. However, their progress in this direction is likely to be impeded if both local and international professional funding and political agencies do not raise their level of support. Specifically, the difficulties encountered are:

- maintaining an adequate flow of school-leavers qualified for degree registration;
- recruiting high calibre faculty to sustain the accounting degree programme;
- securing specific funds to augment university budgets and so raise the investment in accounting curriculum practices;

- directing specific funds to the private sector to encourage additional investment in training and thus improve the quality of the transition from formal
  tertiary education to work; and
- raising the provision of postgraduate and post-experience training in education to ensure currency of the professional competencies in graduates of five
  or more years standing.

The role of the international sector in assisting Fiji and P.N.G. in meeting
these difficulties will obviously depend on the nature of financial aid relationships these countries will accept. Assuming a free access of international commitments, the following kinds of assistance would seem desirable:

- the provision of financial assistance and staff to boost the quality and experiences of the curriculum in senior high schools, possibly through specific
  aid grants by Australian and New Zealand governments;
- the development of a network of universities and colleges in Australia and
  New Zealand that would be prepared to "adopt" the universities and provide
  a regular commitment of staff and curriculum materials and thus reduce the
  recruitment and teaching problems;
- the provision of regional professional education centres to bring together
  professionals and academics, local and international, to conduct post-experience training and to promote in-house development of accounting manpower.
  Such centres could be funded by international development agencies and be
  supported by professional accounting bodies from Australia and New
  Zealand; and
- the establishment of a regional M.B.A. programme run annually on a
  summer school basis at principal island centres. These schools could be
  staffed by local and international academics. The programme could be
  modularised for both on-site and distance teaching (satellite) and course
  credits for the M.B.A. could be accumulated over a period of four years. The
  academic coordination for such a programme could be handled through a
  principal university in the Pacific, e.g., Hawaii, and the necessary funding
  secured through international foundations, specialising in educational development. Units in the programme could be framed as either terminal or credit
  courses and be adjusted to meet the business conditions and demands prevailing at each centre and in the year of instruction.

In addition, public and professional support will need to be increased to make
local conditions more amenable for the development of accounting education.

Two areas needing attention are in public relations and professional development:

(1) Public Relations: Throughout large sections of the local communities the
perception of the role of accounting and accounting education and their significance to economic development are often confused and unclear. This lack of clear
comprehension, together with a limited commitment by local accountants to
their professional body, hampers the development of professionalism and investment in accounting education; considerable constraints (unsympathetic clientele
and governments) emerge, placing unreasonable limitations on the practice of

accounting. Much effort is required by accountants to continuously promote strong public relations to generate clear images of the importance of contributions of accounting and accounting education in the advancement of the private and public sector enterprises. Assistance from professional bodies abroad is required to provide the technical information base necessary to assist the information activities of local accounting bodies and pressure groups.

(2) Professional Development: A pre-condition for successful ventures in accounting education and professional development is a climate of concern within business and government sectors for the development of accounting and managerial talents. That climate is best generated where deficiencies and limitations in financial management are recognised by policy makers, who are prepared to instigate action to upgrade the quality of accounting manpower. In P.N.G. and Fiji, a useful mechanism to develop accounting talents is the establishment of national training bodies whose brief would be to fund, develop and maintain professional development programmes. To succeed, these bodies must maintain a continuous liaison with education establishments and employers to be able to monitor trainee performance and achievement. The problem of professional development and education is too large to be left under the auspices of single institutions whose resources are frequently too fragile to launch long-term programmes for the development of an accounting work force.

7. Summary

The prospects for overcoming the accounting education problems in the islands are good provided that resources and professional efforts are directed towards the upgrading of the accounting education provision and related agencies. Such initiatives can develop a social and economic momentum which will ensure that the development of accounting education is not diverted by the traditional reactions to progress and development. The success of these island economies reviewed here can in part be guaranteed by a growing educational provision and an active and committed accounting profession which must be supported by enlightened governments, enterprises and local communities.

CHAPTER XVIII

ACCOUNTING EDUCATION IN THE
ASEAN FEDERATION OF ACCOUNTANTS (A.F.A.)*

1. Introduction

The five ASEAN countries have many diverse approaches to their problems, but they have certain strongly similar needs. One of these is in the area of the accounting profession and accounting education. All ASEAN countries require well qualified accountants in both the public and private sector. Each country has determined the stringency of its required qualifications for accountants based on a cost-benefit assessment peculiar to their individual environments.

At present, to be qualified as a certified public accountant, candidates are required to obtain a formal education ranging from three to five years and a period of work experience with or without a professional examination.

The A.F.A. report is not intended to set out any single accounting education model nor to change any existing accounting educational systems of the member countries. Its prime objective is to recommend a minimum common body of knowledge required for the preparation of public accountants. It is not intended to interfere with the existing traditional educational system of the various countries, which the A.F.A. committee clearly intended to avoid. The recommendations reflected in the report, comprise three parts: (1) the formal education necessary to provide for the common body of knowledge in accounting, (2) the qualifying experience, and (3) the CPA examination.

2. The Beginning CPA

What is meant by a "professional accountant" or a CPA? The professional accountant is defined as one who is prepared and authorized to offer his services as a certified public accountant (CPA). This means that he has successfully passed all parts of the CPA examination and has fulfilled whatever the practice requirements may be, if any. He is qualified, in the technical sense, to practice public accounting on his own. However, not all of those who qualify as specified above go into public practice; some are employed by private enterprises and by the government, where the nature of work performed will be different from that of public accountants. Such persons will have received their certificates, be certified public accountants and have the body of knowledge described below.

3. The Profession and Its Educational Needs

To be successful in his professional career the committee observes that prospective certified public accountants should acquire:

- A comprehension of the total system of financial information flow and its relations to other systems in generating, analyzing and communicating

*Based on the 1978 Report of the A.F.A. Committee on Accounting Education.

data useful to management, the public, or governmental agencies.

- Habits of analytical thought which permit identification, accumulation, and interpretation of information required for decision making and control in both the private and public sectors.
- An ability to present financial information in conformity with generally accepted accounting principles.
- Proficiency to audit in accordance with generally accepted auditing standards both for a critical evaluation of the system used in developing the financial data and for fair presentation of the information in financial statements.

In view of the above it is believed that to be most effective, the education required should be broadly conceived and should provide for a variety (alternative of accounting careers) and to develop those qualities that will enable students to achieve success in their professional careers. Moreover, standards should be established as to the level of quality in various aspects of accounting educational programs that would give the graduate a capacity for growth and development within the accounting profession.

4. Accounting Curriculum

The accounting curriculum must be specifically relevant and responsive to the needs of the profession. The committee views education for professional accountants as composed of three parts, namely, general education, general business and accounting discipline.

4.1 General Education Courses

The broad general education in humanities and sciences including a knowledge and understanding of topics relevant to accounting should provide the students with a disciplined foundation for the successful study and practice of accounting. The foundation is intended to provide:

- The capability to continue to learn, develop and grow and the foundation on which to build.
- An understanding of the content and process of scientific thought and systematic approach to problem solving.
- Facility in the use of mathematics and statistics to measure and express economic events in quantitative terms.
- An ability to communicate effectively orally and in writing.
- An appreciation of the institutions and forces of the behavioral decision process, legal, economic and political considerations that influence and interface with accountancy.

The allocation of a minimum number of courses devoted to general education is as follows:

	Semester Hours
Communication	12
Behavioral Sciences	6

Economics	6
Mathematics (modern algebra, calculus, statistics and probability)	12
Introduction to Computer Science	3
Total	39
Other general education	(University policy)

(Generally, one semester hour means one 50-minute class meeting and twice that time of work to be performed by students outside the class.)

The committee does not specify the number of courses in other general education since, as it believes, this would depend on the institutional philosophy and this requirement should be left open to the member's own discretion.

4.2 General Business Courses

Supplementing and building upon the knowledge gained in the general education courses, the general business courses provide an understanding of the major functions of business society and the discipline of accounting and an understanding of some of the social forces which influence business and extend the student's understanding of some of the topics having business application.

The number of courses devoted to this part are:

	Semester Hours
Economic Analysis (advanced micro/macro economic theory including the monetary system)	6
Marketing	3
Finance	3-6
Production or Operational Systems	3
Business Law	3-6
Organization (the working, group and individual behavior)	6
Quantitative Applications in Business (optimization models, statistics, sampling, Markov chains, statistical decision theory, queing, PERT, simulation)	9
Accounting (financial, managerial)	6
Written Communication	3
Business Policy	0-3
Total	42-51

4.3 Advanced Accounting Courses

The accounting portion of the total curriculum should cover concepts and skills required in several areas of accounting, including financial, managerial and governmental accounting, auditing, tax advising, management advisory services, data processing and systems analysis. The overall objective is to provide an understanding of the function of accounting, the underlying body of concepts that comprises accounting theory, and their application to accounting business problems and situations.

The advanced professional program should also cover the impact of regulatory agencies and professional bodies on current and emerging accounting issues.

The committee report recommends a range of 30-45 semester hours of accounting study beyond the two introductory accounting courses as follows:

	Semester Hours
Accounting	
Financial accounting measurement problems	
Financial reporting: theory and problems	
Contemporary financial accounting issues	12-12
Cost determination, cost analysis and control, cost-based decision making	3-6
Tax theory, computation and problems	3-6
Audit theory, standards and problems including ethics and responsibilities	3-6
Electronic data processing	3-6
Accounting electives	6-9
Total	30-45

The proposed accounting curriculum can now be summarized as below:

	Semester Hours
General Education	
Communication	12
Behavioral Sciences	6
Economics	6
Mathematics	12
Introduction to Computer Science	3
Total	39
Other general education	(University policy)

	Semester Hours
General Business	
Economic Analysis	6
Marketing	3
Finance	3-6
Production and Operational Systems	3
Business Law	3-6
Organizational Behavior	6
Quantitative Applications in Business	9
Accounting (financial and managerial)	6
Written Communication	3
Business Policy	0-3
Total	42-51

	Semester Hours
Accounting	
Financial Accounting and Reporting	12
Cost Accounting: Accumulation, Analysis and Control	3-6
Taxation	3-6
Auditing	3-6
Electronic Data Processing	3-6
Accounting Electives	6-9
Total	30-45
Grand Total	111-135

The suggested program would of course permit only limited specialization within the four-year program (minimum number of 111 credits) and the five-year program (minimum number of 135 credits); additional study would be required to achieve substantial specialization with the case and/or problem method of instruction be intensively used.

4.4 Administration

As mentioned earlier, the professional preparation that now exists within the five ASEAN countries varies rather widely, ranging from the three- to five-year university level of accounting education with the following alternatives:

Within the College of Business Administration (or other equivalent names)
- The three-year program
    with qualifying work experience
    with and with no CPA examination
- The four-year program
    with and with no qualifying work experience
    with only one-subject examination (in auditing practices) and the full-fledged CPA examination
- The five-year program
    with qualifying work experience
    with no CPA examination

The present general acceptance of the MBA type of educational program in business does have some implications for accounting as well as other business disciplines. The focus centers on the existence of the two contrasting avenues of study of the business disciplines, one at the undergraduate level and the other at the graduate level.

The committee believes that the undergraduate accounting education will continue, for many years to come, to be an important avenue of education for professional accounting, although the MBA type of graduate program will expand in absolute and relative measures. It is reasonable to believe that the MBA type program will prove itself to be the most effective way of professional preparation and will eventually become more attractive to the prospective CPAs.

Accounting is part of business and accounting education is part of the country's total educational system tied up with the socioeconomic environment. With regards to the administration of the program, the committee is not prepared to recommend any model program of study.

5. The Qualifying Work Experience

With reference to the qualifying experience requirement, we have a range from no experience required to full-fledged experience. The committee feels that more work experience seems to be required as a substitute for shorter college years, a trade-off between formal education and experience. On this subject the committee has the following observations:

• Students who have been broadly educated in business while acquiring their accounting education can quickly learn highly technical, professional aspects on the job.

• A substantial portion of CPA's are not in public practice and with various new methods of instruction, students learn more from formal education than from work experience.

• In the changing, increasingly complex business environment the CPA will begin not as a sole practitioner but as a newly qualified accountant in an established CPA firm.

Benefits would be gained from work experience, but the trade-off might not be a good compromise. In the light of the growing body of business-related knowledge and the changing business environment and practices there seems to be a trend toward placing greater reliance on formal education and less on on-the-job training as a means of professional preparation. With different social and business environments, the committee is doubtful about the effectiveness of work experience and recommends therefore that this qualifying experience be critically reviewed.

6. The CPA Examination

There is a wide range of difference in the requirement for passing the CPA examination, a range from no requirement to a full-fledged examination with the examination of one subject in between the two extremes. It is useful to raise some questions at this point. What are the basic objectives of the college accounting education and is it really intended to test the professional competence in accounting and how successful is it? Is work experience a real substitute for the CPA examination? Because the CPA examination is beyond the formal college accounting education the committee is prepared to give its recommendation on this subject.

The CPA certificate is evidence of basic competence of professional quality in the discipline of accounting. This minimum level of competence is demonstrated by acquiring the common body of knowledge (by passing a college accounting program) and by passing the CPA examination. The committee recommends that the CPA examination comprise five sections of six papers as follows:

Section	Number of Papers	Hours of Examination
(1) Accounting Practice: Part 1	1	4
Accounting Practice: Part 2	1	4
(2) Accounting Theory	1	3
(3) Auditing	1	3
(4) Taxation	1	3
(5) Business Law	1	3

6.1   Accounting Practice and Theory Topics

The theory questions should emphasize the testing of conceptual knowledge in the discipline of accounting while accounting practice problems will emphasize the testing of the application of conceptual knowledge. The topics to be covered are:

Assets and liabilities measurements
Owners' equity
Individuals
Partnerships
Corporations
Analysis of financial statement
Statement of changes in financial position
Branch and home office accounting: local and foreign
Business combination
Consolidated statement
Accounting corrections
Cost accounting (job order, process, standard; distribution: direct, joint
   products; cost-based decision making)
Budgeting, forecasting and capital budgeting
Quantitative application in business mathematics, statistics and probability

6.2   Auditing Topics

Generally accepted auditing standards
Internal control
Audit programs and procedures
Auditing evidence
Auditing theory
Auditor's report
Professional ethics and responsibility
Statistical sampling

6.3   Taxation Topics

Sales tax
Commodity tax
Individual income tax
Business income tax

Income tax computation
Double taxation

6.4 Business Law Topics

Contracts
Commercial papers
Forms of business organization: agency, proprietorship, partnership, and
  corporation
Labor Law

With reference to the question of timing of the CPA examination, the committee is of the opinion that, if the CPA examination program is going to be adopted, candidates should be encouraged to take the CPA examination as soon as they have fulfilled their education requirement and as close to their college graduation dates as possible.

7. Summary

Due to the wide variation of the socioeconomic environments and total educational systems of the member countries, the committee is not prepared to recomment any change that would substantially affect the traditional systems now existing. Thus, in one respect it makes specific recommendations, in the other, it only makes some observations. The committee's report can be summarized thus:

• The role of the professional accountants in society is expanding, making necessary a need for more rigorous education for the common body of knowledge required for all professional accountants.

• The body of knowledge necessary for the entrance into the profession will and should be required as part of the college education.

• The committee has no definite recommendation on the duration of the college professional accounting program; instead, it recommends the structure of the accounting programs in terms of work (semester hours).

• The structure of the professional accounting program consists of 39 semester hours of work of general education courses as specified, in addition to other general education courses as required by the college and university; 42 to 51 semester hours of work of general business courses and 30 to 45 semester hours of work of accounting courses. In all a minimum total of 111 to 135 semester credit hours as specified; other general education courses would make up for the full four- or five-year programs respectively.

• Qualifying experience seems to be regarded as part of the college accounting education in some member countries; the effectiveness of the value of the practical experience should be thoroughly reviewed.

• Changes always take place in business and accounting professions. Educational programs must be flexible and adaptive and this is best achieved by entrusting their specific content to the college and university. However, the committee believes that the scope, purpose and general concern of the formal education for professional accounting are proper concerns of the professional body.

• The CPA examination is considered to be of great value and the real test for the mastery of the body of knowledge. The examination papers should cover the main areas of accounting discipline, namely accounting practice and theory, auditing, taxation and business law. Candidates should be allowed to take such examination as close to their graduation dates as possible.

• The committee has no recommendation on the administration of the accounting program. However, it regards the setup of a separate school of accountancy as the least appropriate. While the undergraduate accounting program will remain the main source of supply of the professional accountants, the MBA type program is becoming the most effective means for professional preparation.

Accounting education is on the threshold of change and the need for the highly qualified professional accountant is clear and evident. A review of forces for change suggests that the education of the professional accountants of the future will require, in some member countries, a tremendous effort. The change would undoubtedly be affected by the college and university educational philosophy and the countries' total educational systems. In view of these forces, colleges should carefully review their present curriculum and long-range goals.

CHAPTER XIX

ACCOUNTING EDUCATION IN INDONESIA: ITS STRUCTURE AND REQUIREMENTS

Adolf J. H. Enthoven*

1. Introduction

This chapter outlines the structure and requisites for accounting education and training in Indonesia. The material was gathered as part of appraisals carried out by the author on behalf of the Ford Foundation (1973), and as part of an educational mission for the World Bank and UNESCO (1977). This write-up does not reflect in any way the official position of these organizations, nor those of the Indonesian government; the responsibility for the underlying evaluation is strictly my own.

Indonesia is an excellent case portraying the needs for better accountancy practices and education, and the methods available to enhance effective accountancy training and research. The Indonesian government, the World Bank and the UN (UNESCO) have recognized the necessity to improve accounting education and they have made major steps to develop accounting education in the years ahead. Indonesia can be considered the first country where such a major joint effort is being undertaken, and the approach used may well set the framework for other developing countries in similar positions. I am confident that the Indonesian effort will turn out to be successful, and help spur Indonesia's economic development process.

The subsequent sections reflect upon the structure of accounting education; thereafter, the accountancy requirements will be assessed.

2. The Structure of Accountancy Education in Indonesia

2.1 University Training

Academic accountancy training is carried out in the faculties of economics of universities, where specialization in accountancy occurs after the second or third year of a five-year terminal master's (sarjana) program. The three-year sarjana muda, comparable to a baccalaureate, is not considered a terminal point in economics (accounting). Consequently a terminal bachelor's degree does not exist at present in Indonesia, although plans have been cast in this direction. The ability for upgrading practitioners and students, by means of an accounting diploma or extension course, is also receiving attention by the Ministry of Education. Post-secondary accounting-economics educational programs are directed and supervised by the Ministry of Education and Culture through a "Consortium of Economic Sciences" (CES).

---

*Adolf J. H. Enthoven is Professor of Accounting, Chairman Accounting Department, and Director, Center for International Accounting Development of The University of Texas at Dallas.

About half of the 26,000 economics students in public institutions concentrate on accounting, but recent output is estimated at only 300-350 per year; the other half focus on general economics or business administration.

Accounting education is offered at six state universities (Universities of Indonesia, Gajah Mada, North Sumatra, Airlangga, Pajajaran and Sriwijaya) and at three private universities (Parahyangan, Trisakti, Nomensen). Three other accounting departments are being set up at the Universities of Syiah Kuda (Aceh), Brawijaya (Malang) and Diponegoro (Semarang). Only graduates (sarjanas with doctorandus-Drs. degree) from state universities or other equivalent higher learning institutions are recognized as qualified ("registered") accountants, in accordance with the Ministry of Finance "Accountant's Act 34 of 1954." Private universities are recognized by the government only up to the sarjana muda degree; their sarjana is a non-accredited degree. The students who pursue the sarjana program at private universities have to pass a state examination conducted by the "Committee of Experts" in order to become "registered accountants." The "Committee of Experts," nominated by the Ministry of Education on the proposal of the Minister of Finance, decides upon all qualifications for admittance as "registered accountant."

2.2 Government Accountants Training

Training for government accountants is carried out at the Ministry of Finance's operated State School for Government Auditors (S.T.A.N.) in Jakarta. Its future structural-administrative setup has not been clearly decided upon. S.T.A.N. has been approved by the Ministry of Education as an academic institution with sarjana degree status, but does not offer the Drs. (doctorandus) degree. The courses up to sarjana muda last three years; students then go to the various ministries for several years practical experience, whereupon, after due selection, they return to the S.T.A.N. for two years for completion of their studies. Upon completion and practical service, they become "registered accountants" according to Law 34 of 1954. Students receive payment during their studies, although they have to sign a long-term contract with the government, amounting to five times the length of their study.

In addition to its regular program (three plus two years), S.T.A.N. runs short program courses. Furthermore, it has, since 1975, a nine-month crash program to become Adjunct Government Accountants, for sarjana muda's in economics from universities. These government persons need to be exposed to government accounting methods and practical aspects, which are generally not covered at universities.

The present government bookkeeping system is still the single entry system inherited from the colonial administration, which is inadequate for modern public administration. As an indication of the inadequacy of present accounting practices, summary financial statements lag by at least two years and have not been prepared for most fiscal years. The government plans to undertake a study to determine means to modernize the government accounting system and procedures. It plans to complement this with another study for business management education to develop a national strategy in this area.

2.3 Middle-Level and Semi-Professional Training

The principal sources of middle-level training (assistant accountants) are the private accounting academies. There are at least 16 throughout Indonesia. Previously, there also were government academies, but these have now been integrated into the universities. The academies have to be registered with the government, and they may be either "recognized," "equivalent" or "registered." The "recognized" ones are able to offer sarjana muda degrees, although continuing on to universities is pretty well excluded. However, a great demand exists for assistant accountants with such terminal diplomas (degrees). The final examinations of these private academies are also supervised by the Ministry of Education.

Middle-level accounting (and administrative) training is also offered outside the official degree programs at universities by means of non-degree programs (for example, PAAP: Pendidikan Akhli Administrasi Perusahaan). The PAAP programs are of a business-administrative nature, giving a variety of middle-level accounting courses; they tend to be rather practical-oriented. In accountancy, diploma level training leading to semi- (para) professionals and assistant or adjunct accountants is not well recognized in Indonesia as a terminal point. Limited scope exists for students, once they have such semi-professional degrees, to become professionals or specialize in different accountancy fields (for example, computer sciences, systems, controllership management accounting). Specialization is also a weakness at professional levels. Teaching staff, materials and facilities tend to be deficient in both the public and private institutions. Standardization of the variety of programs and examinations is still unsatisfactory, and there is a lack of coordination among middle level institutions. Transfer to universities is virtually excluded.

2.4 Lower Level Training

The Ministry of Education administers examinations in bookkeeping, consisting of Brevet (Bon) A and B, in order to obtain a certificate as a "recognized" bookkeeper. Previously a private institution correspondence program existed, which has been abandoned. The formal bookkeeping training is essentially provided by commercial bookkeeping colleges; the principal type of commercial colleges are the Sekolah Menengah Ekonomi Tingkat Atas (SMEA). Several bookkeeping schools exist, and one of the better ones is Yagara Pandidikan Pembuktan in Jakarta. The course contents are mainly based on translated Dutch texts. (However, it needs to be mentioned that many enterprises carry out their accounting/ bookkeeping methods based on Dutch concepts.)

2.5 Other Accounting Courses

Miscellaneous accounting courses, essentially basic financial and cost accounting, are also offered at various non-degree extension programs of universities and at management (development) training centers. For example, The Management Institute of the Economics Faculty of the University of Indonesia offers short three- to six-week courses in management accounting, cost accounting, financial accounting. These courses tend to be of a managerial and technical nature. The business administration programs at universities also offer basic financial, cost, and managerial accounting.

2.6   Administrative Setup of University Programs

The existing administrative and course structures in economics-accountancy are a mixture of the original Dutch system and the U.S. system. Deans and heads of departments have great autonomy in setting administrative requirements, programs and courses; while course content (and approaches) is largely up to the individual instructor. Supervision over and coordination between courses, and even institutions, tend to be minimal. However, integration and coordination between various levels of accountancy is being pursued by the Consortium (CES).

No uniform-minimum standard sarjana muda degree in economic sciences exists as yet, although this is to be established in 1979 by means of a uniform examination. But a related problem is the gap between high school and post-secondary school training; for example, English at high schools is generally poorly taught, although most economics and accounting textbooks at universities are in English.

Diploma level programs for either assistant-financial accountants, cost accountants or other types of accountants by desired concentration area have not been developed at universities, academies or other institutions. Such middle and lower level diploma or certificate courses, and related needs and demands, are to be part of an *Accountancy Survey* (see below). Regional accounting centers for upper, middle and lower level training have not yet been developed, nor do adequate correspondence and updating courses exist.

2.7   Enrollments, Outputs and Growth

Some general observations pertaining to economics-accountancy enrollments are presented below:

• Aggregate acceptance of applicants in economics (e.g., accounting) during the period 1971-1975 has been around 2 percent, although at the Universities of Indonesia and Gajah Mada around 5 percent. (At all state and private universities together, the acceptance rate in economics during 1975 was 30 percent, representing 3,000 students.) Enrollment in the Faculty of Economics at the University of Indonesia during the year 1977 was 1,277, and breakdown is as follows:

	Men	Women	Total
Preparatory Level (Persiapan)	101	46	147
Repeaters (Prep. Level)	48	43	91
Bachelors (Sarjana Muda)	321	163	484
Masters (Sarjana)	446	109	555
Total	916	361	1,277

Around 50 percent of the sarjana students are in accountancy. Total enrollment in the Faculty has been stable, due to inability to handle more students.

• 40 percent of the sarjana degrees awarded by the Faculties of Economics were in accounting; for sarjana muda's this was 50 percent.

• Expected enrollment between 1978-85 of 126,750 would amount to twice the average present annual rate. With a current acceptance rate of around 25 percent, doubling the increase will require gearing for current annual input.

• Present Ph.D. faculty is 17, and an additional 40-50 Ph.D. faculty (depending on replacement) has to be generated in the near future.

• Average completion time for the sarjana degree is seven to eight years, while a number of graduates never officially graduate. A number are held up at the SKRIPSI (thesis) stage, due to their own working problems, thesis supervision, and related shortage of staff.

• The current annual total output of official graduates in accounting at the sarjana level is approximately 200 throughout Indonesia.

At STAN around 250 are enrolled each year representing an acceptance rate of about 4 percent; students are selected at high school level. The courses up to the sarjana muda last three years, and with a dropout rate of 30 percent for the first year and 10 percent for the second year, approximately 150 obtain this diploma. Past and current annual number of sarjanas awarded was around 45. STAN plans to graduate about 120 sarjanas per year during the 1980's.

In order to become "registered," a candidate has to work for three years with the government; few of those interested in industrial/commercial practice seek employment without doing first the required government service. The total number of "registered" accountants in 1977 was 1,400 of which over 80 percent work for the government.

It has been estimated that current demand for top level accountants is around 5,000-8,000 (in the public and private sectors), and for supporting personnel (middle and lower levels) about four times this figure (20,000-25,000).

Present and future demand is considered vast, and it will be a number of years before supply could catch up with demand, even with the execution of the present crash program in accountancy. The total annual output of graduate accountants during 1975 was estimated at 350, but annual requirements by 1990 will be 1,400, i.e., an annual increase of 10 percent between 1980-90.

2.8 Staff and Staff Remuneration

Salary scales (although recently sizeably improved) have not yet been fully conducive for instructors to focus full time on teaching, research and writings, and institutional service. Teaching assistants are not extensively used due to lack of incentives and inability of graduate students to teach and conduct accounting labs.

At STAN the problem has been also the lack of qualified lecturers in various (mainly government) accounting fields. Teaching materials, books and equipment are another constraining factor. The existing teaching staff predominantly applies traditional methods. The staff at STAN consists of nine permanent and

70 part-time persons, all from the Ministry of Finance; full-time lecturers teach 12 hours per week. As at all institutions, the staff has difficulty upgrading and updating themselves either through foreign periodicals, visits and contacts, including exposure by foreign lecturers towards newer accounting approaches.

2.9 Curricula and Teaching Materials

The curriculum in economics (e.g., accounting) offers a general macro- and micro-oriented basis during the first two or three years of the sarjana muda studies. During the third and/or the Sarjana's fourth and fifth year, the accounting student then follows a general accounting department program, but with little ability for concentration in specific areas of accountancy. Heavy focus is given to financial accounting and auditing, with lesser emphasis on cost accounting, planning and control, controllership, government accounting, accounting systems and procedures (e.g., mechanized accounting methods). The teaching staff largely applies the "lecturing" approach by means of lecture notes. The lecture hours—between 15 to 20 or even 25 per week—are adequate; however, contact hours with staff outside class are minimal, because most lecturers have additional occupations (either in private practice or at other learning institutions). These other occupational involvements, by part-time or full-time staff, and the shortage of qualified staff, have been detrimental to pursuing up-to-date and relevant developments in accounting, research and related writings (including translations), case study developments, conducting of accounting seminars and workshops. The absence or obsolescence of accounting-oriented texts and related materials (cases, problems, teaching tools) has been a major problem for programs and courses. Most texts are in English; however, most students have difficulty comprehending these texts, while few can read Dutch. Few translations from Dutch and American texts have occurred, or have been written in the local language, hampering teaching effectiveness.

The accounting/economics sarjana programs at universities covers a span of five to nine years for most students, with an average of around seven to eight. Many students are held up at the sarjana thesis stage due to personal, supervisory and reference material problems.

Presently one general type of accounting (fairly theoretical) is turned out by the universities at the sarjana level, while at the sarjana muda level, at state institutions, there is no accounting termination point. It is considered conceivable, with a restructuring of programs, courses (both theoretical and applied), internal efficiencies (e.g., materials), that accounting learning at the universities could be speeded up and improved. Currently no more graduate programs in accountancy exist, which could enable graduates from other programs to proceed with obtaining an economics-accounting degree and/or become registered accountants. Limited functional exchanges occur between academic institutions, and between various levels of training. Exchange of information and developments is hampered by proper vehicles (e.g., magazines, etc.) for communication between institutions. The number of academic institutions that offer accounting programs has already increased during the last years; however, the increase of such programs has not yet been done in conjunction with an "inventory of needs" and a potential restructuring of programs.

STAN class hours are about 30 per week, and classes are also predominantly conducted by the lecturing method. The courses run by STAN are geared to the government's accounting needs. Courses include computer accounting, government budgeting, managerial accounting, and tax accounting, in addition to the regular financial and cost accounting courses.

At middle level programs, the courses are of a general accounting nature, without ability to focus on cost/management, financial/auditing, systems/computers or other desired forms of concentration. Texts, teaching materials and inadequate staff have also plagued the middle level academies; many lecturers from universities are on the staff of the academies (or private universities) potentially hampering the qualitative contents of teaching, research and guidance, including the preparation of course material at all levels, although relieving instructors shortages.

Lower-level commercial colleges offer a general type of commercial program (e.g., calculus, typing, shorthand, bookkeeping). Students can enroll in such colleges after three years of high school; the courses last three years (full time) and most graduates (who get a certificate) find employment in private or governmental offices. Some go into high school teaching.* The material for the SMEA courses is developed by the Ministry of Education. Bookkeeping courses—Brevet A and B—although somewhat revised during recent years, are still not considered satisfactory, especially in regions outside Jakarta. No good correspondence programs presently exist.

2.10 Student Flows

The mentioned shortages and deficiencies in teaching staff (few have Ph.D.'s), inadequate physical facilities, equipment and teaching materials, and lengthy accounting programs, have hampered the absorption of more economic/accounting students. As a general rule, around 5 to 10 percent of students applying are accepted at the major state universities, while approximately 50 percent of economics students choose the accounting concentration later on. However, it has been questioned how many more students presently could be accepted without lowering qualitative standards radically. Universities and academies complained about the poor quality of students coming from high schools. The dropout rate of students in the economics and accountancy departments at universities is relatively high; between 25 and 40 percent per year during the initial years and between 10 and 20 percent thereafter. This is considered attributable to lack of intellectual preparation and guidance, financial problems and inability to carry out studies while holding part-time or full-time jobs.

---

*A new type of continuing SMEA—the SMEA Pembina—was established in 1976 to enable students to proceed with studies at academies or universities after appropriate entrance examinations. It is expected that about 30-50 percent of the SMEA-Pembina graduates will continue their studies at private or state institutions; this potential did not exist under the old SMEA system. The intent is to make all SMEAs a Pembina program of four years (instead of three) with more focus on a variety of commercial topics.

The ability to increase quantitative and qualitative outputs, at all levels, is constrained by the lack of qualified teachers and current methods' applications (e.g., "inbreeding"). Any planned increase in quantitative outputs may go, to some extent, at the expense of quality, both from an institutional and student capacity point of view. However, other contemplated approaches may cure this deficiency in the near future.

3. Accountancy Requirements in Indonesia

3.1 Some General Observations

As may be noticed from the previous section, accountancy education and training in Indonesia does require a *comprehensive* and *systematic* approach, covering all levels and institutions of accounting. A great diversity of accountancy programs presently exist. The structuring of the teaching of accountancy fields (e.g., financial, auditing, managerial, government) will have to be closely coordinated, including educational and practice oriented activities and courses. The institutionalization of accountancy professionals (educators and practitioners) is to have the necessary support from the respective parties. Accountancy education, training, practices and institutional professionalization may require closer linkage in order to develop qualified accountants at all levels and by areas of concentration, necessary for a country's (Indonesia's) needs and objectives (economic plans). Such appraisals are expected to result in an "accountancy development plan," based upon both (1) the socioeconomic plans and (2) a relevant accountancy manpower inventory of present positions and future needs. Such a comprehensive accountancy development plan may cover a 5 to 15 year period, and presumably will be coordinated through an accountancy advisory committee representing the most significant factions, institutions and training centers concerned with the development of accountancy education and practices. The Indonesian accountancy strategy pertaining to such a plan is expected to have the following components: major requirements for strengthening accountancy training would include effective staff training; development of more practical and relevant courses and programs with greater opportunity for specialization at upper and even middle accountancy levels; more effective teaching materials and aids, including accounting "laboratories" with some mechanized facilities (e.g., on-line computer setups); encouragement of research, writing and translation of foreign texts and articles; and creation of postgraduate (post-sarjana) accountancy training programs.

3.2 Accounting Manpower Inventory and Plan

The Consortium for Economic Sciences (CES) of the Ministry of Education and Culture has already drafted a project statement outlining a survey on needs for accountants. Its objectives are to: "survey the actual needs for accountants and their specialities at present, and a projection of future demand should be undertaken, including a study of which branch of accountancy would require intensification."

3.3 Academic, Institutional and Technical Level Training

Programs, course contents and methods of teaching at universities are demanding extensive reappraisal. It will include current teaching approaches and material, together with the best vehicles for developing various types of accountants. This may pertain, for example, to: specializations to be offered at both the sarjana and sarjana muda level, speed-up of programs, establishment of a bachelor's degree in accounting, graduate programs in accounting for entrants from other disciplines, coordination between courses, pursuits of research and writings (including cases), seminars and workshops to be conducted, upgrading programs for lecturers, increased administrative and operational efficiencies. Internships are to be set up, and accounting chairs established. The objectives of accounting education in Indonesia are expected to be clearly spelled out, and ways and means reflected to do this most effectively and efficiently, taking into account the future role of the types and levels of academic and other trained accountants. Such an appraisal will be part of the *Accountancy Inventory and Plan*.

Accountants at professional and semi-professional levels also can be updated by institutions other than universities; for example, the professional accounting organization, (Ikatan Akuntan Indonesia - IAI), could be implemented in offering practice oriented courses for persons working in industry (commerce) and in accounting firms. Their instructors could be expected to come from accounting firms or industries. Such institutional-professional courses could lead to various qualifying (certificate) tests needed for accounting practitioners at different levels and functions.

Training programs should aim at improving the qualifications of accountancy teachers and practicing accountants at all levels. At the university centers, courses for university and academy instructors and practicing accountants may have to focus better on accounting and management information systems, data processing, operational auditing, and management and national income accounting. Training for bookkeeping and teachers is to begin with elementary accounting and upgrading in basic bookkeeping methods.

As for governmental accounting training (STAN), an assessment also will be made of the future nature and contents of its programs, based upon the types and levels of accountants required at various governmental functions. These appraisals are to be part of the accountancy survey and plan. Its present teaching staff comes from the Ministry of Finance, but foreign assistance may also be needed in order to help train personnel for improving governmental accounting, auditing and budgeting systems, including the training of public enterprise accountants and its internal/external auditors. STAN's training programs may emphasize management auditing and accounting, financial accounting, government and budget accounting, data processing and information systems, and national accounting.

Middle level and lower level training is largely carried out by private institutions, and requires better harmonization and supervision including more uniform standards for examinations. Whether middle-level training also could be effectively carried out at universities, leading to sarjana mudas in various functional areas of accountancy, is being appraised.

Bookkeeping courses also are being re-evaluated and, for example, whether they could effectively be carried out by correspondence programs in outer regions. Not only correspondence (postal) type training, but further regionalization of all middle and lower level courses is to be appraised in Indonesia.

3.4   Accountancy Development Centers

Degree and diploma level accountancy training institutions are under scrutiny whereby better training and upgrading of staff will be of high priority. Upgrading is needed at all levels, and presumably could best be executed at certain academic accountancy development centers. Such centers are to serve instructors and administrators at universities (state and private), academies, SMEA, and even commercial and bookkeeping colleges. Financial accounting, management accounting, accounting systems, internal/external auditing, planning and control (feasibility studies), computer accounting and auditing, controllership, etc., together with administrative controls and structures, are to be incorporated into such centers' training modules. Such development centers are to be part of universities with established accounting setups, and would consist of one main center and two subsidiary centers. The centers are to work closely together, exchange information and specialized staff, and complement each other in programs and administrative matters. Gradually other centers are to be established to cater to expanding regional training needs. A davelopment center also will be established for governmental accounting training.

The main purpose of these centers will be the development and upgrading of accounting instructors at various training levels and by area of concentration. Each center would cover a multiplicity of regional (private and state) educational institutions. Programs may run for 3 to 6 months, and serve 25-40 persons in alternative fields of knowledge. However, these will not only cater to the upgrading of instructors but also to the updating of skills of financial and operational accountants, auditors, controllers, systems personnel, managers and administrators.

The staff manpower inputs at all these development centers should be of high caliber. For example, at the university(ies) it should be qualified academicians with doctoral (DR) or Ph.D. degrees; at the governmental level, persons with extensive governmental accounting, auditing, and budgeting teaching experience and practice. These technical assistance inputs may come from diverse sources:

- University centers: foreign academic personnel skilled in various fields of accountancy, and extensive exposure to accountancy, its research, and educational developments and requirements.
- Government center: foreign government accounting bodies and government training programs.

In addition, to develop and upgrade teachers, the functions of accounting development centers are expected to:

- appraise curricula, syllabi, text materials, teaching methodologies and aids, library requirements, equipment utilizations and needs (e.g., computers and other machines);
- perform textbook writing and translations, case development, etc. Teaching materials development would include translating or writing standard textbooks, writing Indonesian case studies and developing course materials (outlines, study notes, problems and visual aids) for accountancy subjects (i.e., for university/academy instructions, for upgrading practicing accountants, and for bookkeeping instruction).
- develop correspondence programs for middle and lower level courses;
- issue research publications and journals plus bulletins for interested parties;
- function as clearinghouses for publications, exchange of personnel, research programs, employment of teachers, etc.;
- pursue research in the various branches of accounting, e.g., appraisals regarding future accounting development requirements (for Indonesia), including accounting manpower planning
- select students for specialized programs abroad, and determine foreign technical assistance needs;
- develop crash programs at diploma, graduate and other levels;
- conduct general and specific courses, seminars and workshops for a variety of groups.

The pursuit of such center activities is expected to be gradual.

A planning and performance monitoring system may have to be established. Each accountancy development center would be responsible for supplying data on annual training programs, numbers of participants, materials development and research projects. A system for obtaining feedback on the relevance of training and materials provided may also have to be established; data would be analyzed by the centers' directors so that recommended improvements for training programs could be effected.

3.5   Accountancy Coordinating Body

The different functional accountancy areas, and the institutions that serve these, are to better linked. Three broad functional areas can be distinguished:

(1) Educational and Training: largely spearheaded by the universities; education and training institutes may be part of an accounting educators association.

(2) Professional Accounting: composed of persons working in private or public industrial and professional entities. A strong accounting profession is desired for national, regional and international purposes.

(3) Governmental: composed of accountants associated with governmental accounting activities, teaching and practice.

Each of these three fill a significant socioeconomic task; however, the need has arisen to have those functional areas and institutions coordinated under a parent body, council or committee which would guide, appraise and assist these entities and their operations. This coordinating body would assist in the appraisal of their programs, courses and areas of coordination, the allocation of certain human, material and financial resources, and other aspects pertaining to accountancy knowledge, skills and practices in Indonesia.

4. Summary

A more unified approach is desired, involving the whole structure and process of accountancy education, training and professionalization. Internal efficiencies could be spurred in this manner, while assistance through international and bilateral agencies would be more easily forthcoming with such a well-structured and cohesive accountancy pattern. It is expected to result in changing present arrangements, or even certain legalistic aspects and current requirements.

The present demand for accountants at all levels and branches (specialization) in accounting far outreaches the prevailing and near future supply in Indonesia. A vast effort therefore is being made to improve the accountancy educational facilities and programs at higher, middle and lower level institutions, and related structural and operational aspects.

Some major constraining factors in increasing the existing and near future supply of accountants by level and category have been:

- The availability of competent teaching staff, both quantitatively and qualitatively.
- The prevailing structural setup of the educational institutions, e.g., their internal efficiencies, program patterns and course requirements.
- The absence of a carefully laid out "accountancy development plan" based upon an inventory of existing and projected supplies and demands, which could serve as a basic framework for action, e.g., potential changes.
- The effective coordination between educational and training institutions and the public and private practice world, in order to gear the training and outputs to the specific requirements of society.

In order to be able to increase, both qualitatively and quantitatively, the outputs of accountants, certain basic considerations are envisaged by Indonesian authorities. These tend to be of the following nature:

- To prepare a comprehensive survey and projections of accountancy demands and outputs. This survey is to set forth the demands and supplies at all levels and areas (fields) of accountancy, and is to delineate the functions and types of accountants.
- To install an accountancy advisory board (council) to direct accountancy development—education and practice—in Indonesia in view of the socio-economic requirements as delineated in the above survey.
- To set up accountancy development centers at specified universities to upgrade existing instructors, and perform a variety of related developmental, training and research activities.
- To expand accountancy programs at a number of universities throughout Indonesia. Further expansion of such training activities will be pursued in the years ahead at all local levels.
- To expand the training and research capabilities of the Ministry of Fi-

nance's State School for Government Auditors (STAN) to take care of increased government requirements and to potentially free accountants for future private use in future years.

The adequate fulfillment of these *initial requirements*, associated with a *restructuring* of the accountancy education and training programs, practice requirements and associated *potential legal amendments*, will lead to greater and better output of Indonesian accountants for all sectors of society in future years.

In addition to effective staff training by the proposed development centers, a major function of the "Accountancy Advisory Council" will be to look at the whole interrelated structure of education and training in accountancy and determine changes required. The objectives of accounting education in Indonesia will be clearly spelled out, and ways and means reflected to do this most effectively and efficiently, taking into account the future role of the types and levels of academic and other trained accountants. These will be part of the accountancy development plan and strategy covering a 5-15 year period.

It is expected, in my opinion, that in another 10 to 15 years Indonesia could have effectively "caught up in the area of accountancy with other countries." As outlined in this annex, a vast effort is needed by both Indonesia international agencies and foreign experts to help spur this process. To this extent both the Indonesian government and the World Bank have committed themselves to an effective accountancy development program in Indonesia. It is a comprehensive and costly project, but it certainly will pay off in the years ahead, and the accountancy improvements will help the economic development process.

CHAPTER XX

ACCOUNTANCY AND ACCOUNTING EDUCATION IN KOREA

PART A

by

Korean Institute of Certified Public Accountants

PART B

by

Mr. Sang Oh Nam*
Assistant Professor of Accounting
School of Management
Seoul National University

PART A

ACCOUNTANCY IN KOREA

1. Historical and Political Background

Korea is an ancient country with a history of 5,000 years. The early days of Korea are shrouded in the clouds of mythological stories. However, the origin of Korean people and Korean history begin usually with the "Three Kingdom Era" (Koguryo, Paekje, and Silla Dynasties). By 668, the Silla Kingdom had unified the Korean people.

The Silla Dynasty was succeeded by Koryo, which ruled from 918 and was replaced by the Yi Dynasty, which ruled from 1392 to 1910. Then came the Japanese Annexation of Korea until independence was gained in August, 1945. The defeat of Japan in 1945 did not bring all Koreans freedom. The Russians occupied the northern half, above the 38th parallel, and the Americans the southern half.

The North launched a surprise invasion of the South on June 25, 1950; that was the Korean War. After bitter destructive battles a truce was signed in 1953, leaving the border nearly where it was before the war.

In 1960, a nationwide uprising by students was touched off by the rigging of an election by Syngman Rhee's government, which had been in power since 1948.

*The author wishes to thank the Korean Institute of Certified Public Accountants for support in writing this paper.

Syngman Rhee stepped down from the presidency and following a new general election, the Democratic Party formed a new government, which was taken over by General Chung-Hee Park, on May 16, 1961.

During President Park's rule, the first five-year economic development plan was introduced in 1962. Since then Korea has emerged as one of the fast growing countries in the world and maintained one of the highest rates of growth in modern economic history.

President Park was assassinated in October, 1979. Through the transition government led by Kyu-Ha Choi, General Doo-Hwan Chun has been newly elected as President of the Republic. President Chun has started realignment of industry for boosting the international competitiveness of the nation's big industries and commendable educational reforms.

2. The Development of the Economy and Business Systems

Since the first five-year economic development plan was introduced in 1962 as a coordinated economic plan, Korea has achieved dramatic progress in various fields including over $12,000 million in yearly exports, a balance in international trade payments, a sharp increase in rural income, expansion of heavy and chemical industries and social overhead capital, and the introduction of a medicare system and other social development projects.

Between 1962 and 1978, the GNP, growing at an average of about 9.3 percent per annum, increased from $2.3 billion to $46.0 billion in current prices, while per capita GNP rose from $87 to $1,242 in current prices. Now the fourth five-year economic plan has been launched, from 1977 through 1981.

Korea is fast becoming a heavily industrialized country and is already a major trading country. Korea's economic development is reflected in the rapid expansion of 40 percent annually to a total of $12.7 billion in 1978. Commodity imports have also expanded markedly, rising from $390 million to $14.5 billion, an annual increase of 27 percent.

Since the early 1960's the Korean economy has come a long way from being the mere recipient of "pump-priming" assistance in the form of foreign aid, soft loans, and taxation privileges and other incentives to become a viable repayer and reinvestor.

In a successful effort to attract foreign investment, several "export estates" have been set up. Inducements include tax advantages, guaranteed remittance of profits and principal, and facilities designed for the comfort and convenience of foreign managerial or technical staff members.

The securities market also had striking development during the last decade. Public offerings have increased rapidly following the enactment of a law in 1973 requiring certain private companies to "go public." There were 356 listed companies with capital of $3,955 million at the end of 1978. The value of bonds listed on the exchange amounted to $2,000 million at the end of 1978. The total value of listed securities at the end of 1978 of $5,959 million showed a twenty-fold increase over seven years.

However, in the wake of the reemergence of worldwide stagflation following closely upon the second oil shock, the Korean economy also experienced (as other Western countries) accelerated inflation, slowdowns in economic growth and unemployment, and a deteriorating balance of payment situation. Thus Korea suffered a rapid recession beginning in the latter half of 1979 due to frequent oil price hikes and the unstable oil situation. But Korea is expected to return to the position of fast economic progress when the world economy recovers.

Business systems of Korea are similar in nature to those of other capitalistic nations. The characteristics of capitalism, free competition, profit seeking and private ownership, are all assured. However, the government plays a key role in regulating business enterprises. For example, the government take various measures like stepped-up support for heavy and chemical industries, the strengthening of international competitiveness of local enterprises, technological renovation and development of skilled manpower and the fostering of small and medium enterprises. As a measure to help strengthen the competitiveness of Korea's manufacturing industry on the international market, the government designated key group companies as general trading companies. Those companies are business leaders in Korea. Such groups of companies like Daewoo, Hyundai, Samsung and Lucky, which were also listed in *Fortune's* 500, have such general trading companies. They receive special government supports for their growth, because their growths are vital to Korean economic development.

Such a strong government leadership prevails to every corner of Korean business circles. The government influence on the accounting profession is the same in this line.

3. The Characteristics of Korean Accounting

There are some characteristics of Korean accounting which are conceived as distinctively different from those of U.S. accounting. The characteristics are as follows:

(1) *Accounting is still in the stage of developing.*

Accounting in Korea is gradually developing. In short, the Korean accounting principles could be termed government-enacted principles which should be followed in financial reporting, in comparison with the generally accepted principles of the United States or other advanced countries.

As a token of underdevelopment, some importing accounting iformations are not fully disclosed and the utilization of audit report is not yet popular. The underdevelopment is partially due to a slow acceptance of Western accounting education; however, accounting education in Korea is gradually improving and so is the accounting profession.

(2) *Strong government influences on accounting principles formulation and practices are noted.*

In Korea, the task of accounting principles formulation belongs to the government sector. The accounting profession, especially KICPA, the only organization of professional CPAs, has influenced substantially in the formulation of accounting principles.

The accounting profession in Korea is controlled and regulated by the Security

Division of the Ministry of Finance and Korean SEC (and its arm, the Securities Supervisory Board). These two organizations control and regulate Korean accounting and auditors in the wake of controlling the securities market.

(3) *Tax accounting dominates business accounting in Korea.*

In Korea, tax accounting is predominant. Even though auditors have tried to avoid the impact of tax accounting, tax law has negative effects in the application of business accounting principles.

Some of the major differences between business accounting and tax accounting are:

a) reserve for retirement and severance benefits;

b) allowance for doubtful accounts;

c) special depreciation;

d) revenue recognition; and

e) various reserves to defer tax payments.

(4) *Some of the special features include:*

a) Periodical revaluation of fixed assets is allowed whenever wholesale price index increases 25 percent or more, for both tax and accounting purposes.

b) Financial statements are usually prepared on an individual company basis rather than on a consolidation basis. Consolidated financial statements are mandatorily required only as supplementary information.

c) Some accounting procedures are permitted to promote business activities by government. For example, special depreciation is allowed to manufacturing companies for faster depreciation; development expense and other deferred charges are capitalized instead of expensed.

d) Statements of (proposed) appropriation of retained earnings are prepared as one of the basic financial statements. Dividends are not recorded as payables until declared in the shareholder's meeting in subsequent years.

e) Income taxes currently payable are recorded as current expense.

f) Marketable securities and investments are generally carried at cost.

g) Effect from accounting change is applied only prospectively.

h) Significant and extraordinary losses from foreign exchange fluctuations incurred on long-term liabilities are generally deferred.

4. Professional Regulatory Bodies

The accounting profession in Korea is controlled and regulated by the Securities Division of the Ministry of Finance (MOF) and the Financial Management Division of the Korean Securities Supervisory Board (an arm of the Korean Securities Exchange Commission, KSEC) through the Korean Institute of Certified Public Accountants (KICPA) and under the following laws, decrees and regulations: Securities Exchange Law, Certified Public Accountants Law, and KICPA's Bylaws and Regulations.

In Exhibit 1, the regulation process of the Korean accounting profession shows two flows. First, for listed and registered companies, the MOF and the Korean SEC regulate companies through the KICPA.

From the exhibit, it is clear that the regulatory power belongs solely to the public sector. The MOF is responsible for the formulation of accounting principles as well as implementation. But the government's dominance has led Korean accounting to the tax-oriented accounting, rigid accounting regulations, and slowness of accounting principles revision work. So far, the development of accounting has not yet quite kept up with the developments or changes of economic environment or business management techniques because of its rigidness and inflexibility.

EXHIBIT 1

Professional Regulation Process

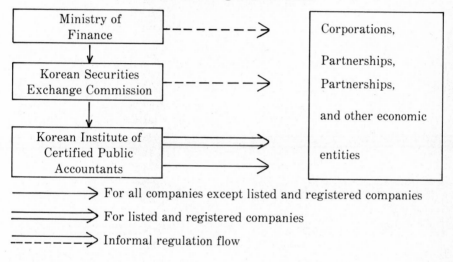

——————> For all companies except listed and registered companies

══════════> For listed and registered companies

— — — — — —> Informal regulation flow

5. Accounting Principles and Its Formulation Process

There are two sets of accounting principles in Korea, one for general use and another applicable to stock exchange listed companies. The former is "Business Accounting Principles" and Financial Statement Rules (companion set) and the latter is "The Accounting Principles for Listed Companies" and "Financial Statement Rules for Listed Companies" (companion set).

These two sets of Korean GAAP are actually same in content and in format with the exception of very minor differences. But there exists a possibility that these two principles could be differently formulated. Recently the Ministry of Finance has requested the Accounting System Advisory Committee (ASAC) of the Korean SEC for revision. The important revision would be the mandatory requirement for preparation of comparative financial statements, recognition of statement of changes in financial position as one of basic financial statements, and treatment of prior period adjustment as an adjustment to beginning retained earnings and expensing research and development costs.

The original *Business Accounting Principles* was pronounced in 1958 and revised in 1976. The *Accounting Principles for Listed Companies* was pronounced in 1974 and revised in 1976. Since there are no significant differences between these two principles, many people are questioning the reasonableness of dual accounting principles.

In addition to these principles some laws and regulations affect current Korean accounting practices, as follow:

Commercial Code
Various Tax Laws
Financial Control Regulation for Listed Companies (issued by KSEC)
Asset Revaluation Law
Laws and Regulations Governing Special Industries.

Standards-setting bodies in Korea are shown in Exhibit 2.

EXHIBIT 2

Accounting Standards and Standards-Setting Bodies in Korea

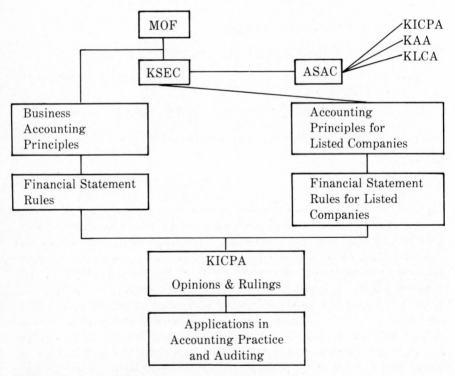

MOF:　Ministry of Finance
KSEC:　Korean Securities Exchange Commission
ASAC:　Accounting Systems Advisory Committee
KICPA:　Korean Institute of Certified Public Accountants
KAA:　Korean Accounting Association
KLCA:　Korean Listed Companies Association

From Exhibit 2 we can know the following things. First, the Ministry of Finance supervises the entire formulation work of principles, so the responsibility of formulation belongs strictly to the government sector. Second, Korean Securities Exchange Commission plays a major role in the formulation of accounting principles for listed companies. The Accounting Systems Advisory Committee is the arm of KSEC and this organization does actual work of formulation and interpretation for listed companies. Third, the Korean Institute of CPAs, Korean Accounting Association (academic organization) and Korean Listed Companies Association (KLCA) usually sends opinions or proposed drafts to KSEC and MOF for consideration in revision work. Thus, these organizations play a kind of advisory role to KSEC and MOF. The original *Business Accounting* and the *Financial Statement Rules* were formulated by the Business Accounting Rules Committee of the Ministry of Finance. But this committee no longer exists, and the MOF still has the power to revise principles. It is expected that the creation of a new FASB type accounting standards body or the Accounting Systems Advisory Committee may substitute that organization.

6. Professional Accountants in Korea

6.1 Economic Development and Professional Accountants

It is only in recent years that an accountantship is regarded as a socially recognized profession in Korea.

In line with economic developments and change of accounting environments, the Korean business society gradually recognizes the importance of auditing and auditors' responsibilities. Especially, auditing has developed as the securities market expands.

1973 was the important year for CPA as well as for the capital market. In 1973, important economic measures such as the Capital Market Promotion Act, Going-Public Encouragement Act, Foreign Capital Inducement Act, Special Decree on Korean Economic Stability and Growth, and above all, the Securities Exchange Law was newly formulated or revised. Under the provisions of the Securities Exchange Law, listed and registered companies are subject to receive compulsory audit from outside independent CPAs. With this measure, CPA opinions, once disregarded by businessmen, were gradually recognized. Their opinions must be disclosed to the public by attachment to financial statements published in the newspaper. If a company receives an adverse opinion or a disclaimer of opinion, a special notice of attention to the applicable stock is issued to the public and various penalties and punishments are assessed to the company. Furthermore, appropriation of retained earnings at the annual shareholders meeting should be based on the audit-adjusted numbers. As a result, management realizes gradually the importance of auditors' opinions.

6.2 Services of Accountants

Korean CPAs perform similar services to those of American CPAs. They perform auditing service, tax service and management service. But the nature, content, and the way of rendering services are somewhat different.

In essence, most of Korean audits are statutory audits. Audit for listed and registered companies is performed in accordance with the Securities Exchange Law. Also, audit for credit beneficiaries is performed in accordance with the statutory requirement that companies of loans in excess of W2 billion controlled under the Bank of Korea must be audited. Statutory audits are the basis for audit job allocation among CPAs. However, there is a tendency toward an increase in voluntary audits in recent years.

Recently, the new government has suggested that CPAs should perform audits of universities, colleges and other private schools and companies exceeding certain size, i.e., paid-in capital of W500 million or total assets of W3 billion. Therefore, there will be a great demand on CPAs and activities of CPAs will be expanded.

6.3   Korean Institute of Certified Public Accountants

The Korean Institute of Certified Public Accountants is the only professional accountants' organization in Korea. It is organized by CPAs who have passed CPA examinations and registered with the Ministry of Finance and the KICPA. The objects of the institute are to improve the dignity of the CPAs, promote the practice of the CPAs, and extend the mutual friendship among the members.

The KICPA is organized with a chairman, two vice-chairmen, two statutory auditors, six directors, a secretary and administrative staffs. The three main committees include Research, Ethics, and Audit Quality Review. The Research Committee has seven subcommittees to deliberate on matters of accounting principles, auditing, taxation, legal, international accounting, management consulting, and public and government accounting.

There are 1,260 members at KICPA as of September 30, 1980. Under the Securities Exchange Law and the CPA Law, CPAs are required to form partnerships or accounting corporations with the approval of the Ministry of Finance and become the only CPAs qualified to audit companies in Korea for KSEC, bank and government purposes. The government has been encouraging larger CPA firms by restricting the size of companies that can be audited by firms with less than 30 CPAs.

The KICPA has a number of training programs for its members. Each year the institute generally has one general three-day seminar and about ten two-day seminars on specific accounting, auditing and tax matters.

The important promulgations of the KICPA are opinions, rulings, auditing standards and professional ethics code. The KICPA also publishes a journal titled *Accounting* yearly.

Foreign CPAs can practice in Korea. Foreign CPAs are required to take oral examinations on the Korean commercial code and tax regulations in order to qualify in Korea. Their activities are, however, restricted.

Six foreign CPA firms have a presence in Korea through membership or some forms of association with the Korean accounting corporations. They are: Arthur Young & Co.; Coopers & Lybrand; Peat, Marwick, Mitchell & Co.; Price Waterhouse & Co.; Touche Ross & Co.; and SGV of the Philippines.

6.4 CPA Examination

To be a CPA, Korean students must take three CPA examinations given by the MOF. Because Examination One is exempted for students with two years of college education, college students usually take Examinations Two and Three.

Examination One is designed to test the candidate's general educational level. The subjects covered are Korean, mathematics, English, and principles of law.

Examination Two is important to college students. The test is designed to test the candidate's knowledge and application of accounting and other commercial subjects. The subjects are intermediate accounting, auditing, cost accounting, accounting theory, business administration, principles of economics, and the commercial code.

Examination Three is the test of the candidate's practical ability to carry out CPA work. The candidate must serve two years of articleship before taking this examination. The subjects are advanced accounting, advanced auditing, managerial costing, financial analysis, and tax accounting. Successful candidates are issued CPA certificates from the Ministry of Finance.

Each examination is given once a year in Seoul. The candidate must pass all subjects at one time to advance to the next examination. The average passing rates of the examinations are Examination One, 11 percent; Examination Two, 5 percent, and Examination Three, 32 percent. It is known that passing the CPA examination is extremely difficult. The MOF is currently in the process of revising the CPA examination regulations to eliminate various criticisms.

PART B

ACCOUNTING EDUCATION IN KOREA

1. History of Education and the Education System

Education in Korea has recorded significant growth during the last thirty years. Total registrations in various levels of schools showed a sixfold increase to the present 8.7 million persons from 1.4 million in 1945. Particularly, the number of college students increased from 8,000 to as many as 260,000 during the same period, a thirty-threefold increase. The period also saw an increase of education facilities to 9,498 from 3,018 and a rise of teaching staff to 200,000 from 20,000. Such a remarkable increase of students, facilities and teaching staffs has provided Korea a prime source of manpower for economic development.

Korea's education system was greatly influenced first by the Christian missionaries and secondly, and ultimately, by the Japanese, at the turn of the century. Modern education was first introduced to Korea by Christian missionaries in the 1880's. In 1884, a number of missionaries of various denominations arrived in Korea and began building modern schools as part of their missionary activities. By the contributions of missionaries, several private universities were established.

During the Japanese annexation period, the nation's basic education system of elementary, secondary and college education was first established. The Seoul National University was thus founded as a model university. In this respect, the Japanese have contributed to Korea to some extent, but their contributions were frequently disregarded, with the much-criticized oppression.

The Korean education system was also influenced by the U.S., particularly after the liberation from Japan. At the end of World War II, the U.S. military government, which existed in Seoul from 1945 to 1948 and until the establishment of Korean government, planted the American education system in Korea to provide the Korean people with democratic education under the principle of equal opportunity. Since then, U.S. influences on Korean education systems have increased in many respects with the close tie between Korea and the U.S.

The Republic of Korea's school system is divided into elementary school, secondary (middle and high school) school, and college or university. The six-three-three-four schooling system was thus adopted in Korea. Higher education includes universities, graduate schools, independent colleges, and junior colleges. Except for medical studies, which take six years, undergraduate courses are four years.

As of the end of 1978, there were 74 four-year regular colleges and universities, 90 graduate schools, 11 two-year teachers' colleges and 10 two-year junior colleges across the nation. Of the higher learning institutions, 140 were private, 55 were state-run and one was public school.

In 1978 the combined enrollment in the nation's higher learning institutions stood at 308,730. The figure broke down to 277,783 for four-year regular colleges and universities, 19,150 for graduate schools, 4,308 for junior teachers' colleges, 4,803 for junior colleges and 2,686 for miscellaneous vocational colleges.

Meanwhile the number of faculty members totaled 12,586. The figure compared 11,953 faculty members recorded in the previous year.

2. History of Accounting and Accounting Education

According to the historical findings, the accounting history of Korea goes back to the times before Luca Pacioli's writing on double-entry bookkeeping. It was during the Koryo Dynasty (918-1392) that Korea's unique bookkeeping system was first invented and used. It is estimated as sometime in the 12th century, but not in the 15th century. The system is known as Songdo Bookkeeping System or Sa-Gae Songdo Chibu-Bup. The system is similar to the double-entry system in principle.

Because of lack of communication, Korea's own bookkeeping system was not known to the Western world until 1918, when *The Federal Accountant*, an Australian professional journal, reported on the system in an editor's note. Now, the Songdo Bookkeeping System which had been invented, developed and used by Korean businesses for hundreds of years is completely ignored and only the Western system is taught in schools. Thus Pacioli's system replaced the old

Korean system, because the Koreans practically abandoned their own system and adopted the Western system.

During the Japanese rule, the Western bookkeeping system was introduced to Korea. It was mostly taught at the commercial high schools. After the war, accounting was also adopted as one of the subjects at colleges of commerce. Most of the accounting subjects appearing at that time were principles of accounting (elementary), cost accounting, auditing, and financial analysis. These are introductory courses, not developed as U.S. textbooks under the same course titles. Therefore, no courses of intermediate or advanced levels of accounting were taught in the class during that time.

After World War II, accounting was taught at most universities' departments of business administration (formerly departments of commerce) as well as at high schools. High school accounting is taught in two ways. At public high school, bookkeeping, which is considered a part of commerce, is classified as one of three industrial subjects (others are agriculture and manufacturing industry). High school students must take and study one of these three subjects. At commercial high schools, accounting is treated as one of core courses and every student must take it.

At the undergraduate level of universities accounting is taught as one of business studies in the department of business administration, so undergraduate students of business studies do not have to specify their major as accounting or some other business area. But at the graduate level, a business student must decide a specific field as his major field among six business areas which are accounting, marketing, production, personnel, finance and international business. Thus students who major in accounting can only appear at the graduate level, not at the undergraduate level.

The department of accountancy was first established at the Sogang University in 1976. The installation of an accounting department in Korea is evaluated as important as the establishment of the college of accountancy in the U.S. As a result, the accounting department can be segregated from the department of business administration and accounting can develop beyond the boundaries of business studies. As of March, 1980, departments of accountancy had appeared at 54 universities and colleges with governmental approval. Such a rapid increase in number of accounting departments was due to social needs for business studies and accounting, and efforts of university officials. Even the government considers the establishment of a special college for taxation in 1981.

There are certain problems and criticism concerning the establishment of accounting departments. Many students prefer the department of business administration to the department of accounting. Thus major universities such as Seoul National University, Yonsei University and Korea University are reluctant to install the accounting department.

Establishment of accounting departments pose problems and criticism. First, it is too premature to establish such a specialized department at the undergraduate level at universities in Korea. It is argued that students should not specialize in a single field like accounting and should get the broad knowledge of business studies. Second, students with accounting majors find it hard to locate jobs. Their jobs are restricted to mechanical accounting, and they frequently are not allowed to have broad management jobs. Third, the social status of accountants is fairly low at the present time. Thus, students tend to be businessmen, government officials, or persons with more highly respected jobs rather than accountants. Fourth, there are many problems in present accounting education. Those problems are also conceived as barriers for the development of accounting departments. Problems are scarcity of accounting teachers, not-well-developed accounting curriculum, and scarcity of quality accounting books. Without such groundwork for accounting education, it appears too early to discuss the installation of accounting departments at the undergraduate level. Fifth, from the logic that accounting students should pass the CPA examination as law students must pass the bar examination, most of accounting students should have CPA titles upon graduation. But because of difficulties in passing the CPA examination, only a few students (as of now) will pass the examination. Therefore, grumbles will be growing among students and students will shun application to the accounting departments.

Korean accounting is greatly influenced by Japanese and American accounting. As Japanese accounting was influenced by German accounting, particularly in the past, it can be said that Korean accounting was also influenced by German accounting to some extent. The Japanese have influenced Korea in various aspects after the Korea-Japan annexation. The Japanese ruled Korea for 36 years. Those years were the critical times for Korea, because during that time Korea was on the verge of approaching Western countries and was beginning to import a new culture from foreign countries. Accounting was one area that was influenced by the Japanese during that time. From that time Koreans tended to accept the Japanese social system easily, with slight modifications. This tendency is supported on the ground that Korea has not yet developed as Japan, and Koreans have a similar cultural background to the Japanese. As a result, many Korean laws, commercial codes and accounting principles were formulated in reference to the Japanese system. Thus, important laws, principles and regulations like *Business Accounting Principles, Accounting Principles for Listed Companies*, income tax laws, etc., were formulated in this way.

However, there are some arguments that Koreans ought to import social or accounting systems directly from the more developed U.S. or U.K., not indirectly through Japan. There are also some outcries that Koreans should develop their own social or accounting systems for unique accounting situations.

The influence of U.S. accounting on Korean accounting education is gradually greater at this time. There are some reasons for this trend. First, Korea has maintained friendly relations with the U.S. after World War II. but with Japan there is always a distant relationship. Korea is closely related to the U.S. politically, economically and socially. Second, as mentioned previously, Koreans start to look for more developed social or accounting systems from the U.S. than Japan. Third, many students and scholars have returned to Korea after receiving an education in the U.S. They are expected to develop Korea's own accounting systems or education. Their background of American education will lead Korean accounting education to the American style.

3. Curriculum

As in other countries, the bachelor of business administration or master of business administration degree programs at Korean universities are based upon a broad educational foundation combined with courses in business and economics.

A total of not less than 140 credits is required for the BBA degree in Korea, an average semester course load of 17.5 credits. In principle, higher learning institutions are free to choose their own curriculum under above-credit limit. However, the curricula of Korean universities are similarly formulated.

At Seoul National University, which is the leading university in Korea, the subjects are classified into three main categories: (1) general education, (2) specialization (major), and (3) general electives. The course requirement for the BBA degree at Seoul National University can be divided as follows:

42 credits must be in general education subjects, as prebusiness courses

63 credits must be in specialization (major) subjects. Included are 33 compulsory core courses of business

35 credits may be in or outside business and economics area

---

140 credits

The general education subjects are prebusiness courses for business students. Students are required to take 42 credits from these subjects. The general education subjects are roughly three kinds. First, some subjects such as National Ethics, Korean History, Physical Education, and Military Drill are specially designated as compulsory by government regulation. Second, there are the so-called tool subjects, such as language and statistics. And third, there are introductory courses of major disciplines, such as Introduction to Political Science, Principles of Economics, Introduction to Logic, and Introduction to Philosophy, etc.

The specialization subjects refer to those which are offered by each department. Students are required to earn at least 63 credit points out of the listed specialization subjects. Some of the specialization subjects are designated compulsory. In the department of business administration, eleven subjects are compulsory. They are Principles of Economics, Principles of Management, Principles of Accounting (introductory), Business Statistics, Financial Accounting, Quantitative Analysis, Organizational Behavior, Financial Management, Production Management, Marketing Management and Personnel Management.

Those subjects which do not fall into any of the above categorized as the general electives. Elective courses in accounting for all business students are financial accounting, management accounting, cost accounting, intermediate accounting, auditing, accounting theory, tax accounting and financial analysis. Those accounting subjects such as advanced accounting, accounting systems, accounting information systems, accounting history, government accounting, and social or macro accounting are rarely included in the accounting curriculum.

At most Korean universities, graduate students are required to take 24 or more credits to earn a master's degree. Particularly at Seoul National University, graduate students must take 30 credits at least to fulfill the master's requirement.

There are some variations in master's degree requirements at Seoul National University. Students with undergraduate background in business can earn the degree by the fulfillment of 30 credits and four semesters' stay. But nighttime (part-time) students of nonbusiness background should spend five semesters in school by limiting total credits to be taken in one semester. This differentiation is designed not only to give part-time students the alleviation of study load per semester but to impose heavier and more rigorous burden on nighttime students during the total study period.

The master's degree program begins with a sequence of fundamental management courses. A student may major in accounting if he or she has, at the beginning of the second year or at the start of any semester thereafter, completed the following core courses: principles of economics, business statistics, principles of accounting, financial accounting, personnel management, marketing management, production management, financial management, quantitative analysis, and organizational behavior. The compulsory courses for accounting majors are: management accounting, cost accounting, auditing, tax accounting, and a seminar in accounting. Elective courses are: accounting theory, accounting information systems, social accounting, and accounting history.

To get a degree, an accounting major must pass a comprehensive examination in business and write a thesis on accounting.

There are many problems in the Korean accounting curriculum at undergraduate level as well as at graduate level.

First, accounting curricula are not yet fully developed. Especially graduate and advanced courses are not well developed. Curricula should be developed on the basis of detailed research and extensive discussions. There were no such efforts to improve the accounting curriculum.

Second, there are not many differences between undergraduate and graduate programs. As seen before, many undergraduate subjects of accounting were repeated at the graduate level. The graduate subjects of accounting are not much different in scope and content from undergraduate subjects.

Third, some advanced knowledge of accounting is not introduced or taught in the class. For instance, important accounting courses such as advanced accounting, management accounting, governmental accounting, accounting for nonprofit organizations, national income accounting, etc., are areas that must be studied and taught at least at the graduate level. No Korean book has ever been published on these subjects. In Korea, management accounting is well behind financial accounting. This is because the financial reporting was emphasized. The function of accounting was only considered as measuring and reporting of financial data, not including the use of accounting data for managerial decisions. The financial statement was primarily regarded as useful for tax reporting via financial reporting. Therefore, accounting schools were late in incorporating management accounting in their curricula.

Fourth, the doctoral program is not yet well formulated. This problem arose partly because there are few Ph.D. candidates in accounting in Korea and partly because there are few qualified accounting professors in Korea. It is anticipated that the problem will be resolved with the increasing demand on accounting teachers and the return of foreign educated Ph.D. students.

Fifth, there are a host of problems in the development of accounting education in Korea. Curricula are not well developed; there are a few high-level textbooks; there are shortages of capable professors; and case studies are not developed. Even though this condition is far better than other developing countries, the level of accounting and accounting education is far behind the U.S. or U.K.

Sixth, curricula for accounting major students of the newly established departments of accountancy are not yet well developed. There are not many differences of curriculum between students of the accounting major and the business major. Again this problem arose due to the shortage of professors and textbooks, and the delay of advanced knowledge of accounting. Therefore, there are not many unique characteristics in the departments of accountancy.

4. Accounting Teachers

There are about 120 accounting teachers at Korean universities and colleges. All of them are members of the Korean Accounting Association, which is the only organization of university and college instructors in accounting.

The accounting teachers can be divided into four categories by rank:

(1) *Full-time instructor:* qualification is the master's degree from a recognized academic institution in Korea or another country.

(2) *Assistant professor:* qualification is the doctoral degree from recognized academic institution in Korea or other country or the instructor with three years of teaching experience and writing.

(3) *Associate professor:* qualification is the same as for instructor above, plus four years of teaching experience and writing.

The doctoral degree is a requirement for a permanent teaching position in all universities in Korea. However, most of the universities have a requirement of at least a master's degree in business administration (specializing in accounting) to teach accounting.

The salary levels of accounting teachers are moderate considering the wages and salaries in Korea. In Korea, salary levels of university and college professors are the same, at the same rank with the same years of service, regardless of specialized (major) fields. Thus, the salary of an assistant professor of accounting is the same as the salary of an assistant professor of chemistry with the same years of teaching experience. However, there are some variations of salary level between national university professors and private university professors.

The approximate annual salary levels of Korean accounting professors are: professor, $12,000; associate professor, $10,800; assistant professor, $9,600; and full-time instructor, $7,400.

As in other countries, it is hard to recruit accounting teachers in Korea. Students favor going into business circles or government rather than being professors. Few graduate students can get the Ph.D. in accounting in Korea. Foreign (particularly U.S.) educated students, although few in number, seldom return to Korea. Another reason for difficulties in recruitment arises from the fact that it is difficult to get the Ph.D. accounting in the U.S.

Considering the difficulties of recruiting accounting teachers in Korea, it is necessary to create support for training programs of accounting education development. A few years ago such a program was suggested by the study group of the World Bank (IBRD). With this suggestion the Korean government agreed with the World Bank to initiate a special management education program. The loan agreement was signed in 1979 and the loan program started in 1980.

The program is divided into two education areas. The first is the management teachers development program, by which candidates of accounting teachers are selected among Korean educated master's degree holders and then sent to the U.S. for Ph.D. study. The second is the management teachers retraining program, by which selected teachers are sent to U.S. universities as visiting scholars or researchers for retraining. With the completion of this program, it is expected that new accounting Ph.D.'s will return to Korea in the near future and most of the present accounting teachers will be retrained and acquire higher levels of accounting knowledge from more developed U.S. universities.

Presently a majority of Korean accounting teachers are holders of the master's degree. Moreover, most of these degrees were obtained from Korean universities. However, this situation improved in comparison with the past, when most of the accounting teachers held bachelor's degrees from Japanese or Korean universities. They were in fact bookkeeping teachers and they were only capable of teaching elementary accounting. They did not receive sufficient education because they were of the generation of Japanese rule and Korean war. The situation has changed since the Korean war. With better education for students, the number of holders of the master's degree in accounting or business administration has increased. There were considerable demands on the higher level of degrees in accounting. But unlike other fields, there are very few accounting Ph.D.'s in Korea. Therefore, each accounting department of Korean universities must be satisfied with master's degree holders as accounting teachers for the time being. The number of Ph.D. professors will increase in the future as each university demands a higher degree level for the qualification of accounting teachers.

5. Textbooks and Teaching Materials

The textbook is another problem area in Korean accounting education. One of the critical accounting education problems is the paucity of accounting textbooks in quality as well as in quantity. Because the textbook is a prerequisite for the development of curriculum and better teaching, the textbook problem must be solved with the problems of curriculum and teaching materials. Especially in a developing country like Korea, the development of textbook and teaching materials is urgently needed. But it will take some time to have quality books and well written teaching materials.

In the past, most Korean accounting books were written only within the boundaries of bookkeeping. Most books deal with accounting problems and solutions, concentrating on financial accounting areas of elementary and intermediate level, and elementary cost accounting areas. The advanced level of accounting, management and other specialized accounting areas have not been covered. However, with the economic development and the growth of the accounting profession, both Korean business society and the accounting profession need more advanced and specialized knowledge of accounting. Also at most Korean universities, courses of management accounting, advanced accounting and some other specialized subjects of accounting have appeared. To meet these demands, there must be some efforts to develop those textbooks and teaching materials.

There is some need to develop case studies in Korea. So far, not many cases have appeared. There are not many classes which use case study as a method of instruction. Korean cases must be written by Korean professors. Because Western cases are made to adapt to Western environment, it would be inadequate to use them without modification in Korean classes.

The quality of accounting books in Korea is still considered low. Most of the books published previously were just the translation of Japanese or American textbooks; thus there was a problem of originality. This situation may be considered a first phase of textbook development in a developing country. However, in recent years several books, but not many, are published with some originality of Korean authors.

It seems desirable that Korean accounting books, as in other developing countries, should be written on an original basis by referring to Western textbooks. In the process, the concepts, principles and methods of Western countries should be adjusted to the Korean business environment or may be accepted without modification if they can be applied without resistance. The blind importing of Western concepts and theories may cause problems in real situations or may be inapplicable.

Since there are not many good accounting books in Korea, some American books are used. For example, Hendriksen's *Accounting Theory*, Horngren's *Introduction to Management Accounting and Cost Accounting*, and Kieso & Weygandt's *Intermediate Accounting* are popular among students. But there are not many students who can purchase those English written books because of the expense and unavailability due to the long shipping time. It would be beneficial to developing countries if some best-selling accounting books were printed in paperback and distributed to those countries. As the demand on those books is sizeable in Korea, it would be profitable for the publishers.

A list of Korean authored accounting textbooks is shown in Exhibit 3.

EXHIBIT 3

Korean-authored Accounting Textbooks

Principles of Accounting, Jhong - Ho Lee, Yong - Joon Lee, Chin - Deok So

Financial Accounting, Soo - Young Chung, Hae - Dong Lee, Jin - Sup Lim, Gui - Hyun Yang

Cost Accounting, Yong - Joon Lee, Se - Hwan Yoo, Jae - Suk Shim

Auditing, Hyung - Joon Park, Chin - Deok So & Ke - Sup Yoon, Ja Song and Chong - Am Chung

Accounting Theory, Sang - Oh Nam, Sung - Ha Cho, Ik - Soon Cho, Jhong - Ho Lee

Tax Accounting, Chan - Soo Shin, Ssang - Jong Song

Intermediate Accounting, Sang - Moon Choi

On the graduate level, there is a severe deficiency of textbooks and course materials. In fact, no books have ever been published for graduate students. As mentioned earlier, there has not been much difference between undergraduate and graduate levels of accounting education. Thus accounting books for undergraduate students are frequently used for graduate students. Such a repetition of undergraduate education on the graduate level has been a source for grumbling by students. Some professors use English written textbooks or reference materials which are limited in Korea in the class. Therefore, the development of textbooks and course materials for graduate students is greatly needed.

6. Accounting Research and Korean Accounting Association

Previously, accounting research in general was not emphasized in Korea; it was virtually nonexistent. There was no need for research; the reasons are as follow. First, in the past, Korean economy and the business environment were not as sophisticated as now. Thus it was not necessary to do research or investigate the real world of business. Second, the past accounting principles were formulated simply by referring to Japanese accounting rules. Therefore, accounting rules of those times could be formulated without the help of accounting research. Third, the securities market was not as fully developed as it is now, and accounting information was not considered important to the investors and other financial statement users. However, those situations have changed. Korea's economy is growing fast and the business environment becomes more and more sophisticated and complex. Under these different situations, accounting principles need to be formulated on the basis of accounting research. Investors and other financial statement users are gradually demanding more accounting information. Thus there appears the pressing need for accounting research.

The topics of accounting research should relate to current accounting problems in Korea focusing on the pecularities of Korean accounting. The probable topics of accounting research could be illustrated as follows:

(1) *Research relating to international accounting area:*
Treatment of foreign exchange gains and losses
Accounting for multinational enterprises
Comparative accounting

(2) *Research relating to the capital market*

Access to foreign capital market
Accounting issues in the Korean securities market
(3) *Research relating to peculiar accounting treatment*
Asset revaluation
(4) *Research relating to auditors' opinions and other auditing problems*
(5) *Research relating to accounting principles*
Validity of income tax allocation in Korea
Accounting for group companies: consolidation vs. combining of statements

Until now, most of Korea's accounting research was conducted on a descriptive or analytical basis, and not on a quantitative, mathematical or computer-based basis. As the trend of accounting research moves to this direction, the future accounting research should be conducted in such a way.

Accounting research in Korea is usually conducted on an individual basis. There is no particular group or organization of accounting research in Korea. For example, the Accounting Research Institute of Sogang University is essentially a teaching institution. The sources of research funds are government, private foundations and corporations. The government is encouraging provision of research funds to university professors.

There are two national journals for accounting research in Korea. One is the *Korean Accounting Review* which is the publication of the Korean Accounting Association. The other is *Accounting,* which is the publication of KICPA. As the name implies, *Korean Accounting Review* is similar to the *Accounting Review of AAA* and *Accounting* is similar to the *Journal of Accountancy* of AICPA. Both journals are published annually. In addition, professors can publish articles in their university's journals. In Korea, most universities have their own journals.

The Korean Accounting Association (KAA) is the organization of university and college professors in Korea. It was organized in 1973. The members to date number 120. The purposes of KAA are (1) to encourage and support research activities in accounting, (2) to hold an annual meeting and special meetings for presentation of articles and discussions, (3) to publish an accounting journal, research studies and monographs, (4) to exchange and supply research data between members, and (5) to cooperate with other national or international organizations. The activities of KAA so far are not satisfactory, but there is a great expectation from academicians, accountants, and businessmen, as well as government officials. There is no fraternity organization like Beta Alpha Psi in Korea.

PART C

EVALUATIVE COMMENTS

Although many problems of accounting and accounting education of Korea are presented here. Korea seems to be in the upper bracket of Third World countries in the areas of financial reporting and accounting education. Korea can be said to be one of the foremost advanced countries among developing countries from the standpoint of accounting and accounting education. Korea is striving for improvements in these areas and the future of Korean accounting and accounting education looks brighter. With the help of continued efforts of the Korean government (MOF), KSEC, KICPA and KAA, Korea will achieve the better state of accounting in the near future. As stated earlier, Korea was once under the influence of Japanese accounting rules. Korea now proceeds to the world of better and more advanced accounting by developing its own framework of accounting, adaptable to Korean business environments, and by importing recent accounting directly from Western countries.

In summary, this paper presents problems and improvements in accounting.

The problems and improvements in accounting and accounting education in Korea are as follow:

- *Accounting*

   (1) The accounting principles and practices should be upgraded to international standards or U.S. standards.

   (2) The government should delegate some regulatory authority powers to KSEC or independent private organization or KICPA. The orientation of public sector regulation should gradually move to the private sector. Consequently, it is desirable that KSEC and KICPA must play a more active role in accounting circles.

   (3) Problem areas of present accounting should be solved and improved. Tax-oriented accounting and disregard of management accounting (accounting for managerial decision) are examples.

   (4) Disclosure of financial information and reporting practices should be improved.

   (5) The improvement in CPA examination system is needed.

- *Accounting Education*

   (1) The development in accounting education must be made corresponding to the development of the economy and the change of business environment in Korea.

   (2) The education of undergraduate level and graduate level must be differentiated. Especially, graduate level education must be extended.

   (3) Establishment of departments of accountancy at the undergraduate level is premature.

   (4) Accounting areas other than financial reporting must be developed with the help of accounting education developments. Management accounting, advanced accounting and other specialized accounting areas (e.g., accounting for not-for-profit organizations, income tax allocation) are examples of these areas.

   (5) The present curriculum must be improved both at the undergraduate and

graduate levels.

(6) The quality and quantity of accounting teachers should be improved. An education plan for fostering new accounting teachers among master's degree holders and a professor retraining program will be beneficial.

(7) The textbooks and teaching materials should be improved and developed. Case studies of Korean business firms must be collected and developed.

(8) Accounting research must be actively conducted in the area of unique Korean accounting situations.

There is some need for creating an international organization of accounting academicians. As we know, there are a number of international organizations for CPAs, but none exists for accounting teachers. It is desirable to establish an international accounting association or some regional association of accounting teachers, such as the Southeast Asian Accounting Association. By the creation of these types of organizations, the accounting education in developing countries will be greatly improved. For instance, the exchange of accounting data and accounting research results, joint accounting research, and discussion of accounting and education problems between countries will be possible. The International Accounting Section of AAA will be helpful in this respect. But this organization seems to have some limitations.

BIBLIOGRAPHY

Hapdong News Agency, *Korea Annual 1979*, Seoul, Korea, 1979.

Korean Institute of Certified Public Accountants, *Bulletin*, 1976.

Korea Trade Promotion Corporation, *Korea in Brief*, 1979.

Peat, Marwick, Mitchell & Co. of Korea, *Accounting in Korea*, 1979.

Samuel S.O. Lee, "Songdo (Kaesung) Bookkeeping System," Proceedings of the Academy of International Business Asia-Pacific Dimensions of International Business, University of Hawaii, Dec., 1979, pp. 184-192.

Seoul National University, *Curricula for Undergraduate Courses, Seoul National University*, Seoul National University Press, 1976.

Byung-Wan Sun, "A Study on the Basic Direction of Accounting Education in Korea and Curricular Formulation," Chun-Buk National University, 1978.

CHAPTER XXI

ACCOUNTING EDUCATION IN MALAYSIA

by
C. L. Mitchell*

1. Background

1.1 Political/Social Factors

Malaysia is populated by Malays, Chinese and Indians. Malays constitute 53 percent of the population, Chinese 36 percent and Indians 11 percent. The majority of the Malays live in rural areas whereas most of the other two races live in urban areas. Of the total population of twelve million, 70 percent live in rural areas.

When Malaysia achieved independence in 1957 a social contract was made between representatives of the two major races in the country. This contract in part was imbedded into the constitution, but on the whole was not formally recognized. But in conformity with the British tradition, it became part of the "unwritten constitution."

It was agreed that the people of Malay descent would occupy a special place and have special privileges in the political, military, law enforcement and government administrative sectors of the economy. On the other hand it was accepted that the people of Chinese descent would be more dominant in the business, professional, educational and financial sectors. This unwritten agreement was a continuation of the status quo which had evolved from the traditional urban/rural positions of the two races, their inherent characteristics and their views on the importance of education in their culture.

It was constitutionally accepted that in the long run Bahasa Malaysia would be the common language of the nation. However, in the short run it was recognized that English would continue to be the dominant language of business, the professions, finance, and higher education due to the international interdependencies in these areas and the rural origins of the Malay language.

During the 20 years since independence two general changes have occurred. The Malays have aggressively pursued their spheres of influence; the Chinese have been continuously required to share with the Malays the spheres in which they were previously dominant. Additionally the rate of introduction of Bahasa Malaysia as the language of the nation, and in particular in education, has been accelerated.

*C. L. Mitchell is Professor of Accounting at the University of British Columbia (Canada). For several years, he was CIDA professor at the University of Malaysia.

1.2 Economic Background

The Federated Malay States were developed under colonial rule as a source of rubber and tin for the Western world. These two industries, based on the natural resources of the country, were the major focus of economic activity and foreign exchange earnings for many years. Singapore was established and prospered as a centre of the entrepot trade. Since independence, Malaysia has attempted to diversify its economy to provide economic stability, and employment for its growing population. This diversification has taken a variety of forms but on balance has been extremely successful. The present economy is largely based on rubber, tin and palm oil with a lesser degree of reliance on forest products and secondary manufacturing. Agriculture is the largest sector of the Malaysian economy in the country and it is more or less self-sufficient in food.

Malaysia has a history of highly developed international trade institutions and strong social, government and commercial systems.

1.3 Relevance of the Economic Background to Accounting

A successful economic diversification policy and increased government information requirements resulting from an active participation policy has led to a dramatic increase in the demand for accountants from government, public practice, and private industry. One measure of this demand is that the shortage of accountants exceeds that of doctors. Evidence of this fact is the significantly higher incomes earned by public accountants over those earned by the traditional king of the Western world's professions—the doctors.

At the same time as the demand for accountants has increased, little effective action has been taken to increase the supply. And the minimum effort that has been made has been frustrated in part by the Bahasa Malaysia language policy, professional pride, and government pressure to introduce Malays into the professions.

2. Accounting Development

A reliable and comprehensive evaluation of accounting systems in Malaysia is beyond the scope of the resources available to this study. Two primary sources have been referred to for this purpose—the Enthoven Study (1975) and the Mitchell Study (1974). These sources have been complemented by a series of individual discussions with accountants with Malaysian experience.

Enterprise and government accounting in Malaysia is still dominated by the practices introduced by the British. It has been adapted since independence but primarily to conform to advances in Australian, Canadian and British practice, influenced substantially by nationals of those countries seconded under foreign aid projects. National income accounting conforms to the theory of the United Nations but the shortage of skilled accountants has retarded its implementation.

Auditing practice, while still based on the British model is adapting to the multinational practices of large auditing firms based primarily in the United States. The absence of legal requirements on auditing procedures permits a rapid translation of these practices. The absence of adequate legal or professional disclosure standards has resulted in many unacceptable disclosure practices.

Following the tradition of the United Kingdom Chartered Accountant, public accountants in Malaysia offer a product line considerably broader than that typically offered in North America by public accountants. Accountants frequently render service as trustees, financial advisors acting on boards of directors, and management advisors, as well as auditors.

Due to the recent development of secondary industry, the absence of an adequate supply of skilled accountants and managers, and the dominance of multinational companies in secondary industries, developments in internal accounting systems have been primarily limited to those systems developed years ago for the rubber and tin industries and those systems transferred from head offices of multinational corporations, occasionally adapted to the local environment.

Government accounting in Malaysia is severely handicapped by lack of leadership and qualified accountants. No solution appears possible to this problem until government is prepared to increase the status and salaries of government accountants to a level approaching that provided in private practice and industry.

There are two professional accounting bodies in Malaysia. They are the Malaysian Association of Accounting (MIA) and the Malaysian Association of Certified Public Accountants (MACPA). Membership figures for the year ending December 31, 1979, are shown in Table 1.

TABLE 1

	Qualified Members	Student Membership
Malaysian Institute of Accountants (MIA)	2,000	-
Malaysian Association of Certified Public Accountants (MACPA)	1,206	1,008

Plans are being formulated to substitute for these two bodies an Institute of Chartered Accountants or another named body.

The MIA is a statutory body set up by the government to regulate the accounting profession. Except for a registration function it is largely dormant. It carries out no examining function and admission is entirely by qualification through other institutions.

The MACPA is a privately registered society and includes both public practitioners and non-practitioners. It carries out an examining function, but, most members have obtained admission through foreign qualifications. Only 120 have qualified through writing local examinations. The association provides no formal means of accounting tuition but requires a minimum of three years of approved experience (plus a further year after qualification for those wishing to practice). Tuition for those qualifying through foreign examinations, and for many seeking direct qualification, is through foreign correspondence schools. A university degree is not required and recruitment is mainly from non-university students.

3. The Present State of Accounting Education

The accounting instructional staff in Malaysia is handicapped by the inability of government and educational institutions to recognize the market price of qualified accountants. Several foreign assistant programs have been implemented to assist the formation of educational and training programs for accountants, but their continuing operation has been frequently thwarted by the loss of qualified instructors from the educational to the private sectors. A current educational inventory of institutions participating in accounting education follows.

3.1   Qualification of Accounting Instructors

Malaysian institutions with the number of instructors and the qualifications of the full-time accounting faculty are shown in Table 2.

TABLE 2

Institution	Total No. of Instructors	Instructors hold Bachelor's	Master's	Ph.D.	Professional Accounting Qualification
Univ. of Malaya	11	11	8	-	8
Univ. of Kebangsaan	5	5	4	-	
MARA Inst. of Technology	33	20	2	-	24
Tunku Abdul Rahman College	3	-	-	-	3

Many of the accounting instructors have recently completed professional development programs, some of which are supported by foreign government aid. Three professors from the University of Malaya, three from the University of Kebangsaan, and one from Tunku Abdul Rahman College have completed foreign government sponsored programs. In addition, two faculty members from the MARA Institute of Technology have completed professional development programs for accounting instructors.

3.2   Structure of Accounting Programs and Curriculum

The number and types of accounting programs in Malaysia are shown in Table 3.

TABLE 3

Institution	Tenure	Qualification Awarded
Univ. of Malaya	4 years full time	Bachelor of Accounting
	3 years full time plus	B.Econ. plus
	2 years part-time	Diploma
Univ. Kebangsaan	4 years full time	B.Econ. (Accounting Honours)
	3 years full time	B.Econ. (General degree with no major)
MARA Inst. of Technology	3 years full time	Diploma in Accounting
	4 years full time	Foreign professional qualifications ACCA, ICMA
Tunku Abdul Rahman College	3 years full time	Diploma in Commerce with majors in Accounting, Business Management or Cost Management Accounting
	3 years full time	Foreign professional qualifications ACA, ICSA and ICMA

All of the institutions of higher learning (see Table 2) require 13 years of schooling prior to admission. The number of hours of lectures, tutorials, labs and outside study per week required in each institution varies. The Universities of Malaya and Kebangsaan use lectures and tutorials, whereas the MARA Institure and Tunku Abdul Rahman College use lectures and labs. The academic year at the two universities consists of 30 weeks and at the other institutions 39 weeks.

The coverage of accounting topics in the accounting programs is shown in Exhibit 1. Additional accounting topics are included in the business programs to the extent shown in Table 4.

TABLE 4

Required	Univ. of Malaya	Univ. of Kebangsaan	M.I.T.	TAR College
Introductory and Financial Accounting	1 course	1 course	3 courses	1 course
Management Accounting	1 course	1 course	2 courses	1 course
Optional				
Management Accounting	1 course) optional			
Financial Accounting	-			

237

EXHIBIT 1

Coverage of Accounting Topics and Accounting Programmes

Accounting	Malaya Bachelor of Accounting (percent)		Univ. of Kebangsaan (4-yr full-time) Bachelor's program) (percent)		M.I.T. 3-year Diploma in Accountancy (percent)		TAR College Diploma in Commerce (A/C) (percent)	
Introductory and Financial	18.9	(7)	16.2	(6)	17.6	(6)	13.6	(3)
Management Accounting	8.1	(3)	5.4	(2)	11.9	(4)	13.6	(3)
Theory	5.4	(2)	2.7	(1)	2.9	(1)	-	-
Systems and Computers	5.4	(2)	5.4	(2)	5.9	(2)	4.6	(1)
Auditing	8.1	(3)	5.4	(2)	5.9	(2)	9.1	(2)
Taxation	8.1	(3)	5.4	(2)	5.9	(2)	9.1	(2)
Law	5.4	(2)	5.4	(2)	8.8	(3)	13.6	(3)
Business Administration	8.1	(3)	13.5	(5)	8.8	(3)	13.6	(3)
Economics	19.0	(7)	27.1	(10)	5.9	(2)	4.6	(1)
Quantitative Methods	5.4	(2)	5.4	(2)	8.8	(3)	9.1	(2)
Others	8.1	(3)	8.1	(3)	17.6	(6)	9.1	(2)
	100.0	(37)	100.0	(37)	100.0	(34)	100.0	(22)

Number of courses in parentheses.

There are no correspondence courses available but there are a number of subscribers to overseas courses (mainly English).

3.3 Textbooks

There are no locally authored textbooks in accounting at the university level in Malaysia. The government has adopted a translation program to stimulate the translation of foreign texts into Bahasa Malaysia but to date only one accounting text has been translated but is still not available for students. No publisher is willing to print it, primarily due to the size of the market and absence of copyright laws. A Canadian project team has prepared extensive English mimeograph teaching notes and case study materials for use in the University of Malaya. This material reflects current North American, Australian and British practice adapted to the local environment. As a consequence of the above, the major formal texts used are those prepared in England or the United States. They fail to reflect the unique features of the Malaysian environment.

3.4 Accounting Research

Accounting research and development in Malaysia is virtually non-existent. This is caused by the presence of apathy on the part of the accounting profession, university, and the government and by the high level of demand for the limited resources and talents of qualified and interested accountants. At this time the limited resources should be allocated to transmitting the present knowledge rather than creating new knowledge. It is doubtful if substantial changes from this priority can be made for several years.

4. Comments

To implement language and racial policies and to control student revolutionary movement, the national government is intimately involved in all levels of education. The resultant heavy hand of bureaucracy has a deleterious impact on morale and motivation within educational institutions.

Fundamental to the problems of accounting in Malaysia are the racial and language policies of government. This situation is likely to continue at least for a lengthy transitional period. The racial policies have biased the enrollment in educational institutions to favor Malays. Generally, the academic performance of the Malays is inferior to that of other ethnic groups. As a consequence, the standards of educational institutions are declining. The language policies have led to the imposition of Bahasa Malaysia (a language with limited technical vocabulary) as the medium of instruction. The majority of teachers and many students are not qualified in this language and as a consequence the quality of the instruction and the standards of accomplishment can be expected to deteriorate.

REFERENCES

Adolf J.H. Enthoven, *An Evaluation of Accountancy Systems, Developments and Requirements in Asia*, Ford Foundation, 1975.

C.L. Mitchell, *Corporate Financial Reporting in Malaysia*, Kuala Lumpur Stock Exchange Berhad, 1974.

APPENDIX

The Malaysian Association of Certified Public Accountants (MACPA) was formed in 1958. The first members of the association were members of the Association of Chartered and Incorporated Accountants in Malaya which was later dissolved in favor of the MACPA and Members of the Malayan Branch of the Association of Certified and Corporate Accountants. The initial membership of the association was about twenty. It has now grown to more than one thousand.

With the acceleration of economic development in Malaysia, the MACPA has not been able to train sufficient students to qualify as accountants by its exclusive method of articleship to members in practice. The MACPA has initiated a development scheme which preserves its original objectives but broadens the base for training students to qualify as accountants without compromising its emphasis on the value of practical experience. The development scheme provides for three streams of students, namely streams one, two and three.

The three streams are:

Stream 1: Student who has signed a training contract with a member of the association in practice.

Stream 2: Student who has signed a training contract with a member of the association not in practice, but in the employment of commerce, industries, government or semi-government organizations.

Stream 3: Student in full-time or part-time studies and who is following an approved course of study at an institution of higher learning or correspondence college. To date, the only courses approved by council in the institutions of higher learning for Stream 3 registration are the Diploma in Accounting and the Bachelor of Accounting of the University of Malaya and the CPA course offered by MARA Institute of Technology.

The education of the student is twofold. The association stresses an education "on the job" acquisition of academic knowledge. There are correspondence schools which provide postal tuition and good books which cover the subjects required by the syllabus of the association.

The subjects under the respective parts of the CPA examination are as follows:

Foundation Examination
Financial Accounting I
Introductory Auditing and Data Processing
Economics and Business Organization
Law I

Professional Examination I
Financial Accounting II
Management Accounting I
Statistics and Quantitative Methods
Law II
Taxation I

Professional Examination II
Financial Accounting III
Management Accounting II
Financial Management
Auditing and Investigations
Taxation II

After the successful completion of the association's examinations and the training contract period, a student under stream 1 or 2 may apply for admission to membership of the association. A stream 3 student after the completion of the association's examinations would be required to further obtain a three-year period of approved practical experience as a registered trainee under the supervision of a CPA member before being eligible for admission to membership of the association.

CHAPTER XXII

ACCOUNTING EDUCATION IN PAKISTAN

by

A.M. Ansari and A. Aziz*

1. Country Background

Pakistan emerged as a sovereign state in the Indian subcontinent on August 14, 1947. The basic reason for the creation of this new country was the two-nation theory under which Muslims wanted an independent country including the areas in which they were in the majority. The birth of the country was accompanied by severe social, economic and political problems. A massive exchange of population took place between the two countries—the Muslims migrating from India to Pakistan, and the Hindus from Pakistan to India. This led to a sharp increase in the population of the area forming Pakistan coupled with a vacuum in the managerial, professional and technical fields. Hindus who dominated in activities such as manufacturing, trading, banking and government service were lost to India in exchange for a predominantly agricultural Muslim immigration from that country. The political instability which the new nation inherited by virtue of its divided geography eventually led to the dismemberment of the country, and the eastern wing of the country seceded in 1971 to become Bangla Desh.

The economy of the country is basically agrarian, with 70 percent of its population living in villages. This has been responsible for the high priority given to the agricultural sector by the present as well as all the past governments of the country. Along with agricultural development, other sectors of economy have seen sizable comparative growth. Whereas the growth in agriculture has been about 100 percent since Pakistan came into being, the output of manufacturing and mining sectors has increased by 400 percent and 800 percent respectively over the same period. In similar fashion the contribution to GNP of sectors such as transportation and communication, construction, services and trade have been on the increase. In spite of all this growth, Pakistan is still an underdeveloped poor country. Its annual per capita income of about U.S. $200 is one of the lowest in the world.

In 1972, the Pakistan People's Party (PPP) took drastic economic measures and promulgated an Economic Reforms Order. This gave the government control over the management of thirty-two basic industries. The owner managers were replaced by professional managers. In fact, the Board of Industrial Management** was constituted to reorganize these nationalized industries. Again,

*A.M. Ansari is Executive Director of the Institute of Cost and Management Accountants of Pakistan; A. Aziz is associated with the University of Karachi.

**This board was dissolved by the current martial law regime two years ago. The government has also denationalized some of the industries to reverse the trend of dwindling output under the management of government officials. However, the president, General Zia-Ul-Hag declared that this government does not contemplate denationalizing all the taken-over industries.

in September 1973, vegetable ghee units, with the exception of those having foreign participation, were nationalized, and their management entrusted to the provincial government through separate boards of management. In 1974 came the Banks Nationalization Ordinance, under which Pakistani commercial banks were nationalized. The Pakistan Banking Council was established to formulate policy guidelines, lay down performance criteria, coordinate the banks' activities, and evaluate their performance. The immediate task given to the council was to provide a branch bank for every town or village having a population of 5,000 or more.

Other reforms carried out by the previous government included nationalization of insurance business, maritime shipping, and the marketing of petroleum products. Administrative and law reforms were also introduced. The former broke the monopoly of civil servants for senior appointments in the Federal Secretariat; even the senior-most posts can now be held by professionals such as economists, accountants, lawyers, educationists, etc. Land reforms were enacted to reduce the landholdings of big landlords, and the land surrendered by virtue of these reforms was given over to landless tenants without charge. Additionally, health reforms announced in March, 1972, have brought better medical facilities closer to the masses through the construction of more hospitals and dispensaries. The labour reforms introduced by the People's Party government gave labourers better wages and greater participation in profits and management. The education reforms have resulted in more uniformity in curricular system of education, examination and textbooks. Although it is difficult to evaluate the effect of these reforms at present, most of them have achieved their short-run objectives.

The present government, which took over in April 1977, has tried to consolidate the reforms introduced by the previous government and efforts are also being made to bring improvements in the economic and social policies and programs wherever such improvements are possible and desirable.

2. Accounting Institutions in Pakistan

2.1 The Accounting Profession

Prior to the independence of Pakistan, the accounting profession predominantly belonged to non-Muslims. There were less than a hundred registered accountants who were left in the country after the mass population shift settled down. In addition, there were about a dozen cost accountants who held membership in the Institute of Cost and Works Accountants of London, or of India. The major purpose served by the registered accountants was the certification of financial accounts of public companies under the Companies Act of 1913.

The Ministry of Commerce maintained a Register of Accountants and conducted examinations for registered accountants under its supervision. In 1961, an ordinance was passed to regulate the profession of accountants. Under the same ordinance, the Institute of Chartered Accountants of Pakistan was established, and the Ministry of Commerce handed over the task and responsibility of conducting examinations to this institute. The membership of this institute at present is above 700, and about one-fourth of the members are practicing as public accountants. Most of the practicing accountants limit their functions to auditing and taxation, but a few have expanded their activities into management consultancy and the designing of accounting systems. These additional services got a fillip when the nationalization of large industrial enterprises was undertaken.

The accounting profession in Pakistan has benefited in a big way from the establishment of the Pakistan Institute of Industrial Accountants, now known as the Institute of Cost and Management Accountants of Pakistan (ICMAP) in 1951. The membership of the institute is above 600 at present, with more than 4,000 students on its register. This institute, which was founded by a group of accountants under the leadership of Mr. Mohammed Shoaib, a former Finance Minister of Pakistan, was reconstituted in 1966 under the Cost and Management Accountants Act. The institute is not only doing very well in the country itself, but has also assumed the role of a semi-international body holding its examinations in African, Persian Gulf and Arabian countries. (Since last year the ICAP has also started holding examinations in these countries.) It also undertakes training of some African students at its education centre in Karachi, and arrangements are in hand whereby the institute will provide training facilities to Ugandian nationals at Kampala.

In addition to these institutes, some practicing accountants, among them a number not having membership of any local or foreign professional accounting bodies, joined hands about four years ago to establish the Institute of Certified Public Accountants of Pakistan (ICPAP). Many of the founder members of this institute occupied high posts in the governmental accounting and finance offices. This helped them get government recognition of the institute as one of the professional accounting bodies. The examinations for the institute, at present, are being conducted by the Board of Technical Education, Karachi. This examining body is recognized to hold examinations for lower level employment in various trades. For this reason, it is the joint opinion of the Institute of Chartered Accountants of Pakistan (ICAP) and the Institute of Cost and Management Accountants of Pakistan (ICMAP) that the Institute of Certified Public Accountants of Pakistan does not qualify as a professional institute and hence should not have been empowered by the government of Pakistan to award CPA status. Both the institutes (ICMAP and ICAP) have approached the government not to let the Institute of Certified Public Accountants of Pakistan (ICPAP) to confer the CPA, a worldwide recognized professional accounting qualification. The dispute is still pending, but in the meantime ICMAP and ICAP have advised their members not to seek membership of ICPAP and to withdraw from ICPAP if they have already become its members.

On the other hand, the founder members of the ICPAP feel that there is an acute shortage of qualified accountants in Pakistan, not only for employment in Middle Eastern countries but also for local consumption. In their opinion, the ICMAP and ICAP are not in a position to cope with the increasing demand for professionally qualified accountants. However, at present, the number of candidates taking ICPAP examinations is quite small—sometimes even less then ten.

This institute is still in infancy and none has qualified to become a CPA through sitting for its examinations. As such, its position as a body regulating the accounting profession does not exist. The ICAP and ICMAP are members of IFAC, CAPA and the International Accounting Standards Committee (IASC). They are cooperating in the implementation of international accounting standards in Pakistan. They also publish their magazines quarterly.

In addition to these two institutes regulating the accounting profession in the country, the government has set up the Securities & Exchange authority of Pakistan to enforce more standardized accounting patterns by industry. To help evolve better norms, concepts, and codes of conduct in the accounting profession, the authority requires that industry adheres to specific reporting procedures. All companies listed on the stock exchanges in Pakistan (about 300) have to submit half yearly and annual financial statements to the SEAP for analysis and review.

The exact number of professionally qualified accountants has never been established, but it can be stated with considerable confidence that the total does not exceed 1,800. Of these, 856 are members of the ICAP, and 618 have the membership of ICMAP. The rest are either Pakistanis holding the membership in British institutions or non-Pakistanis mainly employed by foreign companies operating in Pakistan. About 300 M.B.A.'s and M.Coms. are also working as accountants, but they are neither permitted to act as public accountants nor recognized as professional accountants.

However, all of the accountants are not at present working in Pakistan. Many of them have taken jobs in African and Mid-Eastern countries because of higher salaries; a few have even gone to Canada or U.S.A. This exodus, normally called the brain drain, coupled with nationalization of industries and progressive industrialization of the country, has caused a shortage of qualified and experienced accountants.

2.2 Local Educational Institutions

At the time of emergence of Pakistan, there existed only two commerce colleges in the area now forming Pakistan. At these institutions, B.Com. was the highest degree obtainable. Being keenly aware of this, successive governments encouraged the establishment of more and more commerce colleges and commercial institutes to meet the growing need of accountants because of rapid industrialization. Mostly this expansion in facilities for education took place in the private sector at college level and public sector at lower levels with significant concentration in the city of Karachi where a major portion of industry and commerce are located. However, all the commerce colleges were brought under the management of provincial governments in 1973 through the "nationalization of education" scheme.

The institutions offering accounting, at present, may be grouped under five heads:

(1) Those preparing for professional qualifications such as ACA/FCA, ACMA/ FCMA and CPA.

The Institute of Chartered Accountants of Pakistan (ICAP) prepares students and conducts examination for ACA/FCA qualifications, whereas the Institute of Cost and Management Accountants of Pakistan (ICMAP) prepares for the ACMA/FCMA examinations. The Institute of Certified Public Accountants of Pakistan provides the opportunity to obtain the CPA. All three institutes are headquartered at Karachi. The first two have a number of branches all over the country.

(2) Those preparing for the master's degree in Business Administration/ Commerce.

Eight universities, dispersed all over the country, offer educational programs leading to a master's degree in Business Administration and Commerce. However, both the programs, i.e., M.B.A. or M.Com., are conducted separately. A list of these universities is produced in Exhibit 1.

(3) Open University.

In addition to the universities mentioned in Exhibit 1, Pakistan has also established an open university. This is Allama Iqbal Open University, which has its headquarters in Islamabad and offers courses all over the country by correspondence. The university has so far offered undergraduate courses in accountancy and auditing. Courses in areas of finance management and cost accounting are being developed.

(4) Those preparing for B.Com.

The programs leading to a B.Com. degree are undertaken by 30 colleges affiliated with various universities. About 50 percent of these colleges are located in Karachi, with the rest dispersed all over the country. A list of these colleges is provided in Exhibit 2. The number of colleges offering commerce courses is increasing each year.

(5) Those preparing for certificates or diploma courses.

These programs are conducted by schools known as commercial institutes. Their objective is to provide semi-trained accountants at a fast rate; a person takes one year to complete a certificate course, and two years for a diploma course. These institutes are run by the Department of Technical Education in various provinces, and in most of the cases there is at least one such institute at each district headquarters in the country. Their number at present is 120. In addition, there are a few privately run schools, preparing candidates for the London Chamber of Commerce examinations. Moreover, the evening program of the Institute of Business Administration, University of Karachi, offers one-semester certificate courses in accounting at different levels.

Of all these institutions, the Institute of Cost and Management Accountants has the largest operations. It has about 4,000 students on its rolls, and turns out about 60 fully qualified accountants every year. This is followed by the Institute of Chartered Accountants of Pakistan, with about a thousand registered students, and producing about 40 accountants annually. Next comes the Institute of Business Administration, University of Karachi, with an annual intake of about 150 students in its morning program and 350 in the evening program. It produces about 80 M.B.A.'s every year. At other institutions, the number of M.B.A.

and M.Com. students varies from 30 to 100.

Similar variation in the number of enrolled students exists in the case of B.Com. at colleges; it may be from 50 to 500 (with an average of about 100) sitting in the examination each year. These examinations are conducted by universities and the pass percentage falls between 30 and 40. The number of students enrolled with the commercial institutes varies from city to city. It may be as low as 10 in far-flung areas of Baluchistan to as high as 500 in cities such as Lahore and Karachi.

EXHIBIT 1

COLLEGES TEACHING ACCOUNTING

Government College of Commerce and Economics, Karachi
Government National College, Karachi
Government Liagmut College, Malir, Karachi
St. Patrick's Government College, Karachi
Haji Abdullah Haroon Government College, Karachi
Aisha Bawaney Government College, Karachi
Government Jamia Millia College, Karachi
Government Urdu College, Karachi
Government City College for Men, Karachi
Jinnah Government College, Karachi
Sirajuddaula College, Karachi
Sind Muslim Government Arts/Commerce College, Karachi
Government Premier College, Karachi
Government Allama Igbal College, Karachi
Government Shaheed-e-Millat College, Karachi
Government Sind College of Commerce, Hyderabad
Government Sachal Sarmast Commerce College, Hyderabad
Government Ghazali College, Hyderabad
Government College, Sukkur
Government College, Larkana
Government College, Nawabshah
Government Islamia College, Sukkur
Government College, Khaipur
Government College, Hala
Hailey College of Commerce, Lahore
Government Islamia College, Lahore
Government Hashmi Memorial College, Lahore
Municipal College of Commerce, Lyallpur
Government College, Rawalpindi
Quaid-e-Azam College of Commerce, Peshawar
Government Islamic College, Karachi
Government Commerce College, Islamabad

UNIVERSITIES TEACHING ACCOUNTING

University of Karachi, Karachi
  Department of Commerce
  Institute of Business Administration

Jamshoro University, Hyderabad, Sind
  Department of Commerce

Gomal University, Dera Ismail Khan
  Department of Business Administration

Punjab University, Lahore
  Hailey College of Commerce
  Department of Business Administration

Quaid-e-Azam University, Islamabad
  Department of Administrative Sciences

Peshawar University, Peshawar
  Quaid-e-Azam College of Commerce

Baluchistan University, Quetta
  Department of Commerce

Bahauddin Zakaria University, Multan
  Department of Business Administration

2.3 Government Involvement in Education

The government has considerable financial involvement in education. All education is heavily subsidized in the country. The management of educational institutions also rests with government under the "nationalization of education" scheme. The universities, although with considerable autonomy, have their chief executives, called vice chancellors, appointed by and reporting to the Education Ministry. The colleges are controlled by the same ministry through boards of education located at the provincial headquarters. The commercial institutes come under the Directorate of Technical Education which forms a part of the Ministry of Education. The three professional institutes, i.e., ICMAP, ICPAP and ICAP, are run by councils elected from the membership, with some seats reserved for the government nominees. The financial subsidy to these institutes is provided by the Ministry of Finance.

The coordination in the activities of the colleges offering education up to B.Com. and the institutes of commerce is provided by the curriculum wing of the Ministry of Education. A similar task is undertaken by the University Grant Commission for University Education leading to the master's degree level. However, all the universities, including the Institute of Business Administration, have complete independence in setting standards of examinations and drawing course outlines. Because the universities are following the semester system, individual teachers have considerable part in attaining the standard of training imparted.

249

2.4   Educational Standards at Entry Point

The entrance requirement for professional institutes in the country is a degree in commerce or any other subject. The passing marks required in the degree examinations vary between 33 to 40 percent at various universities. These percentages are the legacy of the British rule in the subcontinent. However, the achievement of minimum passing marks does not mean that a standard comparable to corresponding British standard of education has been attained. At present most of the universities in the country are in the process of transition to the semester system with the hope of alleviating the low educational attainment standard.

3.   The Accountancy Educational Inventory

In conducting this study, data have been collected from all the universities, degree-granting and intermediate colleges and commercial institutes of the country. In addition, information obtained from the two professional bodies of Pakistan has also been incorporated.*

3.1   Qualifications of Accounting Teachers

The accounting teachers, all of whom are Pakistanis, may be divided into three categories: (1) university and college teachers, (2) commerce institute teachers, and (3) teachers conducting preparatory classes for professional accounting examinations.

All the universities, which also control education at the college level, have a requirement of at least a master's degree in commerce or business administration for teachers of accounting to intermediate, degree, or postgraduate classes. A doctorate, however, is preferred. Some accounting teachers have acquired professional qualifications, yet no special recognition is given to them. This has led to a reduced number of university teachers sitting for such qualifications.

At the level of commerce institutes offering diplomas and certificates in commerce, the requirement is flexible. A teacher may be an M.Com. or M.A. (Economics) with B.Com. The latter combination is in fact preferred because the holder of such a qualification can teach both economics and accounting, and thus has a larger utility for an institute.

At the educational centres of the ICMAP and ICAP part-time teachers are employed. They are working as either accounting teachers in local universities or colleges, or as professional accountants. The latter are, in principle, preferred at these centres.

Table 3 summarizes the qualification of accounting teachers in the country.

---

*The ICPAP does not conduct any significant educational programs except examinations through the Board of Technical Education, Karachi, as yet.

TABLE 1

QUALIFICATION OF ACCOUNTING TEACHERS

Qualification	Full-time teachers at universities/colleges/ commerce institutes	Part-time teachers at ICMAP/ICAP
Ph.D./DBA	-	-
M.Com.	86	3
MBA	11	1
ACA	2	7
ACMA	5*	5

In addition to the colleges, universities and professional accounting institutes, accounting is also being taught at the training institutes and staff colleges of the banks and the government. The Auditor General's office has established training institutions and academies for the education and training of government accountants and auditors. There is also a proposal to establish a National Accounts Academy at Karachi, which will provide continuing education and regular accounting courses for government accountants and auditors. Most of the instructors in the staff colleges and banks are full-time bank officers with postgraduate degrees in commerce or business administration. Services of the part-time teachers are also availed by these institutions. In the training institutes of government accountants, departmentally qualified accountants are engaged as teachers.

Most of the accounting teachers in the country, especially in colleges, are young. They have either replaced the more experienced and senior staff who have left to take up job assignments in business or foreign countries, or filled in posts in freshly established departments of commerce and business administration at various universities. Invariably, the younger faculty members have never had a chance to work under the guidance of experts, and thus their development has been haphazard. In a number of cases, some teachers were required to teach accounting because of shortage of appropriate personnel although such persons did not take any advanced courses in accounting during their academic career. These elements have resulted in substandard accounting faculties at most of the institutes.

The development of teaching staff has been almost totally neglected in the recent past. Facilities for attending seminars or obtaining higher education are not made available by the government; neither are scholarships provided for advanced training abroad. However, incentives are provided in the national pay scales for the teachers to obtain higher education. All teachers are allowed study leave for two years once during their career. Accounting teachers earning an M.B.A., M.S., or M.A. from a foreign university are granted two advance increments in their salary scales. Similarly, those completing doctorates from abroad

*Three more teachers have passed the final examination of the institute, but have not been elected members as yet.

or at a Pakistani university are given four advance increments. To take advantage of these benefits, a small number of teachers has left for the U.S. at their own expense.

Although accounting teachers are not provided with any incentive, such as advancement in their careers, or enhanced salaries, to complete professional examinations, a few college and university teachers have enrolled themselves with the Institute of Cost and Management Accountants of Pakistan. In addition, no firm of public accountants offers any facilities for providing practical training to the accounting teachers. Similarly, no such teacher is working as consultant to business or government organization because the accounting consultancy work is almost monopolized by public accounting firms.

In connection with the professional development of teachers, ICMAP and the Management Association of Pakistan have been offering some assistance. In each of their management development programs, they generally invite one or two teachers. In any case, the number of teachers benefiting from these programs is quite insignificant.

Although things have been really bad in the sphere of professional development in the past, healthier signs are becoming visible now. Recently the Institute of Business Administration, University of Karachi, formulated a policy under which any teacher could design and conduct a management development program with a portion of revenue received as fee from participants going to the teacher concerned. Similarly, the Institute of Cost and Management Accountants of Pakistan has provided financial benefits to accounting teachers conducting executive development programs. Additionally, the University Grants Commission, in order to force teachers to develop themselves professionally through research, has announced a promotion policy under which a minimum number of research articles published in journals of international repute has been specified for promotions to the posts of associate professors and professors at universities and colleges.

3.2 Instruction Techniques

The lecture is the pervasive method of teaching at all levels. However, at ICMAP and at M.B.A. and B.B.A. (Honors) levels, lectures are supplemented by case studies, laboratories and workshops, report writing, visits to commercial and industrial organizations, seminars, and internship during vacation. ICMAP has received some visual aid equipment from the government of Canada.

Correspondence courses are offered at ICAP and ICMAP. At ICAP these courses are compulsory for each student, while at ICMAP students have an option between lectures of coaching classes and correspondence courses. The Open University uses the media of radio and television as well, besides the correspondence courses and programmed textbooks. Radio and television programmes are offered by the Open University on national hook-up.

Practical field training is a prerequisite only at the professional institutes to become eligible for membership, or at the institutes/departments of business administration for the award of the M.B.A. degree. In other cases, no practical experience or internship is required. The B.Coms., M.Coms., and Certificate and Diploma holders come out of their colleges, universities and commercial institutes without ever having visited a business concern. This results in the production of bookish accountants completely ignorant of the basic practical problems in the field.

Lack of practical training is not only a problem for the students, it is equally so for the accounting teachers. With the exception of those who hold professional qualifications such as F/ACMA or F/ACA or an M.B.A. from a local or foreign university, accounting teachers in general do not possess any practical experience. They are as blind to the real needs of the profession as are their students. Together, these factors contribute to the production of outdated accounting juniors.

3.3 Structure of Programs and Curricula

Accounting curricula is part of the Commerce and Business Administration education in Pakistan. None of the universities offers a degree in accounting. The structure and curricula of Commerce and Business Administration courses, to a great extent, are uniform in all universities. For a Master's degree in Commerce or Business Administration, six academic years are required. Accounting course load as a fraction of total course load for each qualification is:

Degree		Duration of Course
C.Com.	1/5	One year
D.Com. (Diploma)	1/5	One year
I Com.	2/10	Two years
B.Com.	3/10 to 5/10	Two years
B.B.A. (Hons.)	3/20 to 5/20	Two years
M.Com.	2/9 to 3/9	Two years
M.B.A.	3/20 to 5/20	2/3 years
A.C.A.	7/13	4 years
A.C.M.A.	10/19	3/4 years

Statistical data are not available to estimate the duration of course in case of CPA, because none has been produced by the ICPAP as yet.

The subjects covered by the various examinations conducted by the universities and the professional institutes are given in Exhibit 2. Certain subjects which are common at various examinations are covered at different levels, e.g., auditing is covered at a lesser level in B.Com. as compared to A.C.A. However, it may be noted that courses of ICAP and ICMAP are under revision.

EXHIBIT 2

SUBJECTS COVERED BY VARIOUS EXAMINATIONS

Examination	Accounting Subjects	Other Subjects
M.B.A.	Financial Accounting Cost Accounting Advanced Cost Accounting Managerial Accounting Distribution Cost Analysis Auditing and Income Tax Financial Management Analysis of Financial Statements Advanced Accounting	Management Managerial Economics Statistics & Mathematics for Management Operations Research Research & Report Writing Marketing Management Business Policy Production Management Industrial & Commercial Law
M.Com.	Cost Accounting Auditing Managerial Accounting Taxation	International Economics Monetary Theory & Fiscal Policies Statistics Research & Report Writing Transportation Management Marketing Management Company Law
A.C.A.* (Institute of Chartered Accountants of Pakistan)	Bookkeeping & Accountancy (two papers) Auditing Advanced Accounting (two papers) Cost & Management Accounting Taxation	Mercantile & Company Law (three papers) General Commercial Law Knowledge Economics & Statistics
ACMAP (Institute of Cost & Management Accountants of Pakistan.)	Accounting (two papers) Cost Accounting (two papers) Advanced Accounting (two papers) Advanced Cost and Management Accounting (two papers) Financial Management (two papers) Income Tax Auditing & Company Law	Economics Industrial & Commercial Law Production Technology & Management Business Mathematics & Statistics Quantitative Techniques & E.D.P. Office Management & Report Writing Management

*Subjects covered by CPA examinations are in line with ICAP examinations.

Financial accounting is covered at all levels of education. The extent of coverage is almost the same in each case, but the depth differs with the stage of education. The topics covered at various levels include accounting reports, recording process, accounting for assets and liabilities, partnerships and corporations including mergers and consolidations.

Auditing (as a part of accounting education), however, is given much less emphasis in all examinations except the professional ones. The ICAP has two full-fledged three-hour papers which are compulsory for all candidates. The contents of these papers are audit programs, working papers, techniques, evidence, legal documents, internal control, verification of assets, liabilities, income and expense accounts, and auditors' reports and investigations.

Cost accounting and management accounting are taught as two differenct subjects at the M.B.A., B.B.A. (Hons.) and M.Com. levels. The ICMAP has divided this area into Fundamentals and Advanced Cost Accounting Papers. The ICAP has a joint three-hour paper in management and cost accounting. The subject matter in each case is adequate. Also, topics such as cost-benefit analysis, capital budgeting, analysis of financial statements and differential costs are given good coverage. However, at the B.Com. level, cost accounting is taught at an elementary level, and only basic concepts of the subject are included in the curriculum.

As a part of accounting curriculum, national accounting is taught at Sind University. At the rest of the universities, a brief introduction is provided to the subject in macro-economics courses. Social (societal) accounting is not taught at any level in the country.

Eight universities offer degree courses in business administration. The ICMAP also has two papers on Management, while ICAP courses do not have any papers on Management or Business Administration. The teaching of Business Administration is carried out on modern lines; standard American textbooks are used. The course work is almost comparable to any one followed at a medium-class graduate school of business administration in the U.S. Apart from accounting, other core courses include: Mathematics, Statistics, Economics, Law and Quanititative Techniques.

Public Sector Accounting is not included in the curriculum of any of the universities. ICMAP has included Government Accounting as a part of its Financial Management paper. However, in the proposed revised syllabus for ICMAP examination a full paper is being introduced on Governmental and Public Sector Accounting. The importance of Public Sector Accounting has been realized by ICMAP, and special seminars and courses on Financial Management in Public Sector Industries are being offered.

Whereas the training for professional accountants conducted at the ICAP is on traditional lines following the old British pattern, the educational program of ICMAP is being kept up-to-date. Auxiliary subjects including mathematics, statistics, quantitative techniques, electronic data processing, research and report writing, industrial administration, and management and law. These subjects are covered at a fairly good level.

Because of greater demand of M.B.A.s for accounting and finance positions, the accounting load chosen by the students preparing for this degree is much larger than the required course work. All of the universities prescribe a minimum of three courses of one semester each: financial accounting, cost accounting and managerial accounting. Optional courses in accounting taken by a significant majority of students are: advanced accounting, analysis of financial statements, advanced cost accounting, and auditing and taxation. All of these subjects are taught with the help of standard American textbooks. Managerial accounting is taught by case method whereas lectures supplemented by laboratory work and home assignments are used for other subjects.

In addition to M.B.A., accounting courses are also covered extensively at postgraduate level in M.Com. classes in every university.

The course outlines developed at various levels of education follow mostly standard American texts or old curricula retaining and exhibiting British influence. Because of major differences in the economic structure of Pakistan from British and American economies, often subject matter irrelevant to local needs is added, whereas the essential one is not given due attention. For example, liquidators' accounts, insolvency accounting, and installment accounting (which have no place in local practice) are emphasized to the entire exclusion of important topics such as development and societal accounting.

In addition to the nature of course work, the depth of coverage has been shallow for the last few years. Almost every year there have been political, social or natural incidents leading to closure of educational institutions for the major portion of the academic year. The teachers and students are hard put to cover, and cover-as-you-can, the syllabus prescribed by the various examining bodies. The net outcome is inadequate coverage at a low level resulting in students' oft repeated demand of grace marks to pass the examination.

3.4   Textbooks and Training Materials

In 1947, when Pakistan emerged as an independent country, Indian and British books on accounting were being used as textbooks by universities and colleges in Pakistan. In the early fifties, with the increased number of students in accounting, and also because of difficulties in importing books from India, books on accounting written by Pakistanis started appearing and gradually replaced British and Indian textbooks. Now at the undergraduate level in most of the universities, books written by Pakistani authors have been adopted as textbooks.

There are also books written by Pakistani authors on auditing and tax accounting. These books discuss the subject in the light of Pakistani laws and practices. American textbooks are generally prescribed for postgraduate and professional examination syllabi.

The Institute of Cost and Management Accountants of Pakistan set up a committee to adapt standard accounting textbooks to local needs in 1971. Under this arrangement, the following books were adapted and published: *Cost Accounting* by Matz, Curry and Frank and *Principles of Accounting* by

Niswonger and Fess. No other foreign accounting textbook has been adapted so far. However, some teachers do interject local examples in classroom discussion when using American textbooks.

The dearth of suitable textbooks and other teaching materials such as cases, journals and periodicals is acute. Per capita income being low in the country, and the exchange rate adverse, most of the students are not in a position to buy standard American textbooks. British books have been almost totally replaced by the American books. On the other hand, libraries' textbook sections are not adequately stocked because of meagre financial assistance granted to the educational institutes for replenishment and replacement purposes. It is not surprising to see some libraries stocking the 1957 edition of *Accounting Principles* by Noble and Niswonger for issue as a textbook to students at the graduate level. Incidentally such textbooks were provided by various U.S. organizations under aid programs.

A similar shortage of journals, periodicals and magazines exists in the country. Most of the educational institutions discontinued their subscription to foreign publications because of paucity of funds and adverse exchange parity rates. This has resulted in both the students and teachers being completely unaware of what advances are taking place in accounting abroad.

Local cases are also not available for discussion in accounting classes. The Pakistan Case Clearinghouse, which did commendable work when Professor Meginson (on his U.S. AID sponsored advisory job) was available for guidance in Pakistan in 1969-70, has been completely inactive for the last seven years.

3.5 Accounting Research and Development

Accounting research and development have been quite insignificant. Only the Institute of Cost and Management Accountants of Pakistan and the Institute of Business Administration, University of Karachi, have been active in the field on a small scale. The topics of research generally relate to current business problems. Efforts are being made by ICMAP to establish a research foundation, in memory of Mr. Mohammad Shoaib, the first president of the institute. ICMAP also arranges research-oriented lectures by eminent accountants from other countries. The lectures are called Shoaib Memorial Lectures. So far, three memorial lectures have been delivered, which have also been published by the institute. Prof. Adolf Enthoven delivered the first Shoaib Memorial Lecture in 1976 on "The Future of Management Accounting in Developing Countries." The second lecture "The Integration of Managerial and Financial Accounting" was delivered by Prof. R. J. Chambers in 1977. The third lecture by Prof. J. M. S. Risk on "New Accountancy" was delivered in 1980.

3.6 Other Aspects of Relevance

The professional accounting bodies in Pakistan have their own educational programs. The ICMAP holds regular classes in the evening at ten centres throughout the country, and also coaches its students through correspondence courses. Candidates for the ICMAP examinations have to register for one of the two types of training at least for the first sitting.

The ICAP also holds refresher classes prior to the commencement of its examinations. The students are, however, trained essentially through correspondence courses.

4. Evaluation of Inventory

4.1 The Problem

Since the inception of Pakistan, serious efforts have been made to improve the profession of accounting at all levels. Starting with only two colleges imparting education up to the B.Com., the country has built a sound system of accounting and commerce educational institutions. The early fifties saw the emergence of a number of colleges offering B.Com. education and commerce departments at various universities coaching for M.Com. degrees. The professional education was given impetus by the establishment of the Institute of Chartered Accountants of Pakistan and the Pakistan Institute of Industrial Accountants (now known as ICMAP). Both the institutes operate with more than a score of training centres where coaching classes are held along with correspondence courses conducted from their head offices at Karachi. Business education leading to an M.B.A. degree was imparted only at the Institute of Business Administration, University of Karachi, until 1972. However, in that year, when the institute was virtually reserved for students from Sind province, other provinces started setting up their own similar institutions. The last five years have witnessed the establishment of departments of business administration at seven other universities. All of these newly established departments suffer from an acute shortage of teachers in all subjects, particularly accounting. They have tried to remedy this through the employment of part-time teachers drawn from business and government enterprises. The multiplicity of these institutes, colleges and departments, has resulted in the production of larger but inadequate numbers of B.Coms., M.Coms., and M.B.A.'s. However, the number of professionally qualified accountants has not shown a corresponding increase. This may be due to a high rate of failure at the professional accounting examinations.

In addition to higher level accounting training, the government has been active in providing increasing facilities for lower level accounting education by providing a commercial institute almost in every big town. Moreover, in-service training facilities have been made available to government and private enterprise officers and lower staff working in the ministries of finance and other allied areas, by establishing a finance academy, and two institutes called the National Institute of Public Administration and Management Institute.

In spite of all the resources made available for the accounting education and training, the output of the institutions, though large in quantity, is mainly poor in quality with a few exceptions.

Only two of the institutions imparting accounting education, the ICMAP and the IBA at the University of Karachi, may feel some degree of satisfaction on the type of training and the quality of their product. All other institutions have the basic problem of poor quality of their output. The following may be listed as the causes of this basic problem:

(1) Paucity of senior accounting teachers who can guide the new staff in their development.

(2) Very limited availability of training opportunities with business and industry to gain practical experience for both the teachers and the students.

(3) Dearth of suitable textbooks and training material.

(4) Low standard of education of students at the entry point.

(5) Inclusion of irrelevant and exclusion of essential matter from course work required for various examinations.

(6) A high student/teacher ratio at the undergraduate level.

It is evident that accounting standards are poor both at the academic and professional levels.

Having identified the causes of this problem, it is stressed that attention should be given to the following:

(1) Staffing accounting faculties with senior level academically and professionally better qualified persons.

(2) In-service training of accounting teachers comprising of teaching techniques and practical experience.

(3) Redesigning of course coverage to suit the needs of the economy.

(4) Provisioning of suitable modern textbooks, periodicals and ournals, and the creation of local cases and research work.

(5) Improvement in overall standards of education at all levels.

(6) Reduction of the student/teacher ratio, especially at the undergraduate level.

Given the situation in which Pakistan is placed at present, the task seems difficult but attainable. The resources available to accounting institutions are meagre because of the low priority given to the subject by the government. It is difficult to retain properly qualified accounting teachers because of better job prospects in non-teaching employment. The matter is further complicated by the lack of interest presently being shown by American, Canadian and British universities in providing assistance for higher education to the accounting faculties of their Pakistani counterparts.

Accounting education in Pakistan lacks coordination. It is necessary that a council, comprised of the representatives of the universities and the professional accounting bodies should revise the curricula of the accounting courses taught at different levels, integrating them into a properly coordinated system, avoiding the unnecessary duplication. The coordination between the universities and the professional accounting bodies like ICAP and ICMAP requires special attention.

None of the universities has a separate school of accountancy. As early as 1952 the University of Karachi was considering the proposal of assistance from New Zealand government for setting up a school of accountancy in Karachi. However, this did not materialize.

Conclusion

Pakistan began with an acute shortage of accountants, accounting teachers and educational institutions imparting accounting education. Concerted efforts to remove the inadequacies in this area by public and private bodies and individuals, however, have resulted in the development of a requisite infrastructure. Whereas more personnel and facilities have become available, the quality, unfortunately, has been slipping steadily. Moreover, the emigration of many professionally qualified persons to the Middle East and Africa has worsened the situation. Now, Pakistan stands in need of more and better qualified teachers, modern textbooks, local case material, foreign journals and magazines, and above all, larger funds to fill the adverse gap between the supply of and demand for properly trained accountants. Some of the problems could be solved through the cooperation of the American Accounting Association (AAA). The AAA could help make available the services of about half a dozen senior accounting teachers to Pakistani universities and professional institutes. This could be done through some sort of faculty exchange program under the sponsorship of U.S. AID or Ford Foundation.

Other institutions which may help in this program are the International Bank for Reconstruction and Development and the Asian Development Bank. In addition, Pakistani Development Banks such as Industrial Bank of Pakistan, the Pakistan Industrial Credit and Investment Corporation and the National Development Finance Corporation can provide necessary financial assistance, particularly the rupee (local currency) component of the required investment. These teachers may be entrusted to achieve the following objectives:

- To establish the M.S. and Ph.D. (in accounting) programs at the University of Karachi on a sound footing.
- To acquaint the accounting teachers at various levels in Pakistan with modern methods of teaching.
- To guide and supervise the writing of local cases and textbooks.
- To assist in initiating and establishing research programs on problems of the local accounting profession, and
- To train accounting teachers in the areas of development, societal and governmental accounting and help establish them as normal courses.

Apart from these short-term programs, ICMAP's facilities can be used for the long-range development of accounting education not only in Pakistan but also in the Middle East and Near East regions. The institute has the experience and expertise of conducting its activities at the international level. However, to enable it to play its role as a regional center, its facilities need to be expanded. More staff would be needed. Some of them may have to be trained abroad. In addition to its buildings and library, educational material would also be required. As an expanded body, the ICMAP could work as a coordinating body between various regional accounting associations in Asia and Africa. It could also function as a regional case clearinghouse on a local as well as regional basis. Its membership transcends international boundaries and the facility of reviewing cases would be available to it in good measure.

Also, with the assistance of various universities and institutions, the AAA could procure used textbooks, journals and periodicals of U.S. origin for appropriate libraries in Pakistan. If possible, complimentary subscriptions to journals and periodicals could be made available to the professional institutes and universities. Further, AAA could provide complimentary membership for certain accounting teachers, and involve them in regional research programs.

If the required help were made available, Pakistan, by virtue of its fairly well-developed system of education, not only could solve its own problems but also could assist other regional countries in improving their inventory of accounting education.

CHAPTER XXIII

ACCOUNTING EDUCATION IN THE PHILIPPINES

by
Jesus A. Casino*

1. The Setting

1.1 Land and People

The Philippine archipelago is made up of 7,100 islands of which about 1,000 are inhabited. With a land area of 300,780 square kilometers, it is a medium-sized country, about two-thirds the size of Spain. There are three main geographical divisions, Luzon to the north, Visayas in the middle, and Mindanao in the south. The hub of trade, industrial, educational and cultural activity is in metropolitan Manila, a conglomerate of four cities and nine municipalities with the city of Manila as center.

The total population as of the last census in 1975 was 42 million people. This is growing at the rate of 2.8 percent a year.

Filipinos are basically of Malay stock, but Philippine culture has been influenced in varying degrees by the Chinese, Hindu-Islamic, Hispanic, and Anglo-Saxon peoples who come to the Philippines to settle, trade, explore and colonize.

The Philippine constitution provides three official languages: Pilipino, English and Spanish. English is the dominant official language and the primary medium of instruction, although Pilipino has been increasingly utilized in instruction in recent years.

1.2 Government

The Philippines is a relatively young republic which gained independence in 1946 after some 350 years of Spanish colonization, nearly 50 years of American rule, and four years of Japanese occupation during the second World war.

The 1935 Philippine constitution provided for a democratic form of government with executive power vested in the President, legislative power in the Congress, and judicial power in the Supreme Court and inferior courts established by law.

Because of mounting discontent and disorder, martial law was imposed in September, 1972, and legislation was incorporated into the executive function with the occasional participation of citizens' assemblies.

In 1973, a new constitution was ratified which provides for a parliamentary system of government wherein the legislative power is vested in the National Assembly, the executive power in the Prime Minister and the Cabinet, and the judicial power in the Supreme Courts and lower courts.

*Dr. Jesus A. Casino is Professor of Accounting and Director for Research and Development, Philippine School of Business Administration, Manila, Philippines.

1.3 Economic Profile

The Philippines is still basically an agricultural country although the economy has been shifting gradually to an agro-industrial base. Agriculture comprising agricultural crops, fisheries, livestock, poultry, and forestry accounts for 27 percent of the gross domestic product, employes one-half of the labor force, and generates nearly 60 percent of export earnings. The industrial sector comprised of mining, manufacturing, construction, and utilities accounts for 34 percent of gross domestic product, 15 percent of the labor force and some 40 percent of export earnings, of which 12 percent represents exports of mineral products.

The economy is based on the free-enterprise system with the private sector playing a dominant and dynamic role. However, in recent years, the government has tended to be more aggressive and interventionist in managing economic activities in order to promote orderly and rational economic growth.

Since independence, the economy has grown by 6 percent in real terms. Growth has been characterized by increasing industrialization and diversification of domestic and export production. It has also been marked by instabilities largely due to domestic policies and external developments. But the economy has shown considerable resiliency in the face of adverse economic conditions. Per capital income is U.S. $521, which puts the Philippines among Asia's middle-income countries.

Like other developing countries, the Philippines faces problems of an exploding population, inequitable distribution of wealth, unemployment and underemployment, and a shortage of investment capital. The country depends on external sources for most of its energy requirements, and recent increases in the price of oil have created serious economic dislocations. On the other hand, there are substantially rich and still largely untapped natural resources. Commercial quantities of oil have recently been found, and geothermal and other indigeneous sources of energy are being developed. The country's labor force possesses a relatively high degree of literacy and educational attainment.

A noteworthy development is the growth of the country's financial system which has become one of the most sophisticated in Southeast Asia. There has also been an awakening among Filipinos of the advantages of investing in securities with the emergence of the corporation as the dominant form of business organization and the encouragement by government of greater widespread ownership of shares. To complement local capital resources, the government has adopted a policy of encouraging a steady inflow of foreign equity investment in areas where it can contribute soundly to economic development.

1.4 Economic History

The beginnings of Philippine economic development may be traced to the last few decades of the 18th century when Spain started to develop the natural resources of the country. The opening of the Port of Manila to world trade in 1834 spurred the development of agricultural production for export and the country began to produce not only for itself but also for the Spanish empire and the world.

The Americans continued the development that had begun during the Spanish regime. However, while Spain allowed Philippine goods to move into the world market, the United States monopolized Philippine exports through a policy of "free trade relations." Under this policy, agriculture made impressive gains, foreign and domestic trade flourished, mining and forestry began to develop, plants to process natural products for export and handicraft establishments were established.

The economic prosperity that accompanied free trade relations was, however, artificial and basically unsound because it made the Philippine economy virtually dependent on the U.S. market. When import tariffs, quotas, and taxes were imposed following the grant of a Commonwealth status in 1935, the economy suffered a slump. The second world war completed the damage to the economy.

When the war ended, the Philippine economy was in ruins. However, a full-scale rehabilitation program together with favorable export prices spurred rapid economic recovery. By 1950, production had been substantially restored to pre-war levels.

In the first half of the decade of the fifties, manufacturing developed far more rapidly than other sectors of the economy as a result of tax incentives, foreign exchange and import controls, and a strategy of producing light "import substitute" consumer goods for the domestic market. Favorable market prices and the expansion of land under cultivation increased agricultural exports, but domestic food production lagged. Towards the later part of the decade, economic growth slowed down due to monetary and foreign exchange problems, the saturation of the urban markets and the slow expansion of the rural areas. In 1962, foreign exchange controls were lifted and the peso was devalued.

In the sixties, efforts were taken to modernize the agricultural sector in order to increase food supplies, raise rural incomes, and lay the base of mass purchasing power in the rural areas. A breakthrough in rice production was achieved with the use of new and high-yielding rice varieties. In the industrial sector, "import substitute" manufacturing continued at a reduced pace. Economic growth as a whole proceeded at moderate rates marked by instabilities in the sixties which culminated in a second devaluation of the peso in 1970.

The economic slow-down continued into the early seventies, aggravated by adverse weather conditions, civil disorders, a decreased world demand for domestic export products, and an international monetary crisis. Imposition of martial law in 1972 and its accompanying reforms reversed the downward spiral and infused new vigor into the economy.

In recent years, active measures have been taken to promote exports and to encourage diversification of export markets. There has been a noticeable increase in nontraditional exports as well as a shift in the composition of traditional exports from purely raw materials to processed and even finished products. Industrialization has reached a higher stage with the introduction of major projects involving basic and heavy industry which are currently in different stages of preparation and operation. The rural areas are being developed to achieve greater food self-sufficiency and provide a wider source of raw materials for industry. Towards this end, the government has instituted a major agragrian reform program, expanded infrastructure, particularly irrigation and feeder roads, and provided credit extension work, and marketing facilities.

The long-term economic plan seeks a balanced growth between agriculture and industry. But the economic picture for the eighties tends to be clouded by the continuing uncertainty over prices and supplies of oil, world-wide recessionary trends, barriers against the free flow of goods and services from the developing to the developed world, and other external factors.

2. The Accounting Profession

2.1 Structure of the Profession

2.1.1 The Accountancy Law

The accounting profession in the Philippines is governed by law. The first accountancy law was enacted in 1923. This was amended at various times up to 1975. The most extensive revisions took place in 1967 with the passage of Republic Act 5166 entitled, "The Accountancy Act of 1967." In 1975, further amendments were introduced in Presidential Decree No. 592 entitled, "The Revised Accountancy Law."

The Revised Accountancy Law of 1975 provides for the standardization and regulation of accounting education, examination for registration of certified public accountants, and the supervision, control, and regulation of accountancy in the Philippines.

Provisions of the law are implemented by the Board of Accountancy, subject to the administrative supervision of the Professional Regulation Commission (PRC).

2.1.2 The Board of Accountancy

The Board of Accountancy is composed of a chairman and six members appointed by the President of the Philippines upon recommendation of the Professional Regulation Commission. Members must be certified public accountants, morally qualified, in the practice of accountancy for at least ten years, and not directly or indirectly connected with any school granting degrees that may qualify graduates for admission to the CPA examination, or offering CPA review courses. (1)

The Board of Accountancy prescribes minimum requirements for the admission of candidates to the CPA examinations, conducts the examinations, evaluates results, and issues a certificate of registration as Certified Public Accountant to those who have satisfactorily passed the examination and complied with requirements. Subject to the approval of the PRC, it promulgates rules, regulations, and standards for the practice of accountancy, and is responsible for the enhancement and maintenance of high ethical and technical standards in the profession. It is empowered to investigate CPAs who violate the Accountancy Law and to reprimand those who have erred, or to suspend or revoke registration certificates for cause. (2)

2.1.3 Professional Regulation Commission

The Professional Regulation Commission was created in 1973 as part of a general reorganization of government machinery, to oversee the activities of all professions, including accounting. It is headed by a Commissioner and two Associate Commissioners who are appointed by the President of the Philippines.

2.1.4 Requirements for the Practice of Accountancy

Only persons who are holders of CPA certificates issued by the Board of Accountancy may practice accountancy in the Philippines. The CPA certificate is issued to those who have satisfactorily passed the examination given by the Board of Accountancy, or have otherwise complied with the requirements of the Board.

A person is deemed to be engaged in the practice of accountancy if he holds himself out as a CPA possessing the professional knowledge and skills pertaining to the science and practice of accountancy, and qualified to exercise the professional skills and/or render professional services as a certified public accountant. (3) This definition of accounting practice recognizes that the profession consists not only of those engaged in public accounting, but also those employed in private firms, in the government, in government-owned or controlled corporations, or in educational institutions, whose positions require that the holders be certified public accountants.

2.1.5 The CPA Examinations

To be allowed to take the CPA examinations, a person must be: (4)

(1) A citizen of the Philippines or a citizen, subject, or national of a country which, by specific provisions of law, allows citizens of the Philippines to practice accountancy after an examination, on terms of strict and absolute equality with the citizens, subjects, or nationals of said country.

(2) At least twenty-one years of age.

(3) Of good moral character.

(4) Holder of the degree of Bachelor of Science in Commerce or its equivalent, from any institution of learning recognized by the government, provided minimum credits are earned in certain courses specified by the Board of Accountancy through the Professional Regulation Commission.

The examinations are conducted by the Board of Accountancy in coordination with the PRC, at least once each year, in the cities of Manila and Cebu, and if conditions warrant, in other places.

The examinations cover the following subjects with the corresponding weight in units: (5)

Subject	Weight in Units	Minimum Hours
Theory of Accounts	2	3
Business Law and Taxation	2	3
Management Services	2	3
Auditing Theory	2	3
Auditing Problems	2	3
Practical Accounting Problems I	2	3
Practical Accounting Problems II	2	3

The contents and coverage of the subjects are described in detail in a syllabus prepared by the Board of Accountancy.

To be entitled to registration as a certified public accountant, a candidate should obtain a general weighted average of 75 percent, provided no rating in any subject is less than 65 percent. In the event a candidate obtains a rating of 75 percent in at least four subjects having a combined weight of eight (8) units, he shall receive a conditional credit for the subjects passed, and may take an examination in the remaining subjects within two years from the preceding examinations. (6)

A candidate who fails in two complete examinations is required to re-enroll and complete at least 24 units of CPA examination subjects in a college or university recognized by the government, before he can take another set of examinations. (7)

2.1.6 Professional Organizations

The accredited national professional organization of CPAs in the Philippines is the Philippine Institute of Certified Public Accountants (PICPA). Membership in PICPA is open to all Philippine CPAs on a voluntary basis.

Other professional bodies catering to the specialized needs of CPAs in major areas of practice are the Government Association of CPAs (GACPA) organized in 1972, the Association of CPAs in Commerce and Industry (ACPACI) and the Association of CPAs in Accounting Education (ACPAE), both organized in 1973. Accounting bodies whose membership is not confined to CPAs include the Management Accountants' Association of the Philippines which is affiliated with the National Accounting Association in the U.S., and Philippine chapters of the Institute of Internal Auditors and the Financial Executives Association.

Under the Revised Accountancy Law of 1975, all CPAs are to be integrated under one professional organization in order to raise the standards of the profession and enable it to discharge its public responsibilities more effectively. (8) In 1976, PICPA was accredited by the PRC as the bona fide national organization recognized by the government for the purpose of officially integrating, coordinating, and representing the accounting profession in the Philippines. Other voluntary professional accounting bodies will co-exist with PICPA and will pursue their objectives and activities in ways which are compatible with the objectives of integration. Efforts are now being exerted to enroll all Philippine CPAs as members of PICPA.

2.1.7 Accounting Standards

Philippine CPAs are governed by rules of professional conduct promulgated by the Board of Accountancy. PICPA has assumed responsibility for codifying accounting principles and auditing standards. Corporations whose shares of stock are sold or offered for sale to the public, and those with twenty or more stockholders must comply with regulations of the Securities and Exchange Commission regarding the form and content of their financial statements.

Accounting standards followed in the Philippines are similar to those adopted in the United States. This reflects the influence of nearly fifty years of American rule. It also recognizes the leading role played by the profession in the United States in the development of universally accepted accounting standards. As an associate member of the International Accounting Standards Committee, PICPA is committed to support IASC standards. Through the ASEAN Federation of Accountants it is also actively engaged in the harmonization of accounting principles in the ASEAN region.

While benefiting from American experience in framing accounting standards, the Philippines recognizes that it must seek solutions to accounting problems that are appropriate to the country's economic problems, degree of development, and culture. Thus, PICPA has, from time to time, taken positions on accounting issues differing from, or not covered by pronouncements in the U.S. These include, for example, bulletins entitled, "Accounting for the Effects of the Floating Exchange Rate" issued in March, 1970, and "Revaluation of Fixed Assets" issued in November, 1971.

2.2 Historical Background

2.2.1 The Early Years

Accounts and records must have been kept in one form or another by the early pre-colonial Filipinos. When the Spaniards reached the Philippines, Filipinos already had written languages. There was domestic commerce among barangays and islands, and foreign trade with China, Japan, Siam, Cambodia, Borneo, Sumatra, Java, and other islands of the old Malaysia. A Spanish document of 1586 noted that the Filipinos were "keen traders and have traded with China for many years." Chinese writers indicate that the Filipino traders were scrupulously honest in their commercial transactions. (9)

The Spaniards introduced the "entrada y salida" method of bookkeeping and during the last few decades of the Spanish regime accounting gained importance with the establishment of the first banks, financial institutions, and large international trading houses. Demand for trained personnel led several vocational schools to include bookkeeping and related courses in their curricula. However, accounting did not attain the status of an organized profession at this time.

2.2.2 Birth of a Profession

The first public accounting firms were set up at the turn of the century by British chartered accountants who came to the Philippines as employees and officers of business firms and later went into public accounting practice upon expiration of their contracts. These were followed by American CPAs and by some Filipinos who obtained CPA certificates in the U.S.

By 1923, accounting practice had become sufficiently important to warrant formal government recognition of accounting as a profession. The Philippine legislature enacted Act 3105 which created a Board of Accountancy vested with the power to conduct CPA examinations and determine the qualifications of persons applying for CPA certificates. The first CPA examinations were given in the same year.

As practice developed, problems emerged that had to be confronted by members of the profession acting as a group. This led to the establishment of the Philippine Institute of Certified Public Accountants in 1929. The organizers of the institute were, according to some of the surviving founders, motivated by the desire to raise standards of public accounting in the Philippines, purge the profession of illegal practice by nonCPAs, and oppose legislation being considered at that time to permit the issuance of CPA certificates to certain persons without undergoing the CPA examinations.

Until the outbreak of the second world war, the profession grew steadily, but not spectacularly. Eighteen years after the enactment of the accountancy law, some 1,000 CPA certificates had been issued. The establishment of the country's first stock exchange in 1929, the creation of the Securities and Exchange Commission in 1935, the enactment of the first income tax law in 1919 and of a comprehensive tax system in 1939, all potentially increased the need for accounting and auditing work. But practice remained relatively simple and limited in keeping with the agricultural export-based economy at that time.

2.2.3 Years of Rapid Growth

After the second world war, demand for accounting services grew at a rapid pace, both in quantity and in level of sophistication. Several factors responsible for this follow:

• The government's industrialization program resulted in the establishment of numerous enterprises whose accounting needs had to be serviced.

• The expansion of family-owned enterprises into publicly-owned corporations, the increasing sophistication of the country's financial system, and financing to private enterprise from the government and financial institutions, created a need for adequate and reliable accounting information.

• Various laws were enacted requiring audited financial statements for a number of tax and regulatory purposes.

• The expansion and modernization of government's administrative machinery to take care of the needs of a burgeoning population, called for trained personnel to handle accounting, auditing, budgeting, and tax collecting operations.

• Subsidiaries of multinational companies were introducing accounting practices prescribed by their parent offices.

• A new breed of Filipino professional managers was emerging, trained in modern management concepts and techniques and cognizant of the uses of accounting as a management tool.

• The business environment was becoming increasingly competitive and complex.

• The government was encouraging the use of modern management methods as part of its efforts to speed up industrialization.

Responding to these needs, the accounting profession grew rapidly in numbers, in the avriety and sophistication of its services, and in prestige. Accounting offered varied employment opportunities with relatively good financial rewards and prospects for advancement, and it soon became a popular career choice among Filipino college students.

The profession's rapid growth made it increasingly important to clarify professional standards, strengthen accounting education, and encourage the continuing professional growth of CPAs. In this, PICPA and the Board of Accountancy assumed active and leading roles.

After the war, PICPA established a permanent office and full-time staff. Later, a library was added and chapters organized in different regions of the country. Annual conventions, monthly meetings, and professional development programs were held on a regular basis. A quarterly journal and monthly newsletter was published. Accounting and auditing standards were defined, codified, and published.

To keep pace with the expanded responsibilities of CPAs, the Board of Accountancy, in cooperation with PICPA and the schools, upgraded standards of admission to the profession and initiated various changes in accounting programs and the CPA examinations. Possession of a college degree in business was made a requisite for admission to the CPA examinations. The scope of the examinations was expanded to include Management Advisory Services and separate subjects in Auditing Theory and Taxation. Accounting programs were lengthened and enriched.

2.2.4 Present Status

Next to doctors of medicine, nurses, and lawyers, certified public accountants constitute the largest group of registered professionals in the country. (10) As of December 31, 1979, a total of 39,563 CPA certificates had been issued by the Board of Accountancy. As of the same date, PICPA had 22,152 members in 33 chapters all over the Philippines and one international affiliate in the U.S. A breakdown of PICPA membership shows the following principal occupations:

Commerce and industry	30%
Government service	35%
Public accounting	25%
Education	6%
Others	4%

Accounting has become firmly established as a recognized profession and CPAs are looked upon as providing a valuable professional service, essential to economic development. (11)

Besides their audit and tax services, some public accounting firms have

271

branched out into management advisory services. The large firms have engagements that extend beyond national boundaries. One firm has a network of offices in Asia and engagements in several other countries.

Multinational corporations no longer find it necessary to bring in foreign nationals to handle accounting and financial functions in their Philippine operations. In fact, they are utilizing the services of Filipino accountants for their operations in other countries.

The services and usefulness of accountants have gone far beyond the traditional limits of professional accounting practice. In the last three or four decades, many Filipino accountants have attained prominence and played important roles in the field of education, in the growth and development of banking, insurance, and other financial institutions, in entrepreneurship and professional management, in economic research, and in government.

The profession has also taken an active role in the promotion of regional and international cooperation among acocuntants. In 1957, PICPA organized and hosted the First Far East Conference of Accountants which led to the formation of the Confederation of Asia and Pacific Accountants (CAPA). In 1976, it hosted the First Forum of Accountants of ASEAN member countries which led to the organization of the ASEAN Federation of Accountants.

2.3 The Educational System

2.3.1 Historical Background

The Philippines relies on formal academic study in colleges and universities, rather than apprenticeship, to prepare future members of the accounting profession.

The first formal system of education was introduced by the Spaniards who established schools at all levels. Among the schools still operating today are the University of San Carlos (founded 1595), the University of Santo Tomas (1611), San Juan de Letran College (1620), San Jose College (1872), Ateneo de Manila University (1859), and the University of San Agustin (1894). Higher education was available only at the University of Santo Tomas; the other schools were originally organized to provide elementary and secondary education.

The traditional mode of preparing for business occupations at this time was on-the-job training or apprenticeship. However, the development of the economy in the last few decades of the Spanish regime required an increasingly higher level of preparation. In 1839, the Board of Commerce under the Spanish government established the "Escuela de Commercio" to assist local businessmen in conducting their international affairs. Its curriculum offered training in bookkeeping, commercial arithmetic, English, and French.

A more comprehensive and systematic three-year business program leading to the title "Perito Mercantile" was later introduced at the Ateneo de Manila and the University of Santo Tomas beginning about 1867, at the Manila School of Arts and Trades which opened in 1890, and at similar schools in Iloilo (1891), and Pampanga (1893). The vocationally-oriented curriculum included courses in commercial legislation, accounting, bookkeeping, economics, and business correspondence.

When the Americans came, they sought to make education available to the masses. Towards this end, a nationwide public school system was organized, capped by the founding of the University of the Philippines in 1908. Alongside the public school system, schools founded by religious orders during the Spanish regime were allowed to continue, and new private educational institutions were established.

During the first few years of the American regime, the government established business schools in different parts of the country to train bookkeepers, typists, and clerks needed by the government and business firms. One of these, the Manila Business School founded in 1904, has become the Polytechnic University of the Philippines. The other schools gradually disappeared as business education shifted its orientation from the vocational to the tertiary level.

In 1916, the University of the Philippines began to offer accounting courses at the tertiary level under the Department of Economics of its College of Liberal Arts. In 1919 a four-year collegiate business program specializing in accounting was established by Jose Rizal College, a private institution organized by one of the first Filipinos to obtain a CPA certificate in the United States. Other pioneers in accounting education were De La Salle College (now a university) which began to offer accounting as a major field of study in 1919, the National University in 1921, and Far Eastern University in 1928.

The establishment of a school system which provided educational opportunities for all was enthusiastically received by Filipinos who saw in education a means to improve their economic status and a leverage to achieve upward mobility. Demand for higher education grew particularly in the years after the second world war as students stampeded into colleges and universities to make up for the loss of educational opportunities during the war. Since the government could not provide the necessary facilities, this demand was met by the establishment of more private schools throughout the country. Among the schools organized at this time was the Philippine College of Commerce and Business Administration (now the University of the East) whose collegiate business enrollment soared from 350 students in 1946 to a peak of nearly 30,000 students in the late sixties.

The phenomenal growth of the educational system has been one of the more significant social developments in the Philippines in this century. The Philippines educates as high a proportion of its people as the advanced countries. She has the world's fourth highest percentage of college enrollment relative to total population. (12)

The most popular college program is in business, followed by engineering and technology and arts and science. (13) One of 1.1 million college students in school-year 1979-1980, nearly 30 percent (321,541 students) were enrolled in business courses, and approximately 50 percent of those enrolled in business choose accounting as a major field of study. An estimated 90 percent of those who graduate from accounting programs take the CPA examinations.

2.3.1 General Structure of the System

The present educational structure is basically an extension of the system instituted during the American regime. Entry at the age of 7 is followed by six years of primary education and four years of secondary education. This leads at the age of 17 to four or five years of undergraduate tertiary education. After this, the student may proceed to postgraduate studies which takes two years for a master's program and another two to three years for a doctoral program.

Graduation from a recognized secondary school is a requisite for admission to the tertiary level. In addition, since 1974, the student must pass the minimum standard set by the National College Entrance examination administered by the government.

2.3.2 Classification and Funding of Educational Institutions

Educational institutions are either public (state) or private. Private institutions account for 85 percent of the total collegiate population.

Public institutions are organized and financially supported by the government. These may be categorized into state colleges and universities set up by legislative charter, non-chartered technical institutes, and community colleges.

Private institutions are either sectarian or nonsectarian. Sectarian schools are owned and administered by religious groups and organized as non-stock corporations which reinvest all profits in the school. Nonsectarian schools are organized as stock corporations which declare dividends to stockholders. Since 1969, a few nonsectarian schools have been converted into non-stock, non-profit educational foundations following passage of a law (Republic Act 6055) encouraging such conversions.

Private schools are supported primarily by tuition and other student fees besides the private funds invested by owners. With few exceptions, there are no endowments, government subsidies, or other major sources of income. Increases in tuition fees and their disposition are regulated by the government.

Educational foundations can avail themselves of long-term, low-interest loans from government lending institutions as well as exemptions from the payment of certain taxes on income derived from property used exclusively for the educational activities of the foundation.

Recognizing the crucial role of private education in the Philippines, a Fund for Assistance to Private Education (FAPE) was established in 1968 through a project agreement between the Philippines and U.S. governments. It is endowed with P24 million from the War Damage Fund given by the U.S. Congress to rehabilitate the Philippines from heavy damages sustained during World War II. Fund earnings are used to finance programs designed to upgrade private education by identifying deficiencies in the educational system and undertaking programs that would foster the solution of these problems. Since its inception, FAPE has funded projects in the areas of accreditation, educational policy formulation and information, student recruitment and career choice, exploration of development dimensions in education, graduate centers and fellowships, and an educational retirement plan.

2.3.3 Government Supervision and Regulation

The Philippine Constitution provides that all educational institutions shall be under the supervision of, and subject to regulation by the State.

Chartered colleges and universities are granted autonomy by their respective charters. Internal governance is exercised by a Board of Regents (or Trustees) whose members are either ex-officio or appointed by the President of the Philippines, and whose chairman is, by tradition, the Minister of Education and Culture.

Private colleges and universities are licensed, regulated, and supervised by the Ministry of Education and Culture through its Bureau of Higher Education. No private institution can operate as an educational entity without a permit or recognition granted by the Ministry. Internal governance is a responsibility of the individual school, but policies and programs must conform with regulations and requirements prescribed by the Ministry. Moreover, the Minister of Education and Culture, or his representatives, supervises and inspects these institutions for the purpose of "maintaining a general standard of efficiency consistent with the courses offered." However, supervision is minimal since the Ministry does not have the funds to support the elaborate machinery needed to monitor and regulate the activities of the system.

Course requirements in educational programs for the professions must conform with minimum standards set in each profession. The Professional Regulation Commission, in conjunction with the appropriate examining board (the Board of Accountancy for the accounting profession) and the Ministry of Education and Culture, has the power to prescribe or revise collegiate courses which are a requisite for admission to the practice of a profession.

2.3.4 Accounting Education at the Sub-Professional Level

The development of reputable vocational programs to meet the technical and middle-level manpower requirements of the accounting profession has been largely neglected in the Philippines. The educational system has tended to emphasize professional-level education.

Vocational training is provided in post-secondary technical institutes and in non-degree programs offered by tertiary-level schools, but these generally suffer from lack of qualified teachers, inadequate financial support, and the inability to attract students. The thinking persists that vocational education is only for those who lack the intellectual capacity to tackle the more exacting requirements of a college education. Moreover, educational requirements for sub-professional occupations have been upgraded by most employers who prefer college trained personnel (of which there is an abundant supply) to vocational school graduates.

Some schools have endeavored to fill up this gap in accounting education by integrating sub-professional training into the professional level accounting program. Under this concept, called a ladder-type curriculum, the student is prepared for the profession in stages, each stage representing a particular rung in the occupational ladder, from technician, to sub-professional, to professioal. A terminal certificate is awarded upon completion of each stage, and this is a

275

requisite for continuing to the next stage of the program.

The different steps in the ladder-type curriculum of the Polytechnic University of the Philippines which pioneered in this concept are summarized in Exhibit 1.

EXHIBIT 1

**Ladder-Type Accounting Curriculum at the
Polytechnic University of the Philippines**

Curric-ulum Year	Objectives	Job Targets	Terminal Certificate
First	To develop competencies in initial clerical positions in accounting.	Bookkeeper-cashier Billing clerk Receiving and paying clerk Bookkeeper-typist	Bookkeeper-Cashier certificate
Second	To develop competencies for specialized clerical accounting work.	Senior bookkeeper Payroll clerk Posting clerk Accounting clerk Cost computing clerk	Associate in Accounting diploma
Third	To develop competencies for accounting or accounting-related positions in data processing centers	Programmers Accounting machine operators Keypunch operators	Diploma in business data processing
Fourth	To prepare for professional accounting careers.	Accountant Controller Auditor Financial executive Management or tax consultant	Bachelor in Accountancy degree

2.3.5 Accounting Education at the Professional Level

To qualify for the CPA examinations, a candidate must complete a tertiary-level program of academic studies leading to the degree of Bachelor of Science in Commerce or its equivalent in an educational institution recognized by the government.

Schools with accounting programs: Accounting is one of several specialized fields of study in undergraduate schools of business. There are no separate schools of accountancy.

There are 297 colleges and universities in the Philippines that offer the undergraduate professional-level accounting program. These are classified as to type of ownership and location in Exhibit 2.

276

EXHIBIT 2

Colleges and Universities Offering Professional-Level Accounting Programs

Type of ownership	Luzon	Location Visayas	Mindanao	Total
Public (state)	5	1	1	7
Private sectarian	59	26	38	123
Private nonsectarian	100	30	37	167
Total	164	57	76	297

Source: FAPE Atlas, Vol II, 1975

Program of studies: The length of the typical accounting program is four academic years. An academic year is divided into two semestral terms and a summer term. A semester consist of 18 weeks with at least 100 class days. Summer sessions may be either six or nine weeks in length.

The curriculum specifying the different courses and the sequence in which they are to be taken, is prescribed by the school and approved by the Board of Regents in state colleges or universities, or by the Bureau of Higher Education in the case of private schools.

Students earn units of credit for each course or subject passed. A unit of credit is equivalent to one hour of lecture or recitation each week for a total of 18 hours in a semester. The usual schedule of a lecture or recitation course is three hours a week or the equivalent of three units of credit. Three hours of laboratory work are regarded as the equivalent of one hour of recitation or lecture. The maximum load for a full-time student is between 18 to 21 units per semester, the equivalent of from six to seven three-unit courses. During the summer term the maximum load is nine units.

Under the standards adopted by the Bureau of Higher Education, the minimum requirement for the degree of Bachelor of Science in Commerce or its equivalent is 144 units of credit, of which 60 units should be earned in liberal arts and science courses and 75 units in business courses. The remaining 9 units are free electives.

All programs intended to qualify graduates for the CPA examinations must include the following minimum courses prescribed by the Board of Accountancy through the Professional Regulation Commission (14):

Accounting and auditing	36 units
Business law	9 units
Taxation	6 units
English	15 units
Mathematics	9 units
Management	6 units

The PACSB model curriculum: Most member schools of the Philippine Association of Collegiate Schools of Business (PACSB) have adopted the model program presented in Exhibit 3, which was developed by PACSB with government encouragement. The PACSB model program specifies a total of 162 units of credit, broken down into a liberal education core of 72 units, a basic business education core of 51 units, professional accounting subjects of 33 units, and electives of 6 units.

The core program is taken by all business students regardless of their field of specialization, and is intended to provide a common educational foundation from which to proceed to more specialized study.

The liberal education core seeks to broaden the intellectual interests of students, develop their competence in written and spoken English, and provide them with the education essential for their development into productive and versatile citizens. The business education core seeks to provide foundational knowledge and understanding about the functional areas of business, the analytical tools and techniques utilized in business, and the environmental and social settings in which business operations take place.

EXHIBIT 3

PACSB Model Accounting Program

I. Core Program
    A. Liberal Education core
        1. English .... 15 units
        2. Spanish .... 12 units
        3. Filipino .... 6 units
        4. Social/behavioral sciences ... 15 units
        5. Natural sciences .... 6 units
        6. Mathematics .... 12 units
        7. Liberal education electives .. 3 units
        8. Rizal .... 3 units   72 units

    B. Basic Business Education core
        1. Accounting .... 12 units
        2. Economics .... 6 units
        3. Finance .... 6 units
        4. Management .... 6 units
        5. Marketing .... 3 units
        6. Taxation .... 6 units
        7. Business law .... 9 units
        8. Business statistics .... 3 units   51 units

II. Major subject (accounting) .... 33 units
III. Professional electives .... 6 units
IV. Free electives .... 3 units
V.   Physical education (noncredit) .... (4) units
VI. Reserve Officers' Training Corp. (noncredit) ..... (6) units

    Total Units .... 162 units

The PACSB curriculum allows a school to offer a total of 51 units of accounting and auditing courses which, typically, might consist of the following:

Fundamentals of accounting	6 units
Partnership and corporation accounting	3 units
Intermediate financial accounting	9 units
Advanced financial accounting	6 units
Cost accounting	6 units
Management accounting	6 units
Auditing theory and practice	9 units
Other accounting courses (government accounting, accounting systems, refresher, practicum, etc.)	6 units
Total	51 units

The contents of accounting courses are, in most cases, patterned after the CPA examination syllabus prepared by the Board of Accountancy.

CPA Review: Upon completing the undergraduate program, most candidates undertake an intensive review course to prepare for the CPA examinations. Although not a requisite for admission to the CPA examination, the review course is generally regarded as an integral part of the educational preparation of candidates because of its rigour and comprehensiveness. The course involves between 500 and 600 class hours, allocated to the different CPA examination subjects. Review classes are handled by a number of review schools which are not presently regulated or supervised by the government, although some are affiliated with government-recognized colleges and universities.

2.3.6 Continuing Professional Education

The code of ethics promulgated by the Philippine Board of Accountancy provides that "every CPA should continuously strive to improve his knowledge, skills, and techniques." There is no requirement for CPAs to demonstrate that they are continuing their professional education, but the matter of making this a legal condition for the continued validity of the CPA certificate has been seriously considered.

Professional development is often constrained by lack of interest, inadequate time and resources, and pressure of work, but there is evidence that it is taken seriously by significant segments of the accounting profession. Besides on-the-job training and informal self-study, continuing education is pursued through graduate studies leading to advanced degrees, non-degree professional development courses, in-house staff training programs, and professional development programs of the accounting societies.

Postgraduate studies: Postgraduate studies leading to advanced degrees in business have been offered as early as 1935 when the University of Santo Tomas introduced graduate programs leading to a Master of Science in Commerce, a Ph.D. in Commerce, and a Ph.D. in Economics. Initially, only academicians were attracted to these programs. Since the 1950s however, there has been increasing interest in graduate programs for professional managers.

At present, there are twenty-four schools with master's programs in business, at least two of which offer programs leading to a master's degree in accounting. There are two schools with doctoral business programs. The quality of some graduate schools such as the Asian Institute of Management is such that they have attracted students from neighboring Asian countries.

An MBA degree is now generally regarded as helpful in advancing a professional career in accounting. A growing number of CPAs in business, government, and public accounting have acquired advanced business degrees from schools in the Philippines and abroad. Most seem to prefer programs in general management (rather than accounting), perhaps to balance their specialized undergraduate accounting training.

Professional development courses: Since the 1950s, a number of schools, private training institutes, management consulting firms, and professional societies have been offering short-term, non-degree professional development courses on varied aspects of business. These courses are popular, particularly among those unable to devote time to a full-fledged graduate program. They have played a useful role in keeping participants updated on new concepts and techniques and on current business trends and developments.

In-house staff training programs: The need for organizaed and continuing staff training programs is generally recognized by business, public accounting firms, and the government. These programs take several forms depending on the size of the firm, the time, resources, and facilities available, and the complexity of training desired.

In the smaller firms, staff development may consist of on-the-job training, informal self-study, conference, postgraduate studies, and enrollment in non-degree professional development programs.

The larger business firms make use of scheduled lectures, conferences, case studies, textbook study, field trips, and other features of formal education. Besides the firm's executives, qualified and experienced lecturers are engaged to deliver lectures and act as discussion leaders. A particular course may be given by a single company for its own staff, but at times, various firms in the same business or industry combine their resources to offer such a course.

The large accounting firms have well-planned continuing staff development programs catering to the needs of staff at all levels. Full-time training classes ranging from a few days to six weeks are held during the slack season. Firms with international affiliations have personnel exchange programs whereby promising staff members are sent to other offices abroad to allow them to gain more insight and experience with people of other nationalities and cultures. Staff are also encouraged to pursue graduate studies, attend nondegree programs, and participate in activities of the professional organization, often at company expense.

The continuing professional development of accountants in the public sector is handled by the Manpower Development and Systems office of the Commission on Audit, in coordination with the Budget Commission and the Civil Service Commission. This office formulates long-range comprehensive training plans and prepares and implements annual training programs for all personnel of the Commission on Audit as well as all accounting, collecting, disbursing, internal auditing, and budgetary personnel of the government.

Role of accounting societies: The various accounting societies encourage the continuing professional development of their members and provide opportunities for professional growth through research, publications, seminars, meetings, and conventions.

The most active in this regard has been PICPA. The institute maintains library facilities for its members, sponsors monthly meetings and annual conventions, and publishes a quarterly technical magazine, *The Accountants' Journal.* A staff training program for personnel of small- and medium-sized accounting firms is held from time to time, as are seminars, workshops, and symposia on management and financial accounting, taxation, auditing, and other topics of interest to accountants.

PICPA's professional development activities are presently handled by eight volunteer working committees. It is now planned to integrate these activities and have them managed by a full-time professional staff. The institute's long-range planning committee has recommended the creation of a foundation to develop and maintain continuing professional education programs for CPAs in all sectors of practice, and to conduct relevant research in support of the profession's services.

3. An Appraisal of Accounting Education

The following appraisal of accounting education in the Philippines is confined to the your-year professional level program leading to the CPA examinations. Emphasis is place on conditions obtaining in private colleges and universities which account for 85 percent of the tertiary level student population in the country.

The main source of statistics presented in this section is a 1978 study conducted by the Philippine Association of Collegiate Schools of Business (PACSB) on the state of business education in private institutions of higher learning. For the purpose of this study, PACSB sent out survey questionnaires to 167 private business schools selected on a random basis and received responses from 72 schools. This was followed by team visits to 50 schools which responded to the questionnaire.

It must be stated that standards of accounting education vary among schools. Generalizations should not obscure the fact that while the quality of accounting programs in some schools leaves something to be desired, other schools have maintained their programs at a high level.

3.1 Objectives of Accounting Education

The PICPA has taken the position that accounting education should maintain a sensible balance between long- and short-run objectives. (15)

The primary objective should be to prepare the student for a career in accounting and related fields. This implies that schools should mold the student into a well-rounded professional, rather than a narrow specialist. It also implies the development of those qualities that will enable the student to cope with the problems he is likely to face in his career, benefit from experience, continue his education, and progress to the limit to which his innate abilities will carry him.

As a subsidiary objective, PICPA suggests that the student should also be prepared for the CPA examination and his first job. Given a reasonable review period, the accounting graduate should be able to take and pass the CPA examination. He should also be reasonably qualified for entry level positions in accounting and related fields and, with the necessary orientation and supervision, be able to carry out his initial jobs efficiently and effectively.

The formal written objectives of business schools commonly emphasize long-run objectives couched in general terms, such as "to give the student a well-rounded education in business," or "to train and produce competent professionals," or "to provide general education and training for executive leadership and administrative and career positions," etc.

Despite their formally professed objectives, most schools are pressured into emphasizing the short-run objectives of preparing students for immediate employment and the CPA examination. The government, as a matter of policy, would like graduates to be immediately employable. Students expect to land jobs after graduation, and many employers want graduates who can be productive as soon as possible. The CPA examinations are frequently used to gauge the quality of a school's accounting program, and possession of a CPA certificate greatly enhances the employability of a young graduate.

Overemphasis on short-run objectives has led to criticism that accounting education is "too narrowly specialized." Not infrequently, one hears complaints that accounting graduates are deficient in communication skills, in their understanding of human behavior, in their capacity for analytical thinking, in their adaptability to change, etc.

3.2 The Accounting Curriculum

The accounting curriculum has been revised a number of times in order to upgrade accounting education. Among other things, these revisions have lengthened the accounting program from 120 to 162 units, expanded and enriched the general education portion, and strengthened the technical portion by the introduction of quantitative business techniques and management accounting. The present curriculum is an improvement over the past. However, curriculum evaluation is a continuing process, and several problems remain unresolved.

One problem relates to the need to expose students to practical experience in order to narrow the gap between theoretical training and practical application. The value of experience as part of the total educational preparation of CPAs is generally not disputed. But not all students can be accommodated in the various offices, and not many employers can provide students with the type of experience which they need. In 1967, the Accountancy Law was amended to require that CPA candidates posses one year experience in accounting through employment or apprenticeship, or an acceptable academic substitute. This requirement was removed in 1975 because of difficulties encountered in setting up and enforcing meaningful standards of evaluating the quality of work experience obtained by candidates.

Another problem relates to education and certification in specialized areas of accounting practice other than public accounting.

Because of the influence of the CPA examinations, accounting courses are still heavily oriented towards financial accounting and external auditing. It is claimed that not enough emphasis has been placed on preparing students for careers in the government service and in management accounting. At the prodding of the Philippine government's Commission on Audit, a separate four-year program for government accounting and auditing was developed in 1976. This program is being offered by some schools, but except for those already in the government service, it has generally not attracted many students.

Certification examinations in internal auditing have been given by the local chapter of the Institute of Internal Auditors, and the Philippine Association of Management Accountants is laying the ground work for a Certified Management Accountant's examination patterned after a similar program of the National Accounting Association in the U.S. The PACSB has recommended that the Professional Regulation Commission and PICPA look into the feasibility of offering different types of government examinations besides that for certified public accountant.

These separate developments need to be better planned and coordinated. Instead of setting up separate undergraduate programs in different areas of specialization, the present program should probably be broadened to prepare the student for general practice in the broad field of accounting. Postgraduate education, experience, and a certification examination can then be required to obtain recognition as a specialist in a particular area of practice.

A third problem relates to the proliferation of subject matter. As new material is added to the curriculum, there is a tendency for courses and course contents to increase without eliminating those which have become obsolete or nonessential. This is aggravated by legislation requiring the inclusion of certain subjects in the curriculum, as exemplified by the legislative requirement that all business students take 24 units of Spanish (later reduced to 12 units). In many schools, the curriculum needs to be re-examined to eliminate obsolete topics and unnecessary detail, and to ensure that only the most relevant and significant subject matter is included.

At the same time, new material needs to be introduced and others updated in order to meet the future needs of the profession. For example, PICPA's Committee on Computer Accounting has noted the need to give greater emphasis on computer education. Because of financial constraints and lack of faculty, only three schools offer computer courses to their students. Some perceptive accountants have also urged that the profession look beyond traditional business accounting to the field of socioeconomic accounting. At present, this area is considered the domain of the economist and is discussed only briefly in the macroeconomics course required of all business students.

A fourth problem relates to the need to integrate and coordinate the different subjects in the curriculum. In a system in which students pass or fail individual subjects and no comprehensive examinations are given at the end of the academic year or course offering, each subject tends to be isolated from the others, and students fail to obtain a unified view of the entire curriculum. Interdisciplinary relationships among subjects becomes difficult. Subjects tend to overlap in content because instructors usually do not know what has been covered or stressed in other subjects.

Finally, there are some who feel that private schools should be given greater leeway to experiment, develop, and adopt accounting programs that suit their peculiar facilities, faculties, students, resources, and educational philosophy. According to the PACSB study, school deans feel that government regulations give them little flexibility in curriculum development. On the other hand, the Bureau of Higher Education disclaims any intent to force private schools into one standard mold.

3.3 Accounting Students

The average accounting student enters college at age 17 after ten years of pre-collegiate education. A 1976 survey conducted for PICPA reveals that a large majority of accounting students are young, between 19 and 21 years of age in their junior and senior years in college. Female students outnumber males, 71 percent to 29 percent in the metro-Manila area, and 65 percent to 35 percent outside this area. Accounting seems to be attracting some of the best students as indicated by the fact that more than 50 percent of those surveyed graduated with high school honors. The most important reason given for choosing accounting as a field of study was "greater employment opportunities." (16)

Allowing for the existence of "exclusive" schools, students in the business programs generally come from low income families who are not able to finance a more expensive type of schooling. Fifty-one percent of the respondents to the PACSB survey claim that their students could not afford to buy textbooks.

Over the past two decades or so, a decline in the quality of pre-collegiate education has been noted, resulting in secondary school graduates who are not properly prepared for work at the tertiary level. Because of the poor pre-collegiate preparation, it has often become necessary to give remedial work at the college level to entering freshmen, particularly in the areas of English and mathematics. It has also been observed that the average undergraduate student lacks the maturity, exposure, and experience to fully grasp the managerial decision-making process and its ramifications.

Admission requirements for accounting students vary among schools. Some are very selective, while others admit anyone who meets the minimum qualifications set by the government. Forty-three percent of the schools responding to the PACSB survey indicated that they require students to pass a school-administered entrance examination. After admission, students intending to specialize in accounting are screened further by 66 percent of the respondents. Screening devices consist of any one or more of the following: (1) a minimum grade in basic accounting courses, (2) a minimum average grade in all of the first and second year courses, (3) a qualifying examination, and (4) an interview.

In general, there is a need to upgrade standards of admission and retention in most schools. Admission requirements should be more rigid and uniform. There should be more aptitude tests and guidance counseling to help students determine whether they have the qualities needed for an accounting career and the capacity to pursue professional level college work leading to the CPA certificate.

3.4 Academic Qualifications of Faculty

Regulations of the Bureau of Higher Education require that faculty members handling undergraduate collegiate courses should be holders of, at least, a master's degree. Any deviation from this rule has to be approved by the Bureau on a case-to-case basis. The Board of Accountancy further requires that accounting and auditing courses be handled by certified public accountants.

Out of 2,479 faculty members teaching business courses in schools responding to the PACSB survey, 1.6 percent were doctoral degree holders, 21.7 percent were master's degree holders, and the rest, 76.7 percent, were holders of a bachelor's degree. It is likely that the percentage of accounting faculty without advanced degrees is much higher than the average for the business faculty as a whole. The PACSB has requested the Bureau of Higher Education to exempt instructors in accounting and business law from the master's degree requirement until such a time as the educational qualifications of faculty can be upgraded.

Most business schools are unable to upgrade the educational qualifications of their faculty because they lack the resources to attract qualified faculty and to develop those already on their staff. It is difficult enough to recruit CPAs to join the faculty, let alone CPAs with advanced degrees. It must be stated however, that among the ranks of accounting teachers without master's degrees, there are several whose competence, experience, natural gifts, and devotion to duty more than compensate for their lack of academic credentials. Moreover, there are those who believe that for advanced accounting courses, meaningful experience may be a more important qualification than advanced degrees.

3.5 Teaching Loads

The Bureau of Higher Education regards 24 hours a week as the maximum load for a full-time college teacher with no other regular remunerative employment. For part-time teachers, the maximum load is 12 hours a week. Except for highly technical or specialized courses, at least 60 percent of a college faculty should be employed on a full-time basis.

As actually practiced, faculty members may be categorized into full time, full load, and part-time.

Full-time faculty are those whose total working day is devoted to the institution, who have no other regular remunerative employment, and who are paid on a regular monthly basis regardless of the number of hours taught. As thus defined, there are relatively few full-time faculty. They are found mostly in state colleges and universities, and in some private, mostly sectarian, institutions. In state colleges and universities, they carry a teaching load of from 6 to 12 hours a week, must spend 40 hours a week in the institution and make available 10 hours outside their teaching hours for consultation with students. The teaching load may be reduced if the faculty member is engaged in research, creative writing, productive scholarship, or administrative work.

Full-load faculty are those who carry the maximum teaching load permitted full-time faculty, but who are not committed to spend their time outside teaching hours with with the institution. While they rely on teaching as their principal occupation, some may be engaged in private business, professional practice, or some other remunerative employment. Others divide their time between two or more institutions to increase their teaching loads and overall compensation.

Part-time faculty are those who are fully employed in an occupation other than teaching, and whose regular teaching load does not usually exceed 12 hours a week.

Out of 2,479 faculty members handling business courses in the schools responding to the PACSB survey, 49 percent are full-load and 51 percent part-time. This classification is based on number of hours taught, rather than commitment of a full working day to one institution. A majority (52 percent) of the full-load faculty have regular teaching assignments of from 18 to 21 hours a week. This is increased to a maximum of 24 to 27 hours when exigencies require the assignment of additional teaching loads. For some (8 percent), maximum teaching loads are as high as 30 to 33 hours a week. Part-time faculty have regular loads varying from 6 to 15 hours a week.

Teaching loads exceed standards set by the government because of lack of qualified faculty, but sometimes this is used to increase faculty compensation on a per-hour or per-course basis. A large share of teaching in business schools is carried on by part-time faculty who can pass on the benefit of their experience to students and help them find jobs. On the other hand, teaching suffers because there is often not enough time and stamina for study and research, or sometimes even for class preparation and attendance.

3.6 Faculty Compensation

Fifty-six percent of the schools surveyed by PACSB compensate their faculty on an hourly basis; 15 percent on a per-subject basis, and 28 percent on a monthly basis. Schools give a variety of fringe benefits: vacation leave, sick leave, hospitalization, insurance, retirement pensions, educational and character loans, bonuses, and tuition discounts to students or spouses.

The regulations of the Bureau of Higher Education provide that, as a general rule, faculty remuneration should be comparable with prevailing minimum salary rates for corresponding ranks in government schools in the locality. In general, faculty salaries in private schools are below those in state colleges and universities, and those in the rural areas are lower than those in the urban areas.

Industry and government offer much higher compensation, more attractive working conditions, and opportunities for advancement than can be obtained in colleges and universities. As a consequence, educational institutions are finding it increasingly difficult to recruit and retain competent faculty, particularly in accounting and other specialized courses. This situation has been aggravated in recent years by inflation and the regulation of tuition fees by the government. The problem is critical in private institutions which depend primarily on student fees to sustain operations, including faculty compensation.

3.7 Faculty Development

The rules of ethics promulgated by the Board of Accountancy provide that a CPA in education has the responsibility of achieving professional competence as a teacher.

To provide avenues for professional development, workshops or seminars are conducted periodically by individual schools as well as by professional bodies such as PICPA, PACSB, and ACPAE. Each year, PICPA co-sponsors with a leading accounting firm, a summer faculty training program consisting of formal sessions on a simulated audit engagement capped by actual on-the-job training. Schools offer scholarships, fellowships, and other incentives to enable faculty to pursue advanced academic degrees.

The PACSB study gives us the following picture of the nature and extent of support given by business schools to faculty development in school year 1976-1977:

Total business faculty	2,479
Studies towards advanced degrees abroad:	
Full scholarships	4
Partial scholarships	1
Studies towards advanced degrees within the country:	
Full fellowships	25
Partial fellowships	1
Reduced tuition and other fees	197
Reduced teaching loads with no reduction in salary	16
Attendance at seminars, conferences, etc., subsidized by the school:	
Local programs	439
Programs held abroad	5

In many schools, faculty training programs need to be better planned and coordinated, made continuous and more meaningful.

Meaningful faculty development, particularly in private schools is severely constrained by lack of funds. According to the PACSB study, funds for faculty development are obtained from the school budget (72 percent of the schools), from local private sources (21 percent), from the government (7 percent), and from foreign sources (4 percent). The PACSB study further notes that financial support is inadequate or practically nonexistent. Moreover, schools who fund faculty development frequently run the risk of losing faculty members to business, industry, or the government after they obtain their advanced degrees.

On the part of faculty members, there is not enough incentive for professional development since income is reduced while studying, while payments must be made for books, transportation, and other out-of-pocket costs. The expenses of further development are frequently not justified by the relatively small incremental income that can be derived from advancement in a teaching career, unless one looks forward to other jobs besides teaching.

3.8 Teaching Methods and Techniques

The use of any acceptable method of teaching is allowed provided it is challenging, effective, and it produces the result contemplated by the aporoved course of study. The methods and techniques used and the effectiveness of their application depend to a large degree on the quality and attitude of faculty and students, and on encouragement provided by school administrators.

The more commonly used teaching methods consist of textbook assignments and lectures combined with blackboard demonstrations, recitations, class discussions, and problem-solving. Practice sets are utilized to inject real-life situations in the classroom. Other techniques used to a lesser degree are case studies, role-playing, survey-type research, and organized field trips. Some schools have internship programs.

The blackboard and mimeographing machine are standard equipment in all schools. More sophisticated audiovisual aids such as overhead projectors, film strips, etc., are used in the more affluent institutions.

With some exceptions, there is probably too much emphasis on preparing students for the CPA examinations through memorization and drill, and not enough on developing critical analysis, reflective thinking, and independent judgment. Students tend to be spoon-fed and overly dependent on the instructor. More innovative teaching techniques and approaches must be adopted so that students are motivated to think for themselves and to continue their education even beyond the termination of their formal schooling.

3.9 Textbooks and Supplementary Materials

Any textbook may be adopted provided it reflects current business trends and practices, is up to date in methods of presentation and content, and has not previously been disapproved by the government's Board of Textbooks. The use of Filipino-authored textbooks and teaching materials is encouraged by the government.

According to the PACSB survey, 43 percent of the textbooks used in business schools are written by Filipino authors, 57 percent by foreign (American) authors. Some American textbooks have been adapted to local conditions by Filipino co-authors.

The most commonly used supplementary teaching materials are cases, business articles, industry and technical notes, workbooks, and practice sets.

There is a need to develop more textbooks and supplementary materials that reflect Philippine conditions, are within the range of comprehension of Filipino accounting students, and are available at a price the students can afford. The languge content of American textbooks which are written for students with 12 years of pre-tertiary education is not suitable for Filipino students who have only 10 years of pre-tertiary education.

3.10 Library Facilities

The Bureau of Higher Education expects schools to have library facilities that are adequate in quantity and quality, helpful in serving the needs of scholarship and research, and progressively growing in accordance with institutional development and expansion plans. There are minimum requirements for the number of library staff and books which should be maintained, depending upon enrollment.

A survey of library facilities by FAPE in 1973 revealed that in commerce and business administration, the ratio of total book collection to total enrollment was 2.48 in the private sector and .29 in the public sector. (17) Another study indicates that an estimated 40 percent of library holdings are outdated and no longer useful. (18)

Equally important are conducive reading rooms and a sufficiently lighted and properly ventilated library. There are no available studies on these aspects of library facilities.

3.11 Research in Business Schools

Research is generally acknowledged as one of the basic functions of business schools. However, research activities are hampered by lack of funds, lack of qualified staff, lack of time on the part of the faculty, lack of proper atmosphere, and lack of encouragement given by the government to research in the private sector. (19)

The observation has been made that under conditions existing in the Philippines, the research function can only be properly discharged by state institutions which are funded by the government, and by the few private colleges which derive assistance from foreign foundations. The bulk of private educational institutions which depend on student fees for their subsistence must necessarily commit their resources and efforts to teaching, subordinating if not entirely sacrificing the traditional research function of higher institutions of learning. (20)

Among the schools responding to the PACSB survey, 50 percent reported research activities. In 30 percent of such schools, there is a separate research unit or staff assisted by faculty members. In others, research is undertaken by faculty, either individually or by groups, with little or no coordination or monitoring by the school.

The most common types of research activities are the development of teaching materials, survey type research, textbook writing, and review of literature.

Eighty percent of the schools with research activities provided assistance to faculty undertaking research in one or more of the following ways: use of school facilities, honoraria, reduction in teaching load, facilitating research grants from other sources, provision of research assistants, research grants, thesis funding, and professional chairs. Research activities were funded from tuition fees (70 percent of the schools), foundations (27 percent), and donations (3 percent).

3.12 Performance in the CPA Examinations

The quality of accounting programs may, to some extent, be measured by the performance of graduates in external examinations. Exhibit 4 shows the percentage of candidates who passed the CPA examinations given by the Board of Accountancy in the last five years.

EXHIBIT 4

CPA Examination Results (1975-1979)

Date of Examination	Total Candidates	Total Passed	Percent Passed
Oct 1975	8,253	1,829	22
Oct 1976	10,095	2,294	23
Apr 1977	3,294	883	27
Oct 1977	7,871	2,644	34
Apr 1978	4,077	904	22
Oct 1978	7,799	2,101	27
May 1979	4,599	1,324	29
Oct 1979	8,058	2,605	32

Source: Professional Regulation Commission

The composite figures conceal the fact that graduates of some schools perform exceedingly well in the examinations, while those of others perform poorly. The high mortality of candidates in the latter case underscores the need to tighten admission and retention standards for accounting students. Many of those who fail should probably have been channeled to sub-professional programs or to other disciplines.

Concern has been expressed over the generally poor showing of candidates in the CPA examinations. PACSB has recommended that schools whose accounting graduates show a consistently poor passing percentage should be penalized by having their accounting programs phased out, or by not allowing their graduates to take the CPA examinations.

3.13 Absorption of Graduates in the Labor Market

One of the criticisms hurled against the existing system of higher education in the Philippines is that it has failed to match the output of graduates with the manpower requirements of the economy. It is claimed, for example, that the level of enrollment in business programs and the number of business graduates is much greater than the demands of the labor market, resulting in many graduates who cannot find employment or are underemployed.

On the other hand, there are those who argue that the bases for existing studies have not been wide and broad enough to permit analysis and forecasts with sufficient consideration to waiting periods for jobs, to exchangeability of skills, to effects of technological innovations, to skills and knowledge required rather than to the kinds of workers needed, etc. (21). Because the Philippine economy is volatile, it is doubted whether educational and economic planners can, at any given time and with a reasonable degree of certainty, identify which job opportunities warrant specific training. (22)

A recent study notes that college graduates wait for about six months before landing a job, and within a year after graduation nearly 80 percent get employed. In the employment market, business graduates are the most flexible; they are capable of having a job in any of the standard occupational classes (23). Accounting graduates enjoy even greater employment flexibility than other business graduates. They are, for example, apparently preferred over banking and finance majors for basically credit and finance jobs. There continues to be a demand for qualified accountants as evidenced by the recruiting activities of business and accounting firms, the critical shortage of accounting teachers, and the employment opportunities advertised in the newspapers.

The PACSB study advocates long-term comprehensive planning to orient the educational system to the manpower requirements of the economy. The creation of an interagency committee to define regional manpower requirements at different occupational levels is proposed. Given these requirements, an educational plan will be developed to define the programs and levels of training needed to support manpower requirements and to prescribe policies and guidelines for determining and controlling the level and quality of enrollment in each program. Studies to monitor the absorpiton of graduates in the mainstream of employment will be undertaken periodically, perhaps every five years, for the guidance of students in their choice of a career, and the education sector in program development and resource allocation.

3.14 Accreditation of Educational Institutions

Pioneering work on accreditation in the Philippines has been done by the Philippine Accrediting Association for Schools, Colleges, and Universities (PAASCU) since 1957. PAASCU grants accreditation in Liberal Arts, Business, and Education.

There is general acceptance among business schools of the concept of accreditation as a means of maintaining uniform, high quality standards of business education. Twenty-one percent of the respondent schools in the PACSB survey have been accredited by a recognized accrediting institution; 93 percent feel that there should be an accrediting institution which should specialize in the accreditation of business schools and programs.

4. Summary and Conclusions

Accounting as a profession was introduced in the Philippines by English and American accountants at the turn of the century. In 1923 legal recognition was accorded the profession through the passage of an accountancy act which created a Board of Accountancy, provided for a CPA examination, and prescribed requirements for admission to the profession.

Over the years, the profession has grown in numbers, in the variety and sophistication of services rendered, and in prestige. Accounting has become firmly established as a profession in the Philippines, and CPAs are looked upon as providing a valuable professional service essential to economic development. This status could not have been possible without the large pool of accounting graduates turned out by the country's educational system. Accounting education has played and continues to play an important role in the development of the accounting profession.

Since the passage of the first accountancy act, basic responsibility for the educational function has been assumed by colleges and universities. Future accountants are prepared for the profession primarily through formal academic education, rather than experience. Possession of a college degree in business is a prerequisite for admission to the CPA examination.

In response to social demand, many colleges and universities were established in the Philippines, most of them privately owned. Filipinos learned to value education as a means to improve their economic status and achieve upward mobility. Accounting in particular became a popular career choice. Today, business students comprise nearly 30 percent of the total collegiate population, and approximately 50 percent are accounting majors.

The rapid, largely unplanned growth of schools and enrollments has strained limited resources and spawned declines in quality and other problems that today confront accounting education. There is a critical shortage of qualified accounting faculty. Teaching staffs are generally overloaded with teaching assignments and/or outside employment, with consequently little time for professional development and research. Academic standards vary among schools. In many, there has to be a more rigid screening of students, better methods of instruction, improved facilities, and higher retention and promotion standards. Educational finance is a critical problem and will be a major constraint on any attempts to upgrade accounting education in the future. The problem is particularly acute in the case of private institutions which derive their main support from student fees and are presently in a financial squeeze because of spiraling costs on one hand, and government limitations on student fee increases on the other.

The basic problems of accounting education are deeply ingrained in the educational system as a whole; their solution is tied up with the need to reform the system. Weaknesses and deficiencies in the country's educational system have provoked critical appraisal since the late fifties.

Responding to popular clamor, President Marcos established in December, 1969, a Presidential Commission to Survey Philippine Education (PCSPE) to undertake a thorough study and assessment of education in the Philippines and to make recommendations for policy and implementation. The commission's report was released in 1970.

Surveys of Philippine education have been made regularly since 1925, but few have been taken as seriously as the PCSPE study. Its recommendation provided the basis for Presidential Decree No. 6-A (The Educational Development Decree of 1972), which outlines major reforms in education and establishes a framework for the formulation of educational policies.

Among the major educational reforms contemplated by the government are the following:

• Comprehensive long-range planning will be emphasized to orient the educational system towards national development goals. (24)

• Enrollment in tertiary-level courses will be rationalized to a level consistent with the manpower requirements of the country. For this purpose, mechanisms will be established to properly guide students into fields of studies directly related to jobs demanded in the labor market. (25)

• Effective admission programs will be developed and instituted with a view to improving the quality of entrants and graduates of higher educational institutions. (26)

• Through a system of incentives such as preferential tax rates, government subsidies, scholarship programs, etc., schools will be encouraged to join or form associations for accreditation. Those that fail to be accredited will be directly supervised by the government. (27)

• Both public and private sectors will be recognized by the government as integral components of a national system of higher education, and curricular programs, staffing patterns, and institutional development activities of both public and private institutions will be synchronized. (28)

• Middle-level-skills training needed for national development will be given greater emphasis and importance. (29)

• Government aid to non-government educational institutions is recognized in principle, provided their programs meet certain defined educational requirements and standards and contribute to the attainment of national development goals. (30)

• No new school will be allowed to operate as a stock corporation. (31) Existing schools which are already organized as stock corporations will be encouraged to convert themselves into non-stock, non-profit foundations.

Accounting education in the Philippines is at the crossroads. It must adjust and redirect itself if it is to continue serving the needs of the profession. It must recognize the urgency and inevitability of change in order to be relevant, efficient, and effective. The government has taken the first steps to reform and reorient the entire educational system. But there are clearly no quick and easy solutions in sight.

The basic problem is economics. The critical level of financial resources needed to sustain quality education is simply not available to most schools at this time. Society must pay more than lip-service to the concept of good education. It must be willing to support it financially. But more than adequate financing is needed. Good education is not cheap, but costly education can be poor. There should be more comprehensive, long-range planning that will tackle problems on an integrated and rational basis. Past experience has shown that these problems are interrelated, and that piecemeal, ad hoc solutions seldom produce lasting results, and even create new problems in themselves.

There should also be a greater willingness to innovate, to adapt to new needs and demands, to challenge traditional attitudes and practices and develop new and better ones. In the past, accounting education has expanded largely in its old image; through the years, it has become sluggish and tradition-bound. Finally, there must be a new will and determination to emphasize quality. Educational administrators should have the courage to enforce higher academic standards. Students who have neither the interest in, nor the aptitude and capacity for professional level work should be dropped from the rolls.

It has been observed that the educational crisis confronting the Philippines exists also in other developing and developed countries. Pressures of increased enrollments, rapidly rising costs, and the knowledge explosion are straining educational resources and facilities and challenging the rigidity of traditional educational systems. This phenomenon underscores the importance of international cooperation and assistance for the development of accounting education. The Philippines can profit from the experience of other systems facing comparable challenges, and the Philippines' experience should be of interest to others, particularly the accounting profession in developing countries.

NOTES

1. Presidential Decree No. 692, The Revised Accountancy Law, 1975, Sec. 6.
2. Ibid, Sec. 5.
3. Ibid, Sec. 3.
4. Ibid, Sec. 10.
5. Ibid, Sec. 11.
6. Ibid, Sec. 12.
7. Ibid, Sec. 13.
8. Ibid, Sec. 26.
9. Agoncillo, Teodoro and Guerrero, Milagros C., *History of the Filipino People*, 5th ed., Quezon City: R.P. Garcia Publishing Co., 1977, page 57.
10. National Census and Statistics Office, *Philippine Yearbook 1979*, Manila, pp. 212-214.
11. By proclamation of the President of the Philippines, the third week of March of every year since 1966 has been designated "Accountancy Week" for the purpose of "bringing to the attention of the public the important role played by CPAs in the development of the national economy."
12. National Economic and Development Authority, *Five-Year Philippine Development Plan*, 1978-1982, p. 208.
13. "See ENrollment of 13 M in June," *Bulletin Today* (Manila), May 29, 1980.
14. Republic Act 5166, *The Accountancy Act of 1967*, Sec. 6.
15. PICPA Committee on Education, "Curriculum Standards for Accounting Education," *The Accountants' Journal*, published by the Philippine Institute of CPAs, Manila, Vol. 16, December, 1966, pp. 347-356.

16. Bernabe, Teresa, "Profile of the Accounting Students," University of the Philippines, Quezon City, 1976, (mimeographed).
17. FAPE Atlas Survey as quoted in "A Framework for Private Higher Education Study," conference papers, 5th National Conference on Collegiate Schools of Business, March 29 to April 2, 1977 (mimeographed).
18. Isidro, Antonio, "Educational Diversity and Integration," *FAPE Review*, Makati, Rizal, July, 1976, p. 10.
19. Zwaenepoel, Paul P. *Tertiary Education in the Philippines 1611-1972, A Systems Analysis*, (Quezon City: Alemars-Pheonix Publishing House, 1975), p. 386.
20. Cruz, Santiago de la, Inaugural Address as second president of the University of the East, May 27, 1972.
21. Tenmatay, Augusto L., "Country Report (Philippines)" The Growth of Southeast Asian Universities: Expansion vs. Consolidation, workshop papers and proceedings, Regional Institute of Higher Education and Development, Singapore, December, 1973.
22. Isidro, A., and Ramos, M.D., *Private Colleges and Universities in the Philippines*, (Quezon City: Alemars-Phoenix Press, 1975), pp. 74-75.
23. "Matching the Academe with the World of Work," *The Philippines Sunday Express*, June 1, 1980, p. 11. (This is an excerpt from a study on Higher Education and the Labor Market, taken from FAPE Bulletin)
24. Presidential Decree No. 6-A, *The Educational Development Decree of 1972*, Sec. 3 and 4.
25. Op. cit., National Economic and Development Authority, p. 209.
26. Presidential Commission to Survey Philippine Education (PCSPE), *Education for National Development: New Patterns, New Directions*, Makati, Rizal, 1970, p. 116.
27. Ibid, PCSPE, pp. 112-113.
28. National Economic and Development Authority, *Long-Term Philippine Development Plan up to the Year 2000*, 1977, pp. 117-118.
29. Op. cit., Presidential Decree No. 6-A, Sec. 3-b.
30. Op. cit., PCSPE, p. 146.
31. Report No. 156 submitted by the Committee on Education and Culture to the Batasang Pambansa at its 2nd regular session, 1980, Chapter 3, Sec. 25.

BIBLIOGRAPHY

Books and Pamphlets

Agoncillo, Teodoro and Guerrero, Milagros C., *History of the Filipino People*, 5th ed., (Quezon City: R.P. Garcia Publishing Co., 1977)

Bureau of Private Schools, *Manual of Regulations for Private Schools*, 7th ed., 1970.

Business Education and National Development, Papers and Proceedings of the First National Conference of Business School Deans, 1973 (Manila: Philippine Association of Collegiate Schools of Business)

Carson, Arthur L., *The Story of Philippine Education*, (Quezon City: New Day Publishers, 1978)

Fund for Assistance to Philippine Education, *The Philippine Atlas*, 2 vols., Manila, 1975.

Isidro, A., and Ramos, M.D., Private Colleges and Universities in the Philippines (Quezon City: Alemars: Pheonix Press, 1973)

National Census and Statistics Office, Republic of the Philippines, *Philippine Year Book - 1979*, Manila, 1979.

National Economic and Development Authority, Republic of the Philippines, *Five-Year Philippine Development Plan (1978-1979)*, Manila, 1978.

———, *Long-Term Philippine Development Plan up to the Year 2000*, Manila, 1977.

———, *1979 Philippine Statistical Yearbook*, Manila, 1979.

National Media Production Center, Republic of the Philippines, *Six Years of the New Society*, Manila, 1978.

Presidential Commission to Survey Philippine Education, *Education for National Development: New Patterns, New Directions*, Makati, Rizal, 1970.

The Public Accounting Profession in the Philippines, Casino, J.A., ed., Philippine Institute of Certified Public Accountants, Manila, 1967.

Towards a More Relevant Accounting Education, Papers and Proceedings of the Second National Conference of Business School Deans, 1974 (Manila: Philippine Association of Collegiate Schools of Business)

Zwaenepoel, Paul P., Tertiary Education in the Philippines, 1611-1972, A Systems Analysis, (Quezon City: Alemars-Pheonix Publishing House, 1975).

Periodicals

The Accounting Profession in the Philippines, Souvenir Program, 1st Far East Conference of Accountants, 1957, pp. 175-198.

Fox, Frederick, *Philippine Vocational Education:* 1869-1898, Philippine Studies, Vol. 24, Third Quarter, 1976, published by the Ateneo de Manila University Press, Quezon City, pp. 261-287.

Unpublished Materials

Banaria, Pascasio S., "The Accounting Profession in the Philippines," paper submitted during the Forum of Accountants of ASEAN Member Countries, September 15-17, 1976, Manila (mimeographed)

Bernabe, Teresa, "A Profile of The Accounting Students," University of the Philippines, Quezon City, 1976 (mimeographed)

Papa, Jose L., "Accounting Education and Professional Training of Accountants in the Philippines," paper submitted during the Forum of Accountants of ASEAN Member Countries, September 15-17, 1976, Manila (mimeographed)

Philippine Association of Collegiate Schools of Business, "A Sectoral Study on Commerce and Business Education in Private Institutions of Higher Learning," Manila, 1978 (mimeographed)

CHAPTER XXIV

ACCOUNTING EDUCATION IN THAILAND

by Sangvian Indaravijaya*

1. Educational Background Information

1.1 Structure of the Educational System

The structure of the educational system in Thailand consists of four years of lower primary, three years of upper primary, three years upper secondary education, depending on the streams, and four to six years of higher education at the bachelor's degree level. In the recent National Scheme of Education 1977 the school system consists of six years of primary, three years of lower secondary and three years of upper secondary education prior to higher education and four years of higher education at the bachelor's degree level. The six:three:three school system was phased in for students entering grade 1 and grade 7 starting in the year 1978.

1.2 Administration Organization

The educational administration organization of Thailand is unique in that education is carried out by four ministries. The Ministry of Education is responsible for all secondary education, a small portion of primary education, and most of teacher education and vocational/technical education, which overlaps into post-secondary education. The Ministry of Interior supervises most primary education administered by local authorities. The Office of University Affairs, with ministry status, oversees government universities and private colleges; the Office of the National Education Commission, under the Office of the Prime Minister, is the long-term policy and planning body for all levels of education.

Admission to state universities is by results of examinations. Different colleges of the universities set up their own requirements and most students are required to take examinations in four to five subjects.

1.3 Accounting Education

In the past, accounting in Thailand was offered on the basis of voluntary self-study, correspondence, and group instruction. Accounting has been one of the required subjects in the elementary education, but students are taught only how to prepare simple personal receipts and payments accounts.

It was not until 1935 that accounting at the college level was first offered at

---

*Chairman of the Committee on Accounting Education for Thailand of the ASEAN Federation of Accounting. Other committee members involved with writing this report on Thailand were Amplo Hotrakitya, Arunee Suwanvanichkij, Maruey Phadoongsidhi, Phenkae Snidvongse, Sumalee Sriboonrueng, Suwannee Tangwongsan, Vachira Sabhasri, and Yupha Kanchanadul.

Thammasat University. As the economy expanded, the growing demand for accounting services in both government and private business had resulted in the establishment of the first School of Accounting at Thammasat University in 1938. The following year the Faculty of Commerce and Accountancy (then with the status of the independent department) was also set up at Chulalongkorn University to provide a similar accounting program. Following still later, Kasetsart University, Chiengmai University and Ramkhamheng University also offer programs in accounting for bachelor's degrees.

Besides the five state universities mentioned, preparation for accounting careers is now achieved in a variety of institutional settings: the three-year vocational schools, the five-year technical schools and in all private colleges. Moreover some universities offer programs in accounting at both the undergraduate and graduate levels. These programs are simultaneously related and independent.

1.4 Public Accounting Practices

On October 30, 1962, the accounting profession in Thailand was formally organized with the enactment of the Auditor Act of 1962. It was the first time that the law specifies qualifications and performance standards for public accountants or authorized auditors. The Act creates a "Committee for the Control of Auditing Profession" in the Ministry of Commerce which is vested with the power and function for issuance of audit licenses and regulating accounting practices.

In summary, an audit license is granted to a person who possesses the following qualifications, namely: holds a bachelor's degree in accounting; has acquired a minimum experience in auditing of business enterprises for a short period of time not less than two years and 2,000 hours; and lastly passes the examination specifically designed to test his professional skills and competence in practical auditing and laws relating to the auditing profession.

2. Accounting Policies and Programs

Accounting is a part of business, and the colleges of business administration could not fulfill their mission without some education in accounting. Accounting educational programs in Thailand, as in most countries, are offered as parts of the College of Business Administration, traditionally under some other names such as Faculty of Commerce and Accountancy, Faculty of Economics and Business Administration and Faculty of Social Sciences in some universities. The objectives of the accounting programs cannot, therefore, be identified without referring to the objectives of the college and the objectives and philosophy of the university of which it is a part.

It can be stated that the objectives of the accounting programs vary, from the broader to the more specific. Among them we find the following:

• to develop men and women in terms of morality and ethics so that they will contribute a worthwhile life to society,

• to educate men and women who can think better and express their thinking

with logic and effect; who can better think for themselves and understand themselves; who can understand the problems and challenges of their society and
time; and who are capable to continue to learn, to develop and grow,

● to provide educational experiences that will enable students to develop their
potential for leadership and service in business, government, and academic
areas,

● to prepare students for careers in accounting and in related fields, and to
prepare them to deal effectively with the problems they will face as practicing
members of their professions and as responsible citizens of the social and economic community in which they live, and

● to produce graduates possessing knowledge in specialized fields, general
knowledge, initiative and expertise such that will promote progress in the
pursuit of a professional career in the changing world.

For accounting educational programs to be effective, it is essential that the
objectives of the programs must be clear at both basic and operational levels.
Relating to accounting policies and programs, considerations should be given to
the following:

● Pressures to develop courses which represent training as opposed to education. While it is possible to develop excellence at different levels of programs,
universities must be careful to identify their intentions and the objectives of their
accounting programs. Should universities try to avoid creeping into types of
vocational training that can best be supplied by other institutions?

● Also, there is an increasing emphasis upon departmentalization of teachers
in the College of Business Administration and within the university. When a
department becomes isolated and autonomous, there is a tendency for teachers
within the department to start teaching things which are or should be provided
by other departments or colleges.

● Does a four-year accounting program (for the bachelor's degree) serve its
professional needs effectively? Should the professional accountant need a more
rigorous program than before? There has been a lot of discussion although a
number of problems must be solved if such professional programs and schools
of accounting are to be successful, such as: Are separate professional programs
and schools of accounting a means of facilitating the changes neded to prepare
students for careers as professional accountants? Should such accounting programs be best taught with the existing College of Business Administration?

3. **Accounting Curriculum**

Once the objectives of the accounting educational programs have been decided,
the curriculum to achieve those objectives can be palnned. The future of the
accounting curriculum in a College of Business Administration depends upon
the environment within which the program is functioning and in part upon the
image of accounting education held by educators in other fields in the same
college. At present, it appears that the future of accounting in the College of
Business Administration is very bright. The business community looks favorably upon the position and nature of accounting in the College of Business

Administration.

A logical starting point in considering the accounting curriculum is to understand what the public expects from those who graduate from the accounting programs, whether they will later work in business, government or prepare themselves for professional examinations. Before we go on to discuss the future accounting curriculum it should be observed that as the role of the accountants in society is expanidng, more flexible and adaptive programs are needed if accountants are to be equipped to play this role. Also, there is a trend towards placing greater reliance on formal education and less on-the-job training as a means of professional preparation. That is to say, the body of knowledge necessary for entrance into the profession should be acquired as a part of the college education.

The curriculum discussed hereafter is related to the college accounting education alone.

In planning for the accounting curriculum in Thailand, the Office of University Affairs sets up rather a broad guideline for a program of a total 120-150 credit hours, comprising a minimum of six credit hours each in the areas of science and mathematics, communication, social sciences and humanities and at least 48 credit hours in general business and accounting courses. A separate *ad hoc* committee is set up to accredit each curriculum proposed by both state universities and private colleges. (Thailand is on a two-term system of 16 weeks each; generally one credit hour means one 50-minute class meeting and twice that time of work to be performed by students outside the class.)

The survey of the existing accounting curricula reveals the following:

• There are no significant differences in the objectives of the accounting programs, the common phrase "to prepare students for their accounting and professional career" is found frequently mentioned.

• There is a significant difference in the flexibility of the total programs, i.e., students have more flexibility in choosing the subjects to suit their needs in some universities than the others, where programs are rather rigid; electives range from 6 to 24 credit hours.

• Allowing for the flexibility in the individual curriculum, there is quite a significant difference in the requirements for general eduation; the requirements range from 39-50 credit hours. This is perhaps the main reason leading to the difference in the credit hours of the total program, a range of 130 to 143 credit hours.

• Total requirements for courses in the "general business" group are more or less the same, a range of 33-36 credit hours.

• While the total credit-hour requirements for accounting courses for accounting majors are more or less the same (39-44 credit hours) the flexibility in the students' choices is quite different. At one university, only half the total requirements for accounting courses are required (compulsory) courses, the rest being electives; whereas at others, all accounting requirements are required courses.

• Most of the planners of accounting programs seem to be well aware of the

300

rapidly changing role of accountants. Accordingly, more interdisciplinary courses are included in the curricula.

• The curricula of private colleges, for some reason or other, tend to follow those of the universities they think most suitable to them. Their curricula, however, tend to be less interdisciplinary and emphasize more on procedural aspects of accounting education.

• In the study on the contents of the curricula, the committee views accounting education as composed of three parts, namely: general education, general business and accounting requirements. For convenience, introductory accounting courses are classified under the accounting groups. The results of the study are summarized in Exhibit 1.

• Thus far, we have discussed the contents of the accounting curricula as they are present in the College of Business Administration in Thailand. Within the courses in the accounting group we have deliberately tried to ignore discussing the problems that would be encountered in teaching accounting courses for accounting majors and those specially designed for non-accounting business students.

EXHIBIT 1

SUMMARY OF ACCOUNTING CURRICULUM

General Education	Semester Hours
Communication	10-16
Behavioral Sciences	6-12
Introduction to Computer Sciences	0-3
Mathematics and Statistics	11-17
Humanities	6-10
Other general education	0-2
General Education Total	39-50

General Business	
Economics	6-9
Business Law	3-10
Organization and Management	3-3
Finance	3-3
Marketing	0-3
Production or Operational Systems	0-3
Quantitative Application to Business	3-9
Business Policy	0-3
Other general business	0-5
General Business Total	33-36

Accounting

Financial Accounting: Reporting, Theory,	
Applied and Contemporary Problems	12-24
Cost Determination, Cost Analysis and Control,	
Cost-based Decision Making	3-9
Audit Theory and Philosophy, Audit Problems	3-6
Tax Accounting	2-4
Accounting electives	0-18
Accounting Total	39-44
Electives	6-24
Grand Total	130-143

It should be noted that accounting curriculum contributes only part of the success of the total program. Rigorous, high-quality accounting programs do not depend upon a certain number of courses or amount of credit hours. Recent changes in the improvement of accounting education are attributable to many factors, including improvements in educational materials and the increase in the number of well-prepared accounting teachers. The latter development particularly has contributed to the advancement of more conceptual, analytical education in the classroom.

In planning for the accounting curriculum, planners should be aware of various questions—from general to detailed and from basic to operational. Among them are:

(1) What should be the objectives of the College of Business Administration and of the accounting program in particular?

(2) What should the future accountant be expected to learn at the university and what should he learn on the job, i.e., what is the cutoff between education and firm training?

(3) What is the future role of accounting in public administration activities, particularly in such areas as the central and local governmental units, hospitals, schools and universities and other not-for-profit institutions?

(4) Should more recognition be given to the impact of behavioral sciences, quantitative methods and information sciences on the accounting programs?

(5) Should flexibility, and to what extent, in the accounting courses be considered essential for an accounting curriculum?

(6) Has sufficient emphasis been placed on the assurance that students have acquired skills in effective communication, both written and oral?

(7) What is the future of the accounting profession?

(8) What is the most effective organization for accounting education in the future?

4. Conclusions

We would like to conclude our work at this stage by putting all aspects of accounting education in the following educational standard questions. (Report of Board on Standards for Programs and Schools of Professional Accounting AICPA, adapted):

(1) Standards of the academic environment: relating to the effective functioning of the College, the knowledge, methodology and the autonomy of the college and program.

(2) General standards: relating to the objectives and accreditation of the accounting program.

(3) Admission and retention standards: relating to the admission of students and their continuation in the program.

(4) Curriculum standards: relating to the operational objectives of the curriculum.

(5) Accounting faculty standards: relating to quality and quantity of accounting teachers and the criteria for their performance evaluation, together with supporting personnel.

(6) Financial support standards: relating to the financial administration, physical plant and equipment and library resources.

(7) Standards of performance for graduates: relating to the attributes and knowledge found in a graduate.

Finally, the Accounting Committee does not intend or plan to submit any concrete proposal on accounting education policies and programs and any model program on accounting curriculum and accounting education requirements. However, it realizes that more work is to be done in those areas. At present, quite a number of questions and observations have been put forward, the answers to which are yet to be found.

Admittedly, the Committee itself feels it is still a student of accounting education as much as others, if not more.

AFRICA AND MIDDLE EAST

CHAPTER XXV

REGIONAL ASPECTS AND DEVELOPMENTS IN AFRICA AND THE MIDDLE EAST

1. Regional Background

The African continent's accounting has been heavily influenced by the British and French concepts. However, we find different patterns gradually developing in Africa, as our respective country studies convey.

The developing countries in this part of the world can be categorized as follows:
- U.K. accounting-oriented: East and West Africa
- French accounting-oriented: Africa
- The countries covering the Middle East

2. U.K. Oriented East and West Africa

In East Africa, regional accounting developments were moving along fairly well until the East African Economic Community started to disintegrate several years ago. The Association of Accountants of East Africa had its Secretariat in Nairobi, and extensive efforts were made to coordinate the training of accountants. Exchanges and regular conferences existed between the countries, mainly Kenya, Tanzania and Uganda; however, other countries in the area also participated. Economically and educationally, they were closely linked in the past, constituting the basis for better accounting harmonization and furthering regional accounting education, training and practices. The expectation existed (cf. Enthoven, 1977/79, p 96) that these countries could develop into a confederation along the lines of ASEAN. Unfortunately political differences have hampered the proper regional development in the area so far, although such efforts may well be successfully revitalized in the near future.

In West Africa, Ghana, Nigeria, Sierra Leone and Liberia have recently made an effort toward closer accounting coordination. In due time, these nations also may consider linkages with the accountants and educators in East Africa. The need is great to set up regional accounting training and development centers, and initially one English-speaking accounting development center could be set up in Africa, although justification may exist to set up one in East and one in West Africa. Updating demands have been very strong, and as the follow-up survey indicated in regard to our study, "Accounting Education and The Third World," AAA - 1979, Africa is badly lagging behind in educational developments and improvements (see Chapter VI). The feedback indicated (p. 21):

> One of the major deficiencies referred to in accounting education is the view of the profession in the eyes of both the government and the private sectors, e.g., a lack of awareness by government authorities on the role and necessity of accounting. There is a problem of overemphasis on financial enterprise accounting and little emphasis on managerial, governmental, and even

macro (national) accounting.

General recommendations for the region are as follows: (1) assist countries/regions to achieve their own development; (2) encourage retiring businessmen and teachers to accept positions to teach in underdeveloped nations; (3) scholarships for students; (4) have international and regional agencies divert funds to accounting developments in Third World countries; (5) establish an educational coordinating body like the IAAE; (6) exchange of professors; and (7) effective management and educational training programs.

Educators, assisted by governments and regional development institutions, could be effective in developing better domestic and regional educational structures. The potentials are ther, but first of all a better scrutiny has to be made of the needs (an "inventory") before such accounting planning should take place.

3. French Accounting Oriented Africa

OCAM (Organisation Commune Africaine Malgache at Mauricienne) once also had the roots to develop an effective regional accounting body, but due to certain political and economic differences this body has not developed as was expected. Several countries left the OCAM organization. Although OCAM was not primarily an educational body, it could have taken on this task too.

Many French and English-speaking African countries have felt the need to develop closer ties, and in June 1979, a series of African studies set up the "African Accounting Council." It is open to countries that belong to the Organization of African Unity (OAU). This African Council encompasses 28 both English and French-speaking countries in Africa; it currently includes: Algeria, Angola, Benin, Burundi, Republique Centrafricaine, Cameroun, Ghana, Gabon, Gambie, Guinee, Haute-Volta, Ivory Coast, Ile Maurice, Lesotho, Liberia, Libya, Madagascar, Malawi, Mali, Maroc, Niger, Nigeria, Senegal, Saotome et Principe, Soudan, Tanzania, Togo and Zaire. The council is set up by countries, and not necessarily accounting bodies, because the organizational structures differ by countries.

Different country approaches exist in these "zones of accounting," for example, in French-speaking Africa the professional accounting body, or rather the body that regulates the profession, tends to be part of the Ministry of Finance. In the English-speaking countries, an accounting institute is generally established by a decree or government act. The institute regulates the accounting aspects under the act, and sets its own regulations regarding qualification tests, standards, educational requirements. The emphasis between the two approaches is different, which needs to be taken into account in the development of the African Accounting Council.

In Africa, as in many other Third World countries, the public sector tends to be the dominant one, and the accounting norms and criteria will have to be reflected accordingly. Public sector accounting is one of the most neglected areas of accounting.

The listed objectives of the council are the following:

- To assist in the establishment of bodies entrusted with accounting standardization in African countries.

- To promote and carry out all studies in the field of accounting standardization.
- To encourage education and further training in accountancy.
- To undertake research in accounting matters and associated disciplines.
- To promote the development of the teaching of accountancy and related disciplines.
- To provide for publication, translation and circulation of works on accountancy by African authors.
- To facilitate regular contacts between members.
- To stimulate relationships and exchanges between African specialists and experts.
- To establish communication links with international organizations and with professional associations of other countries whose works and activities are similar to those of the council.
- To promote the use of similar accounting methods in order to facilitate the flow of management information between African countries.

These objectives are pretty wide ranging, and include education, training, and research. However, the ways and means to execute these objectives have not been explored in great detail nor set forth. Priorities will have to be listed, country and regional conditions and requirements outlined, socio-cultural factors taken into account and various "frameworks"—in the form of pragmatic reports—be presented to give courses of action. Mere theorizing about aspects is of limited use, and specific action programs have to be actively worked upon.

The working languages of the council are those used by the Organization of African Unity (OAU). The Secretariat is located in Zaire, and Prof. Kinzonzi Mvutukidi of the University of Zaire has been selected as Secretary-General of the council. The President is Mr. K. Bouchouaka from Algeria. The Vice-Presidency rests with Guinea and Nigeria. All elected hold office for three years.

We are hopeful that this council will be gradually able to implement its objectives, and also achieve better educational structures in the countries and regions of Africa. (Another all-African meeting has been scheduled for December 1980, in Zaire.) A systematic approach needs to be explored and outlined, regarding the vehicles to be used, the time frame and other aspects related to accounting standardization, training, exchange, etc. Such a system may play a sizeable role in the economic development of Africa. In most African countries, accounting is not seen, as yet, as an effective instrument in economic development management.

4. Middle East

The Middle East Society of Associated Accountants has been dormant for some time. However, we understand some efforts are being made to give it new life. Essentially, MESAA covers the Islamic countries of the region. In our opinion, the need for professional and educational coordination in the region is great, and the establishment of a regional accountancy development center, presumably as part of the regional association, could give a tremendous incentive to the enhancement of accounting.

5. Conclusion

Most African countries require a new breed of accountants, with both heavy theoretical and practical exposure in the various areas (concentrations) of accounting. This poses a heavy demand on the educational institutions, because few are equipped for such a task. Regional accounting training and development centers would serve a proper role in first instance. The educational structures on the African continent will have to be assessed almost separately, but closely tied into the regional professional accounting developments such as the African Accounting Council. The latter will have its hands full with practice aspects, while we suggest a separate "African Accounting Educational Association" may look in detail into the accounting educational and research elements in Africa.

CHAPTER XXVI

ACCOUNTING EDUCATION IN EGYPT

by

Metwalli B. Amer and M. M. Khairy*

1. Introduction

Economic activities in Egypt are currently carried out primarily by a large public sector and secondarily by a small private sector. Since the emerging role of the public ownership in the late 1950's, there has been a considerable correlation between the creation of a strong public sector to assume the major responsibility in controlling and directing the economic activities in Egypt and the evolution of the accounting profession and accounting education to meet the new changes, the new responsibilities, and the new requirements. It is very interesting to observe that changes in accounting evidently started with the creation of the public sector.

2. Public Accounting Prior to 1956

Up until 1956, when the Suez Canal Company was nationalized and the sudden Anglo-French-Israeli attack on Egypt took place, public ownership was restricted to some public utilities such as railways, telephones, post offices, and irrigation. The capitalist system with private ownership was dominant in business activities. In this period, public accounting in business and in government was provided by two sources: (1) chartered accountants and (2) the State Audit Department.

Chartered accountants were members of the Egyptian Society of Accountants and Auditors. Anyone who wished to be a chartered accountant, typically, had to satisfy the following conditions:
(1) Had to be a graduate of the College of Commerce of one of the Egyptian universities or equivalent foreign universities.
(2) Had to serve for three consecutive years in a professional office of a chartered accountant.
(3) After the expiration of one-half of the three-year term of service, the candidate had to sit for an Intermediate Examination to test the progress made in professional knowledge.
(4) Before applying for admission as a member in the Society, the candidate had to pass the Final Examination to test his or her professional ability.

The candidate was not permitted to sit for the Final Examination until a period of one year had elapsed since passing the Intermediate Examination.

*Metwalli B. Amer is Professor at California State University; M. Khairy is Professor at Cairo University (Egypt).

There were five subjects for the Final Examination. These subjects covered accounting theory, accounting problems, auditing, taxation, commercial law, general commercial knowledge, and general financial knowledge (including business administration). Each subject was given in three full hours, a total of 36 hours for the two examinations.

Before the government established the public sector, all corporations, partnerships, and individual enterprises whose capital exceeded a certain limit had to engage a chartered accountant to conduct an independent audit annually. Duties and responsibilities of chartered accountants in performing audits in Egypt during the period were similar to those of chartered accountants in England. Needless to say that because of the long British rule of Egypt, the Egyptian Society was much influenced by the British accounting profession.

The State Audit Department was a public agency similar to the General Accounting Office of the U.S. Government. According to the law, any public funds invested in any form of activity had to be audited by this agency. The purpose of this audit was to determine how effectively a governmental institution discharged its financial responsibilities and to what degree these financial responsibilities complied with the laws regulating the operations of public funds.

Before the public sector entered into business activities in 1956, auditing was, therefore, performed either by chartered accountants who performed the attesting function to the financial activities of private enterprises or State Audit Department representatives who were in charge of examining the financial transactions of governmental institutions. Chartered accountants performed their audit in accordance with the standards of auditing established by the profession. Representatives of the State Audit Department performed their audit in accordance with the financial regulations of the country.

With regard to accounting system and measurement, the financial transactions were measured according to the double-entry rules and procedures. The financial transactions of the governmental institutions were measured in accordance with the rules and procedures prescribed by governmental agencies.

The system of accounting education in 1956 had been uniform in the academic institutions across the country and under the direction of the Minister of Education. The degree was called "Bachelor of Commerce" with accounting major (B.Comm.). A student studying for the B.Comm. degree had to go through a four-year program without interruption. All the courses in the curriculum were mandatory. There were about 32 weeks in the academic year and no classes in summer.

Using the College of Commerce at Cairo University as a basis for illustrating accounting education in Egypt, Exhibit I illustrates the courses required by every student studying for the B.Comm. degree with the accounting major. The first two-year program was the general core requirement for all majors in the College of Commerce. The remaining two-year program was the accounting major requirement for all accounting students. The curriculum shows the courses offered during the four years of the 1953-57 program.

EXHIBIT I

Year	Course Title	Lecture Hours per Week	Laboratory Hours per Week	Number of Weeks
1953-54	Economics	2		32
	Business Administration	2	2	32
	Economic Geography	2		32
	Economic History	2		32
	Mathematics	2	2	32
	English Language	4		32
	French Language	4		32
1954-55	Economics	2		32
	Business Administration	4	2	32
	Economic Geography	2		32
	French Language	4		32
	Law	2		32
	Accounting	4	2	32
1955-56	Financial Accounting	2	2	32
	Cost Accounting	2	2	32
	Banking	2	2	32
	Economics	2		32
	Commercial Law	2		32
	Statistics	2	2	32
	Business Administration	2	2	32
1956-57	Financial Accounting	2	2	32
	Economics	2		32
	Commercial Law	2		32
	Insurance	2	2	32
	Taxation	2		32
	Advanced Accounting	2	2	32
	Auditing	2	2	32
	Public Finance	2		32

There are six school days in a week in Egypt, Saturday through Thursday. Friday is the only non-work day.

3. The Emergence of Public Sector Ownership in Egypt

The Suez War of 1956 provided the impetus to the emergence of public ownership in Egypt. Due to the attack on Egypt, the Egyptian government took over British and French enterprises—most of which were commercial banks and insurance companies—into public sector ownership, and thus the public sector emerged.

The government's objective of the public ownership in those days was to exercise control over the limited resources of the country. It was intended to achieve (1) political independence since major banks and financial institutions were dominated by foreign investors, (2) economic development by government planning, controlling, and operating the economic resources, and (3) social well-being by redistributing resources for the masses of people in a country with limited resources and increasing population.

In 1957-58 the government "Egyptianized" some other foreign financing companies to eliminate foreign capital domination in the economy. The shareholders were compensated by the government. In 1960, the two major Egyptian banks, the National Bank of Egypt and the Misr Bank, were nationalized. The public sector participated also with the private sector in establishing major new industries. Perhaps July, 1961, marked the beginning of a new era where the public sector was greatly expanded; the government nationalized four-fifths of the country's investments. With this significant role of public ownership, the public sector needed immediate organization.

4. The Operational and Accounting Structure of the Public Sector

4.1 The "Public Organizations"

The nationalization decrees enabled the public sector to play the major part in economic activities. Starting in December, 1961, the government established many specialized state agencies called "public organizations." Each of these organizations, having the characteristics of holding companies, specialized in supervising companies which dealt with similar business activities. In other words, for each group of public companies or government-owned enterprises which belonged to one type of activity or provided similar products, a public organization was established to supervise this group.

4.2 The Accounting Control Boards

After the establishment of public organizations, each organization established an Accounting Control Board to audit the financial activities of its affiliated companies in the same manner as independent accountants. Some of the accounting firms as well as individual chartered accountants agreed to work on these boards as state employees.

Members of these boards expressed opinions as to the fairness of the financial statements. They were responsible directly to the board of directors of the public organizations to which they reported their findings and presented the financial statements of each company. These members were employed by the organizations on a salary basis. They assumed the duties of chartered accountants in auditing all publicly-owned enterprises. In addition to the traditional attest function, those boards also evaluated management performance and conformity with the plans of the companies belonging to public organizations.

4.3 The Central Auditing Agency

After the public sector assumed the leading role in business activities, the

State Audit Department became the agency which had the legal right to audit
the financial activities of public organizations and their affiliated companies. Its
auditing activities expanded to such a great extent that this public agency had to
be reorganized to meet the new requirements.

In March, 1964, the State Audit Department was replaced by the Central
Auditing Agency which officially and by law became the authorized public
agency to audit the companies of the public sector and government institutions.
It also supervises the various state and public sector agencies in financial, accounting, and technical matters. In addition, it follows up the implementation of
the development plan and evaluates its results.

In the presidential decree establishing the Central Auditing Agency, the
following six central departments of the agency were set up:

(1) The Central Department for the Financial Control of the State's Administrative agencies, which exercises control over ministries, government departments, and local administration units in the following fields: the control of income and expenditure; the audit of pension and bonus accounts; the inspection
of receipt and disbursement records, and the reviewing of commodity stocks. In
addition, it audits loans and credit facilities as well as the final acocunts of the
state budget.

(2) The Central Department for the Financial Control of Public Authorities
and Organizations and Public Sector Units, which is engaged in auditing the
accounts and examining the books and records of the aforementioned bodies, and
checking the auditors' reports and financial accounts of the said bodies.

(3) The Central Department for Following Up the Development Plan and
Evaluating Its Implementation, which exercises control over the projects of the
Economic and Social Development Plan, and follows up the investment, produc-
tion, exportation, employment, consumption, and productivity functions.

(4) The Central Department for Financial Violations, which is responsible
for checking compliance with administrative decisions, and giving opinions in
regard to financial violations by the state's administrative agencies and public
sector units.

(5) The Central Department for Research and Operations which undertakes
research work for the purpose of assisting the Central Auditing Agency to carry
out its functions.

(6) The Secretariat.

Since March, 1964, auditing of public sector enterprises has been performed
by the Accounting Control Boards and the Central Auditing Agency. The demand for the services of chartered accountants by private companies has de-
clined enormously due to the nationalization of many companies whose accounts
are presently examined by the public agency. Many chartered accountants had
to accept government employment in those public auditing agencies.

Members of the Central Auditing Agency and the Accounting Control Boards
of public organizations do not have to be members of the Egyptian Society of
Accountants and Auditors. Hence, they may not meet the professional standards
and requirements governing admission to the public accounting profession.

These members may also lack some of the professional attitude of chartered accountants who should be aware of the standards of professional conduct.

The development of the public sector in Egypt undoubtedly has led to a decline in the role of the public accounting profession in that country. Some believe that the accounting profession itself was effectively nationalized by the nationalization of business enterprises. Fortunately, President Sadat has been encouraging foreign investments in the private sector in Egypt. This attitude may help the accounting profession to gain its lost position and importance in this country in the years to come.

4.4   The Need for a Uniform Accounting System

Under the new accounting structure of the public sector, each Accounting Control Board of every public organization tried to assist the managements of its affiliated companies in designing their accounting systems and in selecting the accounting methods which might suit the measurement of the financial activities of those companies. Since the activities and products of the companies affiliated with one specialized public organization are of the same nature and type, this role of assistance might have encouraged the Accounting Control Board of that public organization to design a uniform accounting system to be adopted by the affiliated companies of that organization. Under such circumstances, there would have been as many uniform accounting systems as the number of the Accounting Control Board of Public Organizations. Comparability among the consolidated financial statements of public organizations would have been meaningless.

Being in a central position to control the financial performance of all public organizations, their affiliated companies, and the Accounting Control Boards, the Central Auditing Agency developed a "Uniform Accounting System" in December, 1966. The new system was adopted and followed by all publicly-owned companies effective the July 1, 1967, fiscal year. Banks and insurance companies were excluded because they have their own prescribed uniform accounting system.

5.   Accounting Education in Egypt

5.1   Faculty

In all universities in Egypt, the following ranks and qualifications are common:
(1) Assistant Instructor (similar to a graduate or teaching assistant in the U.S.): qualification is to be enrolled in the graduate program.
(2) Instructor (similar to assistant professor in the U.S.): qualification is the doctorate from a recognized academic institution in Egypt or other countries. Teaching load is 12 hours per week.
(3) Assistant Professor (similar to associate professor in the U.S.): qualification is the same as for instructor above, plus five years of teaching experience and writing. Teaching load is 10 hours per week.
(4) Professor: qualification is the same as instructor, plus ten years of teaching experience and writing. Teaching load is 8 hours per week.

The doctoral degree is a requirement for a permanent teaching position in all universities in Egypt. Professional experience is not significant for promotion or for obtaining employment.

There is no recognized professional development or continuing education programs for accounting faculty in Egypt. The life in Egypt and the economic conditions are such that each faculty member is kept busy earning a living. Salaries are very low. Writing a book for the course a faculty member teaches is an important source of income. Each faculty member is known in one or two areas of accounting to which he is confined because of workload of writing textbooks for his own students each year. In addition moonlighting, such as teaching a course at another college, preparing a course or a workshop for accountants in publicly owned companies in a training program, or some consulting work, is also a good source of earning. Accordingly, each faculty member is always on the go from one place to the other after money in order to earn a decent living. No time is left for professional development or keeping up to date with what is going on in accounting education and practice in developed countries.

In the area of training, there are seeral public and private agencies conducting training programs for employees in several sectors of the economy. They are:

(1) Public agencies conducting training programs:
   -National Institute for Planning
   -National Institute for Higher Administration
   -Training Administration of the Central Auditing Agency
   -Agency for Productive Efficiency in the Ministry of Industry

(2) Private agencies conducting training programs:
   -Arab Research Administration Center (ARAC)
   -Arab Association for Cost Accounting
   -Arab Association of Business Administration

(3) Others:
   -Organization of Administrative Sciences of the Arab League
   -Management Training Center of the American University in Cairo
   -A few other small consulting offices

Many faculty members are involved in these programs. In addition to the Egyptians who participate in these training programs, many Arabs from rich Arab countries also attend these programs in Cairo and Alexandria. The language used is Arabic. Sometimes the American University in Cairo brings some American professors to lecture in some training programs. The University Management Training Center is equipped with tools which interpret instantly the English lectures into Arabic for the participants who do not know English.

In the late 1960's, several cost accounting professors established a small organization called "Arab Association for Cost Accounting." Its objective has been to standardize cost accounting methods in Arab countries. Although the association still exists, it does not have significant influence nor does it attract many faculty members. The reason is, again, the busy schedule of faculty members required of necessity to earn a decent living. Beyond this association, there is no other accounting faculty organization in Egypt.

The more active organization is a professional one called "Guild of Accountants and Commercialists." It includes some accounting faculty, practitioners, and others working in the field of commerce. It is the most active accounting organization in Egypt.

5.2   Four-Year Undergraduate Program

In the introduction to this report, the four-year curriculum in 1956 at Cairo University was presented. It might be of interest to the reader to see the 1976-77 curriculum at the same university in order to see the changes over 20 years: See Exhibit 2.

EXHIBIT 2

Year	Course Title	Lecture Hours per Week	Laboratory Hours per Week	Number of Weeks
1st Year	Financial Accounting (Individual Enterprises)	3	2	32
	Organization and Administration of Production	4	1	32
	Economics	3		32
	Principles of Law	2		32
	Mathematics	2	2	32
	Economic Resources	2		32
	Languages		4	32
	Introduction to Behavioral Sciences	2		32
2nd Year	Financial Accounting (Corporations)	3	2	32
	Marketing and Administration of Sales	3	1	32
	Economics	3		32
	Business Law	2		32
	Insurance	2	1	32
	Public Administration	2		32
	Business Math	2	2	32
	Languages		4	32
3rd Year	Government and National Accounting	2	1	32
	Cost Accounting	3	1	32
	Personnel and Human Relations	2	1	32
	Purchasing and Stores Administration	2	1	32
	Finance and Financial Management	2	1	32
	Auditing	2	1	32
	Public Finance and Tax Accounting	3	1	32
	Statistics	2	1	32

4th	Accounting Systems	3	1	32
Year	Administrative Accounting	3	2	32
	Cost Accounting	3	1	32
	Auditing	2	1	32
	Tax Accounting	3	1	32
	Micro Economics	2		32
	Operations Research	2	1	32
	Accounting for Specialized Institutions	2	1	32

Over the last 20 years, there have been no significant changes in the credit requirements for the four-year undergraduate programs at the Egyptian universities. All of the courses are still required by every student studying for a Bachelor's degree in Commerce with a major in Accounting. There are no electives.

The first two-year portion of the program is still the general core requirement for all majors in the College of Commerce. The remaining two-year program is the accounting major requirement for all accounting students. The only significant difference between the 1957 and the 1977 curriculum is the inclusion of national accounting, operations research, some data processing and computer technology in the accounting system course, and introduction to behavioral sciences. Students cannot disrupt their four-year attendance in college. They have to continue until they graduate.

5.3 Graduate Programs

The graduate programs at Cairo University, which are typical of Egyptian university programs, are divided into two types: academic, leading to an M.S. and a Ph.D. in accounting, and professional, leading to a diploma in a specialized area in accounting.

5.3.1 The M.Com. in Accounting

A candidate should sit and pass admissions tests in the English language, mathematics and statistics and the computer. The master's degree requires one year of accounting courses. These courses are:

(1) Financial Accounting - 2 hours a week
(2) Tax Accounting - 2 hours a week
(3) Auditing and Internal Control - 2 hours a week
(4) Special Accounting Problems - 2 hours a week
(5) Studies in Cost Accounting - 2 hours a week
(6) Research Methodology - 2 hours a week

After successfully completing the first-year courses, the M.Com. candidate has to write an extensive master thesis. For every master thesis, there is a committee of three: the thesis advisor, a second faculty member, and a third member who is usually a practitioner. After the completion of the thesis, it must be discussed by the three-member committee in a public hearing which is open to the public.

5.3.2   The Ph.D. in Accounting

There is no formal course offering for the Ph.D. in Accounting. It is similar to the British system, which is research-oriented. A Ph.D. committee will be formed and a dissertation advisor will be appointed by the College Council. The Ph.D. candidate conducts an extensive research on his special topic. Once the research is completed and the dissertation is written, the committee will discuss it in a public hearing. The thesis is graded by the committee as a Ph.D with honors or as just a Ph.D. Five to ten years are typical for a Ph.D. candidate to finish his/her degree.

In the professional graduate programs, there are several diplomas offered after the bachelor's degree and after the candidate acquires at least two years of professional experience. Two-year courses are required for each diploma. Some of these diplomas and the courses offered for each are:

(1) Cost Accounting Diploma:

First Year:
- -Cost Accounting Problems - 3 hours a week
- -Accounting Problems - 3 hours a week
- -Presentation and Analysis of Cost - 3 hours a week
- -Production Management - 3 hours a week

Second Year:
- -Standard Cost Systems - 3 hours a week
- -Planning Budgets - 3 hours a week
- -Problems in Cost Accounting - 4 hours a week
- -Research - 2 hours a week

(2) Diploma of Graduate Studies in Accounting:

First Year:
- -Accounting Systems - 3 hours a week
- -Studies in Cost Accounting - 3 hours a week
- -Planning Budgets - 3 hours a week
- -Financial Accounting - 3 hours a week

Second Year:
- -Studies and Problems in Auditing - 3 hours a week
- -Problems in Tax Accounting - 3 hours a week
- -Problems in Accounting - 4 hours a week
- -Research - 2 hours a week

(3) Diploma of Graduate Studies in Government and National Accounting:

First Year:
- -Government Accounting - 3 hours a week
- -Planning Budgets in the Public Sector - 3 hours a week
- -National Economy and Finance - 3 hours a week
- -Problems in Accounting - 3 hours a week

Second Year:
- -Internal Control - 3 hours a week
- -Studies in Costing and Performance Evaluation - 3 hours a week

-National Accounting - 4 hours a week

-Research - 2 hours a week

5.4   Methods of Instructions and Course Materials

In the 1976-77 academic year, the College of Commerce at Cairo University has a student enrollment of 21,600 students. The enrollment figure for the first year alone is nearly 6,000 students. This number is divided into two groups. Each group is put in a big lecture hall with microphones and loud speakers. The professor comes in this hall and lectures for an hour or two through those microphones. The use of modern instructional media such as audiovisual aids in those halls does not exist. There are currently 32 faculty members in the college with professorial rank teaching in the three departments: Accounting, Business Administration, and Insurance. Student-faculty ratio is 21,600 to 32, or 675 students per one faculty member.

Students in some courses, such as accounting, are divided into smaller groups called sections. Graduate or teaching assistants, and if available, instructors and assistant professors help students in those sections by going through the lectures in the big hall. They also solve some problems in problem-solving courses.

In general, there are no home assignments, no taking of attendance, no midterm examinations, and no tracing of year's work. There is only one year-end exam at the end of the academic year for each course. Names of students on the answer sheet are hidden for confidentiality. Due to this emphasis on the final exam as the most single indicator for students' performance during the whole academic year, the year-end finals are an extended process which takes at least two months of hard work by all faculty members. Professors are usually paid separately for correcting those year-end exams due to their great volume.

Due to the lack of pressure or follow-up by instructors, some students do not study their course materials until the end of the academic year. Attendance is very poor due to the big lectures and the failure to record attendance in sections. The use of the library is not common since term papers are not required in the four-year undergraduate programs. Also, each student must purchase the textbook written by the professor teaching that course. These textbooks are rewritten each year with minor organizational changes in order not to circulate used books in the market. Without the income from those books, a faculty member could face hardship in making a living in Egypt. Writing for individual course use is part of the higher education process in Egypt. All that is required from each student is to know what is written in his or her professor's textbook.

5.5   Accounting Research

Research in general is not emphasized because of lack of resources. In accounting, research is technically-oriented. It deals with accounting issues of local nature. The design, application, interpretation, and flexibility of the Uniform Accounting System have been fertile materials for writing in recent years. Several M.S. theses in accounting have been written on those topics. The bulk of faculty writing is for promotion purposes and supplements the seniority criterion which is very important. Faculty writing is published in reviews published by the Egyptian universities' press and in some other periodicals published by some professional associations and leading magazines.

5.6 Local Institutions and Government's Role in Higher Education

There are five major universities in Egypt: Cairo University, Ein Shams University, Al-Azhar University, Alexandria University, and Assiut University.

Recently, the government has established some provincial universities in centrally located and highly populated provinces to reduce the load of traffic from the major universities especially in the city of Cairo and also to meet the need of the continuous increase in population. These provincial universities are located in these provinces and carry their names: Tanta, Mansoura, Zagazig, Helwan, and several more are still under development. In addition to those universities, there are a number of technical colleges and higher institutes with specific educational and vocational functions.

The American University in Cairo is the only private institution in Egypt with a limited number of enrollment. Instruction is given in English and there are some American professors teaching several fields of knowledge including accounting and management courses. Its Management Training Center is very active in developing programs for high officials in Middle Eastern countries including oil producing Arab countries. The university is financed by American sources. It follows the American system of education and instruction. Its programs and curriculum are known for their quality, which is better than the national universities.

All the national universities are publicly financed. Education at all levels is free in Egypt. Students are distributed to universities and colleges within those universities according to their grade percentages in high school. The distribution of high school graduates to all universities, colleges, and technical institutes is done by a central unit from the Minister of Education. Since all those academic institutions are public agencies, the Ministry of Education assumes the role of coordinating higher education policies. The minister usually acts as chairman of the "Higher Council of Universities" with the president of each academic institution serving as a member of the council. The council establishes policies in conformity with the national plans and needs. Faculty and staff of those academic institutions are state employees.

6. Educational Problems

The problems in higher education in Egypt are basically economic in nature. In turn, the economic root of the problem has an influencing effect on faculty members and students. With the lack of opportunity, very low salaries, high cost of living and inflation, everyone is struggling to earn a living to keep up with the necessities of life. Competing for the limited opportunity is a way of life. Seniority among faculty members becomes a very important factor. Senior professors have first choice in selecting the courses where they sell their textbooks to the largest number of students. New faculty members may not write books to sell to their students before three years after receiving their doctorates. They usually get what is left from the senior members of the faculty in course assignment, part-time opportunity, consulting, or moonlighting in general. There is a common feeling of frustration among junior faculty members because of the seniority factor.

These types of problems are common among faculty members. They are socially and economically a part of the academic life at Egyptian universities. Any proposed solutions must come from within since the basic remedy to those problems are related to internal, social, and economic conditions. The remaining part of this chapter is confined to outlining problems of a general nature. The solutions could be provided by outside sources and would be helpful in improving current conditions of higher education. They will not, however, solve the problems originated from the internal, social, and economic conditions.

6.1 Method of Instruction

Lecturing 2,500 students through microphones is a common phenomenon at Egyptian universities. There is nothing that can be done about it with the free education system and the continuous increase in population.

Better equipment in the area of instructional media could be provided to Egyptian universities. Lecture halls can be equipped with modern methods such as audiovisual aids. These aids may attract students to listen and pay attention to the lectures.

6.2 Book References and Periodicals

More than enough locally authored textbooks are utilized in the undergraduate programs in accounting. They are written in Arabic, which is the native language in Egypt. The material in the textbooks is based on Western concepts concepts and methods of accounting ormoifedto meet local systems and rues I iscommon to see more than one textbook in each accounting course due to economic reasons. A three-hour course could be divided between two or sometimes three professors. Each professor writes a book on his part and sells it to the same students who have to know what is in the text to pass the year-end exam.

On the graduate level, there is a severe deficiency of course material. Professors do not write books for the graduate level. Because the number of students is small, not many books will be sold and thus not be profitable. Graduate students do not have much choice except to take notes during lectures, rely on the undergraduate textbooks again, or look for English language reference material—a limited resource in Egypt.

There is an urgent need for American reference books and periodicals in accounting for the libraries in the College of Commerce at Egyptian universities. References such as handbooks, general accounting literature, and books on the graduate level are particularly needed. Periodicals in accounting such as the *Accounting Review,* the *Journal of Accountancy,* and *Management Accounting* are badly needed.

6.3 Faculty Exchange

Because of internal, social, and economic problems faculty members are too occupied by local problems. There is no time available for reflection of what accounting now is or should be in the future. With the continuous involvement in projects to supplement their salaries, faculty members are left no time for reading or conducting any significant research.

The services of some American professors could be used effectively in some major Egyptian universities in teaching graduate courses for graduate students for one or two years. Since language of instruction will be a problem, classes should be equipped with tools for instant interpretation from English to Arabic. Sending American professors to Egypt for that period could be arranged with the Egyptian government which has shown an interest recently in attracting foreign professors and experts for even one semester or year, at a decent financial compensation.

On the other side, some Egyptian professors could be invited to spend a year or two in some American universities. This could be arranged with individual American universities, with the help of the AAA, and some foundations. Possibly also the Egyptian government might take care of the finances. Such an invitation would be very helpful in giving Egyptian professors a chance to keep up with recent developments in accounting.

Also, there is a growing number of accounting faculty members who have received the Ph.D. in accounting from Egyptian universities. To get familiar with accounting in the U.S. and to improve their English, the Egyptian government sends those faculty members to American universities for one year at government expense. The AAA can render a good service by helping those people find universities.

Finally, the Egyptian government is sending a large number of Egyptian students to American universities in order to study for the Ph.D. in accounting. Because of their weak background in English, they have a difficult time in getting admitted in the Ph.D. programs without passing in advance the (TOEFL) exam and the (ATGSB) test. It would be helpful if there were an orientation program or a center to offer them courses in English and other fields to help them pass those tests.

6.4 Professional Development and Training

Professional development or programs for continuing education do not exist in Egypt for academicians and practitioners in accounting. For academicians, there is no accounting association to hold meetings, seminars, workshops, or conferences for all accounting instructors across the country. Economic and financial conditions are also responsible for the lack of interest of the faculty in self-development. For practitioners, the Egyptian Society of Accountants and Auditors and the Guild of Accountants and Commercialists do not have formal programs for professional development, continuing education, or training for higher responsibility work within their trades. The emerging significant role of the public sector has weakened the public accounting profession and the Egyptian Society of Accountants and Auditors. These factors, in turn, have contributed to stagnation in the area of professional development and training in the public accounting profession.

There is an urgent need to exchange ideas and information about accounting among Egyptian academicians and practitioners and their counterparts in developed and developing nations. The forum for such an exchange can be in summer programs, regional conferences, international meetings, or other means outlined in detail in Part Three of this monograph.

7. Summary and Conclusion

Events following the Egyptian revolution of 1952 had a tremendous influence on accounting education and the profession in Egypt. Although the revolution took place in 1952, no significant changes occurred in accounting before 1956. A clear distinction can be drawn between accounting before the revolution and accounting of today. As a result of this obvious distinction, the first phase of the chapter was written as an introduction to public accounting and accounting curriculum before 1956.

The year 1956 was a landmark of change in the economic and social system in Egypt. After realizing that drastic measures had to be taken for economic development, the government decided to nationalize 80 percent of the economic activities, to confiscate some foreign companies after the Suez aggression, and to establish a strong public sector to run the publicly owned companies. Accordingly, the second phase of this chapter dealt with the emergence of public ownership in Egypt.

The third phase of this chapter dealt basically with the present sytem of accounting education in Egypt. Accounting education as it is, not as it should be, was presented. Systems are usually the by-product of several stages of evolution and revolutions in countries and nations. Sometimes it is very difficult for an outsider to understand why things are being done in a specific country one way and not another. To understand existing patterns, it is necessary to understand the cultural, economic, religious, social, and legal systems of that country.

Without this understanding, generalized recommendations to a country could be very harmful. Many of the problems are deeply rooted in its systems of operations and in the habits and lifestyles of its people. Recommendations can only work if the people of a specific country are convinced of their workability and of the financial benefits to themselves.

For those reasons, the last phase of this chapter has dealt with several educational problems in Egypt. The discussion did not refer to problems which can only be solved internally. As mentioned before, many problems were created by internal social, economic, and financial conditions. Unless those conditions change, solutions to those problems will not be found easily.

REFERENCES

Amer, Metwalli B. "Impact of Public Ownership on the U.A.R. Accounting Profession," *The International Journal of Accounting Education and Research*, Vol. IV, (Spring, 1969), pp. 49-61.

Central Auditing Agency. *The Uniform Accounting System*, Cairo, Egypt: Central Auditing Agency, 1967. (In Arabic)

Correspondence in Arabic, with Dr. M. M. Khairy and Dr. Samir Bibawy Fahmy of the College of Commerce at Cairo University, dealing with some sections in Chapters IV and V.

Egyptian Society of Accountants and Auditors. *Statutes and By-Laws*.

Radwan, Abdel-Pasit A. *The Uniform Accounting system, and a Study of the General Principles in Unifying the Accounting Systems*, Cairo, Egypt: Anglo-Egyptian Publishing Co., 1971. (In Arabic)

CHAPTER XXVII

ACCOUNTING EDUCATION IN KENYA

by

James D. Newton*

1. Introduction

It is necessary to begin a discussion of accounting education with a brief review of social, political and economic factors which place the subject in perspective. Kenya calls its economy "mixed," meaning a blend of African Socialism and free market capitalism. In reality, the government appears to be oriented toward a capitalistic system, to the extent possible in a less developed country, though in some ways government spending is assuming greater economic significance. (The public sector comprises about one-third of GDP.)

The extent to which accounting education responds to this mixed economic philosophy varies with the institution involved, from a complete lack of government accounting at the University of Nairobi to a strong orientation toward government accounting at Kenya Institute of Administration (KIA). The relationships between accounting and economic development are generally ignored in all institutions. Likewise the qualifying examinations are based primarily on accounting for private enterprise, with some obvious exceptions, to be discussed, and this orientation is not altogether incorrect, as will also be discussed.

Kenya obtained independence from Britain in 1963. Since that time one of the country's principal goals has been Kenyanization of the economy, meaning essentially replacement of expatriates with Kenya citizens to the maximum extent possible, consistent with sound economic development. It does *not* mean any sort of nationalization. Actual implementation of that policy, including the transition from colonialism, has been carried out with remarkably good judgement for a newly emerged African country. The transition was smooth and without rancor or bloodshed. At the death of the first president, Jomo Kenyatta, in 1978, a constitutional transfer of power took place that could almost be a model for some industrialized countries. This stability, along with a few economic factors to be briefly described, provide the background for accounting education in Kenya. These factors are summarized from the fourth five-year Development Plan recently published by the government (Kenya, 1979).

2. Economic Relationships

The president, in the introduction to the Development Plan, states that the

*Dr. James Newton is Associate Professor at the University of Alberta (Canada) and CIDA Visiting Associate Professor at the University of Nairobi (Kenya).

objectives for the country during this period (1979-83) are individual freedom, growth of the economy, and equitable distribution of increased income and wealth among the people, with a theme of alleviation of poverty. The growth target for the period is annual increase in real GDP of 6.3 percent to K£ 2,193,700,000 by 1983, approximately U.S. $5,900,000,000. The biggest problem is the balance of payments deficit, which is true for most developing countries.

Primary products, essentially agriculture, provide a livelihood for 85 percent of the population and 50 percent of export earnings. The export crops consist mostly of coffee, tea, pyrethrum and sisal, while food crops include corn, wheat, soybeans and fruit, with sizeable livestock production for internal consumption. Manufactured goods constitute the second largest export category, but manufacturing is a net consumer of foreign exchange, due to required heavy imports of machinery. Intermediate and capital goods and oil make up 80 percent of the cost of imports. Export promotion of manufactured goods is a high-level goal in the Development Plan. Tourism, while smaller in monetary volume, provided an 8 percent contribution to foreign exchange earnings in 1976, and thus is a very important industry which will also be heavily promoted in the future.

Kenyanization has progressed to the point that only 1.7 percent of the modern sector employment in 1977 was non-citizens. There were then estimated to be only 15,000 non-citizens out of a modern sector work force of 900,000. These figures must be compared with the population of more than 15,000,000 people in 1979 to be of significance, however, since over 80 percent of productive work in the country occurs in the rural areas outside the modern sector. This work consists primarily of subsistence farming and pastoralism. Moreover, much of the expatriate employment is in scientific or technical aeas such as engineering and accounting, so that the percentages do not reveal the importance of these people to the economy. The Development Plan, however, expresses the intention that up to 95 percent of high and middle level management positions will be filled by Kenyans by 1983.

With respect to the state of the economy, the existence of a relatively sophisticated banking system and the beginnings of a manufacturing capability which can possibly begin to earn, rather than spend, foreign exchange during this five-year period, must be observed in the overall economic context. While import substitution has reduced the percentage of goods for final consumption from over 29 percent in 1964 to less than 14 percent today, the inflation rate is currently running in the neighborhood of 18 percent. While income distribution has been somewhat improved, such that the poorest 25 percent of the population now have almost 7 percent of the national income as opposed to 4 percent in 1969 and the wealthiest 10 percent receive only about 37 percent as opposed to over 56 percent in 1969, these figures can be misleading.

The most severe problem to be faced is the high birth rate. The population is growing at a rate of 3.5 percent annually. This means that the population will much more than double by the year 2000. At the present time, almost 50 percent of the population are under age 15. This demographic reality results in the severe problem of the working poor. More than 49 percent of the nation's people live in households with less than 3000 shillings (U.S. $400) of annual income. The average for these households is 1,800 shillings (U.S. $250) per year. These figures are associated with rural literacy rates of 65 percent for males and 31 percent for females over the age of 15. While free education and income equalization are major goals of the Development Plan, there clearly is a large gap to fill.

3. Certification of Accountants

Prior to Independence in 1963, accounting in Kenya can best be described as British Colonial accounting. In 1949 the Association of Accountants in East Africa had been incorporated under the 1933 Kenya Companies Act. This association of accountants in Kenya, Tanzania and Uganda was open only to members of professional bodies in the U.K., South Africa, Australia and India. Membership was dependent on recommendations from existing members, and its other membership requirements were such that it was virtually an exclusive club of expatriates in East Africa, though some few Africans did manage to acquire the credentials of the necessary professional bodies (Nzomo, p. 39). This body is today of little practical consequence and appears to be winding up its affairs.

In 1969 the government of Kenya set up the Kenya Accountants and Secretaries National Examination Board (KASNEB) to conduct local examinations for candidates interested in becoming accountants or company secretaries. This legislation, in conjunction with the Accountants Act of 1977, provides the legislative basis for accomplishing the government's policy of Kenyanization of the profession. The 1977 Act establishes a registration board to issue practicing certificates and exercise final disciplinary powers (the legislation even contains a code of conduct for accountants), gives retrospective recognition to KASNEB, and provides for creation of an Institute of Certified Public Accountants. Actual establishment of the institute occurred in November, 1978.

The major purposes of the institute, codified in the legislation, are to (1) promote standards of professional competence, (2) promote research into subjects of accounting and finance, and (3) publish books, periodicals and journals in the field. The institute is currently busily engaged with objective (1) and it has established a journal. Other activities, especially standard setting, are receiving little attention, and except where specified by the 1962 Companies Act, accounting standards depend greatly on general acceptance. Undoubtedly the practices of the expatriate public accounting firms and the practices of the multinational corporations exert a large influence in this area.

Even with all mechanisms in place and functioning, the public accounting profession cannot be said to be completely organized, though much progress has been made. The public accountant must possess a recognized qualification and be registered by the registration board. The board is currently issuing certificates to practice and theoretically no one can practice without such a certificate after June 30, 1979, but many appeals have been filed and the fate of those who have been in practice but do not meet existing standards is still in some doubt. In addition, "there is nothing to stop any other person acting as the accountant or auditor to individuals, sole proprietorships, partnerships, private companies, etc." (Nzomo, p. 40).

3.1 KASNEB Examinations

KASNEB offers three examinations:

(1) The Accounts Clerk National Examination for those who wish to obtain qualification as bookkeepers and accounts clerks,

(2) The Certified Public Accountants Examination for those who wish to qualify as accountants, and

(3) The Certified Public Secretaries Examination for those who wish to qualify as company secretaries and administrators in public authorities.

The CPA examinations are normally held twice yearly. The examination is in three parts (six sections). The CPA Part I is equivalent to the Intermediate or Foundation examination of the U.K. accounting professional bodies, while the CPA Part III is designated as Final Professional Level. Standards are reasonably high, and at least one year's full-time study is recommended for each part of the exam, though frequently less time is required. The sections in each part may be taken together or separately at the option of the candidate, but before proceeding to the next part, a candidate must have passed all of the previous part. Provided his overall performance is satisfactory, a candidate who fails in one subject in Sections 1, 2, 4 or 6 may attempt that subject again. He must pass that subject within 18 months of the announcement of results or the whole section will have to be retaken.

The following are subject titles of each part, with basic scope indicated:

CPA Part I

  Section 1

    -Accounting I (Financial accounting principles)

    -Law I (Basic business law)

    -Economics (Micro and macro economics)

  Section 2

    -Business Finance (Basic financial management) or

    -Co-operative Finance and Accounting, or

    -Central Government Finance and Accounting, or

    -Local Government Finance and Accounting.

    (A choice of subjects is given to cater for students who are working in the private sector or who are working in central or local government or in the cooperative movement. Students indicate the stream they wish to take at time of registration.)

    -Statistics (Elementary statistical analysis)

    -Accounting II (Cost accounting principles)

CPA Part II

  Section 3

    -Accounting III (Intermediate and advanced topics)

    -Auditing I

  Section 4

    -Law II (Concentration on Kenyan law)

    -Taxation

    -Management Mathematics (Basic OR)

CPA Part III
  Section 5
    -Principles and Practice of Management
    -Accounting IV (Current topics in accounting)
  Section 6
    -Auditing II (Auditing in greater detail)
    -Accounting V (Managerial accounting)
    -Accounting VI (Financial management and public finance)

Candidates who wish to take the CPA exam must first register as students. In order to be registered, a student may hold any of the following qualifications:

- An East African Certificate of Education (EACE) or equivalent (high school school diploma) with credits in five subjects, including English language or literature, and mathematics. A pass in the general paper of East African Advanced Certificate of Education (EAACE) or equivalent (a post high school level) substitutes for a credit in English language.
- A degree in any faculty of a university recognized by the Board.
- The Preliminary Examination Certificate, but not exemption therefrom, of an approved accountancy or secretarial body.
- One of the following certificates:
  (1) The Stage II Diploma of the Association of Accountants in East Africa.
  (2) The Kenya Government Accountants Examination No. 1.
  (3) The Accounts Clerks National Certificate of KASNEB or equivalent.
  (4) The Diploma in Business Administration of Kenya or Mombasa Polytechnics.
  (5) The Kenya Certificate in Business Administration of Kenya Polytechnic.

In exceptional circumstances, candidates 23 year of age or over may be registered as students without the above qualifications. In all cases, students must maintain continuous registration until completion of all parts of the examinations. Courses in preparation for the CPA exams are available at a number of institutions which are discussed below.

Exemptions from exam subjects may be granted to students who are holders of certain degrees and certificates or diplomas. Exemptions from CPA Part I are granted for anyone who has passed the Intermediate or Foundation examination of the professional accountancy bodies of the U.K., the final exam of KASNEB for Certified Public Secretaries, or the final exam of a number of commonwealth secretarial or accountancy bodies. Likewise a degree from the Universities of Nairobi, Makerere, Dar Es Salaam or London with an accounting concentration exempts the student from Part I of the exam (but note that since the University of Nairobi, for example, provides no courses in government accounting, the exemption effectively means that no examination in other than enterprise accounting is ever required). In addition, partial exemptions from individual subjects are granted for special qualifications, such as a degree in economics or law or a Diploma in Co-operative Management. Exemption applications from registered students who are graduates of institutions other than those specified or who are holders of professional certificates other than those specified are considered on their merits.

The failure rate for KASNEB CPA examinations is quite high, reflecting both high standards and poor preparation. Of 7,263 individual examinations attempted (1970-78) there were 1,605 passes, a pass rate overall of 22 percent. The passes reflect individual parts of the examination, so that to date only 94 persons have passed all requirements and been qualified as CPAs through KASNEB.

While exemptions from KASNEB exams are based primarily on East African or U.K. qualifications, the qualifications for registration as a CPA are somewhat broader. They include the U.K. professional certificates (seven bodies), as well as those of the Institute of Chartered Accountants of India, the American Institure of CPAs and the Canadian Institute of Chartered Accountants, as well, of course, as a final pass in the KASNEB CPA exam.

Thus entry to the public accounting profession or governmental accounting can be accomplished through many channels, and it is apparent that many of these channels are being utilized, as noted above.

4. Educational Institutions

4.1 University of Nairobi

The university, with five campuses in the city of Nairobi, is the only university in Kenya. As such, it assumes a very important role, both in the education of the country's citizens, and in the social and economic planning of the government. The chief officer of the university, the chancellor, is the President of the country. This position is largely ceremonial, however, and administrative responsibility is vested in the vice-chancellor. Governance is through the University Council, an appointive body, thence through the Senate, an elective body consisting of representation from the Faculties. Each Faculty is headed by a dean, each department by a chairman, much like North American universities.

Instruction is in English, the official language of the country. While Swahili is the lingua franca, most students come from rural, tribal areas, where a tribal language is spoken. Almost all students thus speak at least three languages, but while they are generally proficient in English, reading speed and comprehension are at a lower level than in North America or Britain.

The Faculty of Commerce is located on the main campus in the City Centre. Admission to the Commerce program requires eleven years of primary and secondary education, termed ordinary level (EACE) and a further two years of college preparation, termed advanced level (EAACE). The Bachelor of Commerce (B.Comm.) is awarded after completion of a three-year university program, and the MBA after a further two years. Though the M.B.A. has until now required a thesis, the thesis will be replaced by a "business study" which requires field work and is meant to have a more practical orientation than a formal thesis.

Admission to the Commerce program is on the basis of merit, as is admission to all University of Nairobi programs. Top students are identified and selected for the advanced level education, and from this level the best students are again selected for university admission. Such a system is clearly in the best interest of a developing country, since resources are so much more limited than in an industrial country.

The Commerce program with an accounting major is quite rigid, since it consists of only three years of study and all courses are taken in the Faculty of Commerce. The program of study, while lacking the breadth usually found in North American programs, particularly with respect to outside electives, does compare well in depth with the usual business administration programs in such universities. Texts are usually North American or British, and instruction and standards are maintained at as high a level as resources permit, with the result that output quality is often quite good. Output quality is dependent on faculty staffing, as usual, the problems of which are discussed below. While some aspects of the British system remain, the Faculty of Commerce is basically operated on the North American model.

Courses are designated either as full-year or half-year. The students is required to take the equivalent of five full courses in each of years one and two, and six full courses in year three. Marking of these courses is based on a 70 percent final exam and 30 percent course work, with a rigid pass standard of 40 percent. Students earning the minimum passing mark are relatively poor and would not be passed in most North American universities. On the other hand, students earning top marks are as good as those found in the top ranks of good North American universities, so that differences are generally found in the lower pass levels. Overall, 20-50 percent of passing students, depending on the course, might not be passed in good American universities. A basic issue, however, is whether higher standards would be in the best interest of the country or the profession at this time in light of the very strong demand for managerial manpower. An argument can obviously be made either way.

Students who fail a full year course after attempting a supplementary exam offered in early September are only permitted to continue with the following year, carrying the failed course as an extra course, if their overall marks are generally good. Where such failed courses are prerequisites, this is not possible. If overall marks are not satisfactory, or if more than one course is failed after the supplementary exam, the entire year must be repeated, thus making failure of a course or courses relatively more serious than in North America.

The syllabus for the Bachelor of Commerce program, Accounting Option, is:

	Required Full Courses	Required Half Courses
First Year	Introduction to Economics Business Law I Accounting Fundamentals Quantitative Methods I	Business Studies Behavioral Science I
Second Year	Economic Theory Intermediate Accounting	Behavioral Science II Managerial Accounting Organization Theory Finance I Computing Science I Business Statistics I
Third Year	Advanced Accounting Auditing Business Policy	Taxation Cost Accounting The equivalent of two full courses (electives)

Note that there are no electives until third year, no courses outside the Commerce Faculty, and a limited number of electives available. Additional courses in finance, statistics, quantitative methods, or economics are usually chosen for the electives.

The required courses contain the usual amount of cost/benefit analysis and project appraisal material (i.e., not much) found in North American business programs. There should definitely be more orientation toward this set of tools and method of analysis, because it needs introduction into accounting and managerial programs so that it can be thus introduced into government and industry. In government organizations at the present time there is almost none of it in use. It is used in the multinationals to the extent the parent organizations require.

The MBA program is similar in structure and content to such programs in North American universities. Admission is usually based on upper second class honors graduation from a recognized university (considerable discretion exercised), with no GMAT requirements. In past years, most MBA students came with commerce undergraduate degrees, creating problems because there was not enough differentiation between the undergraduate and graduate curricula and not enough depth in the faculty to provide advanced courses for these people. Beginning in 1978-79, the United Nations Economic Commission for Africa (ECA) provided enough scholarships to enable a number of non-commerce degree holders to enroll in the program, thus broadening and enriching the student mix. At the same time, extensive efforts were made to provide a higher level first year program, such that none of the commerce undergraduates in the program attempted to take exemption exams, and several expressed appreciation at the quantity and quality of new material as compared to their undergraduate training.

A second feature of the upgraded program begun in 1978-79 is the requirement that only applicants with two or more years postgraduate experience would be accepted. The result of this change appears to be a much more mature and interested group of students. A number of the students came into the program with accounting backgrounds and accounting experience, but their intention with respect to continuation in accounting has not been clearly expressed by most students. The impact of the MBA program on accounting education in Kenya is thus not apparent at this time.

For 1979-80 another group of forty applicants has been chosen, but actual class size will be subject to scholarship availability, since only about 15 percent of acceptable applicants are self-financed, and scholarships are being sought from a number of agencies. As of this writing (August 1979) only ten scholarships from the University of Nairobi are committed, with the other agencies yet to be heard from.

4.1.1 University Problems and Prospects

The University provides the only source of training for Kenyan citizens at this level, with the exception of foreign training, which affects a very small number of people. An analysis of the problems and prospects for accountants educated at the University requires a review of the situation at the Faculty of Commerce in general, since approximately 80 percent of undergraduates choose the accounting option.

Beginning in 1971, and continuing to the present, the Canadian International Development Agency (CIDA) undertook a program to upgrade the almost non-existent Faculty of Commerce. The substance of the program included provision of expatriate staff, scholarships for education of Kenyans in Canada at the MBA, M.Sc. and Ph.D. levels, and funding of scholarships for MBA education at the University of Nairobi. During this period there were also on staff a number of British Inter-University Council (IUC) instructors and several Fulbright Professors. Total aid thus provided in the form of expatriate staff was:

	Man-years
Canadian	44
American	6
British	9

Likewise, the number of students sponsored by CIDA during the period was:

Total graduate students	70
Trained abroad (Ph.D., M.Sc., MBA)	12
Number joining faculty	18
Number now on faculty	13

As indicated, many of the students returned to the University and are now teaching in the Faculty of Commerce. While the number of Ph.D.'s on staff as a result of the program is far less than hoped, all Kenyans on staff have at least an MBA, several have done doctoral work and are ABD's, and several have Ph.D.'s. The extent of Kenyanization of the Faculty is significant, as shown:

Year	71/72	72/73	73/74	74/75	75/76	76/77	77/78	78/79
Total Staff	10	15	21	28	30	28	27	27
Kenyans	1	2	3	9	16	20	18	16

The reduction in numbers of both categories, subsequent to 1976-77, has been due in large part to the differentials which exist between faculty salaries and those in the private sector. This factor has not only made it difficult to retain qualified staff, particularly in accounting, but has also made it difficult to entice B.Comm.'s and MBA's into training abroad. The difficulty is also a reflection of the appreciation of these degrees by the business community.

With respect to salary differentials, the relatively high cost of living, coupled with very low faculty salaries, makes moonlighting (teaching in various CPA training courses or consulting) almost a necessity. This means in turn that there is little time for professional development or research and publication. Some publications are beginning to appear from the Faculty, but the output is small. High student/teacher ratios further discourage faculty members.

It must be noted as well that of the six appointments at the professor or associate professor levels in 1978-79, none were held by Kenyans. This is also true for all years shown, since these positions have always been filled by expatriates. Thus a critical need is the education and subsequent development of Kenyans for these senior positions.

The Faculty of Commerce is currently at a crossroads, due to almost simultaneous developments on several fronts. First, and most important, is the impending termination of CIDA support after 1979-80. While the University and the government of Kenya are actively seeking continuation of this support, it seems questionable at best whether the necessary level of support will continue. At the same time, IUC support has been decreased and may be cancelled altogether, and the University has reallocated the Fulbright position to another Faculty. Coupled with these developments, which reflect international interest in foreign aid far more than internal conditions in the University of the Faculty, is the possibility that the several staff members from Uganda will return to their own country as a result of recent developments there.

These developments come at a crucial time for the Faculty and could endanger many of the accomplishments made to date. At the least, it seems safe to predict that simultaneous loss of some or all of these expatriates would lead to higher teaching loads and morale problems, and thus further loss of Kenyan staff. At the same time, the needs in terms of demand for graduates are greater than ever.

The Development Plan clearly identifies export growth, industrial efficiency, increased competitiveness in the agricultural sector and greater efficiency in the public sector as high priority goals requiring trained managerial manpower. The public sector is currently hiring as many B.Comm.'s as it can attract. The private sector is also hiring large numbers of B.Comm.'s, particularly those with accounting majors. The public accounting firms are more particular, but demand is still strong. A discussion of the public accounting industry follows.

One estimate of the shortage of accountants in government is provided by the Auditor-General in his introduction to the government's annual accounting report for 1977-78 (Kenya, 1979b). In this report he notes that many of the problems disclosed in the report, both those of accounting and fiscal management, and those involving delays, errors and irregularities, could be attributed to shortages of accounting personnel in all areas of government. He provides an estimate of the lack of staff for each ministry in government as of June 30, 1978. These shortages, in terms of percentage vacancies, range from a 27 percent vacancy rate in the Ministry of Information and Broadcasting to 67 percent in the Ministry of Health. In line with these figures, it has been noted that, in spite of the importance of parastatals in both Kenyan GDP and exports, some of them do not have a single trained manager, implying the absence of qualified accountants as well.

In specific terms, it is estimated that the government would at this time hire 200 B.Comm.'s if they were available. More specifically with respect to accounting graduates, for the 1979-83 Development Plan the anticipated need is for 2,000 accountants; for the country as a whole 20,000 accounting people at all levels are needed over that period (Smith and Mirus, pp. 4-5).

In line with projected needs in the economy as a whole, enrollments in the Faculty of Commerce have grown rapidly in the past few years. Projections for 1979-80 are for 610 undergraduates and 40 MBA's, while a conservative growth estimate results in a forecast of 1,160 undergraduates and 94 MBA's in 1986-87.

Again, since 80 percent of undergraduates choose the accounting option, the projection for university educated accountants is significant over the next few years (Smith and Mirus, p. 11). Thus the demand for commerce graduates, and accountants in particular, is strong, and is matched by heavy demand on the part of prospective students for a commerce education (more than half the applicants to the Faculty of Commerce are normally rejected).

The principal need, therefore, is to train more Kenyans for faculty positions. In the worst case, with all aid-granting agencies withdrawing and all Ugandans and other African expatriates leaving, the possibility of accomplishing this on any significant scale appears remote. It could of course be done solely by the Kenya government, but with so many competing demands for extremely scarce resources, it appears highly doubtful that anything on the required scale would be adopted. On the other hand, a continued infusion of aid by, for example, CIDA, on the scale currently being proposed, would result in a very viable faculty with the capacity to develop, or continue developing, a sound management education program. This proposal envisions granting six scholarships annually for Ph.D. study abroad. Assuming a 50 percent attrition rate, the result would be 12 new Kenyan Ph.D.'s on staff by 1987-88. Since at least some of the attrition would result in M.Sc.'s, there would also be other highly educated Kenyans available for lower level staff positions. During the training period, CIDA or some other agency would provide enough expatriate staff to meet faculty needs (Smith and Mirus, 1979).

4.1.2 Professional Qualification

As noted, the University of Nairobi is the only university level institution in Kenya. Qualification for the accounting profession, however, depends on completion of either a CPA level (called a chartered level in Commonwealth countries) or a certified level (e.g., British ACCA) which is a lower but still professionally respectable leel of achievement. Either level in Kenya entitles the holder to registration by the registration board and a license to practice accounting. Since a university degree in accounting only provides certain exceptions from the qualification exams, other institutions have been established to complete the training or provide it in full for non-university graduates.

4.2 Government Institutions

The Kenya Institute of Administration (KIA) is the premier government educational body in administration. Students receive training on a residence basis, usually during one-year programs. Most are government employees who are paid full salary while on leave to study at KIA. Payment for tuition and board depends on the unit of government by whom they are sponsored, and they are usually required to bond themselves to that governmental body for a period of time after completion of training or pay a rather large penalty if they leave the employment of that body. In the case of accounting trainees, even the large penalty often does not deter successful graduates from leaving government service after completion of CPA III for the much larger salaries in private industry.

All accountancy training is concentrated on the KASNEB exams, from Accounts Clerks through CPA III. Organization of training courses in all Kenya accountancy training institutions is based on the level sought (e.g., CPA II) rather than on the functional areas involved (accounting, law, etc.). In addition, KIA is organized according to the stream of study selected. Thus a local government CPA II student registers with the Local Government Training Department, while a central government CPA II student registers with the Executive Training Department, in spite of the fact that actual streams are now largely non-existent in the new KASNEB syllabus.

KIA students achieve reasonably high pass rates on the exams, ranging from 40-50 percent on the first attempt at CPA I to 20-25 percent on the first attempt at CPA II, which is obviously a more difficult exam. These rates compare very favorably with some other institutions. The success of KIA students is due in part to the full-time residence programs with small classes (16-26 students) and in part to the degree of screening undergone by applicants.

Some of the training load for lower level exams, Accounts Clerks and CPA I, has been assumed by the Government Training Institutes (GTI) at Maseno in western Kenya and Mombasa on the coast. These institutions will eventually have responsibility for all CPA I training, leaving KIA to do the advanced courses. Instructors at KIA and the GTI's are civil servants, and fall administratively under the Office of the President.

Part-time government institutions offer accounting training at various levels, with various levels of success. The University of Nairobi Extra-Mural Division, an extension program, offers courses from Accounts Clerks through CPA III. Student numbers are small but success rates are reported to be high, though no statistics are available. Kenya and Mombasa Polytechnics offer courses at the CPA I and II levels, with generally lower rates of success. There are fewer than 200 students in accounting at the polytechnics.

4.3 Private Institutions

The high demand for people with accounting training, coupled with the 1977 Accountants Act which only permits registration of persons with certain qualifications, has led to a large number of private channels through which qualification is sought. These are discussed in rough order of success of the graduates.

The Accounting Tuition Program (ATP) was established in 1976 as a private venture by an expatriate member of one of the Big Eight firms operating in Kenya. It is now operated jointly by major expatriate and local firms acting through a board of directors. Due to the high rate of success experienced by its graduates in passing both the ACCA and KASNEB exams, none of the major firms do any in-house training, but send all trainees to the ATP. Pass rates average 55-60 percent on the ACCA and 70-75 percent on KASNEB, and the ATP claims the highest pass rate for ACCA of any training program in the world.

ATP currently has more than 400 students who attend night classes for 16 weeks and then become full-time students for three weeks prior to the semi-annual exams. Until recently, all accounting firms required their trainees to be registered for the ACCA exams, at least partly because the KASNEB exams fell during the busy season. Now, with a change in exam timing, all firms require the KASNEB qualification, with the result that approximately two-thirds of ATP students are registered for the KASNEB training and only students who began training before the switch to KASNEB remain in the ACCA program. Approximately one-third of the ATP students are from public accounting firms and two-thirds from industry, with a few self-sponsored. Students come from all over East Africa for the courses. Approximately 50 percent of ATP instructors are from accounting firms, for the more technical accounting and auditing courses, and 50 percent from industry, the polytechnics, KIA and the university as moonlighters.

Second in importance among private institutions is probably Strathmore College, a full-time school which trains students in accounting for the CPA (KASNEB), ACCA, ICMA (Institute of Cost and Management Accounting - U.K.) and other accountancy qualifications. Friends College in Kaimosi trains for Accounts Clerks and CPA I. Total output of these schools is small, but their graduates have reasonable success with the exams, though reputedly lower than ATP or KIA.

Of least importance in terms of graduate success are the commercial colleges, similar to secretarial schools, some of which offer part-time courses and most of which offer correspondence training. There were estimated to be some 80 of these in 1975, but there has been some attrition since then and many now train only for Accounts Clerks. Because KASNEB does not keep statistics with respect to pass rates for students from various institutions, all statistics presented regarding pass rates for institutions are estimates by various persons interviewed, but most estimates seem quite consistent between interviewees. In this respect, there is a general agreement that success rates for the commercial colleges are extremely low. One reason may be that the colleges do not hire enough competent people, another may be that the instruction does not distinguish between ACCA, based on U.K. reporting requirements, and CPA, based on Kenya GAAP. While there are many similarities, there are enough differences to cause difficulties on some of the exams. There may be as many as 1,000 persons currently enrolled with the colleges for Accounts Clerks and 600 for CPA, though numbers are difficult to ascertain.

At a lower level, Kenya Technical Teachers College (KTTC), an institution developed to train teachers of all technical subjects, is currently training accounting teachers. While these teachers are basically trained for secondary school teaching, there is some demand for them in lower-level post-secondary institutions.

5. The Public Accounting Profession

Kenya is a multicultural, multiracial society. It consists of at least three distinct, major groups: those with African, Asian (generally Indian or Pakistani) and European (including North American) backgrounds. It is also useful to distinguish between expatriates with European, Asian or African backgrounds and citizens, again with the same backgrounds, but in far different proportions. While the society is totally integrated and racial animosities are almost nonexistent, the government's policy on Kenyanization makes the cultural and racial

337

mix in the profession of interest, since this mix is changing rapidly and will continue to do so.

At present, the structure of the profession is such that it consists approximately of 50 percent Asians, mostly Kenya citizens, 35 percent Europeans, mostly expatriates, and 15 percent Africans, almost all citizens. Of the Africans, some 10 hold U.K. Chartered qualifications, 35 are U.K. certified, and a few are KASNEB CPA's. Most KASNEB qualified people are in industry, because of higher salaries, and in government, because of bonding agreements entered into at time of commencement of training. No KASNEB qualified person is yet at manager level in any firm, with the exception of two partners in small firms.

Approximately 10 percent of qualified (chartered and certified) persons are African, but most firms, including the large expatriate firms, will have at least one African partner by the end of 1979. Approximately 40-50 new trainees were hired in 1979, almost all from the top 50-60 Faculty of Commerce graduates. Almost all new hires now come from the university, and the classes there are almost 100 percent African, even though most firms have traditionally hired Asians.

The concentration of the profession, as well as its multinational makeup, can be seen from a listing of firms, in estimated order of their billings:

1) Deloitte, Haskins and Sells, operating under that name and under the name of Gill and Johnson out of one office, audits approximately 50 percent of the publicly listed companies and has approximately 65 percent of the billings in the profession nationally.
2) Coopers and Lybrand
3) Price-Waterhouse
4) Githongo and Co. (African)
5) Kassim-Lakha Abdullah and Co. (Asian)
6) Murdock McRae and Smith (Touche Ross associates)
7) Pannell Bellhouse Mwangi and Co. (European/African)
8) Peat, Marwick, Mitchell and Co.

Firms 2) through 8) audit another 49 percent of public companies, leaving the remaining 1 percent to be audited by the remaining 10 or so companies, mostly Asian, including Whinney, Murray, Ernst and Ernst. Only Arthur Andersen (which refers to Price-Waterhouse) and Arthur Young of the Big Eight do not operate in Kenya. It seems apparent that, while many accountants are Kenyan, the profession is very heavily expatriate-based.

There are more U.K. than North American subsidiaries in Kenyan commerce. This fact, in conjunction with the British tradition and the Kenya Companies Act, which is based on the 1948 U.K. Act, results in U.K. disclosure requirements and basic use of the U.K. accounting model in Kenya. In reality, only moral force governs accounting standards, such that almost literal GAAP are in use, with the exception of consolidation requirements of individual firms. Application has been made to join the International Federation of Accountants (IFAC), and the IASC standards are currently being applied.

Most firms are computerized, most do at least some Management Advising Service, have on-the-job training in auditing for their employees, in addition to at least some professional development courses. They also collectively audit most of the parastatals, though the government ministries themselves are audited by government auditors. Overall, the public accounting profession in Kenya is both well developed and important in the economy.

6. Registration and Governance of Accountants

The Accountants Registration Board was established by the 1977 Accountants Act. Any person who desires to practice in public accounting must be registered and licensed by the board. To date some 1,030 persons have applied for registration and 686 have been registered. Of these, 322 have been licensed to practice. Most of the remainder of those registered are employed in industry or government, though some are still under consideration for a practicing license. Of those who applied but were not registered, something more than 50 are still under consideration for registration, while the rest have been denied. Those who were refused registration but who were in practice at the time of the 1977 Act will be allowed to earn a living as bookkeepers or in some other limited version of accounting, but their licenses will specify the extent to which they are allowed to practice. While government and industrial accountants are not required to register, many have, including almost all of the 94 KASNEB qualified persons.

The board has basically undertaken three tasks:

1) Deciding who is an accountant. Those qualifications which are acceptable have been previously noted. In addition, Australian and New Zealand chartered qualification and Indian cost and works (C & MA) are under consideration for approval.
2) Deciding who may practice. Here applicants are considered on an individual basis and qualifications and experience are evaluated.
3) Exercising a final disciplinary function. Since the Act specifies a code of conduct, the board makes a final ruling on some cases, though all disciplinary action begins with the Institute of CPA's. Actions of the board may be appealed in court.

Registered accountants are automatically members of the Institute (if they pay the necessary fees), but there are currently more expatriate than citizen members. At the November, 1978 meeting which formally established the institute, nine members of a governing council were elected, to be joined by two appointive members. Of these, four are African, four citizen Asian, and three European (each of which is a Big Eight local partner). Committees of the council are now functioning to accomplish the goals of the Act, including promotion of professional standards, seeking international recognition, carrying out research and establishment of reporting standards, and advising the Examinations Board. The Examinations Board has a membership of both professional accountants and others, including one University of Nairobi member, currently a senior lecturer in the Faculty of Commerce.

7. Summary and Conclusions

The accounting profession and institutions for accounting education in Kenya are relatively well established. The Registration Board, Institute of CPA's and

Examination Board (KASNEB) are functioning in an effective manner and have achieved a considerable degree of status in Africa. The head of the Registration Board, for example, has carried out investigations of the needs of the accounting professions in a number of other African countries, acting as a consultant to the United Nations Economic Commission for Africa (ECA). The government's policy of Kenyanization is being implemented, generally based on cooperation rather than urgency or pressure. While the policy has been a mixed blessing in the economy as a whole on strictly an economic basis, it appears to be succeeding in the accounting profession. Kenyanization in the Faculty of Commerce, for example, has been a goal which could have hindered growth because of rejection of able candidates for Faculty positions, but there is no hard evidence to support this.

The Faculty of Commerce has extensive needs for training of senior-level instructors. The policy of training and hiring people at the MBA level has resulted in some very good instructors, but some which are not so good as well. If CIDA does not extend the contract, which would permit both the training of staff at Ph.D. and M.Sc. levels and a continuation of expatriate support during the training period, the fate of the Faculty as a relatively high quality educational organization is in considerable doubt. Continuation and broadening of the support which has existed in the past is clearly the most critical need in accounting education in Kenya if university educated accountants are to continue to be available to the profession. This need is much more critical than any needs for certification or chartering institutions, since these institutions are in place and functioning reasonably well.

Library and teaching materials at the university are almost all non-African, and in the case of the library, few materials with dates after 1974 are available. Moreover, the material which is available is almost all of the textbook variety, with little or no research material available to Faculty researchers. Texts written by and for East Africans would make a substantial contribution, but even up-to-date foreign publications which contain state-of-the-art material would be a great improvement.

In terms of course content, the relationship of accounting and economic development needs to be stressed. Public and private project evaluation should be stressed. Accounting problems peculiar to Africa and Kenya should be included in course material, which is now almost totally based on foreign texts.

While much has been done to train and license public accountants, little has been done in the area of cost and managerial accounting beyond standard curriculum inclusion. There is no cost and works institute, or similar CMA type effort, and little attention is being given at present to such developments. Given the substantial progress in public accounting, there is much to be proud of but attention should now begin to be paid to a broadened outlook. A program similar to that of the Society of Management Accountants (SMA) in Canada could be undertaken in Kenya, perhaps with the advice and help of the SMA. This program trains people for accounting positions in industry, including some financial accounting, but concentrating on the needs of the management/cost accountant. The program is part-time evening effort which can fully qualify the person with no accounting background in about five years.

Finally, though there are many accountants working in government, the salaries paid simply do not attract and retain the best people. This is true at both the operating levels of government and university, and at higher levels as well. Salaries and other incentives must be developed which will reverse this situation. With the ability to hold good people, specialized training in governmental accounting could be given which would significantly upgrade the level of accounting in government activities. With a continuation of full support for the University Faculty of Commerce, improved salaries, and development of a program to train managerial accounting specialists, accounting in Kenya could become the model for most of Africa.

REFERENCES

Amwayi, F.M.M. (1978), *Financial Reporting Practices in Kenyan Public Companies*, unpublished MBA Thesis, The University of Nairobi, (1978), 163 pp.

Enthoven, A.J.H. (1975), *An Evaluation of Accountancy Systems, Developments and Requirements in Africa*, (Ford Foundation, 1975), pp. 60-68.

Kenya, Republic of (1979a), *Development Plan for the Period 1979 to 1983*, (1979), Part I 523 pp., Part II 186 pp.

_____ (1979a), *The Appropriation Accounts, Other Public Accounts* and *the Accounts of the Funds for the Year 1977/78, Together with the Report Thereon by the Controller and the Auditor-General*, (1979), 846 pp.

Kinyanjui, E.J.M. (1979), "The Institutions Established by the Accountants Act 1977," *Kenya Accountant* (June, 1979), pp. 24-27+.

Masita, S.C. (1976), *The Development of Accounting and the Accounting Profession (1850-1975) and its Application to East Africa*, unpublished MBA Thesis, The University of Nairobi, (September, 1976), 268 pp.

Nzomo, D.N. (1979), "The Accounting Profession in Kenya," *Kenya Accountant* (June, 1979), pp. 38-44.

Smith, R.S. and R. Mirus, *The Need for Continued Support for the Faculty of Commerce at the University of Nairobi: A Discussion Paper*, unpublished working paper, The University of Alberta (July, 1979), 26 pp.

CHAPTER XXVIII

ACCOUNTING EDUCATION IN LIBYA

by
Khalifa Ali Dau*

1. Introduction

Libya has a population of about 2.5 million people with vast economic resources, mainly oil production. Huge efforts for developing the country have
been underway since the First of September Revolution. The latest development
plan, ending in 1980, is estimated to cost about $3 billion. This figure is expected
to be doubled in the next five-year development plan. Starting from scratch, the
Libyan development plan includes a huge number of projects in farming,
housing, transportation, communication, health care, education, manufacturing, etc. For most of the development projects, feasibility studies, accountability,
and cost-effectiveness analyses are required.

The need for accountants, and thus accounting education, is obvious. To fulfill
the immediate needs, however, many accountants have been imported, mainly
from neighboring Arab countries such as Egypt and the Sudan. It was decided
that two levels of accounting education are needed: intermediate and advanced
(i.e., university level).[1]

2. Accounting Education

2.1 Intermediate Accounting Education

This is a four-year program, designed for students with a junior high school
diploma. Its purpose is training students for clerical, commerical and bookkeeping jobs.

There are three institutions that apply this program in Libya, with a total of
about 2,300 students in 1978. The average student-instructor ratio is 36.1, which
is relatively high. The universal requirement for accounting instructors in these
schools is a bachelor's degree.

2.2 University Accounting Education

Although there are two universities in Libya: Garyounis University and Al-
Fatah University, there is only one business college, namely the Faculty of Economics and Commerce (FEC), of the Garyounis University system.

The FEC has five departments, namely accounting, economics, management,

*Khalifa Ali Dau has a Ph.D. from Louisiana State University, and obtained his Certified Management
Accounting (CMA) Certificate in the U.S. He is Chairman, Department of Accounting, Faculty of
Economics, Garyounis University, Benghazi, Libya.

[1] All formal education in Libya is financed by the state.

political science, and statistics. It has an enrollment of about 2,000 students, about 25 percent of which are accounting majors.

Since the spring of 1977, FEC has adopted the American semester system instead of the British nine-month academic year system.

Under the new system, accounting students are required to earn at least 120 credit hours in order to get a bachelor's degree. On the average, a student is expected to graduate within eight semesters. The course makeup of the accounting program at FEC is presented in Exhibit 1. This exhibit shows that 37 percent of the courses required are in accounting. This is much higher than the standard 17.5 percent recommended by the Beamer Committee for a four-year accounting program.[2] It is also higher than the 20 percent standard recommended by the same committee for a five-year accounting program.[3] That is, more emphasis is put on accounting courses as compared with other business and general courses of the accounting curriculum.

EXHIBIT I

Course Makeup of the University Accounting Program in Libya

Financial accounting and auditing	30%
Cost and managerial accounting	7%
Mathematics: basic, statistics, operations research	13%
Law: civil, business, tax, administration	12%
Business administration	8%
Economics	7%
Languages: Arabic, English	7%
Computer programming and system design	5%
Others (elective courses: behavioral science, management, economics)	11%
TOTAL	100%

Availability of funds and scarcity of manpower make computers a handy and necessary tool for the Libyan development. Graduates of the FEC, especially accounting majors, should be well trained in this area. Therefore, more emphasis on computers and information systems is needed.

Within the accounting segment of the curriculum described in Exhibit 1, less emphasis is put on cost and managerial accounting as compared with financial accounting—7 percent to 30 percent. Cost accounting is a field that has not been fully explored, nor appreciated, by developing countries in general, and Libya is no exception. Good cost accounting systems are needed in order to improve the decision-making process, as well as cost controls.

Therefore, more emphasis should be placed upon cost accounting in the accounting curriculum at FEC. This, however, should not be done at the expense

[2] Committee on Educational and Experience Requirements for CPAs, Academic Preparation for Professional Accounting Careers, American Institute of Certified Public Accountants, 1968, p. 17.

[3] Ibid.

of the non-accounting courses of the curriculum, since the percentage of the accounting courses is too high already. It is recommended that some of the extra financial accounting courses, such as oil and gas accounting, insurance accounting, and banking accounting, should be eliminated to leave room for more cost accounting courses.

3. Accounting Faculty, Materials and Research

3.1 Qualifications of Accounting Instructors

The minimum requirement for teaching at the Garyounis University is a master's degree. Therefore, of the twelve accounting instructors at the FEC, seven instructors have Ph.D. degrees and five instructors have master's degrees. All of them are graduates of U.S. schools. About 80 percent of the instructors are full-time faculty members. The faculty to student ratio is 55.1.

Moreover, a growing number of students is expected to join the accounting department, because of the high demand for accountants in Libya. Therefore, the need for more accounting faculty members is evident.

It is a policy of the Garyounis University to appoint some of the best graduates as teaching assistants and send them abroad for graduate programs, mainly to the U.S. and England, because there are no graduate accounting programs in Libya. The accounting department alone has twenty-one students in such programs, working on their doctorates in the U.S. (only one student is in the U.K.).

The teacher presentation approach is the usual method of instruction. Accounting workshops are used usually for principles and intermediate accounting courses. Audiovisual techniques are used infrequently. There is a real need for improvement in this respect.

3.2 Books and Materials

Arabic is the language of study in the accounting department, with the exception of a few courses taught in English. Therefore, Arabic textbooks, imported mainly from Egypt, are used. Only two accounting textbooks have been written by Libyan faculty members. Because of the lack of competition and small markets, most Arabic accounting textbooks are not very well prepared nor well printed. Thus, American textbooks and publications are used as reference in many courses, although they reflect a different accounting environment.

3.3 Accounting Research

Accounting research has been limited, mainly for lack of free time for accounting instructors. Reasons for this are that: (1) they have excessive teaching loads of about 12 hours per week, and (2) many of them are practicing as accountants and consultants. However, financial resources and research opportunities are available. A few accounting articles written by the accounting faculty have been published in "Dirasat: the Economic and Business Review," a journal published by the Faculty of Economics and Commerce, Garyounis University, and in some American accounting journals.

A faculty exchange program with some foreign universities would definitely enhance research opportunities and capabilities of all parties involved. Such programs will also be beneficial to the accounting program at FEC since: (1) the Libyan instructors will be kept up to date in the accounting field, and (2) the Libyan students will be exposed to different ideas and techniques.

4. Summary and Conclusions

The accounting education system in Libya consists of two programs: a four-year intermediate program and a four-year university program. No graduate programs are available. The present university program, leading to a B.Sc., seems to be very adequate, compared with similar programs in other Arab countries and in the U.S. Many graduates of this program have been admitted to graduate accounting programs in the U.S. and received their master's and doctoral degrees with no difficulties. However, the following needs are evident:

- More emphasis on cost and managerial accounting, and information systems.
- More well-trained staff members.
- Better teaching techniques, such as audiovisual aids.
- Good accounting textbooks that are tailored to the Libyan needs.
- Faculty exchange programs with foreign universities.
- A graduate program in accounting.

CHAPTER XXIX

ACCOUNTING DEVELOPMENTS AND EDUCATION IN SOMALIA

1. Introduction

The section on Somalia was derived from the material worked up by Mr. C. P. Cacho, Resident Representative of the World Bank in Somalia. His views expressed in this writeup are his personal views and not those of the World Bank's Resident Representative.

We are appreciative of this material, because it gives a somewhat different perspective of some critical factors in accounting developments and its educational requirements.

Mr. Cacho's outline is a contribution to the thinking on developing capability for financial management in all sectors of the economy. Although this outline recognizes and provides for the need to deal with short-term improvements, the greater emphasis in on measures to satisfy fully the long-term requirements of a developing Somalia through proposals designed to achieve self-sufficiency in suitably qualified and experienced personnel at all levels, in the field of accounting. The writeup reviews the present situation, assesses Somalia's needs, and suggests outlines of approaches to satisfy such needs.

Somalia, as an underdeveloped country, can least afford waste, and it requires above average efficiency in managing scarce resources. However, it is deficient in the skills needed for efficient resource management. The accelerated pace of development since the Revolution has revealed a significant dearth of the skills required for adequate financial management throughout the economy. This broader perspective is the focus of this paper.

The Somali scene indicates that the functions and significances of the accounting profession and education may not be sufficiently appreciated, and that this may have and probably continues to thwart its development.

The Somali word for "accountant" is "xisabiye" which literally translated means "calculator," a word which grossly underrepresents and distorts what a professionally qualified accountant really is and does. The resulting tendency is to apply the term to those who, for example, have done no more than complete the four-year secondary school-level course at the Commercial Secondary School in Mogadishu, or the two-year course at SIDAM. Another result is that the status and remuneration of "accountants" tend to be low and therefore the accountancy/ financial management field is not regarded as particularly desirable by those planning to enter a profession.

2. The Accounting Profession and the Need for Accountants

There is no professional body and no training for the full profession in Somalia. At the intermediate level, SIDAM only recently graduated its first batch of 36

347

and plans to produce about 40 every other year. The University offers a four-hours-a-week, two-semester course in fairly elementary accounting to its economics students. At the bookkeeper level, the only institution that trains book-keepers on a regular basis is the Commercial Secondary School with an output of 60 a year. Short-term, four-month courses are run by the Central Bank's training institute. Given this dearth of training facilities and the very limited output, inadequate supplies at all levels are not surprising.

There are only two fully professionally qualified accountants in Somalia, neither being a Somali. This would put the ratio of accountants to population at 1:1,000,000. (The ratio for the U.K. is 1:765.) Discounting the relative underdevelopment of Somalia and assuming that a ratio of 1:25,000 would satisfy Somalia's needs today, then some 160 fully qualified accountants would be required immediately. At the usual ratio of three intermediate technicians to each fully qualified accountant some 480 trained intermediate technicians to each would presently be needed. At eight accounts clerks per intermediate accounting technician, the requirements for trained accounts clerks would be about 3,340.

These figures are clearly no more than rough orders of magnitude, but they illustrate realistically enough, the uphill climb—a climb that will become increasingly more difficult as time elapses, the economy develops, and the demand grows further, unless a very early and concerned start is made on the way up.

3. Some Policy Aspects

The awareness of the need for action exists within the government. The efforts at SIDAM and at the Central Bank's Training Institute are moves in the right direction. But much more needs to be done.

A Somali body of professional accountants should be established to do the things that professional bodies traditionally do, such as setting standards, setting examinations, designing training schemes, etc. Such a body should have legal support and the enactment of such a law should provide the opportunity for the government, through publicity and other positive tangible measures, to place the profession where it belongs beside law, medicine. engineering and the other well-known professions. Unless this is done, it is unlikely that many will be attracted to the profession and one of the objectives of forming a professional body would be defeated to the country's detriment.

Although many developing countries have had a more advantageous start than Somalia (due to a nucleus of expatriate accountants and accountants trained in the West) the absence of such an advantage ought not to daunt efforts in Somalia.

The founding fathers of a Somali professional body could, for example, comprise the Minister of Finance, Chairman of Planning Commission, presidents of the Central Development, and commercial banks and their deputies, the Magistrate of Accounts and his deputy, the Accountant General and his deputy, the Dean of the University Faculty of Economics, the DG SIDAM, all lecturers in accounting at the university and SIDAM, university graduates who have majored or specialized in accounting, and all resident members of recognized bodies of accountants.

Model constitutions of accountancy bodies elsewhere and of the laws associated with them can easily be obtained. These models can be adapted to suit Somalia's special needs.

4. Training for Accountants

The usual path in most developed countries is an accounting related university degree plus two years of part-time work/study. In many developing countries, the work/study by correspondence courses is still prevalent. In some cases the fledgling national body uses the syllabus, examinations and standards of a recognized body abroad for a few years while it gains strength. In line with the government's policy of focusing training narrowly to meet Somalia's defined needs, it might be possible to tailor a course of training over, say, four full years from university entrance status, including 12 months of supervised work/training on the job. The less complicated tax, corporate, and executorship laws make this feasible without undue dilution of standards. Whether the training is to be undertaken at the university or at SIDAM or both is a matter for later decision. The need for work/training presupposes that there would be a number of fully qualified accountants presumably on technical assistance assignments. This is a requirement to bear in mind very early at the planning stage.

The path explored above would be suitable for new high school graduates going on to a professional career, but not for those already at work, preferably in accounting. These would not be spared from work, and family financial commitments may in any event preclude full-time study. Within a period of say 10 years of establishing the Somali body, the more mature aspirant to professional status should be especially catered for with correspondence courses for those outside Mogadishu and correspondence courses-cum-evening tuition for those who live in the city. Also a special syllabus and exams should be tailored to their special needs. Finally, they would be required to work under the tutelage of qualified accountants during their period of study. After 10 to 15 years all posts of accountant, auditor and others requiring similar skills should be held only by members of the Somali body.

At the intermediate level, the level at about which the SIDAM course aims, 40 graduates are produced every other year. This rate would meet the present need for 480 in 20 years by which time the need would most likely have risen to three or more times that number. Different approaches may be used simultaneously to accelerate the pace of training. They include:
(1) A two-year immediate post high school course at SIDAM or similar institution.
(2) A one-year immediate post high school course at say SIDAM plus correspondence studies to complete the syllabus.
(3) Correspondence studies throughout. Again, this would ensure that those who live away from Mogadishu would not thereby lose the opportunity for training and qualifying.

As far as practicable, while satisfying the examination requirements, practical work/experience under approved guidance should be required before the award of a diploma. As in the case of accountants there should be special provision during say the first 10 years to enable the mature aspirant to gain the qualification on possibly less rigorous academic terms in view of his/her previous experience in accounting.

To provide an incentive to qualify, posts such as assistant accountant should be reserved after 10 to 15 years, only to those who have earned the Accounting Technician Diploma.

The role of the bookkeeper/audit clerk is also not given the serious consideration it deserves. At present only the Commercial Secondary School runs courses for bookkeepers, although those who complete the course are designated "accountants." It is a four-year post intermediate course and produces only 60 graduates annually.

The severe shortage of trained bookkeepers needs urgent attention. Several methods may be used simultaneously to accelerate the pace of training, among them:

(1) Introduction of an adequate amount of bookkeeping courses within some streams in the secondary school curriculum.
(2) Evening courses for post intermediate students who do not go on to secondary school and for others.
(3) Correspondence courses.

Correspondence courses have been suggested for each of the three levels.

The correspondence course route to learning is tough and particularly so for those being trained for the accounting profession. Yet Somalia's needs are such as to make full-time study for all impracticable for the next 10 to 15 years. The cost in lost manhours of work and material resources would be too high.

5. Technical Assistance Requirements

The foregoing suggestions for institutional development and training attempt to deal to some extent with both the short-term needs and the longer term requirements of self-sufficiency. In the near future it appears that certain other avenues should also be pursued. More importantly, some technical assistance seems urgently needed to (1) help bring accounts up to date and audited, (2) introduce proper accounting systems, (3) provide in-service training, and (4) help, through tutoring and supervision of studies suggested above, the development of the fledgling professional body. About ten fully qualified and experienced accountants would be needed for some five years. A suggested distribution would be:

Accountant General's Department	2
Magistrate of Accounts	2
Spread over public enterprises	4
Teaching and helping with public enterprises	2
TOTAL	10

This may be regarded as too big a group of foreigners, but the job to be done is also considerable and needs to be tackled in this manner if financial management is to show marked improvement in the next few years. All things considered, bilateral aid may be the best source for this type of personnel, although other international assistance avenues are to be explored.

6. Conclusion

Much discussion of the subject of improving accounting in all its aspects in Somalia has occurred. Some constructive action has resulted, for example, the two-year course at SIDAM and the program of four-month courses at the Central Bank's training institute. The Central Bank and the Commercial Bank have been helping to improve accounting in the public enterprises by sending members of their staff to the enterprises. But these are inadequate. It may well be warranted to appoint a Working Party to:

(1) examine all the proposals that have been presented formally and informally;
(2) recommend a detailed blueprint for establishing and developing the profession at all levels; and
(3) report no later than four months after appointment.

Assuming that the report is generally acceptable, the Working Party may then be asked to prepare within three to four months a detailed accounting plan including phasing, requirements of manpower and materials, costs, etc., to implement the blueprint. Thereafter, a mechanism as far as practicable using existing institutions and their personnel, could be put into operation under the joint supervision of the Ministries of Education, Finance and Labour and the Central Bank.

NOTE: Implementing the Unified Accounting System (UAS)

Somalia has prepared a Unified Accounting System in response to the need for improved accounting and auditing as aids to enhance the efficiency of the public enterprises. This model is still being explored; it is to be tested and given legal status before it is put in effect. Financial circles have urged early implementation.

Actual effective implementation requires some technical assistance by way of a cadre of accountants, financial managers, training and other facilities for teaching. These aspects were touched upon in the main body of this outline.

F 5616.5

some

CHAPTER XXX

ACCOUNTING EDUCATION IN TANZANIA

by
Robert Dinman*

1. The Setting

Tanzania is a seriously dedicated socialist nation, a circumstance profoundly affecting its institutions, programs, and their implementation. Tanzania is overwhelmingly an agricultural nation producing mainly coffee, tea, cotton, sisal, and cashew nuts from which its foreign exchange is derived. Gemstones and tourism play some part. Food crops, livestock, and limited fishing provide for basic sustenance of the population.

Productive efforts in Tanzania of an industrial, trading, and commercial nature and for infrastructure are carried out largely by parastatal corporations, though smaller businesses, in the retail trade particularly, are privately owned.

President Julius Nyerere, in his Arusha Declaration of February 5, 1967, committed the nation to a socialist revolution and a new order of social and economic justice, and set forth a blueprint for self-reliance, emphasizing the development of agriculture and the social services, the concentration of the nation's 16 million people mainly in cooperative villages, the construction of schools and clinics, and a reduction in the income gap between rich and poor.

Much of this program has been set in motion. Tanzania has been hard-hit meanwhile, and particularly in recent years, by drought and difficult world economic conditions, which have seriously and adversely affected its world trade (export-import) position. Also, Tanzania has been implementing a long-standing decision to relocate the national capital from Dar es Salaam to Dodoma, at a time when resources are particularly hard to come by.

Tanzania is one of the poor countries of Africa. It was the poorest and least-developed economically of the three East African Community member countries. Uganda has since, however, under the Amin regime, fallen into a condition of almost total economic chaos.

Tanzania, Kenya, and Uganda were members of the East African Community. This community, which disintegrated during 1976 and the several years after, had operated jointly: 1) a cooperating and complementary-intended free trade area; 2) a common monetary system; 3) a common income tax system; 4) posts, telephone, and telegraph, and 5) harbors, railroads and airlines.

The crumbling of the East African Community resulted largely from differences in the political philosophies of the three nations, though substantial economic disparities existed in the economic development of the countries and con-

*Professor Dinman was most recently associated with the University of Dar es Salaam. Previously he was Professor of Accounting in Kenya, Indonesia and University of California, Berkeley.

353

tributed to the problem. In any event, published reports and comments consistently reflected, with respect to the community corporations responsible for the above activities, a sorry state of mismanagement, lack of controls and accountability, operating losses, and a failure of the individual member states to honor obligations to the community corporations. As added responsibilities have devolved upon the individual states, Tanzania faces an urgent need to function more efficiently.

The commercial and industrial parastatal corporations of Tanzania and the fiscal affairs of the Tanzanian government also have been characterized too often by mismanagement, lack of controls and accountability, operating losses, and irresponsibility. Some of the more prevalent problems have been insufficiently trained and unsophisticated management, lack of adequate accounting and statistical data upon which to base decisions or achieve necessary controls, serious failures to make use of the productive capacity of enterprises due to such shortages as spare parts, raw materials, electricity or water services, and the trucks needed for transportation of raw materials and finished goods, lack of controls over property and costs, and excessive numbers of employees. The Tanzanian government has been plagued by exceedingly heavy overruns (by ministries) of expenditures against budget-allocated funds, and by enormous amounts of expenditures for which supporting vouchers are simply not available.

A noteworthy aspect of the accounting scene in Tanzania relates to the external auditing function. Tanzania Audit Corporation is a government parastatal corporation whose function is the audit of all other governmental parastatal corporations. Thus, audit review is being made of accounting activities and results of the major industrial, commercial, and institutional enterprises in Tanzania. Tanzania Audit Corporation is still in the building stage of its development, and is not yet staffed to sufficient levels either qualitatively or quantitatively. The only significant professional accounting firm operating in Tanzania is the international firm of Coopers and Lybrand, which handles auditing and related functions for the private enterprises that are still functioning in Tanzania, and such overflow audit of parastatal corporations as Tanzania Audit Corporation is insufficiently staffed to handle. Coopers and Lybrand has begun to organize and offer management consulting services on a substantial scale, a much needed service in Tanzania.

A development that should be discussed in any evaluation of Tanzania and its accounting needs is the settlement of the people on the land into cooperative villages—the so-called Ujaama Villages. The Ujaama Villages are intended to enhance productivity and to bring social services to the people, including water, electricity, schools, hospitals and clinics, recreational facilities, and the like. It is claimed that more than half of the population of Tanzania is already established in Ujaama Villages, and the government continues to press for completion of this process.

We are discussing something on the order of 15,000 to 20,000 Ujaama Villages. Each is to be a socialized productive economic unit. Their success will depend upon competent managers, treasurers, accountants and auditors, storekeepers, and shopkeepers. Many cooperatives and Ujaama Villages have already experienced serious trouble because of fraud and management failures.

We are discussing something on the order of 15,000 to 20,000 Ujaama Villages. Each is to be a socialized productive economic unit. Their success will depend upon competent managers, treasurers, accountants and auditors, storekeepers, and shopkeepers. Many cooperative and Ujaama Villages have already experienced serious trouble because of fraud and management failures.

None of the above is intended to convey the impression that respectable accounting cannot be found in Tanzania. Sound basic accounting practices may be found, for example, in some of the corporations under control of the National Development Corporation; in General Tyre Corporation, which is a joint venture of the American corporation and the Tanzanian government; and in Tanesco, the national electricity corporation, which is successfully utilizing computers.

It becomes clear, however that the top priority accounting need of Tanzania has to do with the soundness of fundamental accounting procedures, practices, and theory. This has not yet been achieved, and Tanzania has been floundering because of it.

2. The Accounting Institutional Environment

2.1 Identification of Local Institutions Carrying Out Accounting Education

Tanzania has been under no illusions as to the need for trained managers and accountants if the nation is, in any acceptable fashion, to solve its development problems. Consequently, Tanzania, with a good deal of assistance from world organizations, governments, and foundations, began some ten years ago putting together the training institutions needed to produce these trained people.

At present, the various management/accountancy training institutions in operation and the accountancy levels to which they are training (located in Dar es Salaam unless otherwise indicated) are as follows:

(1) The professional and semiprofessional levels:
 University of Dar es Salaam
 Institute of Development Management (located at Morogoro)
 Institute of Finance Management
(2) The semiprofessional and technicians levels:
 College of Business Education
 Nyegezi Social Training Center (located at Mwanza)
 Cooperative College (located at Moshi)
 (Cooperative sector only, including Ujaama Villages)
 Dar es Salaam School of Accountancy (government sector only; small
  branches have been established at other locations in Tanzania)
(3) Institutions operating part-time programs at the technicians and semi-
  professional levels:
 College of Business Education
 Institute of Adult Education (Small branches have been established at
  other locations in Tanzania)
 St. Joseph's College (located at Tanga)

The largest of these operations is that of the Institute of Development Management at Morogoro, some 125 miles west of Dar es Salaam. All others are of what might be considered medium size. More recently, it became apparent that the above institutions are not producing enough trained people at the lower technician and semiprofessional levels. In consequence, institutes of accountancy have been planned and are being funded currently to train significant numbers of people at the lower levels thus providing a suitable pyramid base quantitatively for the accounting needs of the nation. The two new institutes of accountancy are to be located at major population and productive centers of the country—Arusha and Mbeya (in the southern highlands).

2.2   The Government Involvement in Education

The government of Tanzania (with minor exceptions such as the Nyegezi Social Training Center at Mwanza, operated by a Catholic mission; St. Joseph's College at Tanga, and some small private business schools), with foreign assistance has created and is operating the management/accountancy training institutions in Tanzania. The University of Dar es Salaam and one other institution are under the jurisdiction of the Ministry of Education. Each of the other management/accountancy training institutions is under the jurisdiction of the separate government ministries which created them as each saw the need relative to its own functions. Unfortunately, these ministries generally know little about education and educational standards, and some appear to have done relatively little to enforce acceptable standards of performance at their own controlled institutions. It is somewhat difficult, under the circumstances to bring the deficient operation at the institutions to light.

2.3   The East African Community's Education Efforts

The East African community was heavily involved in administrative matters and in the operation of the community parastatal corporations. Community headquarters were located at Arusha in Tanzania and about five years ago the large East African Community Management Training Center was set into operation in Arusha as well. This management training center is now the only significant remaining vestige of the former East African Community, and still serves training needs of these three East African nations. The community had long been involved in educational progress—short courses, seminars, conferences and workshops—for its own administrative and parastatal personnel and for those similarly employed by the individual member states. Some of their programs had been done with highly qualified poeple in sophisticated areas, such as performance budgeting. They seem however not to have succeeded noticeably in the past in improving standards of performance within the community or its member states as a whole.

3.   Educational Inventory

3.1   Qualifications of Accounting Instructors

Accounting instructors at the accountancy training institutions have come from three main sources:

(1) Senior expatriate staff—usually American, Canadian, or European—supplied generally through the aid programs of the UN, national governments, and foundations. Most such personnel have significant academic and/or professional qualifications, and have performed well, particularly the Americans, Canadians, and Germans. In some instances, selection has been poor and contributions have been minimal. Two problems have occurred. Firstly, there have been far too few high-powered personnel available to meet the needs of the training institutions for sophisticated teaching adapted to the environment, for building needed programs, and for the guidance and development of lower level teaching staff. Secondly, such personnel normally have not remained long on the scene. A farily large staff this year may be mostly gone next year and vice-versa.

(2) Other senior and intermediate teaching staffs have come from such countries as India and Pakistan predominantly, and some from Sri Lanka and the Philippines where salary levels are relatively low but where there are large numbers of trained people available. Almost all such personnel are hired on Tanzanian contracts, though a few have been supplied through the aid programs of the UN and various governments. Expatriates hired for the accounting and related activities of the Tanzanian government and the corporate parastatals, too, have come largely from this same source. Many, though not all, of these people have professional qualifications obtained in their own countries and accounting experience. They sometimes have MBA degrees obtained at home universities or occasionally in the USA. Experience at the various institutions in Tanzania indicates that these staff members have been a mixed bag—some have been good, some mediocre, while too many have been incompetent. Generally, their approach has tended to be stereotyped and mechanical and lacking in the depth and perspective necessary for a sound professional approach. Many of the best of them have not remained in Tanzania teaching for very long, mainly for lack of financial inducements.

(3) Junior (and more and more, intermediate and senior) staff is Tanzanian. They must eventually take over as expatriate staff phase out of the process. Unfortunately, there were very few Tanzanians available with the training and experience suitable for such teaching appointments. This is understandable since there was neither the tradition nor encouragement for participation by Africans until some while after independence. Asians filled the jobs in business for which Africans might have been trained.

Consequently, Tanzanian staff has had to be brought up and trained from scratch to provide for the teaching needs of the accountancy training institutions of Tanzania. A very substantial proportion (more than half) of present staffs consist of such young Tanzanians. They have been graduates of the University of Dar es Salaam and to some extent now, of some other of the institutions in Tanzania.

A word is in order as to how graduates of the university and diplomats of the management/accountancy training institutions are assigned to work opportunities in Tanzania. Many of them have been sponsored for this higher-level education by their employing parastatal corporations or government ministries, and

357

they often return after training for continued employment with their sponsors. Other graduates and diplomats, and sometimes some of the former, normally are requested by the Government Manpower Allocation Board to make indication of three work choices either with parastatal corporations, government ministries, or possibly, for example, teaching or in other institutions. The Manpower Board finalizes employment assignments based upon the needs to be filled, after giving consideration to the training and the expressed preferences of the candidates for employment. Unfortunately, teaching appointments were made largely by the Government Manpower Allocation Board without much reference to competency. Unqualified people were sometimes thus appointed; a situation which has now somewhat improved. The University of Dar es Salaam has been graduating only about twenty to twenty-five accounting option students per year. This does not leave a very large pool of acceptable university accountancy graduates upon which to draw for teaching purposes of the management/accountancy training institutions.

Accounting graduates of the University of Dar es Salaam were minimally and badly trained until significantly improved staff was acquired some five years ago. This improved staff has largely disintegrated, however. Some of the other institutions have done a most inept job of accountancy training. The educational system from top to bottom is not as strong as that in the USA, and there has been a heavy reliance upon rote learning. The bachelor's degree at East African universities is based upon a three-year program. Vacation periods are usually somewhat longer than those at American universities. Altogether, the accounting graduate at East African universities spends about 60 percent of the classroom time as spent by his counterpart in the USA.

Keeping in mind the weaknesses in fundamental training of the young teaching Tanzanians, it is obvious that the need for further training and development is particularly great. A goodly amount of such training is taking place, and in the following forms:

(1) Graduate study, normally for the MBA degree and more latterly for the Ph.D. degree as well, at an American or British university.

(2) When possible, some professional experience; Coopers and Lybrand and the Tanzania Audit Corporation have provided temporary employment during vacation or even longer periods. Some graduates may already have had parastatal or government working experience.

(3) Preparation for and taking of the CPA examiantions of the National Board of Accountants and Auditors (NBAA) of Tanzania for the professional accountancy qualification of that country.

(4) ACCA study in Great Britain, usually taking several years. Since this has involved little more than the coverage of accounting undertaken for the university BA or B.Com. degrees, its value may be questionable as a substitute for university graduate study.

(5) Inter-institutional meetings of business teaching staffs, which seem now to have fallen by the wayside. A single past workshop for younger staff mounted under these auspices seems to have been useful. Other formalized programs do not exist.

3.2 Instruction Techniques Utilized in Accounting Programs and Courses

Accounting and management instruction in Tanzania has been, with minor exceptions, based upon American or British text materials (occasionally a mixture of the two) and use of the lecture method. Some institutions make some use of laboratory or seminar meetings of smaller groups, enabling expanded discussion and greater coverage of problem materials. Some use has been made of visual aids by at least one of the institutions.

3.3 Structure of Accounting Programs and Curricula

Accounting programs and curricula have of course depended basically upon the nature of the particular institutions, the levels of accounting to which they train, and the sectors of the society they were intended to service.

In October 1973, the National Board of Accountants and Auditors (Tanzania), created by an act of parliament in November, 1972, became fully operational, and in May 1975, it gave the first of its semiannual professional examinations. These examinations are governed by a syllabus prepared by the NBAA with assistance from the accountancy training institutions and professional accountants in Tanzania.

The syllabus spelled out subjects and content to be covered in the three-hour subject papers of each of the examinations, which are described briefly as follows:

- The National Bookkeeping Certificate Examination (NABPCE) consisting of five subjects calculated to provide the foundation necessary for professional training at the technicians' level.
- The National Accountancy Diploma (NAD) examination consisting of Part I with five core accounting subjects and Part II with four supporting subjects at the semiprofessional level.
- The Certified Public Accountant (CPA) examination consisting of Part I and Part II with four subjects in each, calculated to ensure that the output is comparable in knowledge and stature with professional output elsewhere at the professional level.

The subjects covered by the NBAA accounting examination papers and syllabus are as follows:

- The National Bookkeeping Certificate Examination (NABPCE)
  - 01 Bookkeeping, including Elements of Auditing
  - 02 Commercial Arithmetic
  - 03 Commercial Knowledge and Office Management
  - 04 Materials Management
  - 05 Co-operative Principles and Accounting
  - 06 Government Accounting and Financial Procedures
- The National Accountancy Diploma (NAD) examination
  - (Part I)
  - 01 Accountancy
  - 02 Auditing
  - 03 Taxation

    04 Costing and Management Accountancy
    05 Business Administration
    06 Cooperative Principles and Accountancy
    07 Government Accounting and Financial Procedures
    (Part II)
    08 Law (Mercantile and Company)
    09 Economics
    10 Political Education
    11 Business Mathematics and Statistics
- The Certified Public Accountant (CPA) examination
    (Part I)
    01 Advanced Accountancy
    02 Costing and Management Accountancy
    03 Auditing
    04 Systems and Data Processing
    (Part II)
    05 Advanced Accountancy with Executorship and Bankruptcy
    06 Taxation and Social Accounting
    07 Financial Management with Project Appraisal
    08 Management Principles and Practice

The NBAA, for these examinations which it sets and grades through its secretariat, makes analysis of examination results by individual accountancy training institutions, and is thus able to provide an evaluation of the achievement of each of the training institutions in terms of the performance of their students in these national professional examinations. Based upon the results of these examinations, the NBAA awards successful candidates with the NABPCE Certificate, the NAD Diploma, or the CPA Qualification, and serves as national registrar thereof.

Since the students/graduates of all accountancy training institutions take these accounting examinations, and the institutions are judged by the results, all such institutions have conformed their curricula to the Examinations Syllabus of the NBAA. The NBAA thus exerts a strong strategic and guiding influence over all accountancy training institutions in Tanzania.

The NBAA also offers part-time review courses before each of its examinations to assist candidates with their preparation. These review courses are conducted in Dar es Salaam and other regional centers, and they registered an attendance of some 500 candidates by the time of the examinations of November, 1976.

A review of the curriculum provides the following analysis of topical coverage:

Financial Accounting and Auditing. Some aspects of each of these subjects appear at all three levels of the NBAA examinations. Consequently, they are basic and continuing subjects at all of the training institutions. The main problem in these respects is the quality of the teaching and the study materials utilized. Auditing tends to be weakly handled and internal auditing is relatively neglected from the standpoint of national needs.

Management/Cost Accounting. Direct basic content and problems in the management/cost accounting area are normally covered and at reasonable length. The more sophisticated and analytic areas, including cost-benefit analysis and project appraisal, are too often omitted, inadequately covered, or incompetently handled in view of Tanzania's needs. Candidates' papers in the NBAA examinations commonly reflect extensive weakness in the areas of analysis, practical application to new situations, judgment, and decision-making.

National or Economic Accounting and Social Accounting. These areas, too, are generally inadequately or incompetently handled. This tends to be the case as well as with respect to their coverage in the NBAA examinations.

Business Administration. Courses in business administration provide a substantial coverage of American textbooks. Too often however they consist of broad and ephemeral generalization and far too little meaningful content related to local problems and needs.

Public Sector. In terms of accounting, controls, and planning at anything like sophisticated levels, the public sector is virtually completely ignored in Tanzanian curricula and classrooms and in the NBAA examinations. The needs of Tanzania in these respects are urgent.

Other Accounting Related Topics. It has been noted already that the NBAA examinations contain coverage of computers and systems analysis and social accounting and taxation, and that these subject areas are included in the curricula of the accountancy training institutions operating to the CPA (final professional) level. Classroom coverage in general, however, has not been sufficiently sophisticated. Supporting subjects such as economics, statistics, and commercial law (including corporation law) are receiving routine treatment at the institutions. Except, perhaps, for the University of Dar es Salaam, commercial law, including corporation law, appears to have been taught inadequately, considering the showing of candidates in this area in the NBAA examinations.

Extent of Coverage of Accounting Subjects in Business Administration Programs. All of the institutions provide a first year course in accounting fundamentals to their business administration students. Some provide, additionally, a course in management accounting.

3.4 Textbooks and Case Study Materials

Locally authored accounting textbooks are virtually non-existent. The Cooperative College (at Moshi) has produced some mimeographed materials for local use on cooperative law and practices.

Income tax courses are, of course, based upon the Tanzanian Income Tax Act, and some text writing has been done in this field. Some classroom reference is made to other local laws, such as that of corporations.

British and American textbooks are basically relied upon. Any adaptation of their content has depended upon the knowledge and ability of individual instructors to bring the local scene and local problems to bear in the course of their lectures and assignments.

No significant attack has yet been made in the matter of the preparation of case study materials. Some few have been prepared at several of the institutions and as problems for the NBAA examinations. These, however, have not been brought into significant usage.

Time has been a significant factor in classrooms in the attempt to cover the reading, questions and problems in textbooks. Students are thus hard-put to cope additionally with case studies. Instructors might be reluctant to attempt to fit them in as a consequence.

Undoubtedly, wider usage of case studies would help ameliorate various deficiencies occurring in accounting classrooms at the training institutions.

3.5 Accounting Research and Developments

Accounting research has not seriously begun in Tanzania. It is, however, one of the future objectives of the NBAA and its Secretariat. Professional accountants have been too busy to get involved. The drive upon the nation's accounting needs through the creation of training institutions in Tanzania is only about four or five years old. Senior teaching personnel at the institutions tend to be extremely busy. Younger personnel are getting organized and trained.

4. An Evaluation of Education Inventory

Any evaluation of the inventory of accounting education must come to grips with the fact that, as previously stated, the great accounting need of Tanzania has to do with the soundness of fundamental accounting procedures, practices, and theory. This has not yet been achieved.

Enormous resources have been poured into management/accountancy education in Tanzania. There is no shortage of training institutions already operating, being expanded, or on the way. Will these produce the managers and accountants in the quantities and in the quality necessary for successful development of the economy of Tanzania? *Quantities:* yes, given time enough; *quality:* probably not. And why not? Because, despite the very substantial resources being expended, that extra portion of inspiration, knowledge, effort, and money necessary to do the job right has usually not been forthcoming. This brings up the question, then: In what significant ways does the present effort fall short?

4.1 The Basic Problem

The attempt to create trained managers and accountants in necessary numbers for developing countries amounts to an exceedingly complex and critical problem whose solution, obviously, needs the best of sustained thinking and planning, not of amateurs but of experts.

Instead, this problem generally has been dealt with on an opportunistic, catch-as-catch-can, and chaotic basis. This has been pretty much true in Tanzania. The government, through its various ministries, obtained whatever assistance it could get whenever and wherever it could get it. Too often the people concerned at both ends of the problem lacked the knowledge, understanding, and expertise necessary to create sound, viable, and coordinated training institutions.

Furthermore, virtually no serious thought or even consideration has been given—in view of the problems of the total local environment and the modern world—to the matter of what curriculum content is necessary to produce the managers and accountants competent to cope with the needs and problems of a developing country.

4.2 The Curriculum Content

Certainly, the economy of Tanzania with its socialist structure is different from those of other parts of the world—those parts from which the traditional accounting text materials, training patterns, and professsional examinations have tended to come in particular, American, Great Britain and other Western nations.

Undoubtedly, *the real needs of accountancy training in Tanzania differ is some important ways from the traditional accounting content with which teaching staffs have rushed into accounting classrooms* and built the syllabus for the NBAA examinations. This traditional content was what was best known and was the easiest to cope with in the teaching processes. The relevance of this traditional accounting to the real needs of Tanzania's economic development (or that of any developing nation) has not been explored.

It is obvious that some of the accounting areas covered extensively in class-rooms and professional examinations, for example, partnerships, executorship, estate and trust accounts, have far less relevance to the Tanzanian environment than they have to that of Great Britain. It is likewise clear that "internal" audit-ing is at least as important as, and perhaps more important than, "external" auditing in the Tanzanian environment. Yet virtually all teaching efforts are concentrated on "external" auditing. It is quite probably true that proportion-ately more time is spent on financial accounting than on cost/management ac-counting. The success or failure of Tanzania's economy will depend upon the ef-fectiveness of management and the decision-making processes which depend so heavily on the cost/management techniques and ideas; for example, the budget-ing processes (including performance budgeting for government), the setting of sound standards of performance and the related evaluation of performance, cost-benefit analysis, and sound project appraisal. Further, considering the importance of cooperatives and the Ujaama Villages in the Tanzanian setting (except at the Cooperative College at Moshi), little if anything has been done to bring their technical and legal aspects to bear in management and accounting classrooms.

Little of consequence has been done in such somewhat sophisticated areas, for example, as those indicated by Professor Adolf J. H. Enthoven in Volume 1 of his 1976 Ford Foundation Study "Accountancy Systems, Developments and Re-quirements in Third World Countries." These include:

Accounting systems and systems analysis.
Capital budgeting and parastatal financial management.
Government accounting and performance budgeting.
Social and national income accounting.

Certainly, the viability of the attempt to produce the managers and accoun-tants needed by Tanzania must depend to some significant degree upon the con-tent and relevance of the study and training programs utilized.

4.3   Students and Standards

The Tanzanian student of accountancy often comes from a village environment, with an education characterized more by rote learning than by thinking processes, and without a background or tradition of business. Too, his basic language is usually tribal and/or a new national language, rather than English. Educational standards are not high, comparatively speaking, even at the university level. Nevertheless, it is probably true that this student should be taught what is right and practical rather than what is irrelevant to his society. It must be remembered, too, that this student must get thorough training from his classroom experiences, since his subsequent working world will not be as ready or capable of completing his professional education as is the case with an accounting graduate in countries of the developed world.

Forty percent constitutes the pass mark at the University of Dar es Salaam and at the management/accountancy training institutions. It is also the pass mark level adopted by the NBAA for its national professional accounting examinations. This 40 percent pass mark is derived basically from the British university pattern, where it is an arbitrary and symbolic value assigned to an acceptable passing level effort. First-class honors achievement is normally graded at the 70 percent level, and this mark is pretty much considered the top. This system has worked quite satisfactorily at British universities as a qualitative measure for such subjects, for example, as economics and political science.

Unfortunately, that 40 percent has become the accepted pass level at the Tanzanian institutions, though total marks are, in reality as in America, based upon a scale of 100 (rather than British *de facto* 70). Interestingly, utilizing this 40 percent pass mark and grading on the same basis as in American university classes produces what is considered to be an acceptable proportion of passing and failing students at these institutions. Based on American standards, however, only some 5 percent to 10 percent of these Tanzanian students would be considered to be performing at minimum passing levels.

In the NBAA professional accountancy examinations, too, passing papers at the 40 percent or even 50 percent level are simply not, in general, of acceptable professional quality by world standards. The extreme failure rate experienced in these examinations is being ameliorated somewhat through bending of examination content and leniency in grading in professional examinations already less modern and simpler than those of the western world.

Obviously, accounting standards in Tanzania are too low—in the classroom, in the professional accounting examinations, and in real-life performance. Unless standards are improved, the nation is not likely to solve its management/accountancy problem to an acceptable degree. Any hope for such improvement must rest upon a significantly higher caliber effort than now exists.

4.4   The Teaching Staff

Sound teaching performance in accountancy normally requires the theoretical depth and perspective that comes from significant graduate study, a practical understanding of the accounting process that comes from professional working experience, and some teaching ability and experience. In developing countries it requires also understanding, sympathy, and flexibility. There must be an understanding of the student, his background, how his mind works, and his aspirations and an understanding of the society, its motivations, social and economic organization, and its handling of the accounting process. Also there must be flexibility to reshape teaching approaches to the needs and realities of the environment, and to assist in the process of building an indigenous accounting profession.

The kind of teaching and participation capable of producing the accountants and managers needed in the Tanzanian environment simply has not been forthcoming to a significant degree. The accounting diplomats and graduates of the Tanzanan accountancy training institutions are not being trained to a level sufficient to cope either with the needs of the Tanzanian economy or the professional examinations of the NBAA, where failure rates have been horrendous.

Quotation is made from the report dated December 1974 of the Task Force of the National Board of Accountants and Auditors of Tanzania (page 4) as follows:

> Probably the most difficult single problem faced by the training institutions is that of building teaching staffs with a sufficient number of senior people, who have requisite teaching expertise, significant practical accountancy experience, and who possess a professional accountancy qualification. Too much of the current teaching in the institutions is being done by recent university graduates who simply do not have enough knowledge academically, and have had little or no professional experience. This has resulted somewhat in a situation of the blind leading the blind. The substantial investment of the nation in the accountancy training institutions is being somewhat wasted under the circumstances; since the objective is to produce people capable of coping with the nation's problems at the various technicians and professional accountancy levels. What appears necessary is a significant injection of senior staff to be spread amongst the training institutions wherever most needed, if teaching staffs are to provide accountancy training of sufficient quality and quantity. This will take money, but it is a manageable problem. Unless something is done about improvement of teaching staffs at the accountancy training institutions, expansion of the present training institutions or the creation of new ones will serve only to dilute the quality of present inadequate training now going on at the existing institutions.

Larger numbers of knowledgeable and sophisticated accounting academicians must be brought to bear then if there is to be improvement in the Tanzanian situation.

4.5 Summation

The shortcomings suggested have to be related to events of the past. For some decades, donors of many sorts—world organizations, individual governments, and private foundations—have poured enormous resources sporadically into solving the problem of creating the trained managers and accountants urgently required by the developing countries. The available resources have been varied in nature, including sometimes the help of an isolated individual or two, sometimes that of an entire project team and/or the funds for the acquisition of library materials and of equipment and for the training of indigenous teaching staff.

More often than not, these assistance programs have accomplished relatively little. They have often lacked carefully selected leadership and/or project team personnel. They have involved too often people who have not been competent, or have not cared enough to do what needs to be done. Too often, too, this characterization applies to other expatriates who hold direct hire contracts with the institutions. Upon occasion at the host institution, indigenous department heads or staff members have not been concerned by the attempt to do the job effectively or to improve standards. In such cases, it might well have been better to withdraw (or consider withdrawal of) assistance to the particular institution. In such cases too, the conclusion of an assistance program has sometimes been welcomed, with hardly a ripple left behind.

4.6 Conclusion

It has already been suggested that the larger and most basic part of the Tanzanian problem of training accountants would most likely be solved if the teaching at the management/accountancy training institutions were carried out soundly at even the present level of accounting procedures, practices and theory—and with the text materials currently being used. This implies however, a significantly higher quality level of teaching input than that which exists and also the raising of students' performance standards to acceptable levels. If this much were accomplished, some of the rest reasonably could be expected to follow as well, including the reshaping and development of curriculum content, the preparation of case studies and suitable text materials, and appropriate research. If, however, the whole accountancy training problem of Tanzania is looked at, the main elements involved and requiring attention would appear to be the following:

(1) Knowledgeable and coordinated planning of the total training structure.
(2) Better teaching (and improved teaching methods).
(3) Improved and more relevant subject content.
(4) Higher standards of student performance.
(5) Sounder training of counterpart Tanzanian accounting and management academicians.
(6) Creation of teaching materials and the development of research.
(7) Assistance in development of professional bodies.

LATIN AMERICA

CHAPTER XXXI

REGIONAL ASPECTS AND DEVELOPMENTS IN LATIN AMERICA

The accounting educational modules for the countries presented in this section (Brazil, Mexico and Venezuela) show considerable divergence. These three countries are to be considered part of the Franco-Spanish-Portuguese "zone of accounting influence" as referred to in Part Two. While each has had a somewhat different accounting development pattern, certain common patterns do exist.

In general, the status of accounting development in Latin America lags behind the Western nations. In several countries accounting is not recognized legally or publicly as a profession and discipline. In some cases, a body of accounting standards and concepts hardly exists, and bookkeeping rules still constitute the basic frame of reference. Heavy dependence on laws prevails. There is a lack of uniformity in the area of financial accounting; the accounting rules are essentially set by the governments, who often base them upon rather antiquated commerical or tax regulations. Education has been strong in philosophy, but deficient in pragmatic and applied sciences; this has had an impact on both accountng training and development.

Accounting courses are generally offered within the economics departments of universities and colleges and the accounting focus has a tendency to be deficient in preparation, case studies and relevant texts. As the teaching of accounting is not highly regarded, pay scales are relatively poor and few full-time professors exist. Accordingly, accounting development is seriously hampered. Professors have limited time to prepare textbooks and class materials, as they generally must pursue outside work to increase their incomes. Good textbooks in Spanish are scarce. In addition, specialization in such areas of accounting, as management and government accounting, and accounting systems is not encouraged. Possible fundamental solutions to these deficiencies would include more relevant education, training and research; and effective regional cooperation.

A regional body, the Inter-American Accounting Association (IAA) has been in existence for thirty years. (Until 1979 it was called the Inter-American Accounting Conference.) Little was accomplished beyond the scheduling of a series of conferences however, as the different educational and professional levels of the members made progress difficult. The objectives and activities were of limited scope. As set forth by the Inter-American Accounting Conference in 1951,[1] these goals were:

1. To encourage a mutual understanding of and a cooperative approach to common problems of the profession among the professional accountants of the two continents.

[1] Comision Organizadora de la II Conferencia Interamericana de Contabilidad, "Memoria de la Segunda Conferencia Interamericana de Contabilidad," Mexico 1951, pp. 225-227.

2. To encourage the study and discussion of these problems so that all American accountants might unify the principles, methods, and programs, and thus work toward a better coordination of all the diverse aspects of the profession.

3. To disseminate technical information and to foster the interchange of ideas concerning accounting principles and procedures in all their diverse applications.

4. To raise the standards and to maintain the dignity of the profession.

The Inter-American Accounting Association (IAA) is the official representative of the accounting profession in the Americas. The Executive Director is Mr. Jorge Barajas of Mexico and the membership is composed of the following countries and institutions:

Argentina: Federacion Argentina de Colegios de Graduados en Ciencias Economicas
Bolivia: Colegio de Contadores de Bolivia
Brasil: Instituto Dos Auditores Independentes Do Brasil
Canada: The Canadian Institute of Chartered Accountants
Chile: Colegio de Contadores
Colombia: Instituto Nacional de Contadores Publicos
Costa Rica: Colegio de Contadores Publicos de Costa Rica
Cuba in Exile: Asociacion de Contadores Publicos y Privados de Cuba en el Exilio
Ecuador: Federacion Nacional de Contadores de Ecuador
El Salvador: Corporacion de Contadores de El Salvador
          Asociacion de Contadores de El Salvador
United States: American Institute of Certified Public Accountants
Guatemala: Asociacion Nacional de Contadores
          Corporacion de Contadores de Guatemala
          Instituto Guatemalteco de Contadores Publicos Y Auditores
Honduras: Colegio de Peritos Mercantiles y Contadores Publicos
Mexico: Instituto Mexicano de Contadores Publicos
Nicaragua: Colegio de Contadores Publicos de Nicaragua
Panama: Asociacion de Contadores y Contadores Publicos Autoizados
       Asociacion de Mujeres Contadoras
       Colegio de Contadores Publicos Autoizados
Paraguay: Colegio de Contadores de Paraguay
Peru: Instituto de Contadores de Peru
Puerto Rico: Colegio de Contadores Publicos Autorizados de Puerto Rico
Republica Dominicana: Instituto de Contadores Publicos autorizados de la Republica Dominicana
Uruguay: Colegio de Doctores en Ciencias Economicas y Contadores del Uruguay
Venezuela: Asociacion de Contadores (CNTC)

The association intends to promote study, research and creativity in all aspects of accounting, as well as to encourage a broader diffusion, better knowledge and greater interchange of techniques. To aid in this goal, the association has a new official organ, the *Revista Interamericana de Contabilidad.*

The most recent Interamerican Accounting Conference (the thirteenth), held in Panama in September 1979, set up the activities and technical committees of the association and outlined a variety of objectives. These included educational objectives for the training of the public accountant and a definition of the content of the basic areas of study. The conference noted "a permanent concern in the accounting profession about the academic formation of the public accountant, in order to achieve the educational objectives arising from the exigencies of the society he serves." The conference then resolved:

a. That the Inter-American Accounting Association should officially communicate all universities having professional education programs for the public accountant in all the member countries of the Association, the requirements that the community presents the public accountant, as determined at the Inter-American Accounting Conferences.

b. That the Inter-American Accounting Association should take the necessary action in order to obtain compliance with the recommendation of the IX Inter-American Accounting Conference, held in Bogota, Colombia, in 1970, in the sense that the designation, *Contador Publico* should become the general distinctive name of the professional accountant.

c. That the basic areas of a university program for the formation of the public accountant be recognized by the institutions responsible for complying with such higher education programs, as follows: Accounting, Administration (Management), Finance, Auditing, Systems Analysis, Data Processing, Mathematics, Economics, Law, Taxation, and Humanities.

d. That the profile of the public accountant is: a professional with a basic formation in the above-mentioned areas, technically qualified, and with the aptitude for facing problems of management, and to assume responsibilities for adequate decision making in the areas of accounting, finance and other related fields of knowledge.

e. That the accounting profession, organized as national and international associations, must have an active participation in the processes of university formation of the public accountant, through permanent ties and communication with universities and institutes of higher education.

f. That as a minimum measure, to assure and evaluate the technical competence of the public accountant, the professional examination prior to granting the professional license to practice the accounting profession be maintained as a requisite, or be established in those countries where it does not exist as such.

g. That the Inter-American Committee on Education, established by the Inter-American Accounting Association, according to the guidelines of its new bylaws, should include, in its program of permanent activities, the definition of the content and scope of each one of the basic areas listed in this resolution."

In regard to continuing education, the following considerations were listed:

1. That it is generally recognized as a need that the public accountant should keep himself updated through programs of continuing education.

2. That it is advisable that such programs be developed with the collaboration of professional associations and centers of higher education.

3. That the programs of continuing education present particular situations in

each one of the member countries of the Inter-American Accounting Association.

It is interesting to note that IAA also attaches considerable importance to the "extended dimensions" of accounting. In regard to socioeconomic auditing it states (*Revista*, Vol. 1, 1980, p. 39):

Considering:
1. That this is the first time that this subject has been studied in depth at the Inter-American Accounting Conference;
2. That, due to its social projections, it should be the subject of greater study, investigation and disclosure;
3. That, within our epoch of technological and social advances, socioeconomic accounting and auditing should receive attention parellel to the financial aspects of the enterprises;
4. That the accountants in America should develop their capabilities in this new area of great importance for the future administration of public, private and mixed organizations, with the purpose of being in a position to advise the directors and managers of such organizations.

Resolves:
1. To request, from the Inter-American Accounting Association (IAA) authorities, that the study of this theme should be continued, making investigations in order to establish principles for "social auditing."

In regard to the need for better accounting methodology, it states (ibid p. 35):

Considering:
a. That the XI and XII Inter-American Accounting Conferences have recognized the need to revise the structure of the accounting theory and, consequently, the so-called "generally accepted accounting princples."
b. That there is an urgent need to improve the concepts and methods which for that purpose must follow the accounting profession, in order to overcome the deficiencies and confusions existing in the definitions of terms, because they weaken the fundamental processes of our reasonings."

Declares:
1. That a preliminary concept on accounting is that it deals with the measurement, communication, and interpretation of the effects of actions and events—susceptible to quantification and with economic repercussions—referring to the past, present and future of the entities in general, with the purpose of contributing to the control of their operations and adequate decision making. . . .

Six technical committees were set up within the IAA in 1979. These committees were Research, Education, Auditing Standards and Practices, Standards for Governmental Sector, Administration and Finance, and Professional Practice.

The tasks of the Education Committee, according to *Revista Interamericana de Contabilidad* #2, 1980 (p. 23), were as follows:

1. To carry out studies and investigations of all matters referred or related to the academic preparation of the public accountant, including education at the

university level, additional requirements for the admittance to the profession, continued education of the professionals of accountancy, etc., and to issue opinions, recommendations and reports of the IAA through its Executive Committee.

2. To raise the educational standards of the professional accountant by recommending the subjects to be included in the basic curriculum or in any other way related to the teaching of accounting.

3. To study the needs and characteristics of continued education for the professional accountant and to give an opinion on the formal programs at the postgrade level and of the requirements and implications of programs of this nature.

4. To promote continued contact among the universities and the professionals of each country member of the IAA, to assure the excellent cooperation and interrelation between both sectors in their respective objectives.

5. To promote relations among the Association and all the other entities that have established teaching centers for both professors and students of the Latin American area; to obtain coordination of efforts in the organization of courses and seminars, the preparation of the textbooks in Spanish, the assignment of scholarships, the interchange programs of professors; and to coordinate all other activities that comply with the objectives of the Association.

6. To revise and comment upon the pronouncements of the Educational Committee of IFAC and to participate in their working programs.

7. To make recommendations to the Organizing Committee for the contents of the program of each Inter-American Conference of Accountancy.

The President of the Education Committee is C. P. Antonio Castilla P. of Chile. Members are Canada, Chile, Cuba in Exile, Panama and Puerto Rico.

In the educational area, it may be expected that closer educational and research pursuits will be carried out. The development of a more uniform educational system in Latin America is of high priority; external assistance will be required. Regional training centers, in our opinion, would be most effective, and reciprocity of degrees and professional certificates should be a goal.

The Inter-American Accounting Association may be the group to link regional developments and education. However, this interaction of educational aspects could also be part of a separate regional-international accounting educational association as conveyed in our Chapter XII.

Another development of considerable public sector interest has been the coordination taking place in the Latin American Institute of Auditing Sciences (ILACIF). Its mission is the development and technical improvement of the Supreme Audit Institution of Latin American Countries. ILACIF regulations set out as its principal areas of activity: research and development, technical assistance survey, information and coordination, and *training and education*. As for training, ILACIF has offered approximately 35 training events with over 900 officials from Supreme Audit institutions. The courses offered dealt with government accounting and auditing, operational auditing, public works auditing, petroleum industry audits, and internal control evaluations. ILACIF has been working closely with the Inter-American Accounting Association. ILACIF intends to continue its close relationship with the accounting profession in Latin America. Its principal emphasis will be in the area of training in financial management, accounting and auditing. It is unfortunate that the international and regional development organizations, such as the UN, IADB, IMF and the World Bank, have not demonstrated a greater interest in the activities of ILACIF. As the past President of ILACIF, Dr. Luis Hidalgo, conveyed, "these institutions do not appear to understand the importance of the efforts made by ILACIF to professionalize and improve public sector financial management, accounting and auditing among Latin American countries."

The IAA's Governmental Sector Committee states as one of its objectives *(Revista* #2, p. 23), "To study the techniques and procedures applicable to the administration of the public sector and coordinate with official entities that are working in such specialties such as the Latino-american Institute of Fiscal Sciences (ILACIF), etc." Such coordination is very much needed.

The improvements in more effective accounting and auditing in Latin America could be spurred at the academic level; conditions may have to change and extensive outside assistance will be needed. Bilateral programs can be effective, but in our opinion, a more cohesive regional and international assistance program is required. Regional efforts in education may well be more effective than purely international.

In our opinion, IAA, with adequate external support, could become a very effective regional organization to pursue, *inter alia*, educational coordination and enhancement. Its educational committee, in expanded form, could constitute the regional vehicle for the International Association for Accounting Development; although this also could be done separately by the respective institutions of learning, as the IAA is essentially professional accounting and auditing practice oriented.

CHAPTER XXXII

ACCOUNTING EDUCATION IN BRAZIL

by
Sergio de Iudicibus*

1. Introduction

Brazil, occupying 8.5 million square kilometers (3.3 million square miles) in South America, is the largest of the Latin American countries in size, population, and total GNP.

Despite the well-known inequities in income distribution, the country already ranks among the first in per capita income in Latin America—about US $1,500— and is rapidly advancing toward a leadership position, provided certain growth rate progressions achieved during the last 15 years are maintained, in contrast with many Latin American countries.

Brazil has a clear tendency toward predominance of the private sector in the economy. However, as a result of its rapid growth in the last 20 years, and lack of private capital, the government has been compelled, sometimes against its own will, to engage in certain fields of economic activity which it would like to preserve for private enterprise (as for example, public utility companies are today almost entirely owned by the state).

Though in practice it is possible that such participation will continue to exist in variable degrees, it is mentioned that there is an enormous field for private investments, and that a great part of the people in the country is against the "Big Government."

This dynamic characteristic of the private sector and of the growth of the economy as a whole has created a very promising field for the development of accountancy both professionally and academically, although a lot more has to be undertaken in this area.

2. Broad Prospects for Accountancy in Brazil

In Brazil, the profession is divided into two categories: one comprises professionals with secondary school level diploma—the *accountancy technicians;* the other is made up of graduates from accountancy courses at university level and those who were equalized (they earned secondary school level diploma prior to 1946)—the *accountants*.

To have an idea of the dimension involved, the following figures provided by the Accountancy Regional Council of the State of Sao Paulo are given:

---

*Sergio de Iudicibus is Chairman of the Accounting Department, Faculdade De Economia E Administracao, Universidade De Sao Paulo (University of Sao Paulo), Brazil.

Number of Accountancy Professionals Registered in Brazil
(Up to December, 1978)

	Brazil		State of Sao Paulo Only	
				% of total
Accountants with university degrees or equalized	45,004	100%	17,529	39%
Accountancy technicians with secondary school diploma	194,891	100%	66,935	34%
Total of professionals	239,895	100%	84,464	35%

Although the two categories are not totally additive, the rather larger number of professionals in Brazil is worth noting.

One of the problems of the profession in Brazil is that, basically, both categories may perform the same functions in practice, except for auditing and review and legal examinations, which are of exclusive competence of accountants (those with a university degree).

An accountant may become an independent auditor after his registration for a period of three years at the Regional Council of his State. As a general rule, the Securities Committee requires at least five years of experience before an accountant is authorized to act as an auditor for an open capital company.

The main representative of the auditors' organization in the private sector is the Institute for Independent Auditors of Brazil (IIAB). In spite of recent attempts to improve the level and representativeness of its performance, the institute has been largely inactive in practice as well as the research of accounting principles and the "ethical" inspection of the profession. It has functioned in a relatively "political" fashion without much connection with the universities.

However, efforts have recently been made aiming at a greater participation of IIAB auditors in the formulation of accounting principles at a national level.

The recent business legislation for share companies (Law 6404 of 1976) prescribes, in general, norms which are rather consistent with practices of countries more advanced in accounting, as the United States. It emphasizes for the first time:

- Adoption of the equity method for the evaluation of partnership investments;
- Further improving the system of monetary correction as compared with previous legal regulations.

The legal basis on which the profession lies in its application to corporations and other types of businesses is rather strong and can be theoretically compared with the best American doctrine, with the advantage of a rather advanced monetary correction, at least in the form of Price Level. Such law, however, also allows evaluation at market values (replacement), regardless of the general monetary correction (indexation).

Summarizing this item, we reaffirm that the profession's legal basis is sufficiently wide, though it needs a more effective, long-lasting and efficient action by the Institute for Independent Auditors in the formulation and research of accounting and auditing principles and norms which are better suited to our reality.

As to remuneration conditions for accountants and accountancy technicians, we should say that situation of "good accountants" (due to educational and background problems they represent a minimum portion of the universe)compares favorably with the most valorized professions in the market such as that of the engineer and the physician.

However, the profession's image is still relatively dim due to a number of circumstances. Some of these are also present in more advanced countries, such as little emphasis applied to general culture and humanistic disciplines in the curricula and the fact that accountants usually come from middle class families of less privileged strata and of lower culture. There are other aspects which are irrelevant for discussion in this study.

3. Accountancy Education at University Level in Brazil - The Sao Paulo Example

As one could easily imagine, due to the large territorial extension of the country and the enormous differences among the more and less developed states, it is very difficult, if not impossible, to draw a detailed general profile of the magnitude, degree of excellence and implementation of university level accountancy education in Brazil.

In fact, the Federal Education Council requires a certain number of disciplines which are obligatory for all curricula. However, this does not mean that the quality of the programs of such disciplines, and of those who teach them, and other characteristics always meet the minimum performance requirements in every state.

This may be partially explained away by the regional developmental differences as already pointed out. Also, there are more than one hundred schools all over the country graduating an increasingly large number of university level accountants and this makes it difficult to exercise strict quality control. In addition, the deep-seated idea among Brazilians that schools of economy, accountancy, and administration are not sufficiently "noble" to deserve full-time involvement by professors and students makes it hard to maintain uniformity of professorial and student body excellence.

As to graduate (B.A. degree) and postgraduate programs conducted at the University of Sao Paulo (USP) and, with some variations, at the Fundacao Getulio Vargas (FGV) in Sao Paulo, are probably the most advanced models in Brazil. However, the FGV does not graduate "accountants," but "business administrators," both courses and professions being distinct from each other in Brazil. Yet, the quality of some credits in accountancy attained at the FGV Administration Course is equivalent to that of USP. In addition, the Instituto Superior de Estudos Contabeis (ISEC), an organization affiliated to the FGV in Rio de Janeiro, offers an intensive full-time accountancy course to graduates

375

from other areas, successfully reducing course duration to about one year, and adopts a very similar bibliography.

Thus, the example we will present for graduate (baccalaureate) and post-graduate levels (master and doctorate) based on the University of Sao Paulo experience, despite its deficiencies, shall not be taken as the Brazilian average; it is in fact well above that.

In order to give an idea of the lower levels in other regions, we could say that the South of the country reaches about 50 to 70 percent of the quality attained in Sao Paulo, while the remaining regions reach only about 40 to 50 percent. This generalization, however, may be spurious.

3.1 The Graduation (B.A.) Program in Accountancy

The program presented as follows, is taught as a standard series of 8 semesters with an average of four classes a week for each discipline, per semester:

1st Semester
  Complements of Mathematics I
  Introduction to Economy I
  Introduction to Accountancy I
  Introduction to Administration I
  Law Institutions
  Introduction to Computing for Human Sciences

2nd Semester
  Complements of Mathematics II
  Introduction to Economy II
  Introduction to Accountancy II
  Law Institutions
  Introduction to Administration II
  Sociology

Note: The first two semesters are equal for the courses of Accountancy, Business Administration, and Economy.

3rd Semester
  Cost Accounting I
  Introduction to Probability and Statistics I
  Administration, General and Applied to Psychology
  Data Processing
  Administrative Systems
  Economic Theory (Microeconomy)
  Balance Sheet Analysis

4th Semester
  Cost Accounting II
  Introduction to Probability & Statistics II (General Statistics II)
  Intermediate Accounting
  Social Legislation
  Financial Administration
  Commercial and Business Techniques Applied to Accounting

5th Semester
  Advanced Accounting
  Theory of Administration I (Administrative Processes)
  Financial Mathematics I
  Financial Administration II
  Tax Legislation
  Tax Accounting

6th Semester
  Budgetary and Financial Control (Public Sector)
  Managerial Accounting
  Financial Administration III
  Production Administration I
  Financial Mathematics II

7th Semester
  Business Policy I
  Auditing I
  Analysis of Accounting Systems I
  Structure and Technical Analysis of Capital Market
  Controllership
  Accounting and Auditing in the Public Sector
  Brazilian Issues I

8th Semester
  Business Policy II
  Auditing II
  Mechanisms of Financial Institutions I
  Project Formulation
  Mechanisms of Financial Institutions II
  Analysis of Accounting Systems II
  Brazilian Issues II
  Physical Education

It may be noted from the curriculum above that, according to American standards there is much technicalization, lack of depth in humanistic disciplines, and proliferation of subjects. When a discipline, for example, "Introduction to Accountancy I," is followed by "Introduction to Accountancy II," it will be understood as a sequence of the same subject in another semester.

The bibliography adopted may be compared to that employed in the United States at schools of average quality, with a time span of about three years. In fact, many disciplines employ American textbooks, some of them translated into Portuguese. Others have adopted Brazilian books, preferably by authors from the university itself. The latter are rather similar in quality to good American books but are more compact and with some chapters adjusted to Brazilian reality.

We shall say that one of the strengths of accountancy education in Brazil is evidenced by the efforts for publication of textbooks of reasonable quality in the last few years (since 1971), most of them by professors of the accountancy department of the University of Sao Paulo.

Other texts with quality matching that of American standards are rarely found in other states, and most of the material is poor. However, it may be mentioned that nationwide penetration of texts edited by the University of Sao Paulo is increasing.

3.2   Summary of the Master and Doctorate Courses

The University of Sao Paulo is the only institution in Brazil to offer master's and doctoral programs in accountancy. In these courses—which have a satisfactory level specially as to bibliography—works of many famous foreign and Brazilian authors, as well as recent articles of *Accounting Reveiw*, are well known and studied.

Although the course is not held on a full-time basis, the studies are sufficiently intensive. Every formal class hour given by a professor (about 450 class hours for the whole master's program and twice as many for the doctoral) corresponds to three additional hours by the student on average, for research, study, and homework.

Furthermore, the student has to undertake a general qualification examination comprising several disciplines already taken in the master's and in the doctoral programs. Besides, the student has to write a paper at the master's program in order to prove his ability for research (specially inductive research), and another at the doctoral program, demonstrating originality and greater depth.

This system has already awarded about ten master's degrees and is going to graduate the first seven doctors within one to three years. It should be emphasized that the program is new, and that a postgraduation system according to the Latin model has been adopted.

4.   The Most Common Problems

The most important problem lies in the failure to maintain an adequate number of full-time professors.

This is not due to low pay. Actually, the salaries at the University of Sao Paulo are similar to those of some American universities. The fact is that excellent accounting professionals are rare and opportunities offered by companies in Sao Paulo as well as in the rest of the country are many.

While a faculty member who has recently obtained a degree equivalent to a Ph.D. in the United States earns about US $23,000 a year, in the market place he may easily earn up to three times as much.

This is a widespread situation in Brazil, although some federal research centers are now undertaking efforts to hire some Ph.D. graduates in the United States in order to upgrade accounting research standards. These centers can afford to pay a better salary. The situation in private schools is dramatic in this respect, and practically there are no full-time professors in such schools.

5. Professors with Master's and Ph.D. (or Equivalent) Degrees in Brazil

As a result of the situation pointed out, there are few professors with academic degrees equivalent to those granted in the United States. Gross estimates indicate the existence of thirty masters and fifteen doctors.

Another serious problem in Brazil, even in Sao Paulo, is the almost total non-existence of empirical research in accountancy, in part due to the unavailability of full-time professors and in part for the lack of funds for research.

The link between companies and universities in Brazil is feeble and the few universities of higher standard depend almost entirely on public funds, which are always scarce for education in Brazil.

6. Conclusions and Prospects

In spite of the serious difficulties mentioned, the accounting profession is undergoing a clear boom in Brazil. There are no barriers which are so high that resources and assistance from more advanced centers cannot overcome.

Considering the essentially democratic and capitalistic vocation of our society, and yet admitting regional differences and traps we encounter along our path which pose serious restrictions, we shall be frankly optimistic at foreseeing the possible development of the accounting profession and education in Brazil.

It is indeed no overstatement to regard Brazil as a very good test field for the future evolution of accountancy in developing nations.

CHAPTER XXXIII

ACCOUNTING EDUCATION IN MEXICO

by
Ricardo M. Mora*

1. Introduction

Mexico is the most populated Spanish-speaking country in the world; its population has grown tenfold since its independence in 1810 to 60 million in 1976. The metropolitan area of Mexico City (encircling the capital or Federal District) is by far the most developed area and accounts for almost 20 percent of the total population.

Although Mexico came under European influence in 1540 (with the name of New Spain), it is actually a young nation as far as economic activity is concerned. It emerged in disarray from the 1910 civil war. People possessing education, influence, or in politics became the new businessmen. Self-made foreign immigrants, and some transnational corporations contributed to Mexico's economic development.

Most of the business activity was carried out empirically. The entrepreneur was not interested in ascertaining the truth of his financial affairs or in learning such truth from the accounting process. Bookkeepers were hired to comply with legal requirements, but no information of any significance was fed to them. Income tax returns were not always legitimate. There was no concept of unit "cost" or of cost relationships.

Although accounting was introduced to the Mexican college in the 1910's, the real development of accounting did not start until the 1940's, and gained momentum in the 1960's.

In 1938, after a bitter fight, Mexico expropriated the foreign-owned oil companies. This set the base for a government program to shift emphasis to manufacturing. World War II came at the right time for Mexico's exports of minerals and raw materials. Existing manufacturing facilities, such as textiles and cement, worked to capacity.

In 1959, a presidential decree admitted reports of independent public accountants as evidence of compliance by corporate taxpayers with their federal tax obligations. This put the profession in the spotlight. Many graduates of accounting became independent. Further, the decree prompted the Mexican Institute of CPA's to come out with more frequent pronouncements on auditing procedures and accounting principles.

As a result, financial accounting and auditing in Mexico are now generally

*Ricardo M. Mora is Senior Partner with Despacho Freyssinier Morin, Mexico, and Chairman of the 1982 World Congress of Accountants held in Mexico City.

adequate and excellent in the larger companies, the multi-nationals and some Mexican companies that have become sophisticated in their financial reporting.

Management accounting is well behind financial accounting. Probably because of the financial accounting background of their faculties, accounting schools were late in incorporating management accounting in their curricula. Even today, management accounting subjects that are being taught are not collected under such a designation.

2. Institutions in Charge of Accounting Education

In 1914, public accounting began as a college degree program in Mexico. Although the original "commercial accounting" program was a three-year program, its first graduates in 1917 were awarded university degrees. Since then, the program has become a full-fledged program, comparable to medicine, engineering, etc., and it has never ceased to enjoy university status.

By contrast, business management or business administration became a college degree program only in 1967; it is an eight- to ten-semester program leading to a BBA. Curiously, most business administration programs were born as alternate choices in the university departments of accounting.

Licenses to practice public accounting in Mexico are only granted to university graduates of a public accounting program. Thus, accounting is a university degree program by itself, and not a concentration of a business program.

The Mexican Institute of CPA's was founded in 1923, following its U.S. counterpart. It has functioned well, both during its early stages as a voluntary "club" that separated the university's public accountants from the bookkeepers, as well as after the presidential decree (audit reports as evidence of tax compliance) that spurred the formation of CPA state societies, of which about thirty now function under the wings of the institute, and are bound by its pronouncements on ethics, auditing standards and accounting principles.

Membership in the Mexican Instiute of CPA's was larger than 5,000 at the time (in 1976) that it was acknowledged by the Mexican government as the confederation representing the accounting profession nationally. State societies not affiliated to the national confederation have a combined membership of some 1,000 and another 4,000 to 6,000 CPA's are estimated not to belong to the professional association. Thus, the total number of CPA's in the country by the end of 1976 was estimated from 10,000 to 12,000.

Both the institute and its affiliated state societies sponsor jointly or separately many types of short professional development and updating courses in accounting, auditing, taxation, management services, and others. These are open to the membership, plus their staffs, and to students who can afford them.

Because of the proximity to the U.S., and because the middle-aged Mexican accountant is likely to want to participate in continuing education programs, the American Financial Executives Institute, the National Association of Accountants, and the Institute of Internal Auditors, all have local chapters in Mexico which are successful in their training and other programs, particularly the Financial Executives Institute. The American Management Association has a management training center in Mexico, and there some six to ten other profit-seeking training centers that conduct all kinds of one-week and longer management and accounting courses for a fee. At the graduate level, a higher management educational institution offers a master's degree in management and shorter courses to practicing managers and accountants with cases developed by Harvard University, and translated by a similar center in Barcelona, Spain or in its Mexican counterpart, Instituto Panamericano de Alta Direccion de Empresas.

The national organization of CPA's, two or three state societies, the Mexican chapter of the Financial Executives Institute, and the accounting departments of at least four or five leading universities publish monthly or quarterly technical magazines.

Mexico has no accountancy act as such. There is the Professional Act of 1947 which gives to the states the authority to issue licenses of practice to all types of professionals, as long as they hold a bachelor's degree. Because the educational requirements of almost all of the universities in the country are the same, or at least very similar in form, graduation at the university is conducive almost automatically to the granting of a license to practice.

In the case of the public accountants, having a license from the corresponding government agency is a prerequisite to being accepted for tax practice under the 1959 presidential decree. It is not necessary to hold a license, or a college degree, to hold government or private enterprise positions.

As an exception to the statement that development of the accounting profession usually requires strong government involvement, Mexico's accounting profession developed initially to fill a need in private industry; later, in 1959, it was called in to aid taxation authorities as described above, and only in the 1970's has it been engaged to perform annual independent audits of Mexico's some 800 parastatal enterprises.

Other than the report for tax purposes, which is filed voluntarily by the taxpayer, auditing is not compulsory in Mexico by prescription of a companies act. Corporation law is inspired in old Spanish legislation which, in turn, was patterned after the Napoleonic Code. The Mexican "comisario" (statutory examiner) is supposed to oversee all the acts of the board of directors and management; to scrutinize monthly financial statements, and to report at least once a year to the shareholders at their annual meeting. In practice, statutory examiners are either partners of the accounting firm that is appointed to perform the annual (voluntary) audit, or, in the closely-held company, a shareholder who knows nothing about accounting and perfunctorily signs an annual letter recommending that the financial statements be approved along with the actions of the board.

The Mexican stock exchange requires quarterly unaudited data, and annual audited statements, which are usually good informative documents for investors (as well as credit grantors). Unfortunately, there are only some 300 companies listed on the stock exchange, of which not more than 50 are actively traded.

Mexico has been one of the main supporters of the Interamerican Accounting Association (formerly Interamerican Accounting Conference). Although the Interamerican Association is older than 25 years, it has not made much progress, disparity in the professional levels of the member countries being one of the reasons. It is undergoing an "agonizing reappraisal," and is scheduled to enter into a new phase under the management of a full-time executive director residing in Mexico.

From their respective foundations, Mexico has been a member of the International Accounting Standards Committee, and the International Committee for the Accounting Profession, superseded in 1977 by the International Federation of Accountants.

3. Accounting Education in Mexico Today

The following four institutes had in 1976 a student population of 43 percent of the total number of accounting students in Mexico:

- Universidad Nacional Autonoma de Mexico, Mexico City, founded by the Spaniards, the oldest and largest educational institution in the country with a high degree of influence over many other schools, some of which adopt UNAM's programs and curricula.

- Instituto Politecnico Nacional, a federal government institution of technological and higher learning, located in Mexico City.

- Instituto Tecnologico y de Estudios Superiores de Monterrey, a private instituion patterned after the universities in the Southwest of the U.S., with more emphasis on quality and student performance than mere quantities, as UNAM and IPN are obligated to accept.

- Universidad Iberoamericana, a private university in Mexico City with low-key Catholic orientation.

The very old and famous Mexico's National Autonomous University, as its name implies, is autonomous in the sense that it is self-governed. Many other higher learning institutions in the various states follow the same pattern. All of them, however, depend on federal and/or state funds for financing.

In 1976, there were 36 government-financed schools with an enrollment of 42,000 students in accounting programs, and 22 private schools with a population of 7,000 in accounting programs.

Of the total accounting student population, 25,000 or 52 percent attend schools located in Mexico City; the balance of 23,000 is scattered around 28 of Mexico's 31 states.

3.1 Qualifications of Accounting Instructors

It is a universal requirement for accounting instructors to possess a baccalaureate degree. About 95 percent hold bachelor's degrees, and 5 percent hold master's degrees or doctorates, the latter mainly from institutions abroad. (MBA programs in Mexico started only in 1967, and there is only one graduate program in business administration in the whole country.) Only about 15 percent of total faculty are full or half-time. A typical ratio of faculty to the student population is something like 50-1.

Exhibit 1 presents an inventory of Mexican accounting student population in 1976. The source for this information was the Educational Objectives Research

Program of ANFECA, the Association of Business and Accounting Schools. The organization of this association in the early 1960's is, by itself, a good sign in the area of potential improvement in accounting education in the country.

The non-resident faculty would typically spend most of their day in the actual business world and this would permit them to bring back practical experience into the classroom.

EXHIBIT 1

Course Makeup of Accounting Programs in Mexico

	UNAM	IPN	ITESM	UIA*	Average
Financial accounting and auditing	19%	27%	26%	25%	25%
Law: civil, mercantile, administrative, labor, tax	11	16	14	10	13
Mathematics: basic, financial, statistics, operations research	11	10	10	6	9
Finance	9	3	10	10	8
Business administration (other than finance)	9	7	10	4	7
Economics (including aspects of macro accounting)	9	8	8	2	7
Cost accounting	7	4	4	6	5
Behavioral science	2	6	4	4	4
Humanities	4	0	4	10	4
Others	19	19	10	23	18
	100	100	100	100	100

UNAM: National Autonomous University of Mexico
IPN: National Polytechnic Institute
ITESM: Institute of Technology and Higher Studies
UIA: Ibero-American University

By the same token, the typical accounting instructor would not have much time to prepare in advance for his class. The present feeling in Mexico is that the rapid growth in its accounting student population brought down the quality of the average professor. Among the exceptions would be professors who have earned their faculty "chair" through contest. Theoretically, contests should be the rule for appointment of teachers, at least in the two largest institutions (Universidad Nacional Autonoma, and Instituto Politecnico Nacional). In practice, however, contests are called by exception and the participants would normally be faculty members already in the school who compete for permanent tenure.

Until 1976, there were no formal development programs for accounting instructors. In February, 1977, the National Autonomous University established a

*Percentages may vary (with the exception of financial accounting and auditing) depending on the program makeup for each student.

permanent Faculty Updating Center. Some of the larger schools have an education department that periodically conducts courses in instruction methodology (didactics) for the faculty. In 1976, the Association of Business and Accounting Schools started a master's program in the National Autonomous University for the training of professors (some 60) who in turn are supposed to disseminate their newly acquired knowledge as they go back to their schools of origin.

3.2 Instruction Techniques in Accounting Courses

Theoretical subjects are usually covered by the teacher's presentation approach. Practical applications may fall under the "workshop" concept. Very few other techniques are employed. Audiovisual techniques are used infrequently, mainly because of lack of appropriate materials.

The National Autonomous University recently established an open university program under which the student attends the university only for consultation with his assigned tutor.

Many years ago, even before it was recognized as a professional college, Escuela Bancaria y Comercial successfully began administering its mail courses.

3.3 Structure of Accounting Programs and Curricula

A typical undergraduate accounting program is made up of from 8 to 10 semesters, with from 368 to 438 credits. (A credit is equivalent to two study hours per week: one hour inside and one hour outside the classroom.)

Exhibit 2 sets forth the course makeup of the accounting programs at the four educational institutions surveyed for this study. The following table summarizes the average percentages of the four schools:

	Percent
Financial accounting and auditing	25
Law: civil, mercantile, administrative, labor, tax	13
Mathematics: basic, financial, statistics, operations research	9
Finance	8
Business administration (other than finance)	7
Economics (including aspects of macro accounting)	7
Cost accounting	5
Behavioral science	4
Humanities	4
Others	18
	100

Accounting subjects would occupy from 5 percent to 8 percent in a typical business administration program.

EXHIBIT 2
Accounting Student Population in Mexico: 1976

Institution	No. of Schools	Students	Percentage
Instituto Politecnico Nacional (IPN), financed and administered by the federal government	1	14,628	30
Universidad Nacional Autonoma de Mexico (UNAM), self-administered, fully financed by the federal government	1	5,636	12
Universidad de Guadalajara, same as UNAM	1	3,570	7
Other government schools, most of them self-administered; most of them jointly financed by the respective state government and the federal government	33	17,816	37
Total Government	36	41,650	86
Private Institutions	22	6,785	14
Totals	58	48,435	100

Source: ANFECA (Association of Business and Accounting Schools)

Public administration is not a program of the business or accounting departments. At the National Autonomous University the program in public administration is offered by the School of Social and Political Science and it includes no courses in accounting. At Universidad Iberoamericana, a program in public administration, the same as in business administration, may be built by the student to include up to 15 percent of accounting courses.

For a short period of time, government accounting was an elective course in the same ranks as public utility accounting, hotel accounting, farm accounting, etc. Government accounting has long been absent from the typical accounting curriculum.

Macro accounting is not represented in Mexico's business schools' program. It is thought to belong with economics. By the same token, the typical program in the School of Economics would concentrate on macro-economics and neglect micro-economics.

From the above, it will be evident that Mexico could use a program in government and macro accounting, preferably in the accounting school. At the present time, economists and accountants seem to live in different worlds. The economist would think of himself as the expert for most government appointments, including public finance, parastatal enterprise finance, macro-accounting, and public sector accounting. The accountant would typically start from the other end, working his way up from the accounting or control function of private enterprise to similar functions in government-owned entities to the mere bookkeeping end of the governmental balance sheet, annual revenue estimates, and annual expenditure budgets. Macro accounting is not at all germane to the Mexican accountant.

In the area of micro accounting, Mexico's two programs in its business schools (BBA, and Bachelor in Accounting) seem to require more emphasis on cost or management accounting, beginning with the recognition of such a discipline or combination of disciplines. Presently, there would be a couple of courses in cost accounting as if this were a branch of financial accounting.

3.4 Books and Materials

There are some 35 to 40 locally authored accounting textbooks generally in use at the undergraduate level and one or two in graduate programs.

Roughly one hundred non-Mexican works are used as textbooks or reference books in the undergraduate programs. Of these, about 85 to 90 percent are non-adapted translations from American authors; the balance are in Spanish, from Spain or Argentina.

It is safe to say that few, if any, translators are equipped or willing to adapt their translations to the Mexican environment. At the graduate level, students are expected to at least translate English, and are thus furnished English textbooks and case studies.

3.5 Accounting Research

Only the National Autonomous University and, more recently, the National Polytechnic Institute have formal research and development programs. The former has devoted most of its time to field research on various industries and activities for its business administration cases and materials, and accounting has received less attention so far.

Probably the most important output of Mexican research has been the Program for Research on Educational Objectives conducted for ANFECA (The Association of Business and Accounting Schools) by the National Autonomous University in the areas of accounting and business administration.

4. Evaluative Comments

Mexico seems to be in the upper stratum of Third World countries in the area of accounting practice and education, particularly financial accounting and auditing. This position, however, was generally the result of efforts from well-to-do and middle-class accounting graduates who were at the right place, at the right time: Mexico's big economic push came during the 1940's, 1950's and 1960's.

Mexico has one of the largest population-growth rates in the world (about 3.5 percent), and that brought about the need for massive admissions to the schools, to the detriment of quality in education. The rapid growth in the population caught the school system by surprise. Therefore, there were not enough accounting instructors to service all of the students, let alone provide personal guidance. Many instructors were pressed into teaching service from practice on a part-time basis. Also, the program content remained the same for many years, and the schools continued putting out mediocre auditors that were not required and/or had no calling for the profession. The universities became inundated from the lower social levels with faculty members who had faulty basic education and little dedication to textbook learning.

Except for the relatively few private schools, university education is free at the undergraduate level, and the government is reluctant to introduce charges for tuition for political reasons.

Accounting education has survived mainly because of the input from part-time instructors—practitioners who go back to their alma mater out of gratitude or in search of prestige, or to force themselves to continue their education. But this is not a solid foundation. The faculty needs to become a half-time and, as soon as possible, a full-time faculty.

The circumstances seem to be right for specialization beginning at the academic education level. At the very least, accounting students could branch out into internal and independent auditing, management accounting (including the controllership function), or government accounting.

There is also a great need for qualified internal accountants at the middle and lower levels: cost clerks, budget preparers, raw materials managers, etc. Probably because the federally and state financed universities admit almost all degree applicants at a token tuition, private academies and other institutions have failed to address themselves to setting up one- and two-year programs at the technical level.

In general, there is some degree of direct relationship between the accountant's proficiency in either public or management accounting and his comprehension of the English language. Mexico should brush aside chauvinistic attitudes in this respect, and pragmatically recognize that it needs to catch up, and the only way to do this is either (1) to embark upon a frantic program of translations and adaptations, or (2) to make reading of English language texts mandatory for accounting faculty.

The program for professoral development already in the National Autonomous University is a first step in the right direction. This should be supported, strengthened, and, at the right time, enlarged. Colombia's Instituto Colombiano de Administracion (INCOLDA) is thought to be a successful regional training center for business administration that, with the right support, could also apply itself to accounting education.

There is a belief in Mexico that assistance from international development institutions and foundations is not available in the accounting area, but only for business administration. Mexican schools have been recipients of assistance from the Ford Foundation and others, but only in connection with their graduate business administration programs. There is the feeling in Mexico that most international institutions and foundations do not adhere to the idea that accounting information per se exerts enough influence in fostering economic development.

Perhaps the most welcome educational assistance that could come from abroad would be in the form of a small team of professors that would mingle with the Mexican faculty, teach the students, gain the confidence necessary to teach the professors and, through indirect influence, put in valuable suggestions for improvement of course content and programs. At this point in time, knowledge of the Spanish language is essential for an effective assistance program.

Although many kinds of aids would contribute to the improvement of accounting education in Mexico, possibly the one single step that would have a leapfrog effect would be the establishment of regional centers with the financial support of foundations and with the academic support of schools in developed countries. Teaching the teachers would bring with it an obvious multiplying effect.

There is great need of modern books in the Spanish language, either translations adapted to the Mexican environment or, preferably, works by experienced Mexican accountants. As to translations, it is better that the translator be a proficient accountant even though his English might not be perfect rather than the other way around.

Because of its having been born on a university campus in 1914, the accounting profession in Mexico has never gone the route of the U.K. articleship nor of the American state board examination as a prerequisite for certification. Perhaps this is a filter that Mexico should seriously consider introducing. In addition to fulfilling all of the academic requirements, the applicant for an accounting license might sit for a pre-admission examination. In summary, the most evident needs seem to be the following:

- Full-time or at least half-time faculty.
- Students with the ability for accounting in particular, and learning in general. (The introduction of a system of charges for tuition in the public schools would by itself screen out non-serious students.)
- Reading of English textbooks to become mandatory, and/or establishing a permanent program of translation of current books into Spanish.
- Greater emphasis on the study of management accounting.
- Offering of governmental and macro-accounting programs in the business school.
- Professional examinations of candidates for public accounting certificates.

CHAPTER XXXIV

ACCOUNTING EDUCATION IN VENEZUELA

by

Omar Nucete and Mireya Villalobos de Nucete*

1. General Facts

Venezuela is in a unique geographical position, and occupies most of the northern coast of South America on the Caribbean Sea. It is bordered by Colombia to the west, Guayana to the east, and Brazil to the south. It is divided into twenty states, two federal territories and one federal district.

The population was estimated at 13,150,000 in 1978. The national monetary unit is the bolivar and the current rate of exchange is 4.30 bolivares, approximately, to the U.S. dollar. The official language is Spanish and Caracas is the capital of Venezuela.

In a geographic sense Venezuela offers certain advantages; it is a relatively large country with an area of 355,759 square miles and a tropical climate. Venezuela possesses the greatest petroleum reserves and production and refining capacity in the whole of Latin America. Crude oil production, now just above 2.1m barrels per day, ranks the country as one of the top five producers in the world.

Venezuela's oil fields have been developed principally by foreign oil companies under the concession system since World War I. On January 1, 1976, Venezuela nationalized twenty-one oil companies and assumed control over its oil fields. The change from sixty years of foreign control to state ownership of the industry has been achieved smoothly and normal operations have continued with no interruption in the vital flow of oil.

Venzuela is well placed to achieve an economic miracle based on industrial growth and diversification. It has abundant raw materials, rich in iron ore, mined in the southeast highlands towards Guayana, a young, eager population, a democratic government and a prominent place in the Andean Group, the Latin America counterpart of the European Economic Community. Venezuela's joining the Andean Pact was an event of great importance in the economic life of the country. For this reason some harmonization arose from economic, social and accountancy policies. Over the past years the government has begun to apply stiff controls on foreign investment in line with the rules of the Andean Common Market.

Venezuela has developed some great hydro-electric schemes to boost its indus-

*Omar Nucete is Professor of Finance at the Central University in Caracas, Venezuela; Dr. Mireya Villalobos de Nucete is Associate Professor of Finance at the Central University in Caracas, Venezuela.

trial power. Smaller but growing industries include car assembly, shoe factories, etc. Although agriculture clearly plays a minor part in the country's exports, one-third of the population still depends on it for their livelihood.

2. Forms of Business Organization

The Venezuelan commercial code recognizes the following forms of business organization:

• *General Partnerships.* Under this form of organization two or more persons engage in business and all partners are jointly and severely liable for business debts. This form of organization closely resembles general partnership in the United States.

• *Limited Partnerships.* This type of business possesses characteristics of the general partnership and the limited liability partnership. It is formed by one or more active partners who have unlimited liability for business debts, and by one or more silent partners whose obligations are limited to their capital contributions. Both the limited single partnership and limited partnership by shares exist in the country.

• *Limited Liability Companies.* This entity resembles a corporation in that the contributors are liable only to the extent of the amount of their subscriptions to the participation quotas. The capital subscribed must be neither less than Bs. 20,000, nor more than Bs. 2,000,000. Unless the instrument of organization provides otherwise, quota holders wishing to transfer their interest must first offer it to other partners. In order to transfer it to third parties, the consent of a majority of partners representing at least three-fourths of the capital must be obtained. Quotas may not be represented by negotiable shares or securities.

• *Corporations.* It is the most common form of business organization in Venzuela. This type of business corresponds very closely to the corporation found in the United States. It is formed exclusively by stockholders whose liability is limited to the amount paid for their shares. All authorized shares must be fully subscribed, a minimum of 20 percent must be paid for and deposited in a bank, and shares must have a par value. The constitutive document of a Venezuela corporation must be presented to the Mercantile Register (Court of Commerce) and must contain:

(1) The name, address, and occupation of the original subscribers.
(2) The name of the corporation.
(3) The address of the principal office and all branches.
(4) The purpose of the corporation.
(5) The duration of the corporation.
(6) The capital, the number and value of the shares, the number of shares subscribed by each shareholder, and the form of payment.
(7) The time and form for convening ordinary and extraordinary meetings.
(8) The form of administration, the duties of the manager, and the powers reserved for the shareholders.
(9) The portion of profits to be transferred to the legal and other reserve accounts.
(10) Any other agreements entered into by the stockholders.

• *Corporation Authorized Capital (SACA).* The Capital Market Law recently introduced the SACA type of corporation and defines it as a corporation in which the stockholders may authorize the administrators to increase capital to a stated amount through the issuance of new stock.

• *Open Capital Corporation (SAICA).* The Capital Marketing Law also introduced the SAICA type of corporation. This corporation must have a paid-in capital of not less than Bs. 1,000,000. The law stipulates that not less than 50 percent of the capital be owned by not less than fifty persons for each Bs. 1,000,000 of capital, and no group may own more than 10 percent of the capital.

3. Business Records Required by Law

The Commercial Code of Venezuela clearly provides that double-entry bookkeeping should be used in recording business transactions.

According to Venezuelan law, the following business records must be kept: (1) the daily journal; (2) the general ledger; and (3) the inventory book. All books must be kept in the Spanish language and Venezuelan currency.

The daily journal and the inventory must be bound, have consecutively numbered pages and must be registered in the federal treasury department, or, in its absence, with the highest official of the locality, for the notation of the date and the signature of the official on the first page of each book. All other pages are stamped with the respective seal.

Of the three required books, the only one new to the English speaking accountant is the Inventory Book. Inventory, as used here, differs from the normal usage of the term. It does not refer to the quantity of goods on hand; instead it is an inventory of all assets and liabilities. The difference between them being the capital of the enterprise. At the start of the business, the enterprise is obliged to enter into the inventory book a list of all assets and liabilities and annually thereafter the details of the balance sheet must be entered in this inventory book.

4. Foreign Influences in the Development of Accountancy in Venezuela

The principal influences upon the development of accounting in Venezuela seem to be the following:
(1) The Spanish dominance in the past, which established Spanish practices in Venezuela, and the continuation of the same practices and procedures until today.
(2) The establishment in Venezuela of offices of large United States public accounting firms.
(3) the requirements of international financial institutions. (For example: World Bank, Bank of America, Inter-American Development Bank)
(4) The use of textbooks and published accounting literature of U.S. origin (translated into Spanish) in imparting accounting instructions.
(5) Auditing practices and procedures.

5. Capital Market and the Public Accountant

The Caracas Stock Exchange, the nation's only public securities market, is still in its infancy and does not play a major role in financing the private sector at present. On January 31, 1973, the Congress approved the law of the stock exchange. Two of the principal articles that relate to the public accountant are:

(1) Article 27 which states: "The independent public accountants in the execution of their professional work must follow the norms of auditing generally accepted in Venezuela."

(2) Article 29 which states: "The independent public accountants must include in their reports concerning the financial statements a note where they show that they have revised all the information required by the Stock Exchange."

Accounting has two fundamental functions in the Venezuelan capital market: (1) a means of measuring and presenting the performance of enterprise, and (2) a device for safeguarding the assets of the owner-investors.

There is a real possibility that the local capital market will assume a more active role in coming years.

6. Tendency Toward Uniform Accounting in Venezuela

The growing complexity in the administration of private, mixed or state business demands full confidence in information and control channels. To this end, there is a tendency toward uniform accounting in Venezuela—though in specific fields only as yet. For example, some ministries, autonomous institutes and state businesses must present a Balance Sheet and Revenue and Expense Statements in a specific way, designed by the Business Register, to enroll in the Business Register. Similarly, the financial statements of commercial and mortgage banks and savings and loan entities have to conform to a uniform presentation and gather the accounts in accordance with the accounting code. This accounting code is issued by the bank superintendent.

The insurance companies must also have their accounting in accordance with the prescription of the Commercial Code and the Law of Insurance and Re-insurance, and gather their accounts in accordance with the code and instructions which are established by the superintendent of insurance.

The basic objective of the installation of these catalogs of accounts has been to standardize: (1) the denomination, and (2) the presentation of the accounts in order to improve the exact formulation of the financial statements.

7. Accounting Education

"Escuela de Comercio de Caracas," the first Commerce High School, was established in Caracas in 1912. Its name was changed to "Escuela de Comercio y Lenguas Vivas de Caracas."

On October 13, 1937, by a government decree, the "Instituto de Administracion comercial y de Hacienda" High School was founded. It started working with a four-year program in January, 1938. Later its name was changed to "Santos Michelena," and one more year was added to the program. Until the year 1938, there was no coordinated plan for the development of commercial education at high school level. Schools got established and disappeared but in 1938 only two such schools existed, one in Caracas and the other in Maracaibo.

By 1948 there were five schools of commercial education with 1,345 students. The high schools were: Santos Michelena in Caracas, Fermin Toro in Valencia, Guzman Blanco in Maracaibo, Tulio Febres Cordero in Merida, and Alberto Adriani in San Cristobal.

In 1946 a School of Business Administration was created at the Central University in Venezuela. In 1956, this school was divided into Business Administration and Accounting, but until 1959 the graduate accountants obtained the degree as Business Administrator-Accountant. In 1960, the university held the first graduation of students following a separate curriculum in accounting.

7.1 Levels of Accountants

Various levels of bookkeepers and accountants can be distinguished in the public and private sectors.

• *Unqualified bookkeeper.* A person working as a bookkeeper or a clerk who has received a few months of formal training for this function.

• *Qualified bookkeeper.* A person who has passed the certification examination in bookkeeping, controlled by the Ministry of Education. This certificate can be obtained in a high school or an academy.

• *Assistant accountant.* A person who possesses a certificate in bookkeeping and has completed a further two years study at a high school.

• *Qualified accountant.* A person who has obtained his bachelor's degree with a specialization in accountancy at one of the universities after having completed five years of study. (He is known as the Public Accountant.)

7.2 Requirements for the Degree of Public Accountant

To be admitted in Venezuela to one of the universities granting degrees in accounting, a candidate must possess the bachillerato. This degree is equivalent to the high school diploma in the United States. After obtaining admission to the professional accounting courses, the candidate must pursue courses for five years or ten semesters. Upon the successful completion of these requirements, the candidate is awarded the title of "Public Accountant" (Contador Publico).

7.3 University Studies in Accounting

In Venezuela there are fourteen institutions and universities under the Ministry of Education, awarding a degree or other superior qualification in accounting. These are:

University

(1) Universidad Central de Venezuela in Caracas   10 semesters
    (Many other higher learning institutions in the various states follow the same pattern of this very old, autonomous university.)
(2) Universidad de los Andes (Merida State)   10 semesters
(3) Universidad del Zulia (Zulia State)   10 semesters
(4) Universidad de Carabobo (Carabobo State)   10 semesters

(5) Universidad de Oriente (Sucre State)	10 semesters
(6) Universidad Centro Occidental "Lisandro Alvarado" (Lara State)	10 semesters
(7) Universidad Nacional Abierta (Open University, Caracas)	
(8) Universidad Catolica Andres Bello	5 years
(9) Universidad Santa Maria (Caracas)	5 years
(10) Instituto Universitario Pedagogico Experimental de Barquisimeto (Lara State)	8 or 9 semesters
(11) Instituto Universitario Pedagogico Experimental de Maturin (Monagas State)	8 or 9 semesters

Politechnical University Institute

(12) Instituto Universitario de Tecnologia. Region Capital (Caracas)	2 years

University College

(13) Colegio Universitario de Caracas (Caracas)	6 semesters

Private University Institute

(14) Instituto Universitario de Mercadotecnia (Caracas)	5 semesters

7.3.1 Plan of Studies

The plan of studies followed at the Central University of Venezuela (Universidad Central de Venezuela) is given by semesters of 14 weeks each.

Hours per Week

SEMESTER I

Accounting I	6
Economics I	4
Mathematics I	4
General Economic History	4
Pre-Seminary I	3
Total Hours Semester I	21

SEMESTER II

Accounting II	6
Economics II	4
Mathematics II	4
Venezuelan Economic History	4
Pre-Seminary II	3
Total Hours Semester II	21

SEMESTER III

Accounting III	6
General Economic Geography	4
Mathematics III	4
Private Law I	4
Seminary I	3
Total Hours Semester III	21

SEMESTER IV
  Accounting IV   6
  Venezuelan Economic Geography   4
  Mathematics IV   4
  Mercantile and Company Law   4
  Business Introduction   4
                                             ___
            Total Hours Semester IV   22

SEMESTER V
  Accounting Laboratory   5
  Economic Development I   4
  Statistics I, Methodology   5
  Labor Legislation   4
  Sociology   4
                                             ___
            Total Hours Semester V   22

SEMESTER VI
  Advanced Accounting I   5
  Economic Development II   4
  Application of Statistics to Business   5
  Public Law I   4
  Computer Programming I   3
  Seminary II   2
                                             ___
            Total Hours Semester VI   23

SEMESTER VII
  Advanced Accounting II   5
  Accounting Systems   5
  Public Law II   4
  Computer Programming II   5
  Seminary III   2
                                             ___
            Total Hours Semester VII   21

SEMESTER VIII
  Auditing I   4
  Analysis of Financial Statements I   5
  Cost Accounting I   5
  Taxation   4
  Seminary IV   2
                                             ___
            Total Hours Semester VIII   20

SEMESTER IX
  Auditing II   4
  Analysis of Financial Statements II   5
  Cost Accounting II   5
  Budgets I   4
                                             ___
            Total Hours Semester IX   18

SEMESTER X

Auditing III	4
Accounting for Specialized Institutions	4
Government Accounting	4
Budgets II	4
Total Hours Semester X	16

To allow the students to work during the day, the accounting classes are held between 2 p.m. to 10 p.m.

The School of Accountancy and Business Administration at the Central University had about 4,100 students and 310 professors in 1979. Of these professors, 89 were working full time, 17 half-time and 204 by hours.

7.4 Qualification of Accounting Teachers

To be a professor at the Central University it is necessary to take an examination. At the Central University and in many other universities, the following ranks and stipulated qualifications and experience are common:

Instructor: A baccalaureate degree.

Assistant: Two years of teaching experience, plus a dissertation.

Aggregate: Six years of teaching experience, plus a dissertation.

Associate: A doctoral degree plus ten years of teaching experience and a dissertation.

Titular: A doctoral degree plus 15 years of teaching experience and a dissertation.

7.5 Accounting Research

Research in general is not emphasized. Accounting research, especially, has received very little attention so far. The little research that is being done is of pedagogical nature only.

7.6 Instructional Technique Utilized in Accounting Programs

In addition to lectures, some institutions make use of a laboratory. At the Central University, in the fifth semester, students are put in smaller groups for expanded discussion and coverage of problem materials.

7.7 Master of Business Administration at the Central University, Caracas

An accredited bachelor's degree in business administration, accounting, and economics provides appropriate academic background for the Master of Business Administration program. Completion of the MBA program requires 40 credit hours of course work: 21 credit hours in compulsory subjects; 11 credit hours in elective subjects; and 8 credit hours in research, for a student who has satisfied all of the prepartory requirements.

Normally a student with a baccalaureate degree in business is considered to have satisfied all the preparatory requirements.

Holders of a bachelor's degree in engineering, arts of science, law, education and other fields can also enroll for the MBA program but with some additional requirements.

To achieve an MBA it is necessary to complete some preparatory course work of advanced standing by taking the appropriate examination in the following areas:

Linear Algebra and Calculus for Managers
Elements of Economics
Accounting Fundamentals
Probability and Statistical Inference for Managers
The Master of Business Administration is offered with the following majors:
Finance
Information Systems
Management
Administrative Planning

Each candidate must submit an acceptable dissertation. The dissertation should display the candidate's ability to conduct independent research which represents a significant contribution to knowledge in his or her field. A minimum of eight credit hours is granted for the dissertation.

8. The Public Accounting Profession

The Accounting National Technician Association (Collegio Nacional de Tecnicos en Contabilidad) was founded in 1942 and many non-graduate practitioner accountants are its members. The Association of Public Accountants and Business Administrators in Caracas was created in 1958. It consisted only of graduates in Public Accounting and Business Administration.

On September 27, 1973, the Congress approved the Accountant's Law, and late in the same year the Federation of Colleges of Public Accountants in Venezuela was founded in accordance with the Accountant's Law. This association could be considered as the Venezuelan counterpart of the AICPA. Its main objective is to promote and regulate the development of the Venezuelan accounting profession.

Now, in order to be a Public Accountant, one must hold a degree in accounting from a Venezuelan university.

The present rules state that in addition to auditing, the services of a Public Accountant could be utilized in many instances such as preparation of financial statements for judicial usage, for credit purposes, and/or for administrative matters.

APPENDIX

ACCOUNTANCY EDUCATION IN INDIA

by

The Institute of Cost and Works Accountants of India (I.C.W.A.I)

and

The Institute of Chartered Accountants of India (I.C.A.I.)*

1. National and Social Accounting

Accountancy education in India has had a chequered history. As in most other countries, systematic accounting education started with introduction of systems of formalized accounting practices in government which, in this country, took to the British system of governmental accounting including governmental budgets. Naturally, some form of formal accounting education can be traced to different departments of government with which the entrants into Civil Service had to be familiar. The commercial system of accounting also developed on the basis of borrowed systems, heads of accounts and approaches from the British. Though indigenous systems of accounting were practised by different business houses and business groups, these were not accorded formal recognition until very recently. Company legislation in this country was first accorded in 1913 which required maintenance of accounts books, preparation of annual accounts and audit certification for satisfying the requirements of law, shareholders, creditors and other interested public. Act VII of 1913 embraced all types of companies including banking and some forms of insurance. Even the railways in India were first run as companies and had to have corporate systems of accounts keeping and presentation of accounting information in specified formats.

While the systems of accounts-keeping and presentation of accounts for different purposes submitted themselves to a gradual process of development, mostly in recognition to need, often as a formal recognition to the prevalent practices, education for accounting at an academic level started much later in direct response to the need for educating the people to occupy different rungs and cadres in various commercial and non-commercial organizations. University education in commerce marked the beginning of formal education in accountancy at the academic level though even earlier accountancy was taught in commercial institutes as an element of vocational education. Sydenham College of Commerce, Bombay, is an accredited leader in the field of formal education in accounting. On the other hand, holders of the Government Diploma in Accountancy (GDA) and Registered Accountants (RA) were licensed to practice audit

---

*This study on India was extensively written and effectively coordinated by Dr. P. Chattopadhyay, Director of Research (I.C.W.A.I.). Due to certain logistical problems, this study had to be incorporated as an Appendix, although constituting an integral part of our Asia and Pacific section.

and certify accounts. GDA and RA were indeed precursor to the modern Chartered Accountant (CA), equivalent to the CPA in the United States and the CA in England. The pre-war period noticed a fairly rapid development in the context of accounting education and with the spurt in industrialization, accounting education was accorded greater and greater recognition as a part of the syllabi in different university courses at undergraduate and postgraduate levels. The war, to some extent, posed a challenge for accountants for coping with the needs for procurement and deployment of funds for different purposes in the enterprises in question.

Historically, financial accountancy and cost accountancy have had different sources of origin. While the former was much embedded in the law on companies and in meeting the need for information, often vital, for management, shareholders and government, cost accountancy was much more an internal matter in industrial organizations stemming more from the technicalities of production and distribution than from having to meet the requirements of the law. Variously nicknamed, cost accountancy is much more akin to industrial accountancy which has been found to have a long history in different countries such as Italy, UK and USA. The establishment of the Institute of Cost and Works Accountants, London, was in direct response to the need for streamlined accounting systems for production and distribution in extremely trying conditions posed by the First World War and the post-war years. The establishment of the British Institute gave a spurt to many Indians to qualify in the final examinations of the institute and to practise the art and science of cost accountancy, especially in the defense establishments like ordnance factories. Almost twenty-five years later, the Indian Institute of Cost and Works Accountants was registered as a company limited by guarantee. While the Institute of Cost and Works Accountants of India was still in its infancy, in 1949 the Chartered Accountants Act came into force establishing the Institute of Chartered Accountants of India as a statutory body entrusted with guiding and regulating the chartered accountants in the country. The Institute of Cost and Works Accountants of India was also made into a statutory body in 1959 when Parliament enacted the Cost and Works Accountants Act of 1959. The Institute of Cost and Works Accountants of India was given statutory recognition for guiding and regulating the profession of cost and works accountancy in the country and the functioning of cost and works accountants. In 1980 the Institute of Company Secretaries of India has also been accorded statutory recognition by an Act of Parliament.

Though initially patterned after the Comptroller and Auditor General of Great Britain, the Comptroller and Auditor General of India was given formal recognition and independence in the constitution of India with large powers to examine records and to report to Parliament and government for taking such corrective action on specific issues as necessary. The governmental system of accounts-keeping underwent a process of streamlining under the surveillance of the Comptroller and Auditor General of India and different committees and commissions appointed by the government went into different aspects of systems of governmental administration including accounts-keeping for different purposes. After independence, especially after the adoption of economic planning, normal functions of governmental administration extended in different directions and governmental administration acquired a more logical shape of developmental administration in which economic administration was not only given equal prominence to political administration but in many respects greater significance. Accounting for development thus acquired a prime of place not only in the context of economic planning and formulation of different targets, sectoral and overall, but also in that of implementation of these targets, identification of variances and adoption of corrective measures in different ways. Indeed, the adoption of economic planning in this country gave accountancy education a formal spurt, for along with the extensions in the government departments and enlargement of connected functions, a large number of public enterprises were established. These public enterprises have come into being over time in different forms like departmental undertakings, public corporations and government companies under the control of the central and state governments. On the other hand, direct dispensation of funds for different purposes such as construction of buildings, roads, projects, etc., agriculture and agricultural infrastructure such as irrigation and power and also the manufacture of fertilizers, improved seeds, etc., required close watch on two counts. One, the cost-effectiveness of the expenditure under different heads; two, the direction in which funds had been canalized and the extent to which goals therefor had been realized. Excepting a few public corporations of the departments of government and of public enterprises have been under the audit jurisdiction of the Comptroller and Auditor General of India. Among the organizations which have been left out of the audit jurisdiction of the Comptroller and Auditor General of India are the Reserve Bank of India and the Life Insurance Corporation of India.

Accountancy education in India at the university level, at the levels of the professions and at the levels of the government had to accommodate all these massive changes effected over time both in response to and in anticipation of the economic development of the country. Complexities have multiplied. Demands on the system of accounting education have risen continuously. Expectations from accounting education and accounting systems introduced in different organizations have also risen. Pressure on the system of accounting education both in the universities and colleges and in the professions as also in government has grown not only corresponding to the demands already made overt but also in anticipation of the changes in various sectors of the economy. Accountancy education has lent itself to almost a hierarchical pattern in which the overtone of accounting principles and concepts has been noticeably complex but essentially sustained though the practical shape and character that the accounting concepts and principles have taken in the course of application have remained variegated in consonance with the complexities of the operations sought to be accommodated in the accounting formats. Chart I depicts the hierarchical pattern of the system of accounting education starting from the national level down to those of enterprises. In each of these cases, corresponding complexities in the cost and management accounting system, specifically in the systems for control exercised for the purpose of internal management, in some cases also of external surveillance, have been almost equally reflective. Details of both financial accounting and cost and management accounting systems embracing theories, concepts and principles as also their applications require some elaboration which is being attempted in the paragraphs below for underlining the sensitivity of the system of accounting education in vogue in this country.

Interestingly, accounting education has apparently transgressed the barriers of different intellectual disciplines. Accounts have also been seen from different standpoints. While in the hands of accountants or accounting specialists, accounts have remained the finished product, depicting the state of affairs of business as on a date and the profit and loss position for an accounting period, accounts have been treated as sources of information in several other disciplines where accounting data have provided the basic framework or further analysis. While it can be easily conceived that a system of national accounting or social accounting encompasses the accounts of individual units, be they public corporations, companies or unitary concerns or cooperatives belonging to different sectors of the economy, at the levels of these units preparation and interpretation of accounts have been guided by the provisions of law and prevalent conventions. This macro-micro link has been fairly well established in the organized sectors of industry, business and government and also partly agriculture. The problem has arisen essentially with respect to the large chunk of unorganized sectors in agriculture, small business and trading, so that estimation of their inputs and outputs, factor incomes, etc., has posed a problem. That is, however, not peculiar to India nor to a developing country; this problem has beset national income calculation and preparation of national income accounts in all countries. Even in the context of national accounts, more than one system can be thought of as respects accounting designs particularly for the developing countries where the data base is rather inadequate and estimation of input and output or income and outflow has remained a problem requiring application of different statistical techniques. It has been suggested that for a developing country, one can think of four different accounting designs named as: the natural system; the hypothetical system; the realistic system; and the dualistic system of accounts. While these systems are discrete, they also make for simultaneous adoption and application for different purposes. Each of these systems and designs has its advantages and disadvantages that require conscious appraisal in practice. However, the assumptions and guiding factors behind selection of one or more of these designs have been subject to debate which is yet inconclusive.

Comprehension of all the national economic activities in a single accounting format has been a complex task, particularly in view of several factors and forces remaining out of gear most of the time. These centrifugal forces have tended to multiply with the spur in economic development under planning, massive investments made in different sectors of the economy and rather inadequate monetization in the rural sector which continues to play a predominant role in the Indian economy. In the circumstances, attempts have been made to construct national accounts from different points of view, concerned as they are with accounting for gross domestic output, statistical analysis of incremental capital output under different assumptions and construction of sectoral accounts such as gross busi-

404

ness investment and finance account, accounting for national income, accounting for the households, Central Government account, gross domestic saving and investment account, the rest-of-the-world account, and so on. In these exercises, it has been found significant to analyse the structural changes accompanying economic growth, formulation of monetary and fiscal policies responsive to the requirements of the economy, technological aspects of economic growth, coordination of census and national sample survey data with social accounts, efficiency determinants of economic growth, the rural-urban distinction and terms of trade with pointers for growth with social justices, linkages between financial and physical aspects of planning in different sectors of the economy as also in the national economy as a whole, and, above all, sources and utilization of funds towards realization of national economic goals as seen from the point of view of the whole economy and of the individual sectors comprising it.

The national fund flow system and tying up the loose ends noticed in the framework of such a system have engaged serious attention in the country for some time. National income statistics and analysis of individual aspects and contributing factors to the growth and rate of growth of national income have also been subject to detailed scrutiny in the National Planning Commission, in the Central Statistical Organization and in the Indian Statistical Institute with reference to both control and prediction of the stimuli released in the process of planning and the responses generated in different sectors on a widely scattered basis. We advert to some of these details later. However, it is necessary to mention at this stage that all the issues with which professional accountants or managers remain concerned at the levels of enterprises have also been relevant at the national level in a much bigger magnitude. Complexities encountered have also been far too many. Interestingly, however, the problematic areas have been the same, albeit in different sizes, shapes and character.

Thus, quite logically, one appreciates national income specialists dealing with problems like working capital, fixed capital, depreciation, stock and flow, liquidity, raw materials, employment and wages and such other questions with which managers in enterprises remain concerned as a part of their daily chore. These exercises have not only had the benefit of hindsight and time series analysis but also of projective and predictive character; first, as an extension of the historical trends having been extrapolative; secondly, the changes caused in different areas to make the trends dysfunctional and so reconstructing the future pattern on the basis of integration of these changes and new trends noticed in different sectors; and lastly, application of different quantitative tools to predict the directions of the economy on the basis of either sample service or causal relationships of different factors noticed to have played significant roles in initiating growth at different rates in different sectors. Though basically estimated, the predictions and forecasts of input and output as also efficiency in Indian agriculture have generally fallen within a certain margin of error, attesting to the high quality of these estimations and the sophisticated analysis adopted for this purpose.

The annual conference on national income and the reports containing the papers and proceedings thereof have thrown considerable light on the high level of thinking on several of these issues. Incidentally, in the initial years of planning, efforts had to be organized for strengthening the data base of the economy and different economic, statistical, econometric and sociometric tools and techniques had to be adopted for highlighting the results of planned efforts in different sectors of the economy. The perspective Planning Division of the Planning Commission, the Central Statistical Organization and the Indian Statistical Institute have done commendable work in this respect. Economists, statisticians, behavioural scientists and others in this country have been accredited with high level work in the respective fields. Not only that India is ranked among the few in the developing world with a sound data base but also that in many respects Indian data system has been ranked on par with many countries of the developed world. As Professor A. J. H. Enthoven has mentioned, social accounting concerns itself with business enterprises, private households, government, related account such as rest-of-the-world and capital formation and the derivation of their components having as their core matter the application of accounting methodology to macro-economic analysis (Cf. *Accountancy and Economic Development Policy*, North Holland Publishing Company, Amsterdam, 1973, p. 65).

It may be mentioned that in India both procedural and analytical aspects of social (national) accounting have received considerable scholarly attention during the last two decades, resulting in streamlining several loose ends noticed in attempted construction of national accounts earlier, partly because of inadequacy of data at that time and partly because of insufficient knowledge in the area.

National accounts and constituents thereof are taught at the postgraduate levels in Indian universities. Research effort in this area has also been fairly organized. Though the initial studies in the subject came from Indian researchers studying in foreign universities, particularly British, during the last three decades several high level research studies have appeared in India. Two of the more recent studies on the subject are referred to here only for illustration. One of them is entitled *Capital Formation and its Financing in India* by R. N. Lal (1977, a monograph in Economics from Delhi School of Economics, Delhi University). The other is entitled *Social Accounting for Developing Countries* by P. L. Arya (macmillan, 1976). While the former discusses different aspects of capital formation and the mechanism of financing of such capital formation in the Indian context, the author has gone deep into the methodology of computation of national income statistics with particular reference to capital formation indicating the data gaps that exist. The other title surveys social accounting methodology as evolved in different countries and grapples with Indian data leading to construction of sets of social accounts and constituents thereof. Both these studies have fairly exhaustive bibliography seeking to help future researchers in dealing with the problem. Papers and articles on different issues conected with social accounting or national accounting and national income have appeared in different learned journals, both in this country and abroad underlining the significant issues relevant for policy. The successive five-year plans have also had exercises in projected growths of national income and in this respect these studies have had impacts unique in many ways. Both for five-year planning horizons and twenty-five-year perspective planning, projective exercises in this area have been fairly detailed and analytical. In this context, mention may be made of Professor F. Sewell Bray who attempted to construct social accounts of a business enterprise in a book that appeared on the subject several years ago. However, though the linkage between an individual enterprise and the national economy has been somewhat tenuous, Professor Sewell Bray attemped to show the possibility of integration between the sectoral operations and the aggregative national operations on the economic front.

Apart from the question of establishing linkages between different sectors of the economy and between the national economy as a whole and its individual sectors, there are two-way possibilities easily discernible from the present pattern of accountancy education in the country as adopted by different institutions and at different levels of education such as academic, professional and vocational. The problems thought appropriate for serious analysis at the national level acquired similar significance at the sectoral or enterprise levels also call for attention from the national economic point of view. The linkage patterns, typology of accounting and accountancy education and the role accountancy plays in economic development of countries of both the developed and the developing world have been amply demonstrated by Professor Adolf Enthoven in his book *Accountancy and Economic Development Policy* (1973) followed by his second study, sponsored by the Ford Foundation, entitled *Accountancy Systems in Third World Economies* (1977) wherein Professor Enthoven sought to identify accountancy systems in enterprise accounting, government accounting and national accounting underlining the potentials for improvement and the infrastructural needs for such improvement. Though on essentially a scattered basis, these questions have remained under focus in India during the entire era under planning, especially in the context of determination of growth potentials, input-output relationship, inter-industry studies, inter-sectoral linkages and feedback from the point of view of determination of targets of investment, installation of capacity in different industries and activities and establishing a sensitive institutional framework. As noticed by us earlier, several of the institutions concerned with accountancy and accountancy education in some form or the other have been established in direct response to that long felt need.

2. Sectoral Accounting

Under sectoral accounting systems, mention may be made of agricultural accounting, accountancy for mining and extractive industries, construction industries, manufacturing and processing, services, administration, balance of payment, foreign exchange, etc. Sectoral accounting has acquired a great deal of significance since introduction of the first Five Year Plan in India from different points of view. While at the national level, being aggregates of all the sectors, problems similar to those noticed in sectoral accounting have also been noticed, in sectoral systems further elaborations have been called for from different points of view. Partly this has been necessitated by the need for determining objects and targets for sectoral development and partly for assessing the present state of affairs in these sectors. On the basis of established and anticipated causal relationships, under different assumptions investments were planned for raising different quantities of output at given levels of technology and operational efficiency.

Dealing with individual sectors seriatim, one may mention that each of these sectors has shown different responses to the stimuli provided in different ways. While on the subject of agriculture, it is well known that just before the first Five Year Plan the agricultural production in this country was grossly inadequate from the point of view of both food grains and non-food grains, a classification adopted by the Ministry of Food and Agriculture, Government of India. The agricultural statistics betrayed poor organization for data collection, a large extent of guesstimates and interplay of different types of uncertainties between expectations and reality. A primary task for the government was to revamp the agricultural sector, raising it from the morass of underdevelopment in respect of the quantity of crops raised, variety, quality and the prices commanded by the agricultural commodities embracing both food grains and non-food grains. In addition, as a part of the plan effort, governments at the centre and in the states had to operate in a big way for reorienting the outlook on agriculture, from a way of life as noted by the Fiscal Commission just before the start of the plan era in this country to a fruitful economic activity. Massive institutioal changes were planned and implemented during the period covered by the last five Five Year Plans. While the methodology of collection of agricultural statistics has been considerably sensitized and streamlined, as yet the system has remained anything but foolproof. Partly this is because agriculture being the major occupation in the country, more than 70 percent of the people being dependent on agriculture directly or indirectly, the wide scatter of land, crops and the seasonal variations as also methods and implements used in agriculture it was a stupendous task to bring the totality of agricultural efforts in the country to book. Statistical devices for estimation and forecasting had to be applied on a wide scale and inquiries, studies and surveys had to be organized on a fairly regular basis to get a feel of what is going on in Indian agriculture. Though cooperatives have been established in different areas and systems of accounts-keeping by the cooperatives had to conform to the bylaws, not much headway has been noticed except in some parts of the country. A major thrust has, therefore, to come on agricultural accounting systems, maybe somewhat unsophisticated but remaining a faithful recording of all transactions nonetheless.

A great number of activities are embraced by agriculture or farming such as dairying, cattle raising, piggery, poultry, apiary, pisciculture, horticulture, sericulture, brick-making and other activities with which the farmers are directly concerned in some form or the other along with their main occupations. Howsoever unsophisticated, an agricultural accounting system, shall we say farm accounting system, can and should reflect areas of control exercisable at the levels of farmers, control that can be exercised by the village level administrative bodies like panchayats, block levels, panchayat samitis, zila parishads, district level administration and governments at the Centre and in the States. In the context of exercise of control, predetermined norms based either on past experience or on other premises can play an active part in improving the performance of the farm sector. Naturally, the focus on control is distinct from the informational needs that such a regular and systematic method of accounts-keeping can fulfill. The National Commission on agriculture dealt exhaustively with some of these questions, accommodating considerations about both inputs and outputs. Supplying information needs is a role that has been sought to be realized by the Union Government through organization of Farm Management Surveys in different districts of the country belonging to all the states and conducted over a period of time. While they have indeed supplied essential information for purposes of planning, Farm Management Survey reports are hardly a substitute for farm accounts to be maintained by farmers and other authorities concerned with farming activities. While farm accounts provide information with total reliability, alternative methods devised by government have had to depend very largely on estimates of activities, what the farmers remembered rather than from records of transactions maintained on a regular basis. In different contexts, doubts have been expressed about the reliability of information on the farming sector and over a period of time certain improvements have indeed been effected, but as yet a wholly reliable system has not been evolved.

In this regard, one may also mention that doubts and disputes have arisen in this country during the last decade and a half regarding the fixation of the prices of different agricultural commodities with respect both to support prices and procurement prices. While the farmers have contended that the prices fixed by the government have hardly done justice to the costs incurred by them, the consumers, both industrial and domestic, have felt that high prices of agricultural commodities have eaten into the vitals of the economics of operations of several agriculture-based industries. Pointers are also raised about the generally unfavourable terms of trade between agriculture and industry but in the absence of information as reliable as one can obtain from farm accounts, doubts and disputes have lingered. Here one must also concede that in Indian agriculture today, there are two or three Central Government companies such as the State Farming Corporation of India Limited and different State Government companies dealing with farming where the system of accounts-keeping is dictated by the provisions of the Companies Act, 1956 and where management accounting, cost accounting and financial management have reached a fairly high level of sophistication. Similarly, there are cooperatives which are required to maintain accounts of their activities concerned with both physical aspects and financial aspects of their performance and which have a fairly acceptable degree of reliability. However, systematized accounts-keeping has been almost totally absent in the cases of individual farmers and from time to time they have been expected to fill up schedules of inputs and outputs on the basis on which administrative decision-making has been geared, national income has been computed and growth rates, input-output relationship, etc., determined.

As regards the mining sector, with the nationalization of coal industry, the entire sector has been institutionalized in the sense that individual mining concerns or partnership firms have been almost absent and mining companies have been formed under the control of Central Government, State Governments and private parties as regulated by the Companies Act, 1956. Information regarding the mining sector with respect to the physical and financial inputs and outputs of different types of minerals and metals has become a great deal more reliable than ever before. Focus of attention in this context has been on improvements in productivity and operational efficiency on different fronts with particular reference to choice of techniques, economics of different types of technologies, manual operations as against mechanical operations and distribution of such essential mineral products like coal, petroleum, iron ore and so on, part of which gets sold in the country at all-India prices and for part thereof, locational advantages are attached. A major part of the mineral industry in the country has been nationalized and government companies have come up for dealing with exploration of different minerals, particularly coal, petroleum, iron ore, gold, gems and other precious stones, etc.

The typicalities of accounting practices in the state sector of the industry have been marked by treating total period expenditure as the cost of the output raised without reference to either cost relevance of expenditure or the cost objectives of such expenditure. But in India government companies established under the Companies Act have been guided by provisions of the company law and barring exceptions of a few of the detailed regulations incorporated therein, the corporate practices noticed in the so-called private corporate sector have also been relevant to the public corporate sector, e.g., the government companies, which are so defined according to the extent of shareholding by the governments of the Centre and the States and have included both private limited companies and public limited companies, often the word private having been dropped under a waiver clause in the Companies Act. The accounting practices followed by these government companies have generally fallen under what Professor Adolf J. H. Enthoven has detailed as enterprise accounting subject to the fact that the government companies have been subject to multi-pronged audit and parliamentary or legislative surveillance depending on whether they are under the central government or the state governments. Thus, in addition to professional audit conducted as provided for in the Companies Act, these companies have remained subject to audit by the Comptroller and Auditor General of India and periodic study and scrutiny by the Committee on Public Undertakings of Parliament or state legislature of the individual states.

In many ways, therefore, the enterprise accounting system practised by these companies has also remained subject to accountability accounting with reference to employment generated, funds deployed, production raised, prices charged and revenue collected. In this respect, both structures and functions of all government companies have been subject to detailed examination by the administrative ministries concerned, Comptroller and Auditor General of India and the Accountant Generals in different states, the Committee on Public Undertakings and periodic investigations on specific matters such as pricing policies, employment policies, recruitment policies, expenditure under specific heads, filling up of posts, salaries and perquisites, production management, financial management, materials management and so on. These aspects have been studied and elaborated in what have been called horizontal studies by the Parliamentary Committee on Public Undertakings. Another typicality is that minerals have traditionally remained underpriced insofar as the mineral deposits are mined and exploited only at the cost of the royalty paid at very low rates. Separate accounting studies on the typicalities of systems followed in the mineral industry in India have not been highlighted adequately. Corporate enterprises have been clubbed together under industry groups in which the industry typicalities have remained somewhat hidden and the characteristic issues concerned with exploratory accounting have remained somewhat unsung. This aspect is particularly demonstrated in creative activities like oil and gas in which case at the developmental and promotional stages, expenditure would appear unmatched with results and that gap between them acts as a damper in sensitive financial decision making. The motivations to achieve and the actual achievement recorded have required scientific probe in industries like oil and gas. In this respect, the budget grants provided by the Union Government to the Oil and Natural Gas Commission comes as an expenditure while the results in the form of exploration of proved mineral deposits are handled by separate corporations like the Indian Oil Corporation Limited, the Hindustan Petroleum Company Limited, etc. Another problem infests this area of accounting practices. In projects like Bombay High, investments appear suitable for amortization as long as the deposits last. Being handled by separate authorities and being subject to payment of royalty only, the economics of exploration does not come out in clearer contours.

There are some other peculiarities also that are noticed in the context of Indian mineral industry. The role and jurisdiction of authorities like the Geological Survey of India, the Oil and Natural Gas Commission, government companies operating in different fields concerned with mineral industry and governments of the Centre and the States are not always clearcut. In many ways, the efforts and results remain segmented as shown in the annual reports of different bodies. There is yet another problem noticed in this regard. Mineral based industries have also mines under them giving rise to problems of transfer pricing, the accounting treatment of which has remained somewhat inadequate. Accounting for mineral exploration, promotion and development has remained an underdeveloped area in view of the several authorities concerned with these activities and the characteristic features of minerals, their explorations and exploitation, albeit the fact that Indian accounting practices though underdeveloped vis-a-vis the developed countries of the West are a lot more sophisticated than several of the neighbouring countries of Asia, Africa and other continents. One appreciates in this context the merits of management development programmes in the areas of financial management for oil and gas exploration developed by Professor Enthoven and the economics of application of scientific management techniques and accounting practices in this area. It would not be out of place to mention here that in India separate public enterprises accounting system has not been recognized. Depending on the formal variations of the public enterprises like departmental undertakings, government companies and public corporations, the accounting systems have responded to the governmental accounting practices in the cases of departmental undertakings, accounting practices envisaged in discrete legislations for public corporations with reference to their operational characteristics and accounting practices as incorporated in the company law in the cases of government companies. There is thus hardly any difference between the accounting practices of Coal India Limited from those of private sector mining companies, on the one hand, and Steel Authority of India Limited from those of Tata Iron and Steel Company Limited, on the other, the disclosure of details in each case being dictated by the Companies Act, 1956 as amended up to date and Rules and Regulations made thereunder from time to time.

This is at once an advantage and a disadvantage. Evolution of a single public enterprise accounting system could perhaps attend to the objectives of the public enterprises better than they do now. On the other hand, even under such a system, the operational typicalities of each enterprise could hardly be accommodated in a generic pattern. Moreover, the formal variations and umpteen enterprises in the public sector with different authorities controlling them would have spelled the same problems as are being faced in the cases of government companies operating in different areas of activities. Similar considerations also apply to the manufacturing sector consisting of corporate enterprises of different varieties, some public limited, some private limited and some others government companies belonging to both of these varieties. Here again, the sectoral accounting pattern has remained far more streamlined and organized as far as the corporate sector is concerned. For non-corporate enterprises, though accounting systems have indeed been in vogue in quite a few of them, one is not quite sure. For instance, in sectoral income estimates including growth, investment and employment, the corporate and non-corporate sectors have together presented a picture of rather unknown behaviour in many of the units. But in general, information collected of the manufacturing sector by the Reserve Bank of India as far as the corporate enterprises are concerned, the annual survey of industries and different authorities in administrative charge of different industries have collected massive information on an annual basis falling within a fairly acceptable margin of error.

One difficulty from the accounting point of view is that while information on operational sides including value added is available in detail from the annual survey of industries covering both corporate and non-corporate enterprises of larger size groups, size groups determined in terms of investment and employment, financial linkages of the type that one looks for in accounts are not available in one single source. Causal relationships are not easily establishable except on industrywise aggregates. Incidentally, both Reserve Bank of India and annual survey of industries present data on the basis of industry aggregates from which individual enterprise operations can hardly be determined. On the other hand, the type of information that one gets in the annual accounts is not available in the same form in either the Reserve Bank of India data or in the data available from the annual survey of industries. The methodology of collection and integration of information under different heads is also not entirely explained in each case. But from the point of view of national income computation—sectoral or overall—information available from different sources related to the organized industry sector appears adequate.

The foregoing relates essentially to information for the purpose of compilation, computation and aggregation of national income with reference to individual economic sectors. Methodology of national income calculation has admitted of several changes during the last three decades with reference to both accommodation of a bigger regimen of goods and services, more logical price index series and application of sophisticated statistical techniques for building up wholesale price index and consumer price index as also regional price indices. The expression of gross national product, net national product and per capita net national product at current prices and constant prices has undergone a series of revisions enhancing their reliability and applicability for different purposes. Comprehensive educational programmes on all these aspects are in vogue in different universities in India in which collection of economic statistics, sources of such statistics, methodology of computation of such statistical information and interpretation of such information comprise different courses of study at postgraduate levels in the disciplines of economics, quantitative economics and management. In this regard mention is also necessary of the efforts of the Indian Statistical Institute which was involved in the whole process during almost the entire era under planning and which provided valuable side information regarding different sectors of the economy through organizing and participating in national sample surveys on a countrywide scale from time to time. *Sankhya*, published by the Indian Statistical Institute, contains high level discussions on different aspects of national income, sectoral income and regional incomes which have been noted for their conceptual relevance and practicability.

The White Paper on national income published by the Central Statistical Organization every year and the Economic Survey of the Finance Minister of the Union Government presented to parliament during the budget session every year give details of sectoral income estimates, national income estimates and per capital national income providing a basis for the broadbased economic policy of the government. In the sectoral disaggregation of national income, services comprising banking, insurance, consultancy and governmental administration are also highlighted especially with reference to factor incomes and output in feasible cases. Though estimates of national income are given every year and detailed information on services is available as a running series, the sector continues to be rather inadequate as a part of the educational programme for accountancy. The approach is essentially aggregative, detailing out total expenditures and receipts under different heads. The kind of attention that accountancy education requires on these aspects is, however, yet to come especially in consonance with the progress made in accounting for other sectors. We propose to deal with the enterprise aspects of this sector at appropriate places below.

There is, however, a dividing line between the enterprise accounting systems and the governmental accounting systems. A reference to the governmental

413

accounting systems is called for at this stage, particularly because of the overall influence that the government accounting system exercises over the public enterprises of different forms and varieties, public utilities and also on the private sector enterprises with reference to various regulatory powers exercised under different laws enacted from time to time and numerous rules made thereunder. Governmental system of accounts comprises the core matter of education for new entrants to different all-India services concerned with developmental administration, on the one hand, and accounting and audit functions, on the other. Such accounting and audit functions relate to overall finance accounts and audit, defense accounts and audit, railway accounts and audit, revenue accounts and audit and customs and excise accounts and audit. The government of India has introduced performance budgeting systems in different ministries and departments concerned with economic administration as a result of the recommendations of the Administrative Reforms Commission. Accounting innovations effected recently by the government relate not only to the introduction of performance budgeting but also to that of economic classification of budget heads and realignment of heads of receipts and expenditure in government accounts in consonance with the performance budget heads. Attempts are also going on to introduce performance budget systems in different productive organizations and departments of the government where products are measurable in some form or the other and physical aspects of performance can be matched with receipts and expenditure. Academic interest on systems of governmental accounts and budgets has remained at a low key except in the faculty of public administration and public finance in different universities. A casual, non-professional and pedestrian approach to governmental accounting noticed over time is gradually giving way to more sophisticated, sensitive and professional handling. Though as yet marked improvements are not noticeable on all sides, consciousness on this front has been growing as one would notice from the induction of professional men in different cadres and posts related to economic administration.

This consciousness is also, in major part, related to the fact that under economic planning, the lion's share of governmental activities has been related to economic development and economic management of the country's resources, meagre as they are. At one end, the Planning Commission allocates funds to different heads of development and at the other end the governmental bureaucracy is expected to show due aplomb in the actual deployment of these resources for realizing the objectives and targets laid down in the plans. This has also meant that the traditional orientation to governmental accounting systems has been replaced by developmental orientation in which cost effectiveness of expenditure and social cost benefit analysis in the context of funds allocation are engaging a good deal of attention. On different aspects of operations of the government in various developmental and non-developmental areas, organized information is available as a running series in the reports of the Public Accounts Committee, the Estimates Committee and the demands for grants for different ministries placed before parliament every year. This information has high educational value but the university departments of economics, management

414

and commerce where accountancy is taught are yet to realize the full significance of the information available for purposes of assessment of trends, interpretation of information and projective exercises on different counts. In the same vein, one can also mention that as between the Central Government and governments in the states, degrees of sophistication attained in different aspects of accounting have varied with reference both to collection of information and presentation thereof under cognizable economic and administrative heads of expenditure and receipts. A great deal of improvement appears possible, particularly in enhancing the credibility of the operations of the government in varied spheres and in the process of feedback through properly designed information flow. Accountancy education relates not only to augmentation of veracity of information but also to introduction of regular, systematic and scientific operational details helping governments to know and judge how things are going and to take corrective action through timely monitoring. Both budgets and accounts as also analysis of variances admit of a great deal more streamlining than effected so far once knowledgeability as regards accounting method, systems and procedures is infused into the system. This will result in two types of economies. One, the mass of information presented at the year end along with budget and presentation of actuals, revised budget estimates and budget estimates can be reduced considerably and made more responsive to timely action. Two, information would be thrown up for such action before it is too late.

Our account of the systems of accounting in government would not be complete without a reference to the rather recently taken steps to revamp and rejuvenate the Panchayati system of administration operating at village levels. Money flows to the Panchayats through the Zila Parisads, Panchayat Samities and Village Panchayats as also taxes, levies and imposts collected by them would require systems of accounting not quite envisaged in those in vogue either in the Central Government or in the governments of the states. Grants in aid and other receipts by the Panchayats and expenditure incurred by them under different heads, both for normal and developmental administration, would require fairly sensitive systems of accounting for reflecting the operational details of the plans for integrated rural development, capital investment for different productive purposes, revenue realized under different heads and administrative expenditure incurred, all these subscribing to accounting concepts and practices like finding causal relationships between investment and output, etc.

Another area where a great deal of leeway remains to be made relates to the sector of village and small-scale industries, cottage industries and small traders and transport operators. Though individually each of these units of operations is small, in the aggregate they account for a large chunk of the country's national income in terms of national output, investment and employment. The difficulty in bringing this sector in a standard format of accounting practice is primarily that it is too widely scattered to be identified easily, the operations carried on being in the form of small companies, partnerships and unitary establishments. From time to time, the office of the Development Commissioner of Small Scale Industries under the Central Government and the countrywide network of Small Industries Service Institutes and the Directorates of Small Scale Industries in the States have sought to bring to book and throw up as a running series information on their operations, though large gaps have continued to exist over time. To bridge these gaps, countrywide census of small scale industries was organized recently and the information thrown up has been revealing on many counts, underlining their importance for a developing country like India but, at the same time, pinpointing several inadequacies in the system of information related to them. Simple, straight-forward, and requiring minimal of recording, systems of accounting and cost and management accounting could reflect by bringing to book the multifarious transactions that take place and the status of their operations, judged on the basis of information based on the least guesswork or estimates. Though government, banks and other institutions extending financial and other assistance to the sector insist on authenticated statements of accounts, these are essentially temporary exercises, done for specific purposes and not meeting the requirements of the small entrepreneurs themselves or providing the information needs of the administrative agencies concerned with the improvement of this sector.

If one adds the village industries and cottage industries to the small scale sector, the picture afforded is further complicated in view of the typicalities of the village industries sector and the cottage industries sector. For purposes of national income, year to year estimates are made but the margin of error in such estimation remains unacceptably high. Elements of accountancy education imparted to entrepreneurs could have taken care of at least the need for primary recording of different transactions. The difficulties referred to earlier with respect to village industries and cottage industries are spelt by their widely scattered location, varied operations and part-time occupation of the people engaged in these pursuits requiring imputation of values for the hours of effort put in, remuneration at shadow rates, estimation of capital cost of implements and machinery used and depreciation, etc., to be charged. In the absence of accounting information underlining economies of scale and economics of choice of techniques of production and distribution, the adoption of the most appropriate technology has remained a far cry. A particular difficulty in this respect is the fact that professional services are too costly for the individual entrepreneurs in the sector and as yet the idea of combination consultancy or combination management is rather foreign to this country, though in a small way governments of the Centre and the states have introduced some elements of scientificity by establishing industrial estates in different areas of the country and encouraging and sponsoring the growth of ancillaries related to medium and large scale units, both in the public and private sectors. Their impact on the totality of the sector is yet insignificant.

A reference in the context of the service sector is also invited to the variety of services rendered which are clubbed together for purposes of national accounts. As shown in the chart, the services sector has accommodated different types of services like municipal services, governmental administration, state electricity boards concerned with production and distribution of electricity including thermal, hydel and diesel generation, banking embracing central banking, commercial banking in the nationalized sector and financial institutions, insurance inclusive of both life insurance and general insurance and last but not least, transport and communications covering road transport, ocean transport, railways, air transport and post and telegraph services. Disaggregation of the service sector has been called for because of the peculiarities of each variety of operation included in the sector and the institutional framework that exists in the country for looking after these services. Incidentally, in the service sector, the variety of forms adopted by the institutions operating has also underlined discrete accounting approaches to investment, output, revenue and returns. There are government departments, departmental undertakings, public corporations and government companies as also non-government companies which are operating in this sector. The accounting systems pursued by them have responded, therefore, partly to the governmental system of accounting, partly to the accounting pattern envisaged in the respective enactments behind the public corporations and also partly to the system of accounts required under the Companies Act, 1956. In general, the accounting system pursued by these institutions has been traditional, receipts and payments or income and expenditure accounting leading to finding of profit at the year-end rather than decisional accounting or efficiency accounting apart from accountability accounting. As pointed out earlier, in different segments within the sector, sophisticated systems have also been in vogue such as those followed by the State Bank of India, the Indian Railways, Air India and Indian Airlines. In general, however, traditional accounting systems have ruled the scene.

In the next section, we are concered with accountancy education as imparted by different institutions at different levels, referring in the process to the relevant provisions in the concerned legislations and the innovations that they have sought to initiate. Specifically, we deal with the universities and academic education in accounting including both regular courses at postgraduate levels and research efforts by academic researchers in the accounting field. We deal with the accounting professions covering the Institute of Chartered Accountants of India, the Institute of Cost and Works Accountants of India and the Institute of Company Secretaries of India, the three statutory bodies in this country concerned with accountancy education at the professional level. In addition, we also deal with some other institutions, established recently for dealing with management functions in specific areas like Institute of Port Management, Institute for Financial Management and Research, Management Development Institute and others. Research efforts organized by the Institutes of Management at Ahmedabad, Calcutta and Bangalore are also referred to at appropriate places for their relevance to both formal education in accountancy and research in accounting.

3. Universities, Professions and Other Bodies

It is necessary to distinguish at the outset the nature of stress and significance attached to education for accountancy by universities, on the one hand, and professional and other bodies, on the other. While advancement of learning is an

417

avowed motto of university education, proficiency in current application of the concepts, techniques and methods is aimed at by the professions, in both cases the rationale of techniques, methods and practices as also the conceptual background behind them are underscored. However, even in this context, one may stress the hierarchical pattern of university education in accountancy, being a subject taught at the levels of Higher Secondary courses (commerce stream), B.Com level and M.Com level as also in MBA courses run by several universities now. The character of stress given in accountancy education in commerce and management courses admits of some difference. In the commerce stream, the basic objective is to impart enough ground for taking up different jobs after passing the Higher Secondary Examination.

Accountancy at the Higher Secondary level essentially involves an exposure to the fundamentals of bookkeeping and maintenance of accounts, effecting accounting adjustments, preparation of final accounts and understanding the implications of different terms used in accounts. At the B.Com level, the stress forks into two directions. One, to prepare candidates for taking up jobs in industry, commerce and government. Though the modicum of knowledge imparted at this level is higher than that at the Higher Secondary level, the stress continues to be on the mechanics of bookkeeping and accountancy appropriate for different types of organizations, including government. Two, accountancy education at B.Com level is considered preparatory to advanced level accounting courses in M.Com where specialization is permitted in several universities. Incidentally, in B.Com Honours course in different universities, accountancy is included as a stream. In both Honours courses at the B.Com level and M.Com level, accountancy is taught with reference to concepts and theories of accounting, accounting practices in different types of organizations and relevant provisions in the concerned legislations and Rules and Regulations made thereunder. Apart from financial accounting, honours and postgraduate courses include subjects like cost accounting, management accounting, auditing and taxation.

In the management courses like MBA, DBM and MBM (given different nomeclature in different universities) and the postgraduate degree courses run by the Institutes of Management, accountancy is taught essentially as a tool subject, seeking to strengthen the hands of managers in taking better decisions on the basis of a sound and cognizable information system provided in the accounts. Knowledge in accountancy in management courses is sought to strengthen the courses on financial management with which managers are more directly concerned for understanding the decisioning phenomena and their financial implications. Thus it is not so much at the levels of B.Com or management courses that one seeks high level expertise in accountancy education. By the objectives behind these courses, theoretical grounding and conceptual understanding are designed to be imparted at the M.Com level. As stressed by the Special Committee for Commerce Education (under the Chairmanship of Dr. V.K.R.V. Rao), university education in accountancy seeks to provide a high level preparatory ground for branching into further specialization in specific areas through research or to prepare candidates for entering the accountancy professions like The Institute of Chartered Accountants of India, The Institute of Cost and Works Accountants of India and The Institute of Company Secretaries of India.

In the postgraduate commerce departments of various Indian universities, high level research works have been successfully pursued. The levels have been high and generally accorded international recognition, partly as a result of the mechanism adopted for university research works leading to doctoral degrees and partly due to the acclaim given to different published works. Interestingly, almost all the items that appear on the balance sheet have been subjected to intensive focus for research. The conceptual studies in accountancy have often been based on selected case studies and analysis. There have been quite a few theoretical studies also by accounting scholars belonging both to the teaching professions and to industry. The logic behind different accounting theories has been stressed by researchers often contesting current ideas and seeking to establish new ones. Thus, one may recount such academic research efforts as have been pursued in different universities and institutes of management as contributing substantially to the core of accounting knowledge in India.

Research effort in the accounting and financial management field came under focus in Research Surveys organized by the Indian Council of Social Science Research, New Delhi. Incidentally, accounting and management accounting research during the last three decades formed the subject matter of a separate study which embraced the period from 1950 to early 1970s and covered the entire area of accounting and management accounting as reflected in books and papers published in different learned and professional journals and periodicals. In addition, the ICSSR also organized Research Surveys in other areas like public administration, economics, management, sociology, demography, econometrics and geography. In public administration, management and economics, accounting researches covering the fields of public administration, public enterprises, enterprise financial policy and other areas were included. Thus, one gets a fairly detailed account of accounting research in India during the period covered by these surveys. These surveys are intended not only to enumerate the areas where research work has already been done but also to pinpoint issues and problems that call for further research effort. There are, however, several significant accounting research studies that have appeared during the last five years from different universities and institutes overtly seeking to bridge the gap noticed in the Research Surveys. It is generally observed that since the publication of the Research Surveys in different intellectual disciplines under the aegis of the Indian Council of Social Science Research, the quality of bibliographical and annotational work in different accounting areas has vastly improved.

There are different gaps in academic accounting research that have been noticed over time. While the lion's share of limelight has gone to the corporate sector and covering both public and private sector enterprises, there exists in the country a large number of non-corporate enterprises belonging to different scales of operations which have offered a kind of dark continent, partly because of the difficulties inherent in trekking such a wide untrodden field of operations and partly because of the high costs involved in getting regular and systematic information subscribing to an acceptable standard of reliability. A recent census of the small scale sector covering the country as a whole has revealed wide gaps in the context of regular supply of organized financial information regarding these units, cost effectiveness of promotional measures and cost benefit aspects of massive investments that have gone into this sector. From time to time, information, including investment, employment, production and input information, has been thrown up from surveys conducted in different areas under the aegis of the Research Programmes Committee of the Planning Commission. Revealing pointers were brought out in many of these surveys but in the absence of regular and systematic accounts keeping in the sector, such information gets easily dated.

The second gap also noticed widely relates to different policies pursued by such enterprises. Being essentially operated by one man or a small group of men, the rule of thumb has dominated the scene all along the line. Entrepreneurs have been expected to dance attendance to different needs, often calling for a high degree of techno-behavioural skills. While in their own areas of expertise, mostly production technology, they may have given a good account, on the deployment of funds and on measuring profitability a great deal remains to be desired. Last but not the least, application of different accounting and management accounting techniques and the efficacy of individual techniques require thorough study with reference to the rationale behind these techniques, cost of their application and the benefits derivable therefrom with reference to throwing up new knowledge, new interpretation of existing knowledge and extension of these techniques to somewhat new areas. It is believed that a great deal of improvement could be effected on the basis of research studies in these areas. On the other hand, several accounting techniques discussed in almost all textbooks have rather questionable relevance in developing countries like India and their cost effectiveness remains in doubt. This doubt occurs also when there exists more than one technique for dealing with the same problem, often resulting in diametrically opposite conclusions. Academic research in these areas could have straightened the application of these techniques sizing up their costs and benefits and pinpointing issues that should be considered for total or partial application or with reference to the typical assumptions behind them.

In the context of academic education in accounting at the postgraduate and specialized levels, it has become urgent to make greater use of research findings in these areas not only on the basis of the empirical situation in this country but also in other countries, so that techniques and practices included in academic curriculum remain subject to continuing scrutiny and searching analysis. In this sphere, great scope exists in interchange of accounting scholars specializing in different accounting areas, both within the country and abroad. Education in research methodology, analysis of accounting details and interpretation of data thrown up by accounting analysis for purposes of policy require focusing a great deal more than before. Exchange of ideas and empirical information can initiate attempts in different countries of the world to try with different techniques and

to perfect them in different conditions encountered taking into view the typicalities of each country, especially the legal framework. A point worthy of mention
at this stage is the fact that several well reputed academic scholars in the accounting field are also professionally qualified accountants or cost and management accountants, often having membership of all the three professional accounting bodies in India. There are, however, several well reputed scholars in the
accounting field who have done high level accounting research and who continue
to pursue their research efforts in different accounting areas, both conceptual
and empirical, but who do not have professional qualifications. Several of them
are qualified in different academic disciplines and they have sought to integrate
ideas expounded in various intellectual disciplines into a common framework of
accounting analysis. Thus, there are well reputed behavioural scientists,
engineers, economists and mathematicians as well as operations researchers
who have done work with different problems covered by accounting and cost and
management accounting.

Going on the basis of selectivity, the individual heads of assets and liabilities
that appear in company balance sheets and several items appearing in the profit
and loss account have attracted attention of scholars. In this context, mention
may be made of share capital becoming the subject of searching scrutiny by
accounting scholars with reference to valuation of shares, cost of equity capital,
preference shares and company finance, bonus shares and company finance,
internal finance and profit appropriation policies, capital reserves and their
purposiveness, sundry creditors and short term debt policy, institutional finance
and bank overdrafts for financing requirements of short term funds by different
types of organizations. During the last three decades, a good number of studies
have appeared bearing on each of these aspects and going into both theory and
practice in the legal framework of corporate and non-corporate functioning.
Several of these studies have been widely acclaimed as of high order. On the other
hand, and keeping to the same trend, almost every item that appears on the assets
side of the balance sheet has been dealt with by academic researchers, both con-
ceptually and empirically. Thus, fixed assets and capital formation, depreciation, working capital and its management, current assets, corporate liquidity,
carriage of stock of raw materials, finished goods and work in progress, sundry
debtors and corporate credit management, deferred revenue expenditure and
its theoretical and practical implications have been dealt with in scholarly
studies on each of these topics. In dealing with concepts and conceptual formu-
lations, Indian accounting scholars have generally given an account of the state-
of-the-art, typicalities of the Indian situation, distinctions noticed in public and
private sector enterprises, varying patterns of corporate and non-corporate
financial practices and the efficacy of resource deployment by corporate and
non-corporate bodies belonging to both public and private sectors. Assessment
of enterprise efficiency, criteria for such assessment and the interpretation of
results through application of different criteria have also been taken up by
several research scholars in the accounting field.

Interestingly, several financial institutions have started presenting performance information of their assisted companies and several of them have started presenting social cost-benefit analysis, information on value-added and investment-employment relationships in their assisted units. Thus, the annual reports and performance of portfolio companies, the information about which is presented by the ICICI Limited as separate exercises, have provided impetus to academic accounting researchers in two ways. First, organized information on details of performance is available now as a time series, admitting of application of different quantitative techniques for further analysis. Secondly, as finished products they offer highlights of performance of assisted units which are themselves of a high order, explaining as they do the methodology for computation of different types of information, ratios and other modes of interrelationships. The annual reports of the financial institutions present exhaustive details on the basis of which one can go in for different types of academic exercises, both accounting and economics. Abstract analyses of accounting information have also been attempted by several academic researchers in accounting on the basis of time series data presented by the Reserve Bank of India in different issues of its monthly bulletin. Trend studies on different accounting issues and conscious establishment of relationship of accounting information to the national economy have been attempted by scholars belonging to different intellectual disciplines notably statistics, accounting and management. Specific areas of enterprise functioning have also attracted some notice though not on a wide scale. One may mention here of different items of expenditure such as travelling, audit fees and advertisement with reference to their cost relevance and cost effectiveness. In general, for such studies information made available by the Reserve Bank of India in its monthly bulletin has been used on a large scale, while information not generally presented in the annual accounts and having relevance to day to day function has also been subject to some academic inquiry. Topics like monthly cash flow analysis and working capital cycle may be mentioned in this respect.

The subjects on which scholarly attention appears focused at present relate to inflation accounting, management of corporate liquidity, depreciation, valuation of stock and enterprise sickness and its predictability in the prevailing conditions in the country. Doctoral works on inflation accounting have been either already admitted or are being pursued by scholars in several Indian universities with reference both to the methodology of adjustments and the implications from the points of view of maintenance of capital, erosion of profitability, methodology of building up price index series and the emerging patterns of inflation adjustments in the light of the experience of the United States, the UK and Australia. Indeed, the progress from Current Power Accounting to Current Cost Accounting and Constantly Contemporary Accounting (CoCoA) has provided interesting sidelights to the inflation accounting process. On the other hand, the diagnostic problem in industrial sickness and its predictability have been under focus in several scholarly studies authored by accounting experts in the light of the prevalent regulatory framework, responsive policy changes and remedial measures especially with reference to their cost to the exchequer, on the one hand, and prevention and cure of sickness, on the other. Curiously, an accounting explanation to the phenomenon of sickness has been sought to be provided by scholars through such techniques as ratio analysis and interfirm comparison without consciously seeking to line up the findings from accounting analysis with the regulatory policy frame prescribed by the government and the Reserve Bank of India. Predictability of such sickness has, however, been a worthwhile attempt.

The professional accounting bodies in India, as mentioned previously, have had an integrated, multi-pronged and composite approach involving theories and concepts in the accounting and cost and management accounting field, methods and techniques evolved and sharpened in different situations both within the country and abroad and practical application of these theories, concepts, methods and techniques have occupied the prime of place. Scale variations in productive activities even in the same lines, divergence of contents and character of such activities in different industries and sizing up of these variations for presenting a unified scheme of education and training have engaged the attention of The Institute of Chartered Accountants of India, The Institute of Cost and Works Accountants of India and The Institute of Company Secretaries of India in their respective fields. A profession by definition underscores the rendering of specialized services to society. Building up such specialization has been one of the major aspects of the training programmes of these professional bodies in their respective areas seeking to equip the entrants to the respective professions with a thorough grounding of economics, both theoretical aspects and Indian economic problems, economic laws, management, accountancy, taxation, cost and management accountancy, quantitative techniques, industrial relations, marketing, production management and such other topics of relevance to the practising accountant, cost accountant or company secretary as also to those in the teaching profession in different capacities with respect to both theories in these areas and their practical application.

Before dealing with the individual aspects of research and training programmes conducted by these institutes, it is necessary to underline that in India it has been strongly believed that there exists enough scope for the three professional accounting bodies to prove their mettle in their respective areas while, at the same time, more than nodding acquaintance in each other's subjects has also been desired, so that there occurs in a capsule form common subjects in the syllabi of all the professional accounting bodies in the country. The course contents and syllabi designed by these institutes have sought to accommodate a rather peculiar phenomenon not generally encountered in universities. The entrants to the accounting professions in India guided and regulated by all these three bodies have come from different intellectual disciplines and have different educational backgrounds and levels of attainment. The course content and syllabi have sought to stress the operational requirements of professionals in the job and whatever the background, the education has been sought to be complete so that once they have passed the final examination, candidates are expected to have a standard of knowledge and proficiency in the subject areas covered in the syllabi. Academic homogeneity has not been expected and history has borne out that members belonging to different intellectual disciplines such as history, languages, philosophy, physics, chemistry, mathematics, engineering and technology, commerce, economics and operations research have been widely acclaimed as highly proficient accountants or cost and management accountants both in industry and business and government and the teaching professions. A kind of heterogeneity of membership has been marked in the cases of all the professional accounting bodies in the country, which has a good deal of plus and some minus points.

Each institute has its core subjects like accountancy, taxation and auditing in the case of The Institute of Chartered Accountants of India, cost accounting in the case of The Institute of Cost and Works Accountants of India and company law and procedures in the case of The Institute of Company Secretaries of India. Barring these core subjects, there are several subject areas where different degrees of importance have been attached by these institutes depending on the facility of functioning as accountant, as cost and management accountant or as company secretary. A modicum of knowledge has been sought to be imparted in economics, management and the law providing the internal and external framework in which an organization functions. In designing these courses, careful consideration has been generally given towards freeing them from duplication of university courses. The subject areas, gradation of subjects into core and non-core areas and greater emphasis on practical application have marked these courses from the university courses at the levels of B.Com and M.Com. These institutes generally give exemption from individual papers to high grade university graduates in respective areas of specialization. No exemption is, however, allowed in the core subjects. There is also an effective coordiantion being built up as between the three professional institutes. While some progress has already been achieved in the context of grant of reciprocal exemption in different subjects other than core subjects, it is expected that better rapport will be established in the future and steps in this direction have already been initiated.

The courses designed by the three institutes during the last several years have undergone continual revisions essentially from two points of view. First, emergence of new techniques and progress in different related fields have been fast. It was considered necessary to accommodate them in the courses of study pursued by these institutes. Secondly, and more significantly, the courses designed by these institutes had to respond to the requirements of rapid economic development initiated in the country under the Five Year Plans. Developments in the areas of industry, business and government as also in banking, insurance and other services have been massive. Accounting and cost and management accounting techniques call for increasing application to contain the forces generated by economic development at a fast pace, massive investments going into different economic sectors of the country and the need for increasing surveillance with particular reference to efficient deployment of the limited resources available in the country. High cost of gestation, wastes of material, human and financial resources, the desperate need for import substitution and improvement of the socioeconomic conditions of people call for utmost care and skill in the productive sphere. The accounting professions are committed to help the country achieve its objectives with the minimum cost and optimum returns in relation to resource inputs. These requirements of the nation had to be reflected in the courses of study in the first place and then research and continuing education for members. Thus, two-way requirements have been sought to be met, implying that the courses of study had to be under scrutiny all the time for such sensitization as necessary.

A recent study of the prevalent conditions of accounting education conducted by The Institute of Chartered Accountants of India underscored different requirements of the accounting profession in the light of which the courses of study have been sought to be made more responsive. A similar study is in progress in The Institute of Cost and Works Accountants of India also and it is hoped that before long, effective pointers will be raised by the members calling for a similar comprehensive change in the course of study, outlook of the profession and orientation of members towards the tasks that they are expected to fulfill. In the meantime, the Sachar Panel on Company Law recommended drastic changes in the law to make it more responsive to the requirements of the country spelling challenges before the professions of accounting, cost and management accounting and company secretaryship. The contents of disclosure in company accounts, the reflection of physical and financial aspects of company performance and the need for greater surveillance over deployment of corporate resources will cause massive changes in professional outlook. It is hoped that the bill presented in parliament some time back will become law soon. In anticipation of these changes, the professional accounting bodies in this country have already taken such preparatory measures as necessary.

Naturally, as envisaged in the Sachar Panel Report, a great deal more attention will be given in the future to social responsibility reporting, social responsibility understood in terms of different cognizable criteria laid down in the report. In this respect, there are some distinct points of departure from the connotation of social responsibility. In a labour surplus, developing country like India, a greater dose of social service would imply not only servicing the public immediately concerned with corporate bodies, as employees, consumers, and creditors but also others. A part of the responsibility now undertaken by government will also in the near future devolve on corporate bodies. In the circumstances, massive changes are in the offing even in regard to understanding social responsibility. Stress has already been given in the courses designed by the professional accounting bodies to give vent to this new requirement of corporate functioning. Protective measures for consumers, creditors and employees are also expected to be a lot more comprehensive than ever before. In the aforesaid circumstances, not only the students seeking to enter the professions would be given increasing stresses on these aspects but also the existing members would be subjected to this new orientation through a series of continuing education programmes under active consideration of these bodies.

Here one may perhaps mention that the excessive preoccupation with the maintenance of ecology and prevention of environmental pollution as experienced in the West is subject to a thorough reexamination. Indeed, in India as one gathers from not only the Sachar Panel Report and governmental pronouncements in Parliament and public, as also opening up of a discrete department on environmental issues under the Union Government, the social responsibility orientation will have a much more comprehensive span of focus, the light being on whether in a labour surplus economy like India emphases given in different context on various labour saving devices should be repeated, whether the selection of products for manufacture can be divorced from the immediate requirements of the people in urban and rural areas and whether complete freedom should be given to use scarce raw materials for products of little consequence. These are apart from the fact that costs in the context of social costs and benefits in the context of social benefits would require a lot more down-to-earth consideration of details than given so far. Over-emphases with the precincts of individual enterprises even in regard to calculations of social cost-benefits, as suggested by Little-Mirrlees techniques, have already attracted some attention as to whether one should go in for assessment of second-tier performance that is the cost benefit analysis of those given assistance in various forms, either as consumers or as users as inputs for further production. Serious attention of the professional accounting bodies in India has been centred on these burning issues and several research projects undertaken by these institutes reflect on finding out ways and means to do something in this regard, to help government adopt policies most appropriate for the country. In highlighting these issues, the Institutes of Chartered Accountants in India, Cost and Works Accountants of India and Company Secretaries of India have every year chosen as their themes one subject or another of immediate national concern either in response to policy measures already adopted or in anticipation thereof as also in underlining the importance of issues on which policy measures are immediately called for. Thus, whether it is on taxation, both direct and indirect, or on cost audit or on price fixation or on social responsibilities, professional attention has been directed to unfolding various issues on which policy measures already adopted have been considered either inadequate or not as much responsive as desirable. Appropriately, government itself has either sought the views of these professional bodies on different issues of national importance or has initiated changes in such policy measures as suggested or recommended by these bodies. Incidentally, it may also be mentioned that during the mid-sixties, there was a government appointed Management Adviser to the Committee on Plan Projects, National Planning Commission, who was a qualified chartered accountant of considerable standing.

A point of distinction that India can legitimately claim relates, first of all, to the statutory recognition given to the Institute of Cost and Works Accountants of India in 1959 and then inclusion of provisions in the Companies Act relating to maintenance of cost records in manners appropriate for different industries and audit thereof according as directed by Government in the Department of Company Affairs. Twenty-eight industries have been brought under the purview of maintenance of cost records and audit of cost accounts. In this respect, government has laid down formats for these industries according to which the particulars of operations and costs are required to be certified by qualified cost accountants. The uniqueness of cost audit and maintenance of cost records according as desired by the government is underscored by the fact that in a developing economy like India resource scarcity has acquired acute proportions and the most judicious deployment of scarce resources as also application of cost saving devices, techniques and approaches have been called for. The real impact of this approach has been essentially twofold. Maintenance of cost records in a uniform manner helps industries to straighten all matters of importance that show overt and covert tendencies to go out of gear from time to time. Extent of capacity utilization, usage of materials, utilization of labour and overheads facilities and such other questions that impinge on operational efficienty and costs are subject to better surveillance once information on all this is available in a standardized form and under common heads of classification from year to year as also from unit to unit.

Secondly, government itself is assisted in no uncertain manner in knowing and judging the cost trends in different industries and the reasons for any untoward trend, so that either industry correctives or unit correctives could be initiated. In the Department of Company Affairs, continuing examination of cost audit reports helps exercise of better executive control, particularly in relation to those matters where policy changes are called for. The experience with respect to both maintenance of cost records and cost audit extends over a decade now and the very fact that both industry coverage and unit coverage for maintenance of cost records and audit of cost accounts have been extended are proof enough that cost audit has had a beneficial impact. Appropriately, cost audit reports as certified by cost auditors have not been made public and confidence of industries and enterprises is preserved. Indeed, there are several types of information which when disclosed in detail may harm the economics of operations of these enterprises and the logic of government decision in this behalf suggests itself. Not that the type of information contained in a cost audit report is entirely beyond the public eye. Extracts of cost audit reports have been given extensively by the Comptroller and Auditor General of India in several audit reports related to government companies under the control of the Centre and the States whose products have been subjected to these provisions. One particular area where cost audit reports have been highly relevant relates to price fixation by the government of different commodities from time to time. Ad hoc inquiries that ruled the scene earlier suffered from different counts of which ad hoc-ism itself was a primary one.

Behind the steps so far taken by the government have been the relentless persuasions of the doyens of the cost and management accounting profession in the country and on different issues concerning cost audit and its expanse, arguments and clarifications have been given by the senior members of the Institute of Cost and Works Accountants of India helping government to decide on these issues in an appropriate manner. On the other hand, even at the level of the Company Law Board or, for that matter, in the Bureau of Industrial Costs and Prices as also in the office of the Comptroller and Auditor General of India, qualified cost accountants have been there, so that all these steps taken by the government have been distinctly knowledgeable and have had the necessary stamp of professional expertise. The orientation of the cost and management accounting profession in the country and the courses of studies pursued have been responsive to the growing needs in this direction.

During the last decade, considerable stress has been given by the Institute of Cost and Works Accountants of India on research. The Directorate of Research of the institute, established in 1969, has been able to create some enthusiasm in the profession regarding research activities. While there are several members of the profession in the teaching faculties of universities and Institutes of Management in different parts of the country, having shown proficiency in research on different aspects concerned with the profession, the support extended by such members to professional research organized by the institute has been on the increase in recent years. The Research and Publications Committee of the institute has, in the meantime, delineated the research policies and guidelines for benefit of members of the institute. The committee considered different kinds of studies to be pursued by the institute either in the Research Directorate or by outside members. In this respect, the categories of studies emphasized by the committee are as follows:

(a) (i) Conceptual research - seeking to contribute to the development of new concepts, and
   (ii) those facilitating the modification or sharpening of existing concepts and practices.

(b) In exceptional cases the topics which might, however, require more detailed treatment and naturally such studies would imply larger volume could be undertaken and the Research and Publications Committee may specifically authorize them after examining such scope and needs in depth before they are taken up.

(c) (i) Emphasis should be that the studies should be interesting and be readable and easily understandable.
   (ii) Hard to understand or too technical jargons and verbosity should be avoided and brevity, simplicity and directness should be reflected in the prepared materia.

(d) When any of the research projects should include details, strong empirical content to highlight data should be related to Indian background and practices. However, sparingly, data evolved as a product of desk research or creative thinking, dealing with problems of general relevance, shall also be used in their thematic content to embellish or to enhance the directness of the thought process and its cogency to the topical coverage.

(e) Attention should be given on top priority, regading selection of projects, to meet the specific needs of members in practice for sorting out problems faced by them and for affording guidelines which they could follow with benefit. Such problems as are presently faced relate to provisions in the Company Law and the rules made thereunder with reference to maintenance of cost records and audit of cost accounts. In addition, problems of cost and management consultancy should also be given due importance in selecting research projects.

So far the institute has published twelve research studies. In these studies, researchers have sought to stress the state-of-the-art in respective areas, concepts and techniques and their application in handling different types of problems encountered in industry, business and government. While conceptual discussions in these studies have been detailed pinpointing different issues on which the debate continues, the main emphasis has been put on application and empirical analysis. Several of these studies have been acclaimed both in the country and abroad. In the selection of research projects both by the Directorate of Research and by outside members under the sponsorship of the institute, consideration has been given on the relevance of the individual topics, the extension of knowledge that they seek to effect and the application of new techniques that they are designed to attempt, both in existing areas and in new areas. Thus, the research studies of the institute have had the characteristics of both theoretical exposition and practical application in the typicalities of a growing economy like India. The institute has been given two assignments by the Indian Council of Social Science Research, New Delhi, of which one relates to a Research Survey in Public Enterprises which has since been completed and published by the ICSSR. The other project relating to Assessment of Comparative Efficiency in Fertilizer Industry in India, 1961–62 to 1970–71 is under finalization. The list of research projects since completed by the Institutes of Chartered Accountants of India and Cost and Works Accountants of India is appended for reference.

With three well established institutes concerned with accounting, cost and management accounting and company secretaryship, all accorded statutory recognition, India is singularly placed in the developing world to take the lead in initiating links with other countries of the developing world as also of the developed world for an effective exchange of ideas, establishment of forums for research and education and training intended for new entrants as also for professionals in different lines, exchange of scholars, pursuance of common inter-country research projects, organization of seminars and conferences and streamlining concepts and practices in these areas. It is, therefore, in the fitness of things that Professor Adolf Enthoven in a recent paper published in the *Management Accounting* (September, 1980) has underlined the need for an International Management Accounting Body for serving as a coordinating agency and as an international clearinghouse of expertise, information and ideas. The institute, as envisaged, may be linked with the International Federation of Accountants (I.F.A.C.).

RESEARCH PUBLICATIONS OF
THE INSTITUTE OF CHARTERED ACCOUNTANTS OF INDIA

1. Statement on Auditing Practices
2. Price Fixation in Indian Industries
3. Statement on the Treatment of Retirement Gratuity in Accounts
4. A Study on Share Valuation
5. S. Vaidyanathan Aiyar Memorial Lectures by Professor Louis Goldberg
6. Study on Expenditure during Construction Period

7. History of Accountancy Profession in India
8. Integrated System of Cost and Financial Accounts
9. Organization of a Chartered Accountant's Office
10. Payment of Bonus Act
11. Audit of Banks
12. Management Control System
13. Statement on the Amendments to Schedule VI to the Companies Act, 1956
14. Guidance Note on Section 293A of the Companies Act
15. Statement on Accounting for Foreign Currency Translation
16. Compendium of Notes
17. Internal Control Questionnaire
18. Guidance Note on Additional Emoluments Compulsory Deposit Scheme, 1974
19. Monograph on Compulsory Maintenance of Accounts
20. Guidance Note on Coordination between the Internal Auditors
21. Statement on Payments of Auditors for other Services
22. Guide to Cost Audit
23. Statement on the Manufacturing and Other Companies (Auditor's Report) Order, 1975
24. Compendium of Opinions
25. Technical Guide to Audit of Sugar Industries
26. Technical Guide to Cost Audit of Cement Factories
27. Guidance Note on Deferred Payments
28. Guidance Note on Accounting Treatment of Excise Duty
29. Training Guide for Article Trainees
30. Guide to Tax Audit

RESEARCH PUBLICATIONS OF
THE INSTITUTE OF COST AND WORKS ACCOUNTANTS OF INDIA

1. Decisional Phenomena and the Management Accountant
2. The Break-Even Concept and its Practical Dimensions
3. Financing Asset Replacement
4. Inflation Accounting as a Tool to Fight Inflation
5. Inflation Accounting: Tools and Techniques
6. Management Accounting Problems in Small Scale Industries
7. Glossary of Management Accounting Terms
8. Corporate Capital Structure and Cost of Capital
9. Cost and Quality Control
10. Monthly Financial Reports for Operating Managers
11. Cost Accounting in Commercial Banking Industry
12. Farm Management Accounting and Control

CHART I

ACCOUNTANCY EDUCATION

National Accounting
Social Accounting

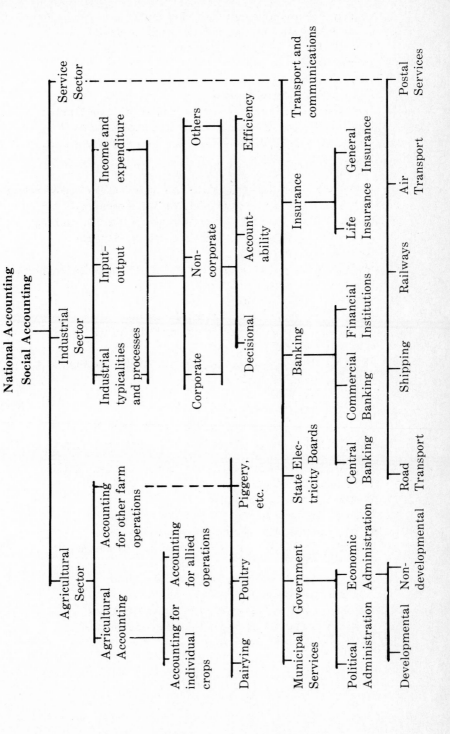

REFERENCES

American Accounting Association. *Accounting Education and the Third World.* Committee on International Accounting Operations and Education, 1976–1978. Sarasota, Florida, 1978.

American Accounting Association. *The Accounting Review.* Sarasota, Florida.

American Institute of Certified Public Accountants. *Horizons for a Profession.* A.I.C.P.A., New York, 1967.

A.I.C.P.A. *The Journal of Accountancy.* New York.

Accounting Standards Steering Committee. *The Corporate Report.* London, 1975.

Bedford, Norton M. *The Role of Accounting in Economic Development.* Society for International Development, Washington, D.C., 1976.

Choi, F. *The International Journal of Accounting.* University of Illinois–Urbana, Vol. 15-1.

Diamond, Wm. *Development Banks.* Baltimore: Johns Hopkins Press, 1957.

Diamond, W. *Development Finance Companies.* Baltimore: Johns Hopkins Press, 1968.

Enthoven, A. J. H. *An Evaluation of Accounting Systems, Developments and Requirements in Asia.* Ford Foundation, New York, 1975.

Enthoven, A. J. H. *An Evaluation of Accounting Systems, Developments, and Requirements in Africa.* Ford Foundation, New York, 1975.

Enthoven, Adolf J. H. *Accountancy and Economic Development Policy.* New York, Amsterdam: North-Holland/American Elsevier, 1973, 1978.

Enthoven, Adolf J. H. *Accountancy Systems in Third World Countries.* New York, Amsterdam: North-Holland/American Elsevier, 1977, 1979.

G.A.O. Report to the Congress of the U.S. *Training and Related Efforts Needed to Improve Financial Management in the Third World.* September, 1979.

Hicks, J. R. *The Social Framework.* London: Oxford Univ. Press, 1942.

Institute of Chartered Accountants of India. *Report of the Review Committee for Accounting Education.* Delhi, June, 1979.

North–South: A Programme for Survival. MIT Press, Cambridge, Mass., 1980.

Perridon, Louis. *Development and State of Conventional Accounting Education Systems.* Fourth International Congress of Accounting Educators, Berlin, 1977.

Tinbergen, J. *Development Planning.* New York: McGraw-Hill, 1967.

Tinbergen, J. *Reshaping the International Order.* A Report to the Club of Rome. Dutter, New York, 1976.

United Nations. *Government Accounting in Economic Development Management.* U.N., New York, 1977.

ABBREVIATIONS

AAA	American Accounting Association
AFA	ASEAN Federation of Accountants
AGA	Association of Government Accountants (US)
AICPA	American Institute of Certified Public Accountants
AID	Agency for International Development (US)
ASEAN	Association of South East Asian Nations
ASOSAI	Asian Organization of Supreme Audit Institutions
CA	Chartered Accountant
CAPA	Confederation of Asian and Pacific Accountants
CIA	Certified Internal Auditor (US)
CIAD	Center for International Accounting Development (University of Texas at Dallas)
CMA	Certified Management Accountant (US)
CPA	Certified Public Accounting (US)
CTC	Center on Transnational Corporations (UN)
DB	Development Banks
Drs.	Doctorandus
EAA	European Accounting Association
ECOSOC	Economic and Social Council (UN)
EDP	Electronic Data Processing
EEC	European Economic Community
GAO	General Accounting Office
GATT	General Agreement on Tariffs and Trade
IAA/IAAC	Inter-American Accounting Association
IAAD	International Association for Accounting Development
IASC	International Accounting Standards Committee
IBRD	International Bank for Reconstruction and Development (also known as the World Bank)
IDA	International Development Association (World Bank)
IFAC	International Federation of Accountants

IIA	Institute of Internal Auditors
ILACIF	Latin American Institute of Auditing Sciences
ILO	International Labor Organization/Office
IMF	International Monetary Fund
INTOSAI	International Organization of Supreme Audit Institutions
MBA	Master of Business Administration
M.Com.	Master of Commerce
MNE	Multinational Enterprise
MS	Master of Science
NAA	National Association of Accountants
NIVRA	Netherlands Institute of Registered Accountants
Ph.D.	Doctor of Philosophy
RA	Registered Accountant (The Netherlands)
SID	Society for International Development
UEC	Union Europeene des Experts Comptables Economiques et Financiers
UK	United Kingdom
UN	United Nations
UNDP	United Nations Development Program
UNESCO	United Nations Educational, Scientific, and Cultural Organization
UNIDO	United Nations Industrial Development Organization
US	United States of America

INDEX

FOREWORD   Professor Dr. Jan Tinbergen

Chapter I   **Introduction and Outline** 1

PART ONE   AN OVERVIEW OF ACCOUNTING
             AND ECONOMIC DEVELOPMENT

Chapter II   **The Significance of Accounting in Economic Development
             Management**

1. The State of Accounting Development 11
   1.1 Stages of Growth in Accounting Systems 11
   1.2 Classification of Accounting Systems 12
2. The Nature and Function of Accounting in Development 14
   2.1 Enterprise Accounting 15
   2.2 Government Accounting 16
   2.3 Macro (Economic) Accounting 16
   2.4 Auditing 17
3. Accounting as a Parent Framework 19
4. Accounting and Economic Policy 20
   4.1 Economic Planning 20
   4.2 Project Appraisals 20
   4.3 Other Socioeconomic Studies 20
   4.4 Capital Formation 20

Chapter III   **Elements Influencing the Development of Accounting**

1. Socioeconomic Influences 23
2. Professional and Institutional Structures 23
3. Legal and Statutory Requirements 26

Chapter IV   **Accounting Education and International Economic Activities**

1. Accounting in the International Environment 29
2. International Accounting Requirements 30
3. Accounting and the Multinational Enterprise 32
4. International Involvement in Setting Accounting Standards 33
5. Accounting Education and International Operations 34

Chapter V   **Accounting Education in the Development Process**

1. The Economic-Accounting Environment.. 35
2. An Educational Appraisal 35
   2.1 Academic Education Needs 36

2.2 Economic Development Accounting 37

2.3 Accounting Educational Methods.. 38

PART TWO   ACCOUNTING EDUCATION IN
            THIRD WORLD COUNTRIES

Chapter VI   **An Evaluation of Accounting Educational Deficiencies
             and Requirements**

1. A General Appraisal of Conditions and Needs 41

2. An Evaluation of Educational Elements 44

3. Scope for an "International Association" for Accounting Development 47

4. Summary of Regional Observations.. 48

    4.1 Asia and Pacific Region 48

    4.2 Africa and Middle East Region 49

    4.3 Latin America 50

Chapter VII   **The Role of Accounting Education, Training and Research
              in Development**

1. The Types of Accounting Education and Training 51

    1.1 Academic Training.. 51

    1.2 Institutional Training 52

    1.3 Technical Training 53

    1.4 Vocational and Other Training 53

2. Research and Development 54

3. Continuing Educational Needs 54

Chapter VII Annex **The Need for Systems Education in Developing Countries**

1. Statement of the Problem 56

2. Consequences 58

3. Reasons for Accounting Deficiencies 59

4. Recommendation for Systems Training Education 60

Chapter VIII **Accounting Educational Programs for Economic Development**

1. Accounting Education and the Development Process 65

2. The Structure and Process of Accounting Education 67

3. International Accounting Education and Economic Development 72

4. The Accounting Curriculum 77

5. The Internationalization of the Accounting Curriculum 79

6. Accounting Education in The Netherlands 81

7. Some Observations on Professional Education 81

8. The Role of the Profession 84

9. Summary 85

PART THREE A FRAMEWORK FOR ACCOUNTING
             EDUCATIONAL ACTION

Chapter IX **Ways and Means of Enhancing Accountancy Education
           and Training**

1. Mechanisms of Transferring Know-How 89

   1.1 An Overview 89

   1.2 Universities and Other Post-Secondary Institutions 90

   1.3 Professional Institutes 90

   1.4 International Development Organizations 91

   1.5 Development Banks 91

   1.6 Training at Multinational Enterprises 92

   1.7 Other Entities 92

2. Training at and by Means of Developed Countries' Institutions 93

   2.1 Exchange of Faculty, Students and Materials 93

   2.2 Professional Institutions 95

   2.3 Accounting Firms 95

   2.4 Governmental and Private Agencies 95

   2.5 International Development Organizations 95

3. Accountancy Development Centers (Regional and Local) 96

   3.1 A Mechanism for Educational Exchange 96

   3.2 Accounting Research and Development 97

Chapter X **Education for Public Sector Financial Management**

1. A General Appraisal 99

2. Governmental Accounting Training 101

3. A Training Program for Public Sector Accounting 102

Chapter XI **Development Banking and Accounting Development**

1. Some General Considerations 107

2. The Role of Development Banks (D.B's) 108

   2.1 Accounting at Development Banks...................................... 109

   2.2 Accounting of Enterprises Financed by Development Banks 109

   2.3 Feasibility Studies 110

   2.4 The Technical Assistance Function of Development Banks 111

3. A Summary of Development Banking's Impact on Accounting................. 112

Chapter XII **An International Association for Accounting Development**

1. The Structure and Activities of the Association 115

1.1 Orientation 115

1.2 The Aims 115

1.3 Membership 117

1.4 Funding 117

1.5 Accounting Education for Economic Development 118

2. A Potential International Role for the AAA 119

2.1 Types of Programs 119

2.2 Proposed Pilot Project(s) in Third World 121

3. Feedback on the Potential Role of Developed Countries 122

4. "International Accounting Educational Survey" 123

5. Conclusion 124

Chapter XIII **International and Regional Vehicles for Action**

1. Domestic and International Approaches for Action 127

2. The International Federation of Accountants (IFAC) 128

3. The International Accounting Standards Committee (IASC) 130

Chapter XIV **Potential Financial Resources for Implementing Framework**

1. General Proposals 135

1.1 The Internal Resources 135

1.2 External Resources 136

2. Specific Suggestions 136

Chapter XV **Summary and Conclusion**

1. Accounting and Economic Development 137

1.1 The Nature of Accounting 137

1.2 Accounting and Development Activities 137

1.3 Accounting Influences and Practices in Third World Countries 138

1.4 Accounting Infrastructure Improvements 139

1.5 Accounting and the Long-Term Development Process 140

1.6 A Move Towards Meta-Accounting 140

2. Aspects of Accounting Education in Third World Economies 141

2.1 Educational Weaknesses 141

2.2 Educational Improvements 141

2.3 Accounting Education and the Profession 143

2.4 International Development and Accounting Education 143

2.5 Educational Programs for Development 144

3. Country and Regional Evaluations 145

4. A Framework for Action 146

4.1 Ways and Means to Improve Education 146

4.2 Education in the Public Sector 147

4.3 Accounting and Development Banking 148

4.4 International Association for Accounting Development 149

4.5 External Vehicles for Action 150

4.6 Sources for Implementing Framework 151

5. Some Concluding Observations 151

PART FOUR   COUNTRY AND REGIONAL STUDIES

Chapter XVI **Regional Aspects and Developments in the Asian and Pacific Area**

1. Regional Background 155

2. Confederation of Asian and Pacific Accountants (CAPA) 155

3. ASEAN and the ASEAN Federation of Accountants (AFA)................... 158

4. Conclusion 169

Chapter XVII   **Accounting Education in the Developing Island Nations of the South Pacific**

1. Introduction 171

2. Background and General Economic Profile................................ 171

3. Specific Accounting Contexts 173

   3.1 Fiji 173

   3.2 Papua New Guinea 174

   3.3 Tonga 177

   3.4 Solomon Islands 178

   3.5 New Hebrides 179

4. Accounting Population 180

5. Accounting Professional Associations 181

6. Accounting Education 182

7. Summary 185

Chapter XVIII **Accounting Education in the ASEAN Federation of Accountants (A.F.A.)**

1. Introduction 187

2. The Beginning CPA 187

3. The Profession and Its Educational Needs 187

4. Accounting Curriculum 188

   4.1 General Education Courses 188

   4.2 General Business Courses 189

   4.3 Advanced Accounting Courses 189

441

4.4 Administration 191

5. The Qualifying Work Experience 192

6. The CPA Examination 192

   6.1 Accounting Practice and Theory Topics 193

   6.2 Auditing Topics 193

   6.3 Taxation Topics 193

   6.4 Business Law Topics 194

7. Summary 194

Chapter XIX   Accounting Education in Indonesia:
Its Structure and Requirements

1. Introduction 197

2. The Structure of Accountancy Education in Indonesia 197

   2.1 University Training 197

   2.2 Government Accountants Training 198

   2.3 Middle-Level and Semi-Professional Training 199

   2.4 Lower Level Training 199

   2.5 Other Accounting Courses 199

   2.6 Administrative Setup of University Programs 200

   2.7 Enrollments, Outputs and Growth 200

   2.8 Staff and Staff Remuneration 201

   2.9 Curricula and Teaching Materials 202

   2.10 Student Flows 203

3. Accountancy Requirements in Indonesia 204

   3.1 Some General Observations 204

   3.2 Accounting Manpower Inventory and Plan 204

   3.3 Academic, Institutional and Technical Level Training 205

   3.4 Accountancy Development Centers 206

   3.5 Accountancy Coordinating Body 207

4. Summary 208

Chapter XX   Accountancy and Accounting Education in Korea

Part A: Accountancy in Korea

1. Historical and Political Background 211

2. The Development of the Economy and Business Systems 212

3. The Characteristics of Korean Accounting 213

4. Professional Regulatory Bodies 214

5. Accounting Principles and Its Formulation Process 215

6. Professional Accountants in Korea 217

6.1 Economic Development and Professional Accountants 217

6.2 Services of Accountants 217

6.3 Korean Institute of Certified Public Accountants 218

6.4 CPA Examination 219

Part B: Accounting Education in Korea

1. History of Education and the Education System 219

2. History of Accounting and Accounting Education 220

3. Curriculum 223

4. Accounting Teachers 225

5. Textbooks and Teaching Materials 226

Part C: Evaluative Comments 229

Bibliography 231

Chapter XXI   **Accounting Education in Malaysia**

1. Background 233

1.1 Political/Social Factors 233

1.2 Economic Background 234

1.3 Relevance of the Economic Background to Accounting 234

2. Accounting Development 234

3. The Present State of Accounting Education 236

3.1 Qualification of Accounting Instructors 236

3.2 Structure of Accounting Progams and Curriculum 236

3.3 Textbooks 239

3.4 Accounting Research 239

4. Comments 239

Appendix 240

Chapter XXII   **Accounting Education in Pakistan**

1. Country Background 243

2. Accounting Institutions in Pakistan 244

2.1 The Accounting Profession 244

2.2 Local Educational Institutions 246

2.3 Government Involvement in Education 249

2.4 Educational Standards at Entry Point 250

3. The Accountancy Educational Inventory 250

3.1 Qualifications of Accounting Teachers 250

3.2 Instruction Techniques 252

3.3 Structure of Programs and Curricula 253

3.4 Textbooks and Training Materials 256

3.5 Accounting Research and Development 257

3.6 Other Aspects of Relevance 257

4. Evaluation of Inventory 258

4.1 The Problem 258

Conclusion 260

Chapter XXIII **Accounting Education in The Philippines**

1. The Setting 263

1.1 Land and People 263

1.2 Government 263

1.3 Economic Profile 264

1.4 Economic History 264

2. The Accounting Profession 266

2.1 Structure of the Profession 266

2.3 The Educational System 272

3. An Appraisal of Accounting Education 281

3.1 Objectives of Accounting Education 281

3.2 The Accounting Curriculum 282

3.3 Accounting Students 284

3.4 Academic Qualifications of Faculty 285

3.5 Teaching Loads 285

3.6 Faculty Compensation 286

3.7 Faculty Development 287

3.8 Teaching Methods and Techniques 288

3.9 Textbooks and Supplementary Materials 288

3.10 Library Facilities 289

3.11 Research in Business Schools 289

3.12 Performance in the CPA Examinations 290

3.13 Absorption of Graduates in the Labor Market 290

3.14 Accreditation of Educational Institutions 291

4. Summary and Conclusions 291

Chapter XXIV **Accounting Education in Thailand**

1. Educational Background Information 297

1.1 Structure of the Educational System 297

1.2 Administration Organization 297

1.3 Accounting Education 297

1.4 Public Accounting Practices 298

2. Accounting Policies and Programs 298

3. Accounting Curriculum 299

4. Conclusions.. 302

Chapter XXV **Regional Aspects and Developments
            in Africa and the Middle East**

1. Regional Background 305

2. U.K. Oriented East and West Africa 305

3. French Accounting Oriented Africa 306

4. Middle East 307

5. Conclusion 308

Chapter XXVI **Accounting Education in Egypt**

1. Introduction

2. Public Accounting Prior to 1956 309

3. The Emergence of Public Sector Ownership in Egypt 311

4. The Operational and Accounting Structure of the Public Sector 312

    4.1 The "Public Organizations" 312

    4.2 The Accounting Control Boards 312

    4.3 The Central Auditing Agency 312

    4.4 The Need for a Uniform Accounting System 314

5. Accounting Education in Egypt 314

    5.1 Faculty... 314

    5.2 Four-Year Undergraduate Program.................................... 316

    5.3 Graduate Programs 317

    5.4 Methods of Instructions and Course Materials........................... 319

    5.5 Accounting Research 319

    5.6 Local Institutions and Government's Role in Higher Education 320

6. Educational Problems 320

    6.1 Method of Instruction 321

    6.2 Book References and Periodicals....................................... 321

    6.3 Faculty Exchange.. 322

    6.4 Professional Development and Training 322

7. Summary and Conclusion 323

Chapter XXVII **Accounting Education in Kenya**

1. Introduction 325

2. Economic Relationships 325

3. Certification of Accountants 327

   3.1 KASNEB Examinations 328

  4. Educational Institutions 330

    4.1 University of Nairobi 330

    4.2 Government Institutions 335

    4.3 Private Institutions 336

  5. The Public Accounting Profession 337

  6. Registration and Governance of Accountants 339

  7. Summary and Conclusion 339

Chapter XXVIII Accounting Education in Libya

  1. Introduction 343

  2. Accounting Education 343

    2.1 Intermediate Accounting Education 343

    2.2 University Accounting Education 343

  3. Accounting Faculty, Materials and Research 345

    3.1 Qualifications of Accounting Instructors 345

    3.2 Books and Materials 345

    3.3 Accounting Research 345

  4. Summary and Conclusions

Chapter XXIX Accounting Developments and Education in Somalia

  1. Introduction 247

  2. The Accounting Profession and the Need for Accountants 347

  3. Some Policy Aspects 348

  4. Training for Accountants 349

  5. Technical Assistance Programs 350

  6. Conclusion 351

Chapter XXX Accounting Education in Tanzania

  1. The Setting 353

  2. The Accounting Institutional Environment 355

    2.1 Identification of Local Institutions Carrying Out Accounting Education 355

    2.2 The Government Involvement in Education 356

    2.3 The East African Community's Education Efforts 356

  3. Educational Inventory 356

    3.1 Qualifications of Accounting Instructors 356

    3.2 Instruction Techniques Utilized in Accounting Programs and Courses 359

    3.3 Structure of Accounting Programs and Curricula 359

    3.4 Textbooks and Case Study Materials 361

3.5 Accounting Research and Developments 362

4. An Evaluation of Education Inventory 362

    4.1 The Basic Problem 362

    4.2 The Curriculum Content 363

    4.3 Students and Standards 364

    4.4 The Teaching Staff 364

    4.5 Summation 365

    4.6 Conclusion 366

Chapter XXXI Regional Aspects and Developments in Latin America
Chapter XXXII Accounting Education in Brazil

1. Introduction 373

2. Broad Prospects for Accountancy in Brazil 373

3. Accountancy Education at University Level in Brazil - The Sao Paulo Example .. 375

    3.1 The Graduation (B.A.) Program in Accountancy 376

    3.2 Summary of the Master and Doctorate Courses 378

4. The Most Common Problems 378

5. Professors with Master's and Ph.D. (or equivalent) Degrees in Brazil 379

6. Conclusions and Prospects 379

Chapter XXXIII Accounting Education in Mexico

1. Introduction 381

2. Institutions in Charge of Accounting Education 382

3. Accounting Education in Mexico Today 384

    3.1 Qualifications of Accounting Instructors 384

    3.2 Instruction Techniques in Accounting Courses 386

    3.3 Structure of Accounting Programs and Curricula 386

    3.4 Books and Materials 388

    3.5 Accounting Research 388

4. Evaluative Comments 388

Chapter XXXIV Accounting Education in Venezuela

1. General Facts 391

2. Forms of Business Organization 392

3. Business Records Required by Law 393

4. Foreign Influences in the Development of Accountancy in Venezuela 393

5. Capital Market and the Public Accountant 394

6. Tendency Toward Uniform Accounting in Venezuela 394

7. Accounting Education 394

7.1 Levels of Accountants 395

7.2 Requirements for the Degree of Public Accountant 395

7.3 University Studies in Accounting 395

7.4 Qualification of Accounting Teachers 398

7.5 Accounting Research 398

7.6 Instructional Technique Utilized in Accounting Programs 398

7.7 Master of Business Administration at the Central University, Caracas 398

8. The Public Accounting Profession 399

Appendix **Accountancy Education in India**

1. National and Social Accounting 401

2. Sectoral Accounting 407

3. Universities, Professions and Other Bodies 417

REFERENCES 433

ABBREVIATIONS 434

INDEX 437